Volumes previously published by the University of California Press, Berkeley, Los Angeles, London, for the Center for Chinese Studies of The University of Michigan:

MICHIGAN STUDIES ON CHINA

Communications and National Integration in Communist China, by Alan P. L. Liu

Mao's Revolution and the Chinese Political Culture, by Richard Solomon

Capital Formation in Mainland China, 1952–1965, by Kang Chao

Small Groups and Political Rituals in China, by Martin King Whyte

Backward Toward Revolution, by Edward Friedman

Peking Politics, 1918–1923: Factionalism and the Failure of Constitutionalism (in press), by Andrew Nathan

CHINA'S ECONOMIC DEVELOPMENT

Michigan Studies on China

Published for the Center for Chinese Studies
of The University of Michigan

MICHIGAN STUDIES ON CHINA

China's Economic Development: The Interplay of Scarcity and Ideology, by Alexander Eckstein

The Chinese Calculus of Deterrence: India and Indochina, by Allen S. Whiting

The research on which these books are based was supported by the Center for Chinese Studies of The University of Michigan.

China's Economic Development

The Interplay of Scarcity and Ideology

ALEXANDER ECKSTEIN

Ann Arbor   The University of Michigan Press

*Grateful acknowledgment is made to the following journals and publishers
for permission to reprint copyrighted materials:*

Aldine Publishing Company, for "The Economic Heritage." Reprinted by
permission from *Economic Trends in Communist China*, edited by
Alexander Eckstein, Walter Galenson, and T. C. Liu, 1968.

American Economic Association, for "Strategy of Economic Development
in Communist China." Reprinted by permission from *American Economic Review, Papers and Proceedings*, May 1961.

The University of Chicago Press, for the following: "Economic Fluctua-
tions in Communist China's Domestic Development" from *China in
Crisis*, vol. 1, bk. two, edited by Ping-ti Ho and Tang Tsou. © 1968 by
The University of Chicago. Also for "Individualism and the Role of the
State in Economic Growth," Copyright 1958 by The University of
Chicago; and "Economic Change in Early Modern China," Copyright
1960 by The University of Chicago. Reprinted by permission from
Economic Development and Cultural Change.

Contemporary China Institute, for the following: "Economic Growth and
Change in China," April–June 1973; and "Is There a Descending Spiral
in China? October–December 1962. Reprinted by permission from
The China Quarterly.

Council on Foreign Relations, Inc., for "On the Economic Crisis in
Communist China." Reprinted by permission from *Foreign Affairs*,
July 1964. Copyright 1964 by Council on Foreign Relations, Inc.

Hitotsubashi University, Institute of Economic Research, for "Conditions
and Prospects for Economic Growth in Mainland China: Some Comments." Reprinted by permission from *Keizai Kenkyu* (The Economic
Review), July 1957.

Princeton University Press, for "Conditions and Prospects for Economic
Growth in Communist China," by Alexander Eckstein, *World Politics*,
parts I & II, vol. VII, no. 1 (copyright © 1954 by Princeton University
Press); parts III & IV (copyright © 1955 by Princeton University Press).
Also for "Economic Development and Political Change in Communist
Systems," by Alexander Eckstein, *World Politics*, vol. XXII, no. 4
(copyright © 1970 by Princeton University Press): pp. 475–95. Re-
printed by permission of Princeton University Press.

To S. K., A. G., A. B., and J. K. F.

Preface

Several years ago, Harold Isaacs in a conversation with me remarked that all social science research is autobiographical. This statement startled me at first since it seemed on the face of it patently wrong. The more I thought about it, however, the more I was struck by the fact that this casual observation was based on deep insight. It really poses the question as to whether and to what extent early conditioning and experiences shape one's life course, pattern of intellectual evolution, values and through these affect the choice of problems to be studied and the approach used.

Growing up in a densely populated, preponderantly agrarian, underdeveloped economy such as that of Yugoslavia, I became sensitized to the ills and problems of rural poverty and economic backwardness at an early age. Recognition of these realities in the politically repressive environment of a royal military dictatorship, which at best made only feeble attempts to cope with these problems, directed my attention to Marxism and socialism while still in high school. These early experiences aroused my interest in economics and more particularly in the economics of backwardness and socialist economics.

Predispositions thus evolved, crystallized into hypotheses and research topics during my stay in graduate school. Starting with a master's thesis on collective bargaining in German agriculture under the Weimar Republic, this focus was also reflected in a subsequent research paper on farm bankruptcy in Santa Clara County in California and in my doctoral dissertation on the economic development of Hungary. The latter solidified my interests in the economic problems of Eastern Europe on the one hand and of socialist systems on the other.

This then led me to an exploration of the applicability and adaptability of socialist forms of economic organization to an underdeveloped country such as China. The pursuit of this interest over approximately twenty years resulted in a series of papers and essays, a selection of which is included in this book.

The preoccupations, choice of problems for study, and the approach to them illustrated by the following essays are naturally not only the product of one's early conditioning and influences, but of training. I was particularly fortunate in being exposed to four great teachers to whom this book is dedicated. Paradoxically I never took any courses from them and my contact with them either personally or through their writings occurred after I completed my graduate work. I was never enrolled as a student in the universities where they taught; yet each in his own way was my intellectual mentor.

Professors Simon Kuznets and Alexander Gerschenkron greatly deepened my understanding of the economic growth and industrialization process. They stimulated me to probe the historical and contextual variables shaping this process and in these ways helped me in crystallizing an approach to the study of underdevelopment. Professor Abram Bergson's work on the Soviet economy provided a standard and a model for non-politicized, theoretically sophisticated measurement and analysis of economic growth and structural change in socialist economies. Professor John Fairbank helped instill in me a devotion and dedication to Chinese studies, an immersion and admiration of Chinese culture and civilization, and an understanding of the historical milieu within which the economy of contemporary China evolved. Moreover, Professors John Fairbank and L. S. Yang were co-authors with me of a paper that is included in this book as chapter 4. I wish to express my thanks to them for permission to reprint it in this volume.

I started work on this book of essays during my sabbatical year at Harvard University in 1969–70. At that time the first draft of the introductory chapter was written and the initial selection of essays for inclusion was made. I wish to thank the Harvard Economics Department and the East Asian Research Center for their warm hospitality that year and most particularly Professors Rosovsky, Reischauer, and Fairbank for their helpfulness. The final selections and revisions were completed during my month long residence at the Villa Serbelloni in the summer of 1972. I would like to acknowledge my debt to the Rockefeller Foundation for making that stay possible and to Dr. and Mrs. William Olson for creating such a warm and intellectually stimulating working environment.

The University of Michigan Center for Chinese Studies was most helpful as always in providing typing and research assistance. Mr. Bruce Reynolds, an economics graduate student at The University of Michigan, rendered an invaluable service in checking footnotes, citations, and tables and in pinpointing inconsistencies in the data and the text. I am particularly indebted to Mr. Nicholas Lardy, another graduate student at the University, for his unstinting help at the proofreading and indexing stage. Last, but not least, I owe an immeasurable debt to Miss Rosalind Daly for seeing this book through the various stages of the production process.

Contents

Part IV
Development Patterns and Strategies

Part V
Economic Fluctuations

Part VI
Epilogue

Figures

Tables

Introduction

When the work on the first papers was started very little was known about the Chinese economy and little was made available by Chinese official sources. The state of statistical information improved significantly in the mid-fifties only to deteriorate again in the sixties. This reality is necessarily reflected in the essays that follow. There are inconsistencies in the data assembled at different times. Often the early information was inadequate and fragmentary and was therefore revised in subsequent essays as more complete or more reliable statistics were released or as further research was done. As a result, the data in the different chapters of this book are at times inconsistent. In general, the statistics released in later years are more usable than those published earlier. Precisely for this reason, chapter 1 attempts to lay out systematically the most important statistical series for the period up to 1970 and on the basis of information available through 1972.

As a rule, the inconsistencies in the data do not seriously affect the analysis and the broad appraisal of trends in these essays. Moreover, these appraisals are not only a function of the state of information at our disposal, but of the perspective we bring to it. This perspective necessarily shifts with time not only as our understanding of the basic pattern of evolution in China improves, but also as the character of the country's development patterns changes and as the economies with which China's performance is compared are transformed. Therefore, if one were writing these papers today certain conclusions and assessments might be modified which does not mean that they were invalid then or are necessarily invalid now.

Much of the early work on the economy of the People's Republic was also highly polemical and the political atmosphere in the United States being dominated by McCarthyism fostered this tendency at the time. It seemed to me then that in spite of these handicaps, conscientious, careful, quantitatively and evidentially based studies of China's economic policies and programs, its economic system, and performance were both possible and essential.

The confrontation of the oldest and most populous society with the task of modernization and industrialization in the context of a socialist system is unquestionably one of the most significant developments of the twentieth century. An analysis of this experience can make a major contribution to our understanding of development processes in presently underdeveloped economies. The lessons thus learned might contribute to development theory and possibly to the design of development policy. Correspondingly, this vast modernizing economy represents an actual or potential laboratory for the testing of hypotheses drawn from development theory and the economic theory of socialism.

The experience of the last twenty years clearly demonstrates that the character of economic development in China and probably to a greater or lesser extent in all underdeveloped economies cannot be adequately understood without reference to the political and social objectives and processes which play such a major role in the formulation of economic policies and affect their implementation as well. These objectives in turn are in part at least a function of the prevailing ideology and value system.

The essays in this book may be viewed as variations around a central theme, namely, that China's economic development since 1949 can best be understood as revolving around a continuous confrontation of Chinese Communist ideology with the realities of the country's economic backwardness. This confrontation contributes to scarcity. Ideology, however, not only has demand effects but through its impact on resource mobilization affects supply as well. Thus, ideology contributes to scarcity and its alleviation as well. At the same time the character of ideology itself is in part modified and shaped by scarcity.

This theme has governed the selection of essays in this book. Most of these were published over the years in professional journals or proceedings of research conferences. The three exceptions are chapter 1, "A Twenty-Year Perspective," chapter 8, "Economic Development Strategies in China," and the Epilogue, chapter 12, "The Chinese Economy: Some

Firsthand Impressions." The first was specifically written for this book and a somewhat different version of it was published in *The China Quarterly*. The second combines two related papers, one of which was published in the *American Economic Review*, while the last was prepared most recently, following my trip to China.

The theme of the book is developed in six parts. The first provides an overview of China's development problems, policies, and performance in the last two decades. It thus sets the stage for an understanding of the essays that follow, each of which deals with a particular aspect of the country's development experience.

Part II develops a framework for the analysis of scarcity and ideology, while Part III probes into China's economic heritage as a means of assessing the role of this inheritance in shaping the character of development since 1949. Parts IV and V examine in turn the interplay of scarcity and ideology in conditioning China's development strategies, patterns of economic growth and economic fluctuations since 1949.

The explorations of individualism and the role of the state in economic growth in chapter 2 can be viewed as but an aspect of the means-ends dichotomy so central to economic analysis. Relative backwardness and the consciousness of such backwardness create tensions between what are perceived to be the potentialities of technological progress and the actual state of the economy. A powerful international "demonstration effect" serves as a reminder of what advances technological progress is capable of yielding. The stronger the urge to close the gap quickly between the actual and the potential, the more acute will the means-ends, scarcity-ideology dichotomy tend to be. The violent eruption of the Chinese economy into a political and industrial revolution can thus be viewed both as a symptom of these tensions and as a way of coping with them, resolving or alleviating them.

Chapter 3 carries this analysis further by exploring in greater detail some of the ways in which ideology can be shaped by economic forces, most particularly how the character of Marxism can be transformed under the impact of pressures imposed by backwardness.

The means available to the Chinese Communist regime for the pursuit of their economic objectives are closely circumscribed by the character of their heritage. Thus, while the essays in Part II focus on the interrelationships between means and ends, the two chapters in Part III concentrate on the inherited means. They investigate most particularly how historical forces shaped factor endowments and the character of economic institutions. Thus, an analytical framework for the study of economic change in early modern China is outlined in chapter 4, while a more empirically based analysis of the actual pattern of evolution is presented in chapter 5.

Parts IV and V explore China's development patterns, strategies and actual performance as shaped by economic inheritance and the interplay of scarcity and ideology. Chapter 6, "Conditions and Prospects for Economic Growth in Communist China," in Part IV probes in some detail into the basic resource constraints limiting economic development in China as viewed from the perspective of the country's past and the comparative industrialization experience of Japan, the Soviet Union, and India. This study of conditions and growth prospects was completed in 1954, at a time when our data and our information on the state of the economy was much more scanty than in the later 1950's or even today. Moreover, this was written from the vantage point of the early years when the new development patterns were not yet fully crystallized in China, collectivization of agriculture had not yet taken place, and nationalization of industry and trade was not yet fully completed. Likewise, the national income estimates in early stages of preparation at the time were not yet published, and we had even less of a population series than became available in later years.

In the light of this and viewed from the vantage point of the early 1970's, this study makes a twofold contribution of considerable relevance and value even now. On the one hand, it analyzes and appraises the developments during the recovery years in some detail, and on the other, it investigates in some depth the factors and forces conditioning economic growth in China. Therefore, although particular figures and some specific observations have been invalidated in the light of information made subsequently available, the exploration of background factors, the description of developments in the early years, the broad growth trends sketched out, and the analysis of the basic relationships conditioning economic growth in China help to illuminate the path followed by this economy in the past two decades.

Chapter 7 builds on the preceding one. It examines some of the implications of the Chinese collectivization experience and how this might affect the analysis of conditions and growth prospects in chapter 6. Chapter 7, "Collectivization and the Prospects for Economic Growth in Mainland China," concentrates on two or three key issues, most notably the differing collectivization paths of China and the Soviet Union and their implications for agricultural development in the two countries.

While chapters 6 and 7 explore development prospects and the variables shaping them as seen from the vantage point of the early years, chapter 8 analyzes the development strategy actually pursued up to and through the Great Leap. It starts with an examination of the role of ideology in shaping economic policy and development strategy. This then leads into an appraisal of the Stalinist model and its differing adaptations in the Soviet and Chinese settings. As Chinese planners began to draw lessons from their First Five-Year Plan experience in order to lay the basis for the second plan, they began to realize that the Soviet strategy was not well suited to China's factor endowments. As a result, they gradually crystallized a new strategy which combined mass mobilization of underemployed rural labor with technological dualism. The chapter then appraises this strategy and explores its applicability to other underdeveloped areas. In this connection it draws on the industrialization experience of Japan. Chapter 8 was prepared in 1961 and therefore many of the observations relate to developments up to that time. Most of these would still be considered valid but would have to be couched in the past, rather than in the present tense.

The last three chapters of Part V concentrate on the subject of economic fluctuations in China. Chapter 9 examines the character and effects of the economic crisis of the early 1960's. Written on the heels of the crisis, it presents a somewhat more pessimistic picture of economic trends in China than if one were analyzing this period from the vantage point of the early 1970's. This chapter is closely related to the one following it, which tries to show that while economic conditions had seriously deteriorated during the crisis there was no evidence to sustain the hypothesis that the whole system was on the verge of collapse or collapsing.

Chapter 11 places the economic crisis of the early 1960's into a broader perspective of economic fluctuations. It develops a theoretical framework for the study of economic fluctuations in China revolving around the basic dichotomy between scarcity and ideology and then goes on to test this theory in the light of the empirical evidence available to us.

Part I
Economic Growth and Change in China

Chapter 1

A Twenty-Year Perspective

Maoist ideology and policy imposed on the realities of China's economic backwardness and the scarcities resulting therefrom have produced a peculiar and sharply contrasting pattern of development during the past two decades. The differences in economic performance were so marked— characterized by rapid expansion in the fifties and stagnation in the sixties—that it almost seems as though one were dealing with economies in two entirely different settings, perhaps even in two different countries.

The central theme to be explored in this chapter and indeed in this book of essays as a whole is that the sharply fluctuating pattern of development in the 1950's and 1960's can best be understood as the product of a continuing confrontation of ideology and scarcity in China. Scarcity, in turn, is a function of interacting demand and supply forces. In the Chinese context, demand is to a considerable extent shaped by ideology. Ideology provides the framework for the definition of economic policy, objectives, targets and programs and the elaboration of a development mix. On the other hand, basic factor endowments and the level of technology prevailing in the economy condition production capacities and the ability to supply goods and services. With a given state of factor endowments and technology, the more demands ideology places on the economy, the greater will tend to be the state of scarcity.

At the same time, the demands generated by ideology will create pressures for expansion of productive capacity in future periods, thus leading to a possible alleviation of scarcity. On the other hand as indicated in chapter 3, the specific character of an ideology can be conditioned by

Adapted from Alexander Eckstein, "Economic Growth and Change in China: A Twenty-Year Perspective," *The China Quarterly,* April–June 1973.

the scarcity setting in which it is embedded, and this certainly applies to the Chinese case.

I. Comparability of China with Other Industrializing Countries

The attempt at deliberate industrialization in China represents an unprecedented case in the history of modern economic growth, comparable only to India. Of the presently developed countries only pre-industrial Japan was comparable to contemporary China in terms of per capita income, average productivity of labor and intensity of population pressure on arable and land resources as shown in Table 1, chapter 5, and Table 7, chapter 6. However, the dynamics of population growth was quite different. Birth rates in Japan appear to have been much lower than in China—an estimated twenty-five per thousand in 1875 and about thirty per thousand in 1896 as compared to thirty-seven per thousand on the mainland in the mid-1950's.[1] Moreover, rates of natural increase were much lower in Japan—substantially less than 1.0 percent per year before 1900 and never above 1.5 percent before World War I as compared to 1.9 to 2.4 percent for 1952–57 in China. Similarly, rates of literacy and the degree of commercialization seem to have been significantly higher in late Tokugawa and early Meiji Japan. As indicated in chapter 5, "The Economic Heritage," literacy rates were not only higher in Japan than in at least Republican China, but also perhaps higher than in mid-nineteenth century England.[2] This would suggest the possibility that Japan in some sense was better prepared for launching an industrialization drive than contemporary China. It could be argued that high rates of schooling and commercialization may greatly affect a society's learning ability, its readiness to absorb new knowledge and new influences, and the rate at which these innovating influences can be diffused throughout the economy.

All other presently industrialized economies have entered the stage of their respective industrial revolutions from a significantly higher per capita income base than China. This appears to be most notably the case for England. Allowing for the tremendous incomparabilities of economies over large stretches of space and time, national product per head for Great Britain may be crudely estimated at about 200 to 250 present-day dollars in 1801.[3] On the basis of all of the available indications this was also the approximate level of per capita income of Western and Northern Europe in the first half of the nineteenth century, that is on the eve of their industrialization.[4] In contrast, during the first few decades of this century and prior to the advent of the communist regime, Chinese product per capita may be roughly estimated as $50 to $65.[5]

Thus on the eve of their industrialization, the countries of Western and Northern Europe were not only significantly smaller than China—both in territory and population—but were also appreciably more advanced in economic terms. The unique character of China's development problem is reinforced by a comparison with the two largest industrialized countries, i.e., the United States and the Soviet Union. The United States is territorially roughly similar to the Chinese mainland, but of course, it has a much smaller population. The Soviet Union is much larger in territory but still significantly smaller in population. Neither the United States nor the Soviet Union ever experienced anywhere the same degree of population pressure as that witnessed in nineteenth- and twentieth-century China. Moreover, the annual rates of population growth were significantly lower in both of these countries, particularly in Russia, than in China. They were on the average around 0.5 percent for Russia from 1913 to 1958 and slightly over 1 percent for the 1860 to 1913 period. In the United States the rates of natural increase were very high at the end of the eighteenth century, about 2.5 percent per year; but these declined to 1.5 percent by 1870 to 1880.[6]

However, the rapid population expansion of the United States was taking place in an economy with unusually favorable factor endowments as witnessed by the fact that per capita product was already by 1840 an estimated $440 (in 1958 prices).[7] The per capita product of Tsarist Russia on the other hand may be crudely estimated as about $170 (in 1860), i.e., about two to three times that of pre-Communist China.[8]

There are a number of underdeveloped countries—some in Asia—which are launching their industrialization drives from as low a per capita product base and in the face of at least as unfavorable "initial conditions" as those confronting China. However, except for India, there is no other national unit which is now or has in the past encompassed such a vast population. Thus, China has embarked on the road to industrialization in a country of unprecedented size. What then is the significance of size and what are its implications from an economic development point of view?

In exploring the implications of size, most economists have focused their attention on its advantages from the standpoint of growth. In this connection, two factors tend to be emphasized most frequently, i.e., economies of scale and resource endowments. It has been pointed out that given two countries at roughly similar stages of development, size of market limitations would tend to be considerably less severe in a large country, with a large population than in a small country. Thus market size is more likely to suffice for the construction of at least a limited number of optimum scale plants in the former as compared to the latter.[9] For example, a fully integrated steel mill may find more readily an internal market sufficient to absorb all of its output in China or India than in a small African country.

Advantages may also accrue to a country with a vast territory since it may be expected to encompass within its boundaries most of the mineral resources needed for modern economic growth. Of course, both sets of advantages cited are fully operative only in closed economies. They may be less important the more freely the countries concerned are engaged in international trade.

Relatively less attention has been paid to the disadvantages of size. These may be particularly pronounced for low income, underdeveloped countries. These disadvantages revolve largely around communications barriers on the one hand and problems of administration and control on the other, imposed by a combination of territorial expanse, vast population and geographic configuration. All of these factors represent obstacles to ready access which tend to hamper the flow of new goods, new techniques and generally the diffusion of innovating influences.

The transport and communications barriers also complicate the task of improving literacy and basic education. This then in turn further reinforces the access barriers. The access barriers also greatly reduce administrative, governmental, and bureaucratic capacity. The traditional imperial administration of China could impose reasonably effective centralized control over the vastness of the mainland, but only because the functions or tasks over which it strove to exercise control and the degree of penetration it sought were quite limited. There is no question that the transport and communications network and technology at the disposal of the Chinese Communist regime was greatly improved as compared to imperial times. However, the degree of penetration and control desired and demanded by the new regime has very much increased as well. One could hypothesize that the degree of control sought may have been raised much more than the regime's administrative capacity to exercise it. This undoubtedly must have been a significant factor in the breakdown occasioned by the Great Leap and in the considerable weakening of centralized controls in China in the 1970's.

One could raise the question whether size is indeed the crucial variable here. Suppose that each Chinese province became an independent state, would this really make a difference and if so, in what way? This certainly would not affect geographic access; that is, transport barriers, distance from the coast and from the main overseas shipping lanes and the continental, inland character of the bulk of the mainland would not be affected. This might suggest that geography may be a more significant factor than size. However, size itself aggravates the access, diffusion and learning problem in several ways. Communications lanes between the center and its parts are clearly lengthened in large as compared to small nation-states. It is more difficult to penetrate every area and every household in a large country with a vast population than would be the case in a smaller unit. This then has implications for diffusion of new influences and techniques, for penetration and for control.

Size might affect development prospects in yet another way. It is a well established fact that large countries tend to have small foreign trade shares in relation to GNP.[10] This in part reflects the fact that in a large country the totality of international, relative to domestic, transactions tends to be small. However, this too then tends to curtail the diffusion of new influences, new techniques, new methods of production, and new goods in large as compared to small countries, at least to the extent that foreign trade serves as a major avenue for the flow of these innovations. This certainly seems to be the case in China. In combining the various elements cited it would be virtually impossible to weigh in quantitative terms the relative importance of size, both in its territorial and population aspects, and of geographic configuration.

II. The Chinese Communist Approach to the Development Problem

Given the handicaps imposed by geography, size, population pressure and low per capita income, how did the new regime deal with the development problem? How did the Chinese Communist policy makers confront the realities of the country's economic backwardness?

It would seem that at first the new regime did not explicitly or consciously face up to this problem. The leadership was probably too preoccupied with certain immediate and urgent tasks: rehabilitating the economy, restoring transport and distribution, arresting inflation and establishing fiscal and financial stability as brought out in chapter 7 and, last but not least, coping with the Korean War.

However, more fundamentally perhaps, there is no evidence that the Chinese Communists appreciated the unprecedented character of the country's development problem. Unlike in the Soviet Union between 1917 and 1928, prior to 1955 there was apparently very little discussion or controversy in China concerning the character of economic institutions and the future direction of development policies.[11]

There are very few indications of groping and of a conscious search for an organizational model and a development strategy suited to Chinese conditions. It was apparently taken for granted that the Soviet model could be adopted more or less ready-made. After all, it led to rapid industrialization in the Soviet Union, and it withstood the test of invasion and a long war. Moreover, the process of creating new economic institutions and development policies was quite costly for the Soviet Union. Thus the Chinese undoubtedly hoped to save themselves the agony and the cost of starting from scratch.

This unquestioning adherence to the Soviet model was probably fostered and to some extent validated by the developments in the early 1950's. The Chinese economy responded remarkably well and rapidly to the measures being taken. Agricultural and industrial production recovered speedily, fiscal and monetary stability was essentially attained by 1951 and the economy as a whole was moving forward very fast. The momentum thus gained in the process of recovery seems to have carried the economy forward well into the fifties.

A number of factors contributed to this wave of expansion. First of all, peace, order and political stability were established. This in and of itself gave the economy a most significant boost. For about one hundred years, ever since the Opium War, vast resources, energies, talent and political acumen were invested in fighting wars—foreign and domestic. The unity of the country was undermined. These resources, energies and talents could now be concentrated upon the pursuits of peace, reconstruction and development.

Second, as of 1949, China's resources were grossly underutilized. This was not only due to war devastation but to the organization of work, the working arrangements and the whole system of economic organization. Thus not only was there underutilized plant capacity and open unemployment of labor due to war disruption, but a great deal of latent and chronic underemployment of both plant and labor was embedded in the very structure of economic organization and incentives. For instance the long drawn-out cycle of inflation was most disruptive for work organization. It contributed to a high rate of absenteeism and low labor productivity as employees were spending part of the work day or the work week in converting money into goods.

In contrast, initial conditions in the new China were most favorable for high work morale. The very act of victory carried with it great hopes of a new order, a promise of a better world not only for the Party leaders and cadres but for the peasantry, the industrial workers and the intellectuals. This must have infused them with a sense of dedication and commitment which spurred them on. These tendencies were greatly encouraged by the Korean War, the patriotic appeals that could be invoked in its name and most particularly—as seen by the Chinese—the victory attained there.

The recovery and psychological momentum referred to above was reinforced by institutional transformation. Nationalization of industrial and other non-farm enterprises coupled with land reform, collectivization and introduction of compulsory purchases of farm products—initiated during the recovery period but implemented on a large scale only after 1952—raised very significantly the rate of resource mobilization. Thus not only was existing plant and equipment more fully utilized, but heretofore unutilized or underutilized inputs were invested in the production process. In this way savings were mobilized for expansion of plant and equipment, labor was more fully utilized to operate this plant and raw materials supply was greatly augmented so that plant, equipment and labor could be kept more or less fully employed. As a result, institutional transformation had a double effect: it increased the rate of resource mobilization and at the same time reallocated these resources from consumption to investment.

Recovery, high initial morale and institutional transformation were inherently once-for-all factors which could and did in fact contribute to marked spurts in production capacity and output. However, a rapid rate of expansion based on these elements could not be maintained indefinitely. This began to become quite apparent by 1955 and particularly by the time of the 8th Party Congress in 1956. In effect, Soviet development strategy may have been well adapted to taking full advantage of these once for all factors. At the same time, its initial success served to obscure the basic development dilemmas facing China and thus encouraged a postponement of their consideration until circumstances forced them to the fore of policy attention.

As the force of these once-for-all factors spent themselves, disequilibria became increasingly marked in different sectors of the economy. The most fundamental of these related to food supply and agricultural raw materials. The share of farm output marketed was raised very appreciably in 1953 when compulsory procurements were introduced, but thereafter they more or less fluctuated around a stable level. This was at a time, however, when urban population and therefore urban food requirements were rising very rapidly under the impact of industrialization. Rapid economic growth also produced some short-run problems as well, in the form of capacity ceilings and raw material supply bottlenecks. Of all these problems, the most fundamental were unquestionably the imbalances created by the sharply divergent growth paths of agriculture on the one hand and the non-farm sectors on the other.

This then raised a whole host of questions in the minds of policy makers. Was the Soviet strategy of industrialization at the expense of agriculture applicable to Chinese conditions? Could collectivization be relied upon to raise output and/or the marketed share in Chinese agriculture? Would collectivization have to be linked to farm mechanization or could the former precede the latter? What type of rewards—material or psychic—would be best designed to foster work incentives? Should the Chinese adopt Soviet industrial technology with its relative emphasis on capital-intensive methods or should they place greater emphasis on employment creation and labor-intensive methods of production? In these terms would it be advisable to pay greater attention to the development of small-scale industry and not concentrate all attention on large-scale methods of production? Finally, in the light of the agricultural supply and labor absorption problem, questions were being raised concerning the wisdom of ignoring the population problem.

Against this background, the economic policy makers and planners of the People's Republic had to confront, so to speak, anew the problem of economic development in a large, densely populated, low income and backward economy. The enormity of the task facing the new regime was accentuated by the ambitious character of the goals the political leadership defined for itself: rapid industrialization, a fast pace of economic advance and catching up with presently developed countries within a relatively short period (e.g., catching up with Britain in fifteen years).[12] Therefore, the overwhelming scarcities characterizing the economy of the People's Republic can be regarded as a product of supply constraints imposed by the country's backwardness on the one hand and the demands placed upon it by the prevailing ideology on the other. The ideology, in turn, can at one and the same time be regarded as a product of this backwardness as shown in chapter 3, and as a major force in modifying and alleviating it.

As the disequilibria, bottlenecks and development problems became more acute, visible and recognized, the growth path and strategy to be pursued by China became the subject of a vigorous, though—in comparison with the Soviet industrialization controversies of the 1920's—less sophisticated and somewhat muted debate. One of its principal protagonists was Ma Yin-ch'u, Chancellor of Peking University, who was an advocate of "balanced growth."[13] Although phrased in somewhat Aesopian language and heavily overlain with Marxist verbiage, in essence Ma cautioned against placing exclusive stress on industrialization narrowly defined. He urged a shift in the priority mix, with greater emphasis to be placed on agricultural development.

This not only meant changing the investment mix, but also improving peasant incentives. It also implied placing a greater reliance on material as compared to psychic incentives or coercive appeals and thus easing the tax and collection pressure on the peasantry, and allowing greater scope for the operation of the private plots and the free markets. In fact, it would necessarily imply at least some change in the expenditure mix, with some lowering of the investment rate and an attendant rise in consumption. Closely linked to Ma's approach to development was his marked concern about population policy. He pointed to population growth as a serious problem for China and urged population control measures upon the planners and policy makers.[14]

As these various issues were raised, particularly beginning in 1955, there gradually crystallized two rather different approaches to economic development. Since these were not only technical problems but were at the core of policy making, they were necessarily political. As such they were at the center of the internal political struggles, partly hidden from view. For that reason, the definition of each approach and particularly the linking of particular leadership figures to one or another school of thought is to a lesser or greater degree based on circumstantial and speculative evidence.

The issues that seem to have divided policy makers revolve around the pace of development, the rate of investment, the intersectoral pattern of investment, the structure of incentives and the importance of technical skills and technical inputs in general in the development process. Attitudes on these broader problems were closely intertwined with positions assumed on quite specific policy issues, such as the desirable pace of collectivization and the wisdom of communization; the degree of centralization of decision in the planning and control system as a whole, as well as within enterprises, collectives and communes; the scope for private plots and free markets in agriculture; the role of "reds" versus "experts" in production, in planning, in education and in other sectors of the society; the role of large versus small-scale industry in fostering economic growth; the need for a population control program; the desired character of the wage structure in industry and the system of rewards in agriculture.

Mao's own predilections seem to have been running more or less consistently in the direction of pushing the pace of collectivization and communization; downgrading material incentives and stressing the importance of normative appeals; confining the scope of the private sector— especially in agriculture; stressing the need for frugality, self-abnegation and raising the rate of saving and investment; urging the mobilization of all resources, including labor, as a means of accelerating development; and last, but not least, placing great emphasis on zeal and commitment to communist values ("redness") as an essential prerequisite of industrialization under socialism.

The dilemma facing Mao has been how to foster rapid industrialization in a backward country, how to cope with the problem of scarcity, while building and perpetuating a socialist or communist society. He has been trying to resolve this dilemma by substituting ideology and organization for technical inputs. Ideology and organization—the first as the motive force and the second as the instrument—are used for resource mobilization, mobilization of labor and capital. The stress in Mao is on the masses, the "mass line," and on input mobilization rather than input productivity, hence the Great Leap.

At the very core of the Maoist vision, as developed in greater detail in chapter 11, is the notion of model communist man, i.e., a man capable of great dedication, self-sacrifice and hard work for the good of the Party and society without expectation of material reward. Moreover, this would be a well-rounded man imbued with basic education, eager to learn and to absorb new methods and anxious to innovate.

If the Chinese masses could be molded in this image, most of the economic policy dilemmas might disappear, or at least be markedly alleviated. Thus if model communist man would not resent working to the limits of his capacity at a more or less stationary real wage, labor could be mobilized to quite a far-reaching extent without necessarily leading to a decline in labor productivity. Similarly, this would permit a high rate of saving and a rise in this rate without significant disincentive effects for labor. Furthermore, since these model men would be infused with a strong learning incentive and a spirit of innovation, the dichotomy between "red" and "expert" would either be minimized or disappear altogether; the very concept of "redness" would incorporate "expertness" as well.

The incorporation of "expertise" into "redness" would then obviate the need for role and skill differentiation. This ideal society would be composed of dedicated communist generalists who could readily shift positions, roles and skills. At the same time given the preponderant reliance on normative appeals as a means of motivating workers, there would be no functional need for pronounced wage differentiation. Thus role specialization and income differentiation could be reduced or virtually eliminated so that the foundations for an egalitarian society would be laid.

There is every indication that Mao fully understood that model communist man was still an exception rather than a rule in China. He was, however, and seems still to be convinced that given proper ideology, indoctrination and organization, the masses could in time be imbued with these values and traits. Therefore, on concrete economic policy issues, Mao's positions would be strongly influenced by his vision of an ideal communist society and by his concern to adopt measures which would be designed to transform human beings and slowly, step by step, lead them on to the realization of this vision.

It is precisely on these concrete policy issues that differences arose between leadership figures and groups. Some of these divergences were marked and clearly visible; others were quite subtle and barely discernible at the time they cropped up.[15] They undoubtedly account for a continuing economic policy struggle which can be traced back to at least 1955 and perhaps earlier. For instance, in 1955 there were sharp differences of opinion between advocates of rapid collectivization and those who were more cautious, who wanted to proceed more slowly and wished to couple agricultural mechanization with collectivization.[16] Since mechanization was necessarily a long-term goal, by coupling the two a strong rationale could be developed for slowing down the pace of collectivization. A similar instance of policy differences revolved around the Twelve Year Agricultural Plan, the Draft Program for which was first adopted by the Supreme State Conference on January 25, 1956. A second and revised version was adopted in October 1957 and the Plan was officially promulgated in final form only at the Second Session of the Second National People's Congress in April 1960.

With the gradual movement into the Great Leap these policy differences were apparently muted from about the end of 1957 to the end of 1958 as all groups became caught up in the mass mobilization spirit, including seemingly many of the skeptics. Even those who advocated (*a*) a go-slow policy in regard to farm collectivization, (*b*) greater reliance on material incentives for motivating peasants and industrial workers and (*c*) more emphasis on "expertness" as compared to "redness" either kept quiet, acquiesced or were swept along by the Great Leap. However, by December 1958 the voices of caution, the economists, the planners and the less romantic elements of the leadership began to be heard once more. This is clearly reflected in the resolutions of the Wuhan Plenum of the Central Committee.[17]

The evidence available would thus suggest that Maoist policies were in ascendance between mid-1955 and the end of 1958. This was not only true for collectivization and farm policies in general, but also in relation to the industrialization drive of 1956 and the launching of the Great Leap in late 1957. It is in no sense negated by the short period of consolidation in the first three quarters of 1957, largely forced upon the regime by a poor harvest on the one hand and by the need to let the economic system recuperate from the strains of the "Big Push" in 1956.

As the high tide of communization faced increasing difficulties, as indicated in chapter 11, all of the doubts concerning Maoist economic policies seem to have been revived. As a result, there was a great deal of uncertainty throughout 1959, as to whether private plots should be tolerated in agriculture, whether free rural markets should be permitted and to what extent the small-scale production of industrial goods such as steel, chemical fertilizer and electric power should be encouraged. These doubts were, of course, reinforced by the poor 1959 harvest and the deteriorating food-supply situation of that year. Finally, the advent of the 1960 crisis forced a reconsideration of economic policy with the Maoist school of thought being pushed into the background. This signaled a sharp reversal of policy, with an emphasis on rationalization of industrial production, closing down and weeding out of inefficient enterprises—both small and large-scale—emphasis on quality rather than quantity, greater stress on input productivity rather than input mobilization, restoration of private plots and free markets in agriculture, decentralization or virtual abandonment of communes as resource-allocating and decision-making units, coupled with greater reliance on material incentives in all sectors of the economy.

These organizational and incentive changes were closely linked with decreases in the rate of investment and a reallocation of priorities, with much greater emphasis being placed on agricultural development. It would be fair to say that with the inauguration of this "agriculture first" policy in 1961, the regime recognized for the first time that growth in farm production could not be achieved through ideology and organization alone. On the contrary it required modern industrial inputs, most particularly chemical fertilizer, certain types of farm equipment and more rural electrification. This new policy had then certain definite implications for industrial development as well. It meant placing much greater emphasis than heretofore on the development of the chemical and farm equipment industry.

This was the dominant policy line at least up to 1964 and to a lesser extent up to 1966, when the Cultural Revolution placed Maoist views once more into the forefront. As a matter of fact, it is reasonably clear that one of the more significant elements contributing to the Cultural Revolution was Mao's concern that the policy of the early 1960's was leading China away from a revolutionary path and away from his vision of a good society. Mao was not so much worried about the priority shifts and the new patterns of resource allocation. He was much more afraid of the reorganization in forms of farm production and the greater reliance being placed on material incentives in farming. Mao feared that this would necessarily lead to the "growth of capitalist tendencies in the countryside" and thus undermine the base of the whole economic, social and political system.

It would be, however, a serious error to view the periodic policy shifts as always representing sharp breaks with preceding practices. In many

cases, the shifts represent changes in emphasis and in degree. For instance, private plots were not abolished during the Cultural Revolution, but their scope and function were more clearly confined than in the 1961 to 1964 period. Similarly, since the end of the active phase of the Cultural Revolution, certain signs indicate that material incentives and technical considerations are again being given greater scope, but at the same time the egalitarian thrust and the far-reaching reliance on normative appeals may still be retained.

We thus see a fluctuating pattern of economic policy in China between 1955 and 1970. I would suggest as a tentative hypothesis that these policy fluctuations were the product of three interacting and mutually inter-related forces: (*a*) a continuing policy struggle in the top leadership, (*b*) harvest fluctuations and changing economic conditions in part associated therewith, and (*c*) an autonomous bureaucratic or policy cycle; the latter—more fully described in chapter 11—revolved largely around the inherent dynamics of mobilization policies which could not be sustained continuously and thus required periods of rest and consolidation. These policy fluctuations can also be regarded as symptoms of the continuing interplay and conflict between ideology and scarcity with a profound impact on the actual course of economic growth and transformation in China.

III. The Record of Performance

Appraisal of the economic performance record of the Chinese People's Republic in the last twenty years involves most difficult problems of quantification and interpretation. The statistical services of the country were built up in the course of the 1950's and as a result for some sectors reasonably good data were generated and published. At the same time, for most of the major sectors the data are sufficiently usable to provide a point of departure for estimates with tolerable margins of error for the 1952–57 period. However, the statistical network so painfully and pain-stakingly built up during the First Five-Year Plan period was seriously undermined during the Great Leap, following which a black curtain of statistical secrecy was lowered upon China. As a result, the official data for 1958 and 1959 are of quite doubtful validity and since 1960 there are very few officially published quantitative indicators. Therefore, all data concerning economic trends in the 1960's are necessarily based on highly fragmentary or speculative information.[18] Bearing these qualifications in mind, the growth performance of the economy will be analyzed here first on the basis of production trends in agriculture and industry, followed by an examination of foreign trade movements and finally based on GNP as a whole.

A. Agriculture

The most important indicators of agricultural production trends are presented in Table 1. Before discussing these, several additional notes of caution are in order.

There is general agreement among most students of the Chinese economy that the official production series, whether expressed in tonnage or value terms, understate output for the early years and therefore overstate the rate of growth actually attained during the 1952–57 period. However, on the basis of available information, there is no reliable basis for adjusting this bias. The discrepancies arising from different methods of adjustment are quite apparent in both the value and the physical production data in Tables 1 and 2.

According to the official value series, total farm output increased by almost 25 percent and thus grew at an average annual rate of over 4 percent between 1952 and 1957. In marked contrast, Liu and Yeh estimate that production increased by less than 9 percent, expanding at an average annual rate of less than 2 percent. It is quite possible or even probable that Liu and Yeh over-correct the bias inherent in the official figures by applying too high an upward adjustment factor to the farm production figures for 1952 to 1955.[19] This can be most clearly seen in relation to grain crops which constituted over half of total farm output value in the 1950's.[20] According to Liu and Yeh grain output increased only by 5.4 percent between 1952 and 1957. Dawson and Jones, on the other hand, estimate that food crop (i.e., grain) production has gone up by 8.8 percent as shown in Table 2. In the meantime, population rose by 12.5 percent and as a result there was a 3 percent decline in grain production per capita even on the basis of the Dawson-Jones figures. However, the most careful adjustments are those by Chao which yield just about the same rate of growth in grain production as in population.

TABLE 1

Indicators of Agricultural Output Growth

Year	Value Indices (1952 = 100)		Production (in millions of metric tons)								
	Official (1)	L–Y (2)	Grain						Soybeans (9)	Oilseeds (10)	Cotton (11)
			Official (3)	Dawson (4)	Jones (5)	Chao (6)	State (7)	CONGEN (8)			
1949	67.3	—	108.1	150	—	—	—	—	—	—	—
1950	79.7	—	124.7	—	—	—	—	—	—	—	—
1951	86.7	—	135.0	—	—	—	—	—	—	—	—
1952	100.0	100.0	154.4	170	170	166	—	—	9.5	3.7	1.30
1953	103.1	101.9	156.9	166	—	170	—	—	9.9	3.5	1.17
1954	106.6	104.1	160.5	170	—	176	—	—	9.1	3.9	1.06
1955	114.8	105.2	174.8	185	—	182	—	—	9.1	4.3	1.52
1956	120.4	108.2	182.5	175–180	185	188	—	—	10.2	4.6	1.44
1957	124.7	108.7	185.0	185	—	186	185	185	10.0	3.8	1.64
1958	—	—	250.0	204	—	—	204	193	—	—	—
1959	—	—	270.0	170	—	—	170	168	—	—	—
1960	—	—	150.0	160	—	—	150	159	—	—	—
1961	—	—	162.0	170	162	—	161	166	—	—	—
1962	—	—	174.0	180	—	—	172	180	—	—	—
1963	—	—	183.0	185	—	—	183	178	—	—	—
1964	—	—	200.0	195	—	—	200	190	—	—	—
1965	—	—	200.0	193–200	200	—	200	185	—	—	—
1966	—	—	—	—	—	—	206	185–195	—	—	—
1967	—	—	230.0	—	—	—	218	205–215	—	—	—
1968	—	—	—	—	—	—	206	190–210	—	—	—
1969	—	—	—	—	—	—	210	195–205	—	—	—
1970	—	—	240.0	—	—	—	215–220	210–220	—	—	—

Source:

(1) State Statistical Bureau, PRC, *Ten Great Years*, Peking, Foreign Languages Press, 1960; this refers to gross production value.

(2) T. C. Liu and K. C. Yeh, *The Economy of the Chinese Mainland: National Income and Economic Development, 1933–1959*, Princeton, 1965, p. 140; this refers to gross value added product.

(3) *Ten Great Years, op. cit.,* p. 119 for 1949 to 1958; A. L. Erisman's reconstructed official estimates for 1960 to 1970 in "China: Agricultural Development, 1949–71," in *People's Republic of China: An Economic Assessment,* U.S.G.P.O., Washington, D.C., 1972, Table 2, p. 121.

(4) E. F. Jones, "The Emerging Pattern of China's Economic Revolution," in *An Economic Profile of Mainland China,* vol. 1, Washington, D.C., February, 1967, Table II, p. 93.

(5) *Ibid.,* Table III, p. 94.

(6) Chao Kang, *Agricultural Production in Communist China, 1949–1965,* Table 8.15, p. 227.

(7) Department of State, *Issues No. 4, Communist China,* Washington, D.C., December, 1969, p. 13. For 1960 and 1970, figures are taken from A. L. Erisman, *op. cit.,* Table 2.

(8) *Current Scene,* vol. II. no. 27 of Jan. 15, 1964, p. 4; vol. V, no. 21 of Dec. 15, 1967, p. 10, and vol. IX, no. 10 of Oct. 7, 1971, p. 2; CONGEN refers to United States Consulate General in Hong Kong. These estimates are compiled by the United States Agricultural Attaché.

(9), (10), and (11), from Chao, *op. cit.,* table 11.1, pp. 262–63.

These figures illustrate the potential seriousness of the food and agricultural raw materials problem even during the First Five-Year Plan period. Rapid industrialization and economic expansion with growing urban food supply, farm export and raw materials requirements could not be sustained for very long in the face of a declining or at best stationary product per capita—particularly so since China was importing virtually no grain at the time. It is no wonder that this was a cause of serious concern for the Chinese policy makers and that it forced a reconsideration of development strategy referred to in the preceding section.

All outside estimates agree with the official farm production figures for 1957; therefore these provide a relatively firm anchor for projecting the series backward and forward. The problem becomes particularly acute for 1958–59 when the official grain production figures stretch one's credulity to the limit. However, just as there is no reliable basis for correcting the downward bias in the grain figures of the early 1950's, so there is no statistically valid method for adjusting these gross exaggerations. As noted earlier, the state statistical system was badly disrupted during the Great Leap and all of the available evidence would suggest that the planners themselves had no reliable information concerning the grain output in those two years. Just as it is most unlikely that farm production could rise by 35 percent in one year, so is it improbable that it could fall by 45 percent from one year to the next.

Therefore, the estimates by Dawson, Jones, the State Department and the Agricultural Attaché in Hongkong represent attempts to derive grain production data independently on the basis of annual weather fluctuations, reports concerning extent of flooding, droughts on the mainland, scattered local reports about crop conditions and increasing chemical fertilizer applications. This then entails piecing together a great deal of partial and fragmentary evidence which may be subject to differing interpretations. It is therefore not too surprising that there are some discrepancies in these series.

My analysis is based on the reconstructed Chinese official series on the one hand—disregarding in it the figures for 1958 and 1959—and the two United States government series on the other. The latter appear as a State and a CONGEN series in Table 1. The differences between these two series used to be quite appreciable, but the United States Consulate General in Hongkong has recently revised its estimates upward and thus has fallen more closely in line with most of the other independent estimates. Actually the State Department and Chinese official series are very close until 1965 and diverge only for recent years. Based on the State estimates for 1958 and 1959 and the reconstructed official series for the other years, it would seem that farm production reached a peak level in 1958 and then declined by more than 25 percent over a two-year period. This means, assuming that the estimates in Table 1 represent a fairly close approximation of reality, that 1960 production had fallen back to the 1949 level. Following this low point, output more or less recovered to the 1957 level by 1963 but exceeded the peak 1958 level only by 1966. This new peak was then, in turn, surpassed by the record 1967 harvest. It is interesting to note that this very good harvest was produced amidst the Cultural Revolution. This can probably be ascribed partly to good weather and partly to the fact that the Cultural Revolution did not penetrate too deeply into the countryside; thus its disruptive effects seem to have been minimal in agriculture. According to official Chinese statements, grain production in 1970 and 1971 exceeded 1967 levels, while United States government estimates would suggest no significant change.

Based on this fluctuating pattern of farm production, what has been the agricultural output trend in China during the life span of the People's Republic? As may be seen from Table 2, for the 1952–70 period, the average annual rate of growth was about 1.3 to 2.3 percent per year, depending on whether the official Chinese or the United States government series are used. This eighteen-year period starts and ends with good harvest years, therefore it may not be too much affected by annual harvest fluctuations. A rather more favorable result is obtained if we confine our analysis to the last seven years starting with 1963, which marks the year by which agriculture seems to have more or less recovered from its great crisis. Thus, the average annual rate of output growth for the 1963–70 period was 2.5 to 3.7 percent. It could be argued that since the 1952–70 period encompasses the unusual Great Leap *cum* Great Crisis years it may not adequately depict the long-term trend performance of Chinese agriculture in its present institutional setting and under "normal" conditions, including average weather conditions. One might therefore speculate that agricultural output performance since 1963 may serve as a better basis for forward projection. It has been a period of relative institutional stability and of continuously rising applications of chemical fertilizer. Thus, barring

TABLE 2

Rates of Output Growth in Agriculture*
(in percent)

I. In Physical Grain Production Terms	Source of Estimates				
	Official	Dawson–Jones	State	CONGEN	Chao
1. Percentage Rise in Output					
1952–57	19.8	8.8	–	–	12.0
1957–65	8.1	8.1	8.1	0.0	8.1
1957–70	29.7	–	17.5	16.2	–
1963–70	31.1	–	19.1	20.7	–
1952–70	44.6	–	28.0	26.4	–
2. Average Annual Rate of Growth					
1952–57	3.7	1.7	–	–	2.3
1957–65	1.0	1.0	1.0	0.0	1.0
1957–70	2.0	–	1.2	1.2	–
1963–70	3.7	–	2.5	2.6	–
1952–70	2.3	–	1.3	1.3	–

II. In Value Terms, 1952–57	Source of Estimates	
	Official	Liu-Yeh
1. Percentage Rise in Output	24.7	8.7
2. Average Annual Rate of Growth	4.3	1.7

*All calculations carried out to one decimal place and then rounded.
Source: Table 1.

major disruption, one could on this basis expect a somewhat higher rate of growth in the 1970's than in the 1950's and certainly more rapid progress than characterized the two decades as a whole.

It must be emphasized that all of these observations are based on grain output alone, rather than on total agricultural product. As noted earlier, grains constituted about 50 to 60 percent of gross agricultural production value. As may be seen from Table 1, industrial crops did less well than grains during these years. On the other hand, fruits and particularly vegetables did apparently better than grains during the 1960's. The trends in livestock numbers and production seem much less clear. In the 1950's these probably grew faster than crop production, but they may have lagged in the 1960's.[21] The combination of these trends would suggest that on balance grains may represent reasonably well movements in total farm output.

It was pointed out earlier that as industrialization progressed at a very fast pace in the 1950's, agriculture was becoming a bottleneck sector in the more or less closed economy of China. The rate of agricultural advance was not sufficient to meet the rapidly growing demands placed upon the farm sector by virtue of the total population growth rate, the expansion in urban population, increasing raw materials requirements for industry and rising exports. The first of these points is illustrated by the fact that while farm production increased by about 30 to 55 percent (depending on which series is used) between 1952 and 1970, population rose by an estimated 45 percent.[22] This would suggest that food supply may have lagged behind population growth, or at best kept slightly ahead of it. By this standard then, the performance of Chinese agriculture was not too satisfactory.

On the face of it this observation seems to be contradicted by visual observation of all those who have visited China in recent years, including this author. Food seems abundant in all cities of China accessible to foreigners, is apparently available in great variety and is for the most part quite cheap. However, the casual visitor has no basis for comparing food supply availabilities today with those of the 1950's. He also does not know how representative of the country as a whole is the sample he is observing. Finally, a rising food supply may be secured through gradual improvements in distribution even without significant increases in output.

However, one gains a rather different perspective if one compares the performance record of agriculture in China since 1949 with that of the Republican period or with the long-term growth rates of some presently industrialized countries. Thus grain output increased only by an estimated 8 percent between 1914–18 and 1931–37 as compared to the aforementioned 30 to 55 percent between 1952 and 1970. Total farm output rose faster in the Republican years, i.e., by about 15 percent.[23] The differences in the performance rates of these two periods appear so marked that they are well beyond the probable margin of error.

China's rate of agricultural progress also appears in a favorable light if compared with agricultural development in Meiji Japan and nineteenth-century England. Japan is usually cited as a case of development in which agriculture played a prominent role, was technologically progressive and advanced rapidly. Yet during the first fifteen years of industrialization (1878–82 to 1893–97), agricultural output in Meiji Japan increased by about 27 percent as compared to an estimated 26 to 50 percent in China between 1952 and 1967. If we take a longer period, i.e., four decades between 1873–82 and 1918–22, farm production in Japan expanded at an average rate of 1.8 percent per year as compared to 1.3 to 2.3 percent in

China for 1952–70.[24] Of course, on a per capita basis Japan fared much better than China because of the significantly lower rate of population growth in the early decades following the Meiji Restoration.

While the rate of agricultural expansion may have been slightly more rapid in Meiji Japan than in contemporary China, the reverse holds for England in the first half of the nineteenth century. According to Deane and Cole, real product in agriculture, forestry and fishing grew at an average annual rate of 1.2 to 1.5 percent during the first few decades of the nineteenth century; it rose to a peak of 1.8 percent per year between 1821–31 and 1851–61, but then declined, falling below 1 percent in the last part of the century.[25] Therefore, viewed in historical perspective, the rate of farm product growth in China may be considered as eminently respectable. Yet placed against the formidable population pressure and the rather rapid rate of population growth it does not seem to have met adequately the requirements of the country's industrialization.

Agricultural progress in China also appears to be lagging in comparison with the rates of growth in farm production experienced by a number of underdeveloped countries, including Asian countries, since World War II.[26] In India, for instance, the average annual rate of growth was apparently 3 percent for 1950–51 to 1968–69.[27] However, this average is misleading since farm output grew at an annual rate of 4 percent in the 1950's but only at 2 percent in the 1960's. Thus, agricultural development in India appears to have followed an opposite course from that in China. While in China the situation has improved significantly since 1963, in India it has deteriorated.

B. Industry

Industry presents a sharp contrast to agriculture in China both in respect to the character of the statistics and the pattern of performance. As noted above, considerable uncertainty surrounds the farm output data for the early 1950's and for the 1960's. Industrial production data, on the other hand, are reasonably reliable up to 1958 and therefore one can approach measures of industrial production trends for the first decade with somewhat greater confidence. However, the situation seems reversed for the second decade. While there are at least some guideposts for the reconstruction of grain production trends, there are no comparable bases for estimating industrial output. Even for the 1960's there are quite good weather data for China and the fertilizer supply statistics (domestic production and imports) also seem fairly reliable. Moreover, occasionally some grain production figures have been released. On the basis of these and some other input data, it is possible to estimate annual output fluctuations and trends on the basis of certain assumptions. Admittedly this is hazardous and subject to sizeable margins of error, yet it is better than having no guideposts at all.

Unfortunately, there are no comparable input data for industry. Physical production series can be reconstructed for a quite limited range of commodities, which in value terms constitute a much smaller share of output than grains do in the case of agriculture.[28] The task of reconstruction in the absence of hard output data is also rendered infintely more difficult due to the much greater variety and complexity of the industrial output bill. This necessarily limits the reliability of the industrial output measures for the 1960's even more than in the case of agriculture.

This applies particularly for the series published by the Department of State as shown in Table 3. On the one hand, given the popular nature of the publication in which it appeared, there was no room for presentation of basic data and methods. As a result, we are left in the dark as to how these series were derived. On the other hand, one is left with the impression that at least for some years these are crude guesses rather than careful estimates. For instance one wonders what is the basis for concluding that the index of industrial production (1957 = 100) declined from 180 in 1966 to 155 in 1967 and 140 in 1968. There is a great deal of qualitative evidence to suggest that industrial output declined in the cultural revolution years; but did it decline by 23 percent in two years?

In contrast, we know much more about the composition, derivation and origins of the Field series.[29] Although it is narrowly based for the 1960's, this index may still be reasonably representative of the annual rates of change in industrial production for the period. It is also superior to the reconstructed official index which is based on gross production value, involving a considerable and possibly changing degree of double counting. As shown by Chao, it may be subject to other sources of upward bias as well.[30] For these reasons, and since Field's series—unlike Chao's and Liu's and Yeh's—extend over the period as a whole, they will be used as the basis for analysis here.

An examination of the data in Table 3 will once more underline the contrast in performance in the 1950's and the 1960's. These show more

TABLE 3

Industrial Output Indices for China, 1949–1966[a]

Year	Official 1	Official 2	Chao 1	Chao 2	Liu-Yeh 1	Field 1	Field 2	State 1957 = 100
1949	39.9	40.8	44.3	50.0	–	41.0	48.5	–
1950	52.0	55.7	57.7	63.3	–	54.6	61.1	–
1951	74.8	76.8	77.0	81.2	–	77.6	81.3	–
1952	100.0	100.0	100.0	100.0	100.0	100.0	100.0	–
1953	131.7	130.2	124.7	122.1	122.9	122.8	125.1	–
1954	153.6	151.4	141.6	139.4	142.2	143.1	142.9	–
1955	165.6	159.8	146.9	149.7	159.0	148.4	143.8	–
1956	217.1	205.0	182.2	179.4	210.8	188.3	178.2	–
1957	240.6	228.3	195.9	189.8	238.6	209.0	195.0	100
1958	–	379.4	272.6	251.5	289.2	282.1	256.3	140
1959	–	528.6	371.4	330.9	373.5	362.3	323.7	165
1960	–	–	–	–	–	–	315–319	180
1961	–	–	–	–	–	–	208–214	140
1962	–	–	–	–	–	–	211–220	110
1963	–	377.0	–	–	–	–	232–244	114
1964	–	433.6	–	–	–	–	259–277	130
1965	–	489.5	–	–	–	–	289–313	150
1966	–	585.4	–	–	–	–	322–353	180
1967	–	–	–	–	–	–	261–290	155
1968	–	–	–	–	–	–	282–317	140
1969	–	–	–	–	–	–	332–289	–
1970	–	–	–	–	–	–	388–449	–

[a]All series numbered 1 refer to factory industry only, while series 2 includes handicrafts and small-scale industry as well.

Source:

Official, from R. M. Field, "Chinese Communist Industrial Production" in *An Economic Profile of Mainland China,* Washington, D.C., 1967, Table 1, p. 273; this is a gross production value index.

Chao, from Chao Kang, *The Rate and Pattern of Industrial Growth in Communist China,* Ann Arbor, 1965, Table 19, p. 88; this is a wage bill weighted index of industrial production.

Liu-Yeh, from T. C. Liu and K. C. Yeh, *op cit.,* p. 66, referring to modern industry and based on net industrial product.

Field's index is based on value-added weights for 1956. Series 1 of the Field index is from his "Chinese Communist Industrial Production," in *An Economic Profile of Mainland China,* Washington, D.C., 1967, Table 1, p. 273, while series 2 is from his "Chinese Industrial Development," in *People's Republic of China: An Economic Assessment, op. cit.,* Table 1, p. 63.

State, from *Issues No. 4, Communist China, op. cit.,* p. 13; unclear whether it refers to total industrial production or factory industry only.

than a threefold rise in industrial production between 1952 and 1959. This was followed by a sharp contraction, so that output fell by about a third in three years. According to all available indications it may have recovered to the former peak level by 1966. Thus there was virtually no net industrial expansion during these years. The situation was almost certainly made worse by the Cultural Revolution, so that industrial output turned down once more in 1967 and 1968, but then recovered quite rapidly in the following two years. As a result in 1970, industrial output levels for the first time clearly exceeded 1959 levels, with a net growth in these eleven years of perhaps 30 percent.

As a result the average annual rate of industrial output growth was around 14 to 19 percent for 1952 to 1957, depending on the index used (see Table 4). This rate is raised even higher for the 1952–59 period. In

TABLE 4

Rate of Growth in Industrial Production
(in percent)

I. Percentage Rise in Output[a]					
Year	Official	Chao	Liu–Yeh	Field[b]	State
1952–57	128.3	89.8	138.6	95.0	–
1952–59	428.6	230.9	273.5	223.7	–
1957–66	156.4	–	–	73.0	80.0
1957–70	–	–	–	214.6	–
1959–66	10.7	–	–	4.2	9.1
1959–70	–	–	–	29.2	–
1952–66	485.4	–	–	227.5	–
1952–70	–	–	–	318.5	–
II. Average Annual Rates of Growth[a,b]					
Year					
1952–57	18.0	13.5	19.1	14.3	–
1952–59	27.0	19.0	21.0	18.0	–
1957–66	11.0	–	–	6.2	6.8
1957–70	–	–	–	8.6	–
1959–66	1.4	–	–	0.6	1.3
1959–70	–	–	–	2.3	–
1952–66	13.5	–	–	8.4	–
1952–70	–	–	–	8.3	–

[a]Based on the more comprehensive series from Table 3 and in many cases, rounded.
[b]Based on the midpoints of the range given in Field.
Source: Table 3.

either case, at the time China's industrial rate of growth exceeded that of virtually all other countries. It also apparently surpassed the industrial rates of growth for the Soviet Union at the time of its first two five-year plans (1928–37).[31] In sharp contrast, the 1960's were characterized by quite slow industrial growth. Thus, while the average annual rate of industrial expansion is estimated by Field as about 18 percent between 1952 and 1959, it dwindled to an average of 2 percent between 1959 and 1970. As a result the rate of industrial growth for the period as a whole—exclusive of the early recovery years—was about 8 percent.

Therefore for the period as a whole China's industrial performance is not much better than that of India. However, the pattern of performance in India is exactly the opposite of that witnessed in China. Thus the average industrial rate of growth in India was over 7 percent per year in the first decade (1951–60), about a half of that of China; but India's declined only to 6 percent in the 1960's in contrast to quite slow industrial expansion in China.[32]

It is interesting to note that the various series in Table 3 indicate marked fluctuations in the rate of growth, as indeed was the case for farm output as well. However, industrial output fluctuations followed agriculture usually with a one to two year lag. This phenomenon is most clearly revealed during the Great Leap and the Great Crisis. Thus while farm output declined in 1959, industrial production peaked in that very year and showed a sharp decline only in 1961, in turn reaching its low point in 1962—a point attained by agriculture two years earlier.

Other notable characteristics of industrial production trends not revealed by these series are the trade-offs between quantity and quality on the one hand and changes in industrial structure on the other. Thus, while there was apparently no net expansion in industrial production after 1960 as indicated above, there was a very significant improvement in the quality of the product. As factory output increased by about two-thirds between 1957 and 1959, marking a very appreciable acceleration in the rate of growth, output quality declined markedly according to numerous accounts in the Chinese press and periodicals. Correspondingly with the onset of the industrial depression, the emphasis on the part of policy makers and industrial managers shifted from quantity to quality; moreover, given the much slower pace of expansion in the 1960's this quality improvement was rendered much easier. Therefore if one could take account of this factor, it is almost certain that the rate of expansion would appear to be slower during the Great Leap than shown in Table 3 and correspondingly the pace of recovery in the 1960's would seem to be more rapid; as a result the sharpness of the contrast in industrial performance during the two decades would be diminished to some extent.

Similarly, these aggregate measures conceal differential rates of change in individual branches of industry. As might be expected, the principal emphasis in the 1950's was upon the development of heavy industry. This is most clearly evident in the case of iron and steel output, and metal processing in general, as illustrated by the fact that its relative weight in total industrial production rose from 16 percent in 1952 to 26 percent in 1959.[33] At the same time, petroleum extraction and processing, chemicals, electric power generation and building materials expanded above average rates. On the other hand, textiles, food processing and consumer goods industries lagged behind and grew much more slowly.

Unfortunately there are only about eleven categories of industrial products for which we have production estimates for the 1960's, i.e., electric power, coal, crude oil, crude steel, chemical fertilizer, cement, timber, machine tools, paper, cotton cloth and sugar.[34] Of these, only crude oil and chemical fertilizer show very rapid advances between 1960 and 1970. These two industries are the success stories of the 1960's. Thus chemical fertilizer production rose from 800 thousand metric tons in 1957 to about 2.5 million metric tons in 1960, and 8 to 14 million tons in 1970. At the same time petroleum extraction increased from about 1.5 million tons in 1957 to 4.5 million tons in 1960 and 18 million tons in 1970.[35]

On the other hand coal, cement, timber, paper and cotton cloth production barely expanded at all between 1960 and 1970. Electric power, steel, machine tools and sugar experienced modest growth with steel output, for instance, rising from 13 to 18 million tons in these last ten years as compared to an increase of 0.6 to 13 million in the preceding years. However, all of these data must be treated with a great deal of caution since they are based on highly fragmentary information of uncertain reliability.

China's industrial development thus exhibits an interesting pattern. Those branches which grew most rapidly in the 1950's expanded much more slowly in the 1960's. In these there was almost certainly a significant improvement in the quality of output, which partly made up for the slowing down in the quantitative rate of growth. On the other hand, the 1960's witnessed the rise of virtually new and most rapidly expanding industries, such as crude oil extraction, chemical fertilizer production and certain branches of defense production. These changes in industrial structure clearly reflected new directions in industrial policy. The growth of crude oil and defense production represented an expression of China's self-reliance policy brought about by the Sino-Soviet break. In both of these industrial branches, China was quite import-dependent on the Soviet Union in the 1950's. In contrast, the rise of a large chemical fertilizer industry was dictated by the much higher priority accorded to agricultural development in the 1960's compared to the 1950's, combined with the recognition that such development depended to a considerable extent upon the channeling of modern inputs into farm production.

C. Foreign Trade

The purpose of this introductory chapter is to review and appraise the available growth performance indicators for China so as to form some basis for assessing the country's development record since 1949. This is also the vantage point from which we intend to approach an examination of the country's foreign trade. That is, our interest in foreign trade is confined to its study as an index of growth performance.

Of all the available measures of China's economic growth, the data for foreign trade are relatively the least ambiguous and most reliable. They are completely derived from the trading partner's side and thus are not dependent on Chinese statistical practice. This method does of course present some problems which need not detain us here.[36] Suffice it to say that conversion into dollars of imports and exports expressed in a variety of national currencies clearly presents some conceptual and statistical problems. The appropriateness of official or some alternative exchange rates as converters raises some particularly complex questions for communist country trade with China. Another source of error arises from the fact that there are no reliable foreign trade data for Albania, North Vietnam and North Korea. It may be roughly estimated that these countries absorbed about 10 percent of China's foreign trade in the 1960's and a lower share in the 1950's. Therefore in compiling total imports and exports, even sizeable margins of error in these country figures are not likely to affect appreciably the China trade totals.

In spite of these difficulties, foreign trade data are unquestionably subject to much smaller margins of error than any of the indicators cited

TABLE 5

Trends in China's Foreign Trade, 1950–1970
(in millions of U.S. dollars)

Year	Exports	Imports	Total Trade Turnover
1950	620	590	1,210
1951	780	1,120	1,900
1952	875	1,015	1,890
1953	1,040	1,255	2,295
1954	1,060	1,290	2,350
1955	1,375	1,660	3,035
1956	1,635	1,485	3,120
1957	1,615	1,440	3,055
1958	1,940	1,825	3,765
1959	2,230	2,060	4,290
1960	1,960	2,030	3,990
1961	1,530	1,495	3,020
1962	1,525	1,150	2,675
1963	1,570	1,200	2,770
1964	1,750	1,470	3,220
1965	2,035	1,845	3,880
1966	2,210	2,035	4,245
1967	1,945	1,950	3,895
1968	1,945	1,820	3,765
1969	2,030	1,830	3,860
1970	2,050	2,170	4,220

Source: A. H. Usack and R. E. Batsavage: "The International Trade of the PRC," *People's Republic of China: An Economic Assessment, op. cit.,* Table 3, p. 343.

for agriculture or industry.[37] Proceeding on this basis, it is apparent from the data in Table 5 that China's foreign trade grew most rapidly up to 1959, but has been essentially stagnating since. After a sharp decline following the Great Leap, both exports and imports began to recover in 1962 so that by 1966 the former peak levels were almost attained. However, the disruption of transport and industrial production occasioned by the Cultural Revolution brought with it another decline in 1967 and 1968. As a result, there was no net growth in foreign trade between 1959 and 1970. Only in 1971 did China's foreign trade match or even slightly exceed the 1959 level in current value terms. However, it was not until 1973 that the former peak was surpassed in real volume terms as well.

Thus an analysis of foreign trade trends confirms and reinforces the findings of the preceding sections, i.e., the contrasting pattern of performance in the first and second decade, attainment of a peak during the

Great Leap—in 1958 for agriculture and in 1959 for industry and foreign trade—and very slow growth or virtual stagnation since. Between 1952 and 1959, total trade more than doubled, with exports growing almost two-and-one-half-fold and imports just about doubling. This represented approximately a 20 percent average annual rate of growth for exports and 16 percent for imports, that is possibly a faster rate than that shown for industrial production.

The pace of Communist China's trade expansion may best be gauged by comparing it with movements in total world trade and in the trade of Japan, India and some other countries. Through 1959, China's trade grew much more rapidly than total world trade, trade of all underdeveloped countries or trade of all Asian countries as a group. Japan's exports, on the other hand, forged ahead at even a faster pace than China did, but its imports lagged somewhat behind that rate.[38]

China's foreign trade performance, however, is somewhat less impressive when viewed from a long-run historical perspective. Mainland Chinese trade attained its pre-communist peak levels in 1928 and 1929. These earlier levels were then not surpassed on the import side until 1955 or 1956. The additional net rise thereafter, between 1954–56 and 1959, was about 60 percent.[39]

While China's foreign trade ceased expanding in 1959, total world trade continued to grow; exports rose by another 50 percent between 1959 and 1966 with imports increasing by 75 percent. As a result, China's share in world trade and her trading rank were diminishing throughout the 1960's. This is further illustrated by the fact that between 1953 and 1966 world exports expanded two-and-one-half-fold while China's sales abroad just about doubled. It would seem that these trends and relationships would not be significantly altered if Chinese exports and imports were based on stable prices. According to United Nations data, the unit value indices for exports and imports of Southern and Eastern Asia, expressed in United States dollars, do not exhibit marked movement between 1953 and 1966. They show a decline in the unit value index for exports from 108 in 1953 (1963 = 100) to 106 in 1959 and 102 in 1966; the corresponding figures for imports are 103, 97 and 101.[40]

China's trade expansion also appears in an unfavorable light in comparison to India. In 1953 India's foreign trade turnover was just about the same as that of China, i.e., about 2.3 billion United States dollars. By 1959 China attained a 4.3 billion level as compared to 3.3 billion for India. On the other hand India's exports and imports were continuing to rise at a time when Chinese trade was contracting. Consequently by 1970, the total trade turnover of India had increased to over 4 billion United States dollars, while China's was slightly lagging behind the 1959 level.[41]

A comparison of Indian and Chinese foreign trade trends reveals several interesting characteristics. First, it underlines a conclusion arrived at in earlier sections, namely that while the Chinese economy advanced very rapidly in the first decade and marked time in the second, economic trends in India were precisely the reverse. Second, it suggests that the rates of growth of these two economies were fairly similar for the twenty year period considered as a whole. As far as foreign trade is concerned, India advanced somewhat faster than China as evidenced by the fact that its total trade turnover rose by about 90 percent between 1953 and 1966 while the corresponding increase for China was only 82 percent. Third, under the impact of these tendencies the Indian economy was becoming more foreign trade oriented than the Chinese. Finally, China maintained a surplus in its trade with the rest of the world ever since 1955 and even through the worst crisis years. India, on the other hand, shows a trade deficit for all years since independence. This is, of course, merely a symptom of the fact that China began to amortize and service the Soviet credits in 1955 without receiving any new economic assistance. Moreover, China became a net foreign aid donor and lender herself while India remained a recipient of foreign aid through all of these years.

D. Gross National Product (GNP)

Thorough and careful estimates for national product and its components were compiled for the 1952 to 1957 period by Liu and Yeh. There is a very high probability that Liu and Yeh overestimated food crop production in 1952 and thereby underestimated the rate of growth of agricultural product and GNP as a whole between 1952 and 1957.[42] At the same time, as was pointed out before, there is virtually complete consensus among all investigators concerning agricultural production levels in 1957. Therefore we adjusted the 1952 GNP estimate downward on the basis of Chao's findings presented in Table 1. This however probably still represents an overstatement for 1952 GNP since the agricultural product levels affect the estimates in other sectors as well, but these indirect effects were not adjusted for in my estimates in Table 6.

TABLE 6

Hypothetical Projection of GNP, Population, and Per Capita Product
in China, 1952–1970
(all value indicators are in 1952 prices)

	1952	1957	1958	1959	1960	1963	1966	1967	1970
1. Index of Farm Production	100	112.0	123.0	102.4	90.5	110.2	126.5	131.3	144.6
2. Index of Industrial Production	100	195.0	256.3	323.7	317.5	238.0	337.5	275.5	418.5
3. GNP in Billions of Yuan									
Eckstein	73.8	100.8	120.6	123.4	114.8	104.9	134.3	126.5	171.4
Liu-Yeh	74.7	100.8	114.2	110.4	101.4	97.4	—	—	—
4. GNP Index									
Eckstein	100	136.0	163.0	167.0	155.0	142.0	182.0	171.0	220.0
Liu-Yeh	100	134.0	153.0	148.0	136.0	130.0	—	—	—
5. Population in Millions									
Orleans	575	625	634	647	655	683	711	722	753
Aird	575	641	657	673	689	718	766	783	836
6. Population Index									
Orleans	100	108.7	110.3	112.5	113.9	118.9	123.6	125.5	130.9
Aird	100	111.4	114.2	117.0	119.8	123.1	133.2	136.1	145.3
7. GNP Per Capita in Yuan									
Eckstein *cum* Orleans	128.4	161.3	190.2	190.7	175.2	153.5	188.9	175.2	227.6
Liu-Yeh *cum* Aird	129.9	157.2	173.8	164.0	147.2	135.6	—	—	—
8. GNP Per Capita Index									
Eckstein *cum* Orleans	100	125.6	148.1	148.5	136.4	119.6	147.1	136.4	177.2
Liu-Yeh *cum* Aird	100	121.0	133.7	126.2	113.3	104.4	—	—	—
9. Foreign Trade Index	100	161.6	198.9	227.0	211.1	146.5	224.6	206.0	223.2

Source: Row 1 is based on Table 1; Row 2 is based on Table 3; Row 3 is derived from the series in Table 1 and 3 on the basis of methods and assumptions outlined in the text. Row 4 is based on Row 3. Row 5 is from John S. Aird, "Population Policy and Demographic Prospects in the People's Republic of China," in *People's Republic of China: An Economic Assessment*, Joint Economic Committee Print, 92d Congress, 2nd Session, Washington, D.C., 1972; and from Leo Orleans, *Every Fifth Child*, London, 1972. Row 6 is derived from Row 5; Row 7 is obtained by dividing the series in Row 3 by the series in Row 5; Row 8 is a translation of Row 7 into index number form; Row 9 is based on Table 5.

Given the paucity of data, such estimates cannot be constructed for the 1958 to 1970 period. The best one can attempt is to identify some crude order of magnitudes for the various years based on certain assumptions. Thus T. C. Liu constructed an econometric model based on parameters derived from the 1952–57 data and then adjusted for the changed realities of the 1960's.[43] For this period Liu's agricultural product estimates are based on an earlier CONGEN series. These greatly underestimate food crop output in the 1960's. Partly because of this, Liu's GNP series as a whole represent underestimates.

For this reason and in order to extend the series to 1970 I derived an alternative projection in Table 6 based on several quite crude assumptions. First, it is assumed that the grain or food crop production series can serve as a proxy for total farm product. As noted earlier, all of the available indications suggest that vegetable production rose more rapidly than grain output, while industrial crops and livestock products lagged behind grains. Thus on balance, grain may understate somewhat the pace of agricultural expansion in the 1960's depending on the relative growth rates of these categories of farm output. In deriving the series in Table 6, for 1952 and 1957, Chao's estimates were used; for 1958, 1959, 1966, 1968 and 1969, United States government data were relied upon; while for the other years, we depended on the reconstructed official Chinese series.

Second, in deriving the projections in Table 6, it was also assumed that the index of industrial production compiled by Field (see Table 3) is representative of trends in the industrial sector as a whole, including manufacturing, handicrafts, mining, public utilities and construction. Third, the presupposition is that the tertiary sectors—transport, trade and services—exhibit the same annual fluctuations and trends as the commodity production sectors combined.

Each of these steps may contribute to sizeable margins of error in these hypothetical projections. This applies particularly to the second and the third; Field's index is narrowly based in terms of coverage and while there is a great deal of interdependence between commodity production and tertiary activities, there is no particular reason as to why this relationship should be a proportionate one. However, we have one independent check on the plausibility of our hypothetical GNP estimates. As noted earlier, foreign trade statistics are reasonably reliable and as may be seen from the data in Table 6 (rows 3 and 9), they behave similarly as GNP. Again while foreign trade and domestic economic activity are interdependent the relationship could be one characterized by lags and of course need not be a proportionate one. Nevertheless, the behavior of the foreign trade series suggests that our GNP estimates may not be totally unreasonable.

The per capita estimates are also subject to error because the population estimates are quite uncertain. Unfortunately there are no systematic annual population data since 1958. Therefore, the population index in Table 6 is based on two alternative projections of China's population growth, one by Leo Orleans and another by John Aird.[44]

Finally, the dollar estimates were obtained by converting the yuan figures at the official exchange rate prevailing at the end of 1952, i.e., 2.46 yuan to the dollar. This raises all of the usual problems of dollar conversion of national currency estimates. Recognizing fully the methodological shortcomings of this procedure, we have no adequate basis for relying on alternative and conceptually sounder rates. One could use a ratio of 1.79 to 1 or 5.91 to 1 based on comparisons of 1952 prices for the United States and China, for a limited sample of consumers and producers goods respectively.[45] Since capital goods constitute at most 10 percent of the total Chinese output basket, the 5.91 to 1 ratio may yield a grossly distorted and rather implausible estimate of per capita product in 1957 of $26 or $27 per capita. On the other hand, it is quite possible that the 1.79 to 1 rate may be much closer to the mark and may more adequately reflect the relative purchasing power of the Chinese mainland product basket. It would yield a per capita product estimate of about $90 for 1957.

Bearing all of these qualifications in mind, the GNP series in Table 6 clearly reflect the sharp fluctuations in rates of economic growth and levels of economic activity. Thus, following a decade of rapid expansion, China's GNP attained a peak level in 1959. It contracted thereafter and declined by about 20 percent between 1959 and 1961. Starting its recovery in 1962, the Chinese economy attained a new peak in 1966. The impact of the Great Crisis can be gauged by the fact that the total rise in GNP was less than 10 percent between 1959 and 1966. Following a temporary setback, occasioned by the Cultural Revolution, a new wave of expansion was launched at the end of 1968, so that by 1970 the economy attained new peak levels of economic activity.

As a result, China's GNP more than doubled between 1952 and 1970, but the bulk of this growth was achieved in the 1950's. The contrasting pattern of performance in the two decades is evidenced by the fact that

GNP rose by about 70 percent in seven years, between 1952 and 1959, but only by approximately 30 percent in the eleven years spanning 1959 to 1970.

According to these estimates the average annual rate of growth for China was about 6 percent during the First Five-Year Plan period. If one recalculated the Liu-Yeh estimates completely so as to trace through all of the sectors the impact of overstating farm output for the early years, this rate may be raised to 7 percent. If we extend this time span to include the Great Leap, the average rate of growth rises close to 8 percent per year for the 1952–59 period. In sharp contrast between 1959 and the next peak in 1966, the average annual rate of growth may have been only around 1 percent. On the other hand, between 1966 and 1970, the rate of growth rose to 5 percent a year, or if one were to adopt the United States government rather than the official Chinese estimates for 1970 grain production, this might drop to 4 percent. Finally, combining the markedly different periods in the relatively short economic history of the People's Republic of China—the First Five-Year Plan period, the Great Leap, the Great Crisis and its aftermath and the Cultural Revolution and its aftermath—seems to yield an average rate of growth of 4 to 4.5 percent a year (not counting the recovery years of 1949 to 1952).

The per capita growth rates and levels projected in Table 6 are of course partly a function of the population series used. Aird's estimates are based on the assumption that in spite of various family planning measures, birth rates have remained fairly high while death rates have dropped quite markedly under the impact of public health measures. Orleans, on the other hand, concludes that the family planning programs and population control campaigns may have led to some reduction in fertility, while the declines in the death rate were perhaps not as marked as assumed by Aird. As a result, while both Aird and Orleans start with the same population base in 1952 and 1953, their estimates diverge for subsequent years, so that according to Orleans, China's population in 1970 would be around 750 million, while Aird shows close to 840 million.

Since Liu-Yeh's projections yield a lower rate of growth and lower GNP levels than mine, combining these with Aird's population series yields a low per capita estimate. In contrast, a combination of my GNP series and Orleans's population estimates results in more rapid rates of growth in per capita income. An intermediate series may be obtained (not derived in Table 6), by combining Aird's population and my GNP estimates.

As shown in Table 6, on the more favorable assumptions concerning GNP and population growth, per capita product in China rose from about 130 yuan in 1952 to almost 230 yuan in 1970. Assuming a more rapid pace of population expansion, the latter figure is reduced to around 200 yuan. In dollar terms, this might mean a rise in per capita product from about $53 to a range of $83 to $93 depending on which population series are used and based on the official exchange rate of Y2.46 to the dollar. On the other hand, if the Y1.79 to the dollar rate is used, the rise is from $66 in 1952 to a range of $114 to $127 in 1970.

The projections in Table 6 indicate that the Chinese economy has been growing at an average rate of 4 to 4.5 percent a year since 1952. In per capita terms, it experienced a 2 to 3 percent rate of growth. If the lower GNP estimates are combined with the higher population growth rates, we approach the lower end of this range, while the reverse combination yields the opposite result.

What all these indicators suggest is that during the past two decades as a whole, China's economy advanced at a moderate rate. The rate of growth in GNP was somewhat higher than in India, which may be estimated as about 2.5 percent per year.[46] The performance gap of the two countries is perceptibly greater when aggregate growth is translated into per capita terms. Thus per capita product rose at an average rate of about 1 percent in India as compared to at least 2 percent in China.

In evaluating the comparative performance of these two economies it must also be borne in mind that India was the beneficiary of large-scale foreign aid throughout this period, while China obtained more modest aid from the Soviet Union in the early 1950's only. Since 1955 China has repaid these Soviet credits and has extended some foreign aid as well. Thus India has continuously been a net importer, while China has become a net exporter of capital. Therefore the attainment of roughly similar rates of growth involved much heavier savings and investment burdens for the Chinese than for the Indian economy.

The growth performance of China as well as India seems modest in comparison with the Soviet Union and a number of eastern and western European countries since World War II, not to mention postwar Japan. It also is less than impressive if measured by the standards of a number of underdeveloped countries including Taiwan, Thailand, South Korea and, until recently, Malaysia. On the other hand, by long-term historical standards of presently industrialized countries, Chinese growth rates may be considered high. Thus they fall within the range of the long-term rates for the most rapidly growing economies such as the United States, Sweden and Japan.[47] Given the low per capita income base from which China launched her industrialization effort and the relatively modest rate of economic growth attained in the last two decades, it is not surprising that she remained a very low income country.

In many respects China's whole development pattern has been unusual as compared to other developing economies. Typically, underdeveloped countries tend to have the preponderant share of their labor force in agriculture (60 to 80 percent) with close to half (40 to 60 percent) of their national product derived from that sector.[48] This was the situation in China as well up to the early 1950's. As shown by the estimates and projections in Table 7, however, by 1970 less than 30 percent of China's national product was derived from agriculture and, as a proportion of the GNP, the industrial sector loomed much larger than farming. Indeed, the intersectoral composition of gross national product in 1970 would seem to resemble that of some relatively highly developed economies. At the same time, there is no indication that the agricultural labor force share of approximately 75 percent has diminished.

These unusually large differences in labor shares and product shares may in part reflect pricing distortions so that GNP valued on the basis of an adjusted factor cost standard might yield a somewhat more "normal" product distribution. This, however, could account for only a small portion of the anomaly. A large part of the marked discrepancy in labor as compared to product shares can probably be accounted for by government policy, which has deliberately been designed to stem the migration of

TABLE 7

Shares of Major Sectors in National
Product, 1952–1970

Sector	1952	1957	1970
Agricultural (A)	45	37	28
Industry (M+)	21	29	37
Services (S)	34	34	35

Sources: Table 6 and 1957 GNP estimates by Liu and Yeh in *The Economy of the Chinese Mainland.*

labor from the country to the city. Moreover, from time to time, back-migration from the urban to the rural areas was strongly encouraged.

As a result, the labor productivity differentials between the agricultural and nonagricultural sectors may have been increased rather than decreased. In 1957 these differentials were already larger in China than for any other country for which we have GNP and labor force estimates.[49] While we have no basis for projecting labor force trends between 1957 and 1970, it is quite possible that the farm labor share may not have changed significantly in the intervening years. If this indeed was the case and if aggregate GNP and sectoral trends followed the path indicated in Tables 6 and 7, intersectoral labor productivity differentials must have increased rather than decreased. How far this process can go without creating acute strains in the economy is an open question.

One cannot sufficiently emphasize the fact that growth rates of 4 to 4.5 percent, which appear moderate by contemporary standards, were characteristic historically of the most rapidly expanding and dynamic economies. This is the rate which propelled Japan into a major industrial country between 1870 and 1940. The phenomenon becomes less surprising if one bears in mind that *at this rate, a country's GNP rises by about sixty times a century.*

If China continued to grow at such a rate over the next hundred years, in the year 2070, her gross national product would be 3,300 billion present-day dollars or over three times that of the United States today. If her population were to grow at the same rate as in the recent past, there would be 6 billion people in China at that time and per capita income would be about $550. It would thus be at the level of presently middle-developed countries.

This would mean that in absolute terms, China would be an enormous economic power. Whether it would also carry this power in relative terms will necessarily depend on what happens in this coming century in the United States, the Soviet Union and Japan. If these countries were to follow their past growth pattern, the gap between China and them would grow rather than diminish.

All of this, however, is a most artificial projection given the enormous imponderables of China's future, as well as the future course of other countries. Population growth in China can in time be expected to slow down, and the rate of economic growth could be above 4 percent. At the same time the rate of growth in Japan, the Soviet Union and the United

States might slow down. In this case China might improve not only her absolute, but relative position as well.

What all this suggests is that if the Chinese economy continues to grow even at a modest rate, just by virtue of her enormous and unprecedented size she is bound to develop in time into a most significant industrial and economic power with far-reaching implications for the structure of the international system.

IV. Concluding Comments

In the preceding section, China's economic performance was assessed primarily in terms of economic growth. This clearly is much too narrow and inadequate a framework in terms of which to view the development of an economy, particularly if one is also interested in the welfare implications of such development.

There is no question that if one analyzed the objectives function of the Chinese leadership, one would find that a reasonably egalitarian income distribution coupled with the preservation of certain socialist values will rank perhaps as high as economic growth. As indicated earlier, the precise weight of each of these goals in the total objectives function may shift from time to time.

Assurance of a minimum standard of living and narrowing of income inequalities are stated objectives of development programs in most of the underdeveloped countries. However, in China, these objectives are assigned a high priority, in deed as well as in word, in contrast to many other countries. Admittedly, these are variables that are much more difficult to measure than economic growth, and income distribution data are notoriously inadequate even for more developed economies. Nevertheless, the overwhelming body of visual, qualitative and admittedly impressionistic evidence coupled with whatever quantitative evidence is available, strongly supports the conclusion that the Chinese have been remarkably successful in narrowing income inequalities and thereby assuring a certain minimum standard to most, if not all elements of the population. This does not mean that wage and income differentials have disappeared, either locally or interregionally, but that they have been considerably narrowed in the course of two decades.

Viewed in this broader perspective, China's economic performance appears much more impressive than that of India and a good many other developing countries. Not only was China's growth, particularly in per capita terms, more rapid than India's, but this was achieved while income inequalities were narrowed and with very limited foreign aid. It is not too surprising therefore that China's appeal as a model for other developing areas is so strong. However, the specific character of this appeal has shifted over time. In the 1950's its appeal derived principally from its rapid growth performance at a time when other developing countries were almost solely preoccupied with growth as the most critical development goal. In contrast, in the 1960's, when most developing countries recognized that growth without appropriate income distribution policies can have disruptive economic, social and political consequences, China's appeal derived principally from its egalitarian policies despite the fact that its growth performance was quite poor (about 2 to 2.5 percent per year between 1959 and 1970).

In effect, in the first decade China was applying the Soviet or Stalinist development model to a densely populated underdeveloped country. Therefore China's development appeal in the 1950's was really based on this model. As noted earlier, the applicability of this model was more or less taken for granted by the Chinese at the time. However, whether it was in fact applicable or not was difficult to test as long as the once-for-all factors played such a crucial role in propelling the economy forward. Only when these were more or less dissipated did Chinese development planners have to face up to the most difficult problems of resource allocation choices and strategies.

Up to that time there was apparently not too much cause for concern by the Chinese Communist leadership in general and Mao in particular about the ideological or societal validity of the Soviet model. "Revisionism" with its preponderant reliance on remunerative appeals had not yet become the dominant way of life, the central ethos in the Soviet system during the Stalinist era. In the first two Five-Year Plan periods (1928–37) and in the years of war preparation and war, the Soviet regime concentrated all of its energies on mobilization: resource mobilization for industrialization and military mobilization for defense. That is, Soviet society of the period up to 1950 could be characterized as a mobilization system incorporating modern technical inputs. As such it had a high degree of congruence for the Chinese Communist leadership.

While revisionist tendencies were operative all along they were more or less suppressed during the Stalinist era. Terror was ever present as a threat and curb on stability, interfering with lasting role, income and class differentiation. Therefore it was only after Stalin's death and after industrialization in the Soviet Union had proceeded some distance that the fruits of economic growth became slowly and gradually diffused throughout society and economy and began to benefit the average consumer. The combination of these two sets of interrelated factors—the disappearance of Stalinist terror, the rise in per capita consumption and the rise in consumer aspirations—mutually reinforced each other, driving the Soviet system in a "revisionist" direction.

Thus there was a congruence of forces coming from two different directions—one arising from developments in the Soviet Union and the other growing out of Chinese conditions—that led to the parting of the ways in the two development paths. By 1955 the Chinese began to realize that the Stalinist model was not applicable to Chinese conditions, i.e., that a development strategy built on industrialization at the expense of agriculture was not viable amidst the resource endowments prevailing on the mainland. At the same time, they saw that the Soviets themselves were departing from the Stalinist path and were instead beginning to travel on a "revisionist" road, a road which was abhorrent to Mao and his followers; it violated their ideological and value orientation and therefore they did not wish to pursue it. This forced them to pioneer a path of their own so that in the end they could not save themselves the agony of starting anew, of starting out fresh and evolving a development strategy of their own.

However, the experiment with an original Chinese Communist strategy embodied in the Great Leap ended in near disaster which has haunted the regime and the economy ever since. The Great Leap was a watershed for the system as a whole. It marked a major defeat and setback, creating a spirit of uncertainty, groping, lack of self-confidence and lack of consensus among the leaders. One might speculate that the traditional unity and collegiality of the Yenan generation was undermined by the Great Crisis following on the heels of the Great Leap. The confidence in Mao's leadership was questioned, and it would seem that Mao was more or less pushed into the background while new and more or less "revisionist" policies were being pursued. These revisionist policies, however, encouraged "capitalist tendencies in the countryside" which were so unpalatable to Mao and so contrary to his value system (see chapter 11). Finally, in part because of this, he decided to recapture his influence not only over broad policy guidance but over day-to-day decision making. This element was almost certainly one of the central issues in the Cultural Revolution.

Seen in this light, the failure of the sixties can perhaps be explained in the following terms: the Great Leap represented an all-out mobilization effort which stretched the resource, organizational, administrative and bureaucratic capacities of the system as a whole beyond its capabilities. This showed up in a multiplicity of ways, such as mistaken directives, mismanagement of projects, planning errors, technical errors in project construction and so forth. It is the planning, organizational and management breakdown that ultimately produced the acute agricultural crisis, which then spilled over into the rest of the economy. Poor weather conditions undoubtedly contributed to this downturn, but it is doubtful if weather was the principal culprit.

This tremendous overmobilization left the whole system of economic, social and political organization seriously damaged. In many ways the economy was brought to a state of prostration similar to that produced by war devastation. However, while in 1949 and 1950 the regime was riding on a wave of victory and forward momentum, in 1960 it was being swept along by a cumulative contraction and depression. The process of recovery was now a much more difficult and painful one than in 1949. Thanks to the new economic policies adopted in 1961 and the ingenuity of the leadership acting with Mao's acquiescence but not under his dominance, recovery was attained within a period of three years, between 1962 and 1965.

Barely had the economy recovered under the impact of the new economic policy when the Cultural Revolution was launched. This revolution can in part be interpreted as a reaction to the policy direction of the early 1960's. Irrespective of its origins and motivations, the Cultural Revolution inflicted serious damage on the economy, particularly on industry and transport. By launching and pursuing the Cultural Revolution, Mao demonstrated that in his determination to combat the rise of revisionist tendencies in the economy and society, he was willing to pay the price of lower economic growth. Thus, while Mao may deny the contradiction between the requirements of industrialization and his vision of a communist society, he is not willing to tolerate policies which will interfere with the realization of that vision even if they were to benefit industrializaton and modernization.

In its simplest terms, the poor performance of the economy in the 1960's can be accounted for by (a) the Great Leap occasioned disaster and the time lost as a result of it and (*b*) Mao's hostility to policies which would have fostered and facilitated economic development. In the final analysis, therefore, the experience of these two decades cannot serve as a reliable guide in forecasting the future course of the Chinese economy. Both decades were highly abnormal in some sense; the first, because of the overpowering impact of the once-for-all factors, at least in the first half if not longer, and the second, because of the Great Crisis which more or less determined the course of economic policy and activity during this decade. Against this background, one would expect a different course of economic development in China after Mao's death, one which will neither follow the pattern of the first nor of the second decade.

The groundwork for this new course seems to be in the process of being laid. Since the termination of the most active phase of the Cultural Revolution in mid-1968, the economic policy directions emerging may suggest some kind of a synthesis of the elements prevailing in the 1950's with those dominating in the 1960's. There seems to be a return to economic rationality, to some kind of an economic calculus, in some respects reminiscent of the first decade. At the same time, management of the economy appears to be more decentralized, with considerable emphasis being placed on the development of small-scale industry, representing features which have come more strongly to the fore in the 1960's.

Part II

Some Theoretical Considerations

Chapter 2

Individualism and the Role of the State
in Economic Growth

I

Economic growth can be viewed as a broadening of the range of alternatives open to society. Clearly, technological and resource constraints are likely to be so compelling and overriding in primitive or underdeveloped economies as to leave comparatively little scope for the exercise of choice—either individual or social. On the other hand, the situation is quite different—at least in degree—at more advanced stages of economic development. At these stages, one of the principal manifestations of this broadening in the range of alternatives is precisely the greater opportunity to exercise choice over the form in which choices in the economy become institutionalized. This, in turn, requires a delineation of the spheres of public vs. private choice and a determination of the relative weight of each sphere.

One of the aspects of individualism and possibly the one most relevant for our purposes, is the scope for individual choice and decentralized decision-making in the economic sphere. In a preponderantly free enterprise market economy the institutionalization of these ingredients of individualism is more or less automatically assured. This does not, however, mean that this system necessarily assures equal scope for the exercise of choice on the part of all individuals in the economic system, or that it provides a greater scope for individual choice than an alternative system might. In contrast to preponderantly free enterprise market systems, in

Read at the January 1957 meeting of the American Council of Learned Societies, Panel II on Economic Growth and the Individual and reprinted from *Economic Development and Cultural Change*, VI:2, January 1958.

economies in which the public sector looms quite large, the scope for individual choice and decision-making may be more a function of the political rather than the economic system. Thus the mechanism through which economic policy is formulated and the role of the ballot box in economic policy formulation become major conditioning factors.

In essence, what this suggests is that there is a potentially positive correlation between individualism and economic development. The extent to which this potential is translated into reality will depend upon the role played by individual choice and initiative in resource allocation, regardless of whether the choices and decisions are in fact arrived at primarily within the confines of the economic or political process. With this context in mind, let us attempt to spell out some of the factors and variables that are likely to condition the role the state may be expected or forced to play in the process of economic growth and its impact upon the position of the individual.

II

In analyzing the role of the state in the process of economic growth, the following elements may be considered as essential:

1. *The hierarchy of objectives, goals, and ends of economic develop-ment*—This necessarily involves an examination of both the qualitative and quantitative aspects, that is, the character, range, and variety of the ends sought as well as the level to be attained. The interplay of these dimensions of content, range, and level will be one of the principal factors defining the ambitiousness of the particular economic development program. In respect to content, several broad categories of objectives or motivations may be cited, for instance, those revolving around nationalism and those related to a striving for rising standards of living. In a sense, these might be considered as ultimate ends which need to be, and are in fact, broken down into a series of derived and possibly more concrete goals. Thus, at the stage when these objectives are disaggregated and sorted out as to the ranges and levels involved, they inevitably tend to become competitive rather than complementary entities in the sense that under

ceteris paribus assumptions, the wider the range, the lower will have to be the level, and *vice versa.*

2. *The time horizon in economic development*—This entails a definition of the rate at which the goals are to be attained. In a sense, it is but another aspect of the hierarchy of objectives, since rapid or leisurely growth may be an explicitly stated end in and of itself.

3. *The means available* for attaining—at the desired rate—the content, range, and level of ends explicitly or implicitly formulated. Here one would have to consider such variables as resource and factor endowments and the state of the arts prevailing in the particular economy.

4. *The structure and character of institutions: social, economic, and political*—This is possibly the most complex of all the categories listed here. The considerations most relevant for our purposes revolve around the rigidity of the institutional framework, its capacity to generate, absorb, and adapt itself to economic change and to the disruptive forces of industrialization. This would mean investigating factors such as the prevailing value system, class structure, social mobility, contractual and legal arrangements, degree and character of urbanization, land tenure system, degree of commercialization and monetization, character and structure of state organization, structure of political power, etc. However, analysis of these variables is greatly complicated by virtue of the fact that some of them are rather intangible, while their particular chemical mix—that is, the nature of combinations and interaction between the different institutional factors—and the reaction produced may be quite unpredictable. In effect, it is much easier to provide *ex post facto* rationalizations or explanations as to why and in what ways certain types of institutional structure were more conducive to industrialization than others, than to assess *ex ante* the height and the tensile strength of institutional barriers and their resistance to economic development.

5. *The relative backwardness of the economy*—From an economic point of view, relative backwardness—and the emphasis should be on relative—involves certain advantages and disadvantages. The disadvantages lie principally in the field of foreign trade, while the so called "advantages of backwardness" may be found in the realm of technology. Thus industrially advanced countries enjoy certain competitive advantages in world markets, and particularly in the markets

of the underdeveloped areas themselves. This in and of itself can under certain conditions become a major handicap in the industrialization of backward countries. On the other hand, as Professor Gerschenkron has pointed out, one of the essential ingredients of relative backwardness is a gap in the levels of technology used and applied. Therefore the backward country can reap large potential gains by importing advanced technology from abroad and thus, in effect, make a technological leap from comparatively primitive to highly advanced levels.

At this point another aspect of relative backwardness may be usefully introduced, namely the gap in material welfare or standards of living, and the gap in national power produced by differences in levels of industrialization. All three of these gaps—in consumption, technology, and power—could be viewed as different aspects of a "demonstration effect" through which the gulf between a potential and actual state is forcefully brought home. Characteristically, it is in this shape that the pressure for industrialization of backward countries is manifested. Once the disequilibrating and innovating forces of modernization, industrialization, and urbanization have been introduced on an appreciable scale,[1] one could say that, *ceteris paribus,* the greater the relative backwardness, the more acute will tend to be the "tension" arising from this chasm between the potential and the actual, and thus the greater will be the pressure for industrialization.

Given the five categories of elements and variables considered above, we are now in a position to state our hypothesis concerning the conditions under which the state will tend to play a greater or lesser role in the process of economic growth. On this basis then one could say that:

a) The greater the range of ends and the higher the level of attainment sought;

b) the shorter the time horizon within which the ends are to be attained, that is, the more rapid the rate of economic growth desired;

c) the more unfavorable the factor and resource endowments;

d) the greater the institutional barriers to economic change and industrialization; and

e) the more backward the economy in relative terms the greater will tend to be the urge, push, and pressure for massive state intervention and initiative in the process of industrialization, and at the same time, the greater will be the need for such intervention if a breakthrough, rather than a breakdown, is to be attained.

III

Assuming that the state is compelled to make a major commitment on behalf of industrialization, what types of measures may the state be expected to adopt and what effect may these have upon the position of the individual, or more specifically, upon the individual choice and decentralized decision-making in the economic sphere? From this point of view, a sharp distinction needs to be made between the elements and the degree of state power applied in the process of economic growth.

In analyzing the qualitative aspects of state intervention affecting the economic sphere, one could perhaps distinguish between five categories of action: provision of social overhead, provision of economic overhead, application of direct and indirect levers and controls, government operation of enterprises extending beyond the overhead sectors, and central planning.

Provision of social overhead might entail maintenance of law and order in the society, provision and enforcement of legal and contractual obligations, supply of educational, health, and social welfare facilities, assumption of military and defense functions, etc. In effect, these are categories of action which to the extent that they are provided at all, are usually furnished by public rather than private agencies.

Provision of economic overhead may involve the institution of central banking and of monetary and fiscal facilities, the development of a highway and railroad network and of other public utilities.

Application of direct or indirect levers and controls may be based on a wide variety of measures, such as introduction of tariffs, railroad rate discrimination, tax privileges and other types of subsidies, rationing of goods and of credit, price controls, etc.

Government operation of enterprises extending beyond the overhead sectors may range from management of some industries, or a few firms in different industries, to public ownership of all means of production.

Central planning may involve more or less total concentration of economic decision-making in the hands of a national planning board.

Admittedly, this fivefold classification is arbitrary, and the line of demarcation between the different categories is quite blurred. Yet, in terms of their effect upon the exercise of individual choice and initiative, they present qualitatively rather significant differences. Thus, most of the items in the first two categories belong to what, in industrializing societies at least, are usually considered as the minimal and essential functions of a state. In contrast, centralized and comprehensive planning combined with total government operation of the economy may be regarded as maximum functions. One of the key questions that needs to be posed in this context is which one, or which combination, of categories will the state use to promote economic development? Whichever means it uses, how massively, to what degree, and with what intensity will it apply its power to the provision of these different categories? Moreover, how will particular kinds and degrees of state intervention affect factor supply, particularly the supply of capital and entrepreneurship?

It may turn out that the more massively and rapidly the state provides what can be considered its minimum functions, the less may be the pressure or the need for it to provide the maximum functions. Therefore the reliance upon maxima may in effect be a function of past and current failure to provide the minima. In these terms, then, one could say that a necessary precondition for the broadening of opportunities for the exercise of individual choice, individual initiative, and the growth of individual values in underdeveloped countries, launched on a developmental program, is a high degree and rapid application of state power for the supply of social and economic overhead, combined with partial controls and planning as circumstances may demand them.

Theoretically one could, of course, visualize a system in which amidst public ownership of the means of production, national planning, and resource allocation was—within wide limits—based upon the operation of free consumer choice and consumer autonomy. Realistically, however, it would be extremely difficult to build sufficient checks and balances into such a Lange-like model to prevent it from slipping into a totalitarian mold. On the other hand, this is much less true in the case of partial planning and partial government operation of enterprises, which in many situations is needed to reinforce the provision of social and economic overheads, if comprehensive government planning and management is to be avoided.

The failure of the state in the minimum fields tends to be more or less directly reflected in capital formation and the growth of entrepreneurship. Thus, in many traditional societies, accumulations of merchant and other forms of capital tend to be dissipated because of: (*a*) the absence of adequate and contractual arrangements to protect these holdings from the more or less arbitrary ravages of officialdom, and (*b*) the failure of the state to institute a social security system, so that old age assistance, poor relief, and similar functions must be privately assumed through the family and kinship system. At the same time, condition (*a*) tends to reinforce the economic risks of various types of business and industrial investments. Moreover, the same condition further encourages the flow of capital into land investment, which in an environment of acute population pressure and agrarian value orientation, represents one of the safest and most profitable forms of holding. However, from the standpoint of the economy, this is merely a transfer payment, ultimately representing a leakage of investment into consumption. In effect, then, this is a milieu in which the state—through sins of commission and omission—tends to undercut actual and potential sources of capital accumulation, while at the same time making its contribution to the narrowing of business opportunities. Under these conditions the scarcities of entrepreneurial and technical talent tend to be further intensified through the neglect of education facilities. Moreover, to the extent that some education is provided, its orientation is frequently inhospitable to the growth of scientific and technical knowledge.

Viewed in these terms, perhaps one of the most important contributions the pre-industrial European city made to the industrialization of the continent was that it provided a legally and more or less militarily protected haven for the accumulation and conservation of capital, and for its investment in fields that were eminently productive from an economic development viewpoint.

Amidst such circumstances, the formidable barriers to modernization and industrialization are likely to be perpetuated, while economic, social, and political tensions mount under the impact of innovating influences ushered in—as a rule—through foreign contact. Unless some means are found for alleviating these tensions through a process of change and adaptation, the potentially explosive forces in society may be expected to burst forth, sweeping away the old order, capturing the state, and using it as a total and far-reaching instrument for mounting an industrial revolution.

On this basis, one could argue that if India, for instance, wishes to avoid a totalitarian path to industrialization, her current plans and efforts do not provide for enough, rather than for too much, state intervention. Thus the large gap in financial resources available for the implementation of the Second Five-Year Plan may be a symptom of the inability and the reluctance of the Indian state to mobilize the means adequate for the implementation of the ends sought. But, even more fundamentally, perhaps, the inadequacy of the government efforts to spread adult education—both basic and technical education—rapidly, may be an important factor in inhibiting the attainment of certain economic objectives, while at the same time it serves to reinforce the great gulf between the small elite and the rural masses—a factor representing marked potential dangers in the political realm.

To sum up this phase of my argument, it may perhaps be useful to attempt to work with the concept of an "optimum level and pattern of state intervention" parallelling other optima—e.g., the optimum propensity to consume—incorporated in different types of economic and social science models. For our present purposes, this optimum would have to be defined in relation to two broad sets of objectives, i.e., striving for rising standards of living combined with an increase and/or preservation of the scope for the exercise of individual choice and initiative. The definition would also have to take account of the specific circumstances in each case, particularly in relation to the qualitative and quantitative aspects of state intervention, and to the variables listed in Section II above.

IV

We have discussed thus far the role the state may need to play in the process of economic growth without any reference to the character of the state and its capacity to perform the tasks required of it. Historically, however, particularly in the underdeveloped countries, the state—and the social structure on which it was based—was one of the very agencies hampering economic development. The same conditions that create the need for massive state intervention, in one form or another, also tend to breed a type of state which is singularly unequipped to intervene effectively on behalf of economic development. That is, economic backwardness is usually associated with political and other forms of backwardness.

Thus in China, for instance, the state has played a passive to actively negative role *vis à vis* the economy. The very concept of economic change and economic dynamism was alien to such a society with the nexus between economic growth and national power and/or welfare only very dimly understood, if perceived at all. The function of the economy was a largely static one, being charged with the primary task of supporting the ruling elite. Therefore, the state assumed very few responsibilities in the economy, beyond assuring that it would provide a stable, continuing, and adequate source of revenue for the imperial household and the gentry-bureaucracy.

The continuing failure of the traditional Chinese state to respond to the challenge of modernization, the institutional rigidities permeating the traditional social structure, the incapacity and unwillingness of the ruling classes to come to terms with change, their inability to understand the character of the innovating influences and to follow a policy of enlightened self-interest, have all served to retard the process of industrialization for so long that cumulative tensions of such explosive proportions were generated that they could no longer be contained, while at the same time perhaps nothing short of such an explosive force could have broken the shackles of the old order and swept away the barriers to economic growth. The violent eruption of the Chinese economy into what seems to bear the earmarks of an industrial revolution under totalitarian control can thus be viewed as an illustration of a resort to maximum solutions in the face of repeated and continued failure of the old state to perform and furnish the minimal functions referred to in the preceding section.

This course of development contrasts sharply with that experienced in Japan, where the breakdown of the old order accelerated by innovating influences produced a realignment of elites. The new elite, which bore some continuity with the old, then set out very deliberately to use the state as an instrument for modernization and industrialization. In doing this, the state from the outset paid major attention to developing rapidly the social and economic overhead sectors and to provide a general framework within which all types of enterprises, private and public, large and small, would grow. The state in effect conceived its role as initiator and promoter of the development process, leaving much of the execution to private enterprise.

While this is not intended to suggest that the Japanese experience can necessarily be duplicated in other countries, and in different circumstances, it is worthwhile to note that the state was able to perform this kind of a role amidst conditions which *ex ante* would have seemed exceptionally unfavorable. Not only were factor and resource endowments poor—in many respects poorer, perhaps not only absolutely but relatively, than those of some major underdeveloped areas today—but institutional barriers were formidable too.

However, an analysis of the conditions under which the state would or would not be *capable* of performing the functions required of it would be beyond the scope of this paper. Rather, I have tried to confine myself more specifically to a spelling out of the conditions under which and the ways in which the state may be *required* to assume a large role in initiating and promoting economic development without jeopardizing the growth of opportunities for the exercise of individual choice and initiative in the economic sphere.

Chapter 3

Economic Development and Political Change in Communist Systems

I. Introduction

In the field of comparative communist studies, theory seems to have lagged behind reality. Until a few years ago we had tended to think of communist polities in terms of uniformities oriented around the concept of a totalitarian model which permeated all communist systems more or less the same way and to the same degree. Although it was recognized that there were cultural differences and variations in the levels of development, these factors were not assigned great weight in modifying and transforming communist polities. On the contrary, the very possibility of a transformation was assigned a low probability.

In contrast with that view, the central hypothesis advanced in this paper is that the stage of economic development imposes certain imperatives of its own on any economic, political and social system, including communist ones. Moreover, the stage of development is one of the crucial variables contributing to the process of differentiation between communist systems.

The basic thesis of this paper is predicated on the premise that there is a significant degree of correlation between economic and political change. This is not intended to suggest that political structures and changes are uniquely determined by economic factors. On the contrary, it is fully recognized that a host of other variables impinge on the polity (e.g. historical factors, political culture, the character of the international system, etc.) but these will be left out of consideration in this examination

Reprinted from *World Politics,* vol. XXII, no. 4, July 1970.

of the relationships between the economy and the polity. It would be erroneous to read into this omission an argument that economic changes are *bound* to produce political changes. Obviously communist and other regimes can consciously or unconsciously decide to maintain certain political arrangements and practices even if they are disfunctional from an economic point of view and even if they entail growing economic costs. Thus in the case of Czechoslovakia, for instance, a highly centralized command system could be maintained in a complex, highly industrialized and strongly foreign-trade oriented economy only at a serious sacrifice in efficiency and growth. This then in turn contributed very significantly to the pressures for economic reform which then became an important factor in producing political change. Following the Russian invasion, the *status quo ante* is being re-established more or less consciously at the expense of economic efficiency and growth.

II. The Analytical Framework

The stage of economic development circumscribes the technological, the production, the supply capacities or possibilities of the economic system. It also circumscribes the set of economic institutions and arrangements which are compatible with the prevailing state of technology used. This does not mean that economic institutions are uniquely predetermined by a particular type of technology; rather it defines a circumscribed range of possibilities. For instance it is most improbable that food production by traditional methods, i.e., based on labor-intensive techniques and relying on non-industrial inputs, will be carried on by large business corporations. Similarly it is difficult to envisage corporate forms of organization for handicraft methods of manufacture.

The level of technology applied will (*ceteris paribus*) necessarily affect the processes and methods of production in agriculture and industry and the level of labor productivity in these sectors. With low levels of labor productivity, the preponderant share of the labor force will remain tied to agriculture and the rural way of life. Similarly, methods of production in industry may be expected to be quite labor-intensive in an underdeveloped economy with the handicraft sector looming large. Thus technological backwardness, in the sense of reliance on pre-industrial methods of production, necessarily implies economic backwardness, which in turn finds its expression in the structure of the economy.[1] Economic backwardness is characterized by large labor and GNP shares in agriculture and correspondingly small shares in industry. Technical backwardness and low productivity in agriculture under most circumstances is also associated with a low degree of commercialization and monetization. This necessarily affects the character of trade and trading institutions as it does of banks and other monetary institutions. The scope of internal trade and banking will necessarily be restricted in an economy based on small-scale methods of production on the one hand and pre-modern methods of transport on the other.[2] The character of commercial and banking organization will also necessarily be affected by the prevailing level of communications technology. Thus the rise of large national trading enterprises and of national banking institutions was greatly facilitated by the development of the telephone and the telegraph.

There is then a close functional relationship between low productivity, high labor and GNP shares in agriculture, local agricultural self-sufficiency, low degrees of commercialization, low degree of monetization and low degree of urbanization. All of these elements tend to be further reinforced by poor transport and communication.

Economic institutions associated with technical backwardness necessarily affect the character of political institutions and arrangements. At the same time, technical backwardness affects political structure and political capabilities directly as well. For example, there is a close association between rural self-sufficiency, low degree of commercialization and monetization, underdeveloped transport and communications and economic fragmentation on the one hand and the distances over which a government can exercise centralized control in considerable depth.[3] *Ceteris paribus,* technical backwardness similarly limits not only the production capacities of an economy but its mobilization capabilities as well. At the same time it also limits the mobilization capacities of the political system as well.[4] It can thus be shown that there is a strong association between levels of technology used, stages of economic development and stages of political development on the one hand, and the economic and political capabilities of a system to meet the demands placed upon it on the other.

The demands placed upon a political system are at least in part fostered by the external environment. An international system of nation-states which surrounds each state-based political system provides one of the sources of external pressure and stimuli. This is reinforced by a cross-cultural and transnational demonstration effect based on standards of living, standards of power and other attributes perceived as characterizing the most developed countries. The demands thus generated require the encouragement, development and/or maintenance of tasks which could be categorized in several alternative ways. The following represent one possible approach to defining these tasks:[5]

1. *National Integration,* most particularly the pursuit of national unity, identity and legitimacy.

2. *National Security and Power,* that is protection of the country's territorial integrity, its boundaries and its sovereignty; in some cases there must be added to this, in part as a natural extension of the foregoing, a pursuit of external and internal power goals.

3. *Improvement in the Levels of Material Welfare* in the country.

4. *Industrialization* or one could phrase this more broadly as economic modernization. However, the two necessarily go hand in hand.

5. *Resource Mobilization,* which in turn requires political and economic control, penetration and participation.[6]

These different tasks are closely interrelated, in some cases complementary but in some competitive and mutually contradictory. At the same time they can be viewed as representing final or intermediate demands. Thus from one vantage point the first three categories represent ends (final demand) while the last two can be considered as inputs (intermediate demand) necessary for the attainment of these ends. However, from some points of view, improvements in standard of living could be considered not only as a consequence but as a necessary prerequisite to industrialization and mobilization on the ground that such improvements would be required as incentives for the attainment of the latter.

It could be said that the character of the polity in a state is a function of this continuing interplay between the capabilities of the system as constrained by the stage of development and the technology associated therewith on the one hand, and the demand mix and demand intensity placed upon it on the other. These capacities and demands may be mutually adjusted or adjusting, i.e. in a state of equilibrium or tending towards equilibrium, or they may be diverging and tending towards a sharp imbalance, a serious disequilibrium. The equilibrium being defined in this context refers to the relationship between the technological capabilities of the system and the demands placed upon it such that it is compatible with a more or less stable political system. Up to a point this disequilibrium may be self-liquidating due to mutual adjustments between capacity variables and demand variables, but beyond a certain point the disequilibrium may become eruptive in the sense that it leads to a sharp discontinuity, a revolutionary transformation, in the character of the polity.

At the same time there is not only a functional relationship between the polity on the one hand and capacities and demands on the other, but the latter two are themselves interrelated. Thus the priorities assigned to the different tasks and the methods used to pursue them will to a large extent be a function of technological capabilities (stage of development) and the particular character of the polity. While the five categories of tasks outlined above may be said to face all states, the priority mix chosen and the degree to which it will be pursued (i.e., the qualitative and quantitative aspects of the goal structure) will depend on whether the nation-state is new or old, communist or non-communist, economically developed or underdeveloped. Correspondingly the extent to which the speed with which the various demands are being pursued will affect the capabilities of the system. For instance, industrialization and economic mobilization measures if carried out successfully will necessarily alter the capacities, the capabilities of the system to fulfill the demands placed upon it.

Within this general framework I will try to explore two particular aspects in the complex of relationships linking stage of economic development to communist polity: (1) the impact on ideology and (2) the impact of technological and economic changes on political style and practice.

III. Stage of Development and Communist Ideology

In the analytical framework outlined above, the political system in a particular country is viewed as the product of certain capabilities and demands, capacities and aspirations. The continuing interaction between these two sets of variables provides the basic engine of change in the system. The capacity side of the system is critically dependent upon the level of technology prevailing in the country and the stage of economic development. This is not the sole determinant of capacities but defines their range and limits.

One of the hypotheses of this paper is that the greater the disequilibrium, the sharper the imbalance between the capacities and the demands, the greater will tend to be the *tension* in the system. This *tension* is largely borne of frustration, for the most part articulated by the intelligentsia. It is the intelligentsia that demands an explanation for and a rapid resolution of the sharp imbalances and disproportionalities in the system. These demands for explanation and rapid resolution borne of frustration create a set of needs and predispositions to adopt an ideology which serves indeed the functions of a "Weltanschauung," of a total, all-embracing explanation and a radical, revolutionary solution. Therefore it could be said that the more acute the state of *tension* in the system, the more total, radical, and revolutionary will ideology tend to be. At the same time it could be hypothesized that the more economically and technically backward a country is the more *potent* will have to be the force of ideology to overcome the accumulated deadweight of stagnation and inertia. As Professor Gerschenkron put it so aptly: "to break through the barriers of stagnation in a backward country, to ignite the imaginations of men, and to place their energies in the service of economic development, a stronger medicine is needed than the promise of better allocation of resources or even the lower price of bread. Under such conditions even the businessman, even the classical daring and innovating entrepreneur, needs a more powerful stimulus than the prospect of high profits. What is needed to remove the mounting routine and prejudice is *faith*." (italics supplied)[7]

The character of the ideology will also condition the character of the demands imposed on the system which, depending on its capabilities to meet these demands, then contributes to aggravating the tensions through a continuous back and forth feedback mechanism. The character of the ideology can, however, also affect the capacities of the system particularly through the relationships between ideology, political mobilization, and economic resource mobilization to be further developed below.

Economic development in general and output growth in particular may be considered a function of (*a*) the quantity of inputs (factors of production) applied, (*b*) the quality of these inputs, and (*c*) the input combinations used and the technology associated therewith. Both (*a*) and (*b*) can in turn be called forth either through coercion and/or through economic, i.e., material, or psychic incentives. Psychic incentives, however, are largely a function of ideology and organization. In this context, the function of ideology and organization is to foster input mobilization, with ideology providing the rationale and the sanction and organization supplying implementation capacity or administrative inputs for this mobilization task. At the same time the organization itself must be strongly imbued by ideology if it is to perform its mobilization task adequately. In effect, then ideology must motivate the organization and, both through the organization and directly as well, motivate the masses for mobilization.[8]

Ideology and organization can foster rising input mobilization and/or rising input productivity to the extent that it can evoke spontaneous adherence, conscious or unconscious, and internalization of the ideologically imbued values of the human actors in the system. More specifically, mobilization is facilitated to the extent that ideology can evoke a genuinely voluntary spirit of self-sacrifice, self-abnegation and subordination of personal strivings to the attainment of collective goals. Put in Freudian terms mobilization is facilitated to the extent that "the individual gives up his ego ideal and substitutes for it the group ideal as embodied in the leader."[9]

The direct relationships between ideology and input mobilization are somewhat clearer than those between the former and input productivity. At any given level of input mobilization, ideology might supply the needed psychic incentives to boost labor productivity up to a point. Defining labor productivity in net marginal terms, i.e., marginal increments in productivity attributable to the labor factor itself at given skill levels, its rise could be due to "harder" work and/or increased efficiency both resulting from improved incentives, in our case psychic incentives. "Harder" work could imply longer hours and more days worked per month and per year. Strictly speaking this should be considered as increased input application, rather than rising productivity. Alternatively, "harder" work might imply greater diligence during the hours worked. Increased efficiency of labor inputs could therefore be due to greater diligence per unit of time worked, greater care exercised during the hours worked, and/or greater interest of the laborer in his work.

Looking at the problem in these terms, rising input mobilization and input productivity may be mutually complementary and reinforcing up to a certain point. However, beyond that point they become competitive. For instance, ideologically imbued mobilization may increase labor participation rates by drawing more women, children, and old people into the labor force. To the extent that the productivity of these elements may be expected to be lower than those of the working age males, increasing participation of the former will tend to lower the productivity of the labor force, but still increase the output of the population as a whole. Alternatively, ideology may induce workers to extend their hours voluntarily and without any elements of coercion. Yet even with such a positive attitude, longer hours of work might be at the expense of man-hour productivity due to fatigue for instance. At the extreme limit, similar considerations may apply to the mobilization of savings. Thus theoretically at least one could envisage that under certain circumstances ideology might be so successful in inculcating attitudes of abstinence and self-denial that households would cut their consumption voluntarily to the point that it may be nutritionally debilitating, thus interfering with the physical capacity to work and thereby lowering labor productivity. Admittedly only a very low degree of probability can be attached to this particular possibility.

Beyond a certain point mobilization may be expected to yield diminishing returns for other reasons as well. The leaders, carriers, and implementors of input mobilization in communist systems tend to be the "reds" rather than the "experts." This lack or downgrading of technical know-how and technical considerations may be expected to reduce even further the efficiency with which the mobilized resources are utilized.[10]

All of these potentially negative labor productivity effects will tend to be aggravated to the extent that ideologically induced mobilization shades over from purely spontaneous adherence into pressured or coercive adherence. Thus coercive or semi-coercive measures of both savings and/or labor mobilization may be expected to yield negative productivity effects even if they do augment the quantity of inputs supplied. In these terms then the *potency* of an ideology may be assessed by the extent to which it contributes to evoking spontaneous rather than coercive adherence as reflected in increasing input mobilization and/or rising input productivity.[11]

What is the relevance of these concepts and this line of reasoning for communist systems? I tried to suggest that the greater the disequilibrium between capacities and demands, the greater will tend to be the *tension* in the system. The greater *tension* will find its expression in a more totalistic, radical, all-embracing, and *potent* ideology which will infuse the actors in the system with a sense of purpose and commitment such as to provide the basis for a far-reaching mobilization designed to alleviate the disequilibrium by boosting system capacity. In terms of this hypothesis, there should be some correlation between stage of development and the particular character of communist ideology. More specifically with a given demand mix and intensity, the lower the capacity of the system to satisfy these demands the more *potent* will the prevailing variant of communist ideology tend to be.

There is a clearly discernible central tendency in Marxist thought even if one grants that it is peppered with ambiguities, inconsistencies and qualifications—in part traceable to an evolution of Marx's views in the light of changing conditions during his lifetime. This central thrust of Marx's system is perhaps most clearly expressed by the following quote: "In the social production which men carry on they enter into definite relations that are indispensable and *independent of their will; these relations of production correspond to a definite stage of development of their material forces of production.* The sum total of these relations of production constitutes the *economic structure of society*—the real *foundation on which rise legal and political superstructure* and to which definite forms of social consciousness correspond." (italics supplied)[12]

Crucial for the problems considered in this paper is Marx's concept of the material foundations, the economic base, the substructure juxtaposed to the superstructure of the legal order, the polity, culture and social consciousness. The relationship between the material base and the superstructure in Marx's thought lends itself to varying interpretations. Certainly one of the possible and historically most frequent interpretations follows logically from the above quoted statement. This is a fully deterministic interpretation which clearly implies that the superstructure, including the polity, is a function of the base, i.e., of the mode and relations of production. Moreover these relations of production have to correspond to a definite stage of development independent of men's will.

It is of course perfectly true that Marx allowed for the possibility that under certain circumstances the superstructure can shape the base.[13] In some of their writings Marx and Engels attached great importance to ideas and to will as levers of social change. Unfortunately Marx and Engels did not face up to this problem in any systematic fashion; they did not spell out the conditions under which in their view the base or the superstructure would be determinant.[14] This ambiguity opened the way to numerous disputations and scholastic arguments between different schools of Marxism.

For purposes of this paper, the validity of these various interpretations of Marx is of no particular significance. Our focus instead is on what interpretations and emphases have been adopted by socialist movements in different countries, using the term socialist in its broadest meaning (i.e., encompassing communist movements as well). In these terms then, it would seem that in the Western European movements—particularly prior to World War I—great stress was placed on the type of interpretations which logically follows from Marx's statement quoted above. Closely associated with this is the notion that since the superstructure, including the polity and social consciousness (including class consciousness), is a function of the base, socialist movements would grow and socialism would triumph in the more highly industrialized countries. Implicit, and at times explicit, in this approach is an evolutionary rather than a revolutionary view of history. After all, the forces of history are propelled by industrialization and by the changing mode of production and relations of production associated with it. Therefore the role of socialist movements is merely to assist the historical forces as they are unfolding.

This view of Marxism and this type of ideological flavor was clearly not suited to the conditions of Tsarist Russia. Under the circumstances of Russia's backwardness a more *potent* ideology was required to overcome the deadweight of stagnation, engineer a revolution and break the *tension*. It is therefore not surprising to find a much greater emphasis placed in Leninism on the importance of will and consciousness. Struggling in an underdeveloped economy, the Leninist version of Marxism became much more activist, much more concerned about shaping the forces of history rather than waiting for industrialization to take its inexorable course, in one word much more revolutionary. It now fell to the dictatorship of the proletariat to foster industrialization and to create the conditions for the advent of socialism, rather than the other way around. Ultimately the revolution had to be engineered, had to be willed. Accordingly ideology had to be shaped and transformed so as to infuse it with a spirit of radicalism, zeal and commitment sufficient to break the barriers of stagnation.

This strain of *voluntarism* and radicalism with the consequent upgrading in the importance of the superstructure as compared to the base is even more pronounced in Chinese communist ideological interpretations. This is perhaps most clearly evidenced by Mao's repeated stress on man as the most precious thing. This spirit is also reflected in the marked emphasis placed by the Chinese communists on "men over machines" and "men over weapons." In effect, quite central to the Maoist belief system is the pre-supposition that will, spontaneity, consciousness infused by and reflected in ideology and organization can serve as substitutes for technology, equipment, and material forces in general, at least within certain ranges.[15] Or put in another way, ideology and organization can provide the sanction, the rationale, and the wherewithal for far-reaching mobilization of labor and capital (savings) which then through *primitive accumulation* can develop the material forces, launch the industrialization drive and thus develop the base.

Given China's backwardness as compared to that of Tsarist Russia and nineteenth century Europe, classical Marxism as a revolutionary ideology was much too weak and of limited applicability to mainland conditions. Amidst these conditions of even greater relative backwardness, the importance of ideology had to be upgraded significantly since it must perform a host of functions in the system. The radical flavor of the ideology is, at least in part, a function of the widening disequilibrium between capabilities and demands characterizing Chinese polity in the twentieth century. Thus communist ideology in China can be viewed as a product of *tension* as well as an instrument designed to alleviate it.

The radical flavor of communist ideology in China combined with the enormous emphasis placed on indoctrination, thought reform, and remolding of thought is again, at least in part, traceable to China's backwardness. Mass indoctrination and mobilization are required to break the inertia of the masses, the inertia built into the very fabric of society and the structure of the economy, and to break the deadweight of tradition. At the same time, the enormous gap between the technical and production capacities of the system on the one hand and the vast aspirations of the Chinese communists on the other requires very strong faith by the leaders and by the masses in the objectives formulated for the society. Thus ideology serves as a secular religion *par excellence,* much more so than seems to have been the case at any stage in Soviet history.[16]

However, this very emphasis on mass indoctrination, mass mobilization and mass participation so characteristic of the communist system in China seems to have produced certain built-in contradictions and tensions of its own. Thus mass mobilization, mass participation, and mass involvement is really seen by Mao as the only possible path to modernization at this stage of China's development. Maintenance of this mass mobilization base requires tremendous ideological and organizational zeal which can only be buttressed over time by a commitment to a state of permanent revolution. However, as the experience of China and other underdeveloped countries has shown, the mobilization and the technocratic paths to industrialization are to a greater or lesser extent mutually incompatible. While a certain measure of ideologically induced resource mobilization may be a necessary requisite for modernization, such mobilization cannot serve as a substitute for technical and material inputs.[17] Furthermore, extreme mobilization efforts are bound to take place at the expense of input productivity and may greatly complicate the application of the technical and material inputs so vitally needed for modernization and industrialization.

Maoism in effect opts for mass mobilization and a strategy of permanent revolution linked to it—of which the cultural revolution is but an extreme manifestation—because it considers the technocratic path to modernization too slow. Moreover, this path would in any case be ruled out on ideological grounds as leading to bureaucratization and an atrophy of the revolution. It is these sets of dilemmas that seem to push Maoism more and more in the direction of what may be termed *totalitarian populism*. It is populist from several points of view. The concept of the "people" and the "enemies of the people" is quite central to Chinese communist doctrine and mass mobilization practice. But it can be considered as populist in a more important sense. Maoism can be considered as a movement committed to industrialization and modernization, which is yet unwilling to countenance the consequences of industrialization. While the Russian populists of the nineteenth century, strongly wedded to a rural value orientation, resisted the consequences of industrialization, Mao resists the application of modern inputs to the industrialization process because he too fears the consequences. He is concerned that technocratically based industrialism will create elitism, shut out the masses, or increase their consumption propensities and undermine the revolution. Thus just as Russian populism was a peasant-welfare oriented ideology born in a backward, agrarian, and autocratic state so is Maoism a people-using doctrine of an even more backward, agrarian, communist state.

IV. Economic Development and Political Change in Communist Systems

1. Stage of Development, Command Economy and Command Polity

Considering the social system as operating through an interplay of capacities and demands and assuming that it functions in an underdeveloped communist economy placed in a world environment populated by communist, non-communist, and anti-communist states, certain consequences follow. Such a system will tend to be committed at one and the same time to rapid industrialization, a high rate of defense expenditure, and a high rate of resource mobilization—of both capital and labor—needed to sustain these high rates of non-consumption.

The pursuit of these industrialization and defense objectives required that they be translated into operational programs. This in turn suggests the need to draft economic plans and to devise instruments for implementing them. In communist systems such plans have been based in the past on highly specific targets reflecting an explicitly or implicitly formulated order of priorities. These, in turn, were then translated into more or less detailed resource allocation bundles with a very high degree of commitment to their attainment. The implementation of these plans and programs requires the use of certain instruments and appeals. These might be normative, coercive or remunerative; that is ideologically and value-based appeals as contrasted with appeals based on force and compulsion or on material incentives and inducements.[18] The more successful the normative appeals are in motivating the actors in the system to behave in certain ways and implement the objectives as postulated by the planners and the policy-makers, the less will be the need to use coercive or remunerative appeals. From the standpoint of the policy-makers, the normative appeals are the most preferred. If successful, they will lead to goal congruence and goal compliance at minimal resource cost. This goal congruence would, of course, be attained if and when the values of the policy-makers were internalized by the population at large.

If normative appeals fail in producing goal congruence, communist leaders will tend to favor reliance on coercive power as a means of closing the gap between planners' and household preference scales. From an economic development point of view the divergence in time preference scales and in the tradeoffs between work and leisure are of particular importance. These affect the rates of savings and labor mobilization respectively. Should coercive power fail to yield the expected or desired rate of mobilization, or if this mobilization rate can be obtained only at the cost of sharp declines in labor productivity, planners and policy-makers will be forced to rely on remunerative appeals—material incentives—as a means of increasing the supply of labor and other inputs. This would mean raising prices, wages and interest rates. From the standpoint of the classical type of communist leadership this last type of appeal is the least preferred for several reasons. Interest rates may turn out to be a very weak instrument for raising the savings level; these rates may need to be increased very much in order to yield the targeted savings rate, and even then there is no assurance that the desired rate will in fact be attained. Moreover, reliance on wage increases as a means of increasing labor supply runs the danger of boosting household consumption well beyond the levels postulated by the planners. Reliance on material incentives is almost certainly bound to yield a commodity and service output bundle quite different from that desired or planned by the policy-makers. Finally, reliance on remunerative appeals tends to endanger the very control structure and value system on which the communist system is based. Material incentives might encourage spontaneous development in pursuit of individual advantage and thus independent of the state's will, a phenomenon profoundly disturbing to the regime.[19]

In fact, at a particular point in time it is most improbable that any one of these appeals would be used in their pure form. It is much more likely that communist regimes will use appeal mixes, the composition of which, would be expected to shift in the light of changing circumstances and the extent to which the prevailing mix succeeds in evoking the desired response.[20] However this may be, to the extent that coercive power is used to institutionalize a high rate of saving, a high rate of mobilization, and the attainment of specific but ambitious production targets of high priority, a centralized command polity will need to be erected to provide the muscle and the backbone to the centralized command economy. Of course, a command polity may and in fact most probably would be constructed for the attainment of non-economic goals as well.

In the early stages of economic development such a command economy and polity may be quite functional as a model for rapid industrialization. At these stages a large part of economic growth can be based on input mobilization, i.e., the mobilization of latent surpluses of labor and capital, even if it occurs at the expense of input productivity. Moreover, economies in the early phases of development are relatively less complex and less sensitive instruments. There is also less refined division of labor, less functional differentiation and less skill differentiation than characterizes more highly developed economies. Also, such economies necessarily borrow their technology from abroad rather than operate at or near the technological frontiers. For all of these reasons combined, a mobilization strategy of economic growth may serve reasonably well at this stage of "primitive accumulation." Moreover at this same mobilization and "primitive accumulation" stage, terror—either physical or psychological—may serve as a reasonably functional means of applying coercive power for the support of a command polity and economy.

2. Changes in the Command Economy and Polity Under the Impact of Economic Development

One of the hallmarks of the development process is growing complexity, roundaboutness, and interdependence in the production of goods and services. Closely associated with this growing complexity is a rapidly rising demand for technical and scientific skills. At the same time, to the extent that more or less latent labor surpluses were present, these tend to be absorbed during the process of economic growth. As these surpluses are absorbed, labor becomes an increasingly scarce factor. As labor shortages develop and skill level requirements increase, standard mobilization techniques will no longer suffice in increasing the supply of labor and particularly in improving the quality and productivity of labor inputs.

As long as there are more or less readily available pools of surplus labor and as long as the preponderance of demand is for unskilled labor, the growing demand for labor can be met through coercive mobilization or through the use of negative incentives even if these techniques lead to declines in labor productivity. Under these conditions, the negative output effects resulting from losses in labor productivity can be made up by stepping up the rate of mobilization.

Once these surpluses are more or less exhausted, it may become very difficult to call forth incremental increases in labor supply by coercive methods. Moreover these incremental increases may be too small to counteract the losses in labor productivity so that under these conditions coercive mobilization may be expected to yield decreases in output.

Normative appeals, by their very character, are difficult to sustain over long periods of time. They can be used for marshalling an all-out mobilization effort, but they may be much less well suited to maintaining the level of mobilization once attained. Moreover, they are blunt instruments that do not lend themselves too well to inducing incremental increases in supply of labor or of particular forms of skilled labor.

For all these reasons combined, mobilization appeals—coercive and normative—will tend to be more functional in underdeveloped countries at early stages of industrialization. Correspondingly as industrialization progresses remunerative appeals, material incentives, will necessarily assume growing importance.

The industrialization process and the rising complexity, roundaboutness, and interdependence of the economy associated therewith brings also with it an increasing division of labor and a growing functional differentiation of occupations, occupational roles and social roles. Closely interrelated with this process is the rise of managerial bureaucracies in enterprises, in government bureaus, in the party, and in social organizations. These bureaucracies and these processes, in turn, produce a technical, professional and managerial elite.

These patterns of change are reinforced by urbanization accompanying industrialization and the corresponding relative, and eventually absolute, decline in the economic importance of agriculture, in the share of the rural population, and the numbers living in villages. These phenomena then produce an urban way of life with a rising demand for a more intimate and more systematic linking of effort with reward. All of these factors in combination then contribute to rising personal aspirations by the population at large, and the more educated portions of it in particular. This, in turn, then is reflected in growing consumer demand and mounting pressures for sharing in the material benefits of economic advance. These economic and social transformations necessarily create mounting pressures for change in the character of communist regimes.

A command economy system with its centralized network of direct controls becomes more and more difficult to manage as industrialization proceeds and as the economy becomes more complex. Thus the system can be retained only at an increasing economic cost and a loss in efficiency. This may be said to be at least the case at our present state of computer and economic management technology.

The management and operation of a complex economy requires a vast quantity of highly reliable information speedily obtained. It also demands rapid processing of this information and quick decisions in the light of changing circumstances. This places an enormous information and decision-making burden on a highly centralized system of economic administration. The problem is compounded by the fact that in a complex and interdependent economy errors and disequilibria originating at one point in the system might proliferate and reverberate throughout it. In one sense, the information and decision problem is but a symptom of bounded rationality on part of the human actors in the system. Theoretically, alternative paths might be pursued in attempts to resolve this problem: one would lead in the direction of decentralization and the other to "computopia."[21]

In considering decentralization it is essential to distinguish between bureaucratic and market decentralization. Under the first, decision-making powers are retained by the governmental authorities but are decentralized within the governmental apparatus. That is many decision-making powers are delegated by the center to lower level governmental organs, either on a functional or territorial basis. In contrast, under the second type of decentralization decision-making powers are taken out of the hands of the government, taken away from the polity, and transformed to the market. The difficulty with bureaucratic decentralization is, that at least judging by the experience of communist regimes thus far, they solve very few of the problems of a large system and create many new ones. The dilemma from the standpoint of communist regimes is how to retain full political control of the system and at the same time gain economic rationality and efficiency. In this quest continuing attempts are made to design decision-making systems which combine centralized control with decentralized administration.

However, decentralized administration and the delegation of powers built into it necessarily leads to goal bifurcation.[22] It is very difficult, if not impossible, to design a system of incentives for a bureaucracy which will assure spontaneous adherence of lower level organs and micro-units to system goals. Quite apart from this as economic development proceeds and an economic system becomes more complex, bureaucratic decentralization might at best alleviate rather than resolve the information problem.

All of these considerations then may push communist regimes into various forms of experimentation with market decentralization. This, however, runs into political resistance because of the surrender of control entailed in pursuit of this path. The way out of these dilemmas could be provided by a "computopia," if it were feasible. Some tendencies in this direction can be detected in Soviet planning practices in recent years. The hope here would be that central planners could retain complete control while simulating the behavior of a decentralized market system. Moreover, in designing such a "computopia" attempts would be made to improve upon the market by internalizing, i.e., by taking into account and solving for, the externalities in the system. If technically and conceptually feasible, the choice of this strategy could assure retention of centralized political control without loss of economic efficiency. Fortunately or unfortunately at the present state of our theory and computer technology this is not a feasible or practicable solution.

The difficulties in the way of pursuing "computopia" then tend to create new pressures for market decentralization and for placing increasing reliance on material incentives. These are definite limits placed on the degree to which coercive power can be stepped up. Resort to terror under these conditions may perhaps even involve higher economic, social and political costs than at earlier stages of development. In a complex industrial and urban economy, managers must have a reasonable degree of security, predictability and regularity to perform their jobs effectively and efficiently. The aforementioned considerations are reinforced by the fact that as an economy advances and catches up with highly industrialized countries it can rely less on technological borrowing. Correspondingly, if it wants to maintain its pace of progress it must rely more on its own innovative efforts. Innovation and the risk taking entailed in it may however be very seriously deterred in an atmosphere and environment permeated by terror.

However, if under the impact of these economic pressures communist regimes do tolerate, permit, or encourage market decentralization this is bound to have political consequences. These political consequences may be expected to be the more far-reaching the further market decentralization is carried. If this process progresses so far as to leave the implementation of economic decisions to the market—with government policymakers and planners only making macro-decisions—a vast economic bureaucracy becomes displaced. In effect the polity is removed from a vast area of administration as direct controls are replaced by indirect controls exercised through the market. Market decentralization, moreover, tends to foster growth of functional autonomy and helps the development of autonomous centers of power in the economy. Thus market decentralization undermines the position of many power-holders in the system and *pari passu* creates new foci of power. The problem is further complicated for communist regimes by the fact that once certain positions of autonomy develop and spread in the system they are very difficult to contain since they generate pressures for a further spread of autonomy.[23]

All of these tendencies combined will necessarily also have some resource allocative affects. With rising demands for increasing consumption, investment and/or defense expenditure rates will be subjected to growing pressure with possible consequences for the country's defense posture and foreign policy conduct. The cessation of terror with the resulting removal of fear combined with growing autonomy in some sectors may encourage some people to begin speaking up and even to express some unpopular thoughts, thus further undermining the totalitarian character of the communist system.

In conclusion, the general thesis of this paper can be summed up in the following terms: approaching the analysis of the social system from the standpoint of economic capabilities in relation to elite goals, it becomes the function of the political system to implement these goals. The capacities of the economic and political system are constrained by the stage of development. At the same time the attainment of elite goals in a modern state requires mass participation and involvement. The forms of mass participation and the methods and appeals used to evoke them are themselves a function of the stage of development. Moreover, it is through the various forms of mass participation that the capabilities of the economic system are developed.

However, as the process of economic growth alleviates some of the disequilibria between system capabilities and demands, it gives rise to some new contradictions in all societies, including communist ones. In the latter these revolve to a large extent around the contradictory demands of centralized political control on the one hand and economic efficiency on the other. These contradictions are also aggravated by rising literacy of the masses, increasing levels of mass education, growing mass consumption demands, and a greater urge for more intimate linkings of effort with reward.

All of these changes combined with structural transformations in the economy associated with the development process render certain types of economic institutions and political practices less functional at more advanced as compared to earlier stages of development. More specifically a centralized command economy based largely on normative and/or coercive power, most particularly terror, tends to become less and less functional. With the removal of terror, upgrading of remunerative appeals, and the growing pressure for market decentralization, the polity becomes more circumscribed in scope, less pervasive. At the same time, and in fact as a result, more rationality, predictability and autonomy is demanded both by the elites and the masses. Under these circumstances there also tend to arise growing pressures and opportunities for interest group articulation and individual self-expression. Consequently the totalitarian features of communist systems may become transformed and alleviated in the process of economic growth. This need not imply the advent of democracy nor the withering away of communist dictatorships, but rather a change in their form.[24]

Part III

The Inherited Economy

Chapter 4

Economic Change in Early Modern China

I. The Chinese Economy in the Perspective of Worldwide Economic Development

This paper tries to characterize broadly the process of economic change in China during the century of disturbance which ended with the collapse of the Ch'ing dynasty in 1911. In approaching this task we focus particularly upon the factors that retarded growth. In order to gain perspective upon this century of economic transformation in China and place it in the context of world economic development, we first outline briefly and schematically several paths which industrialization has followed since 1750 in different parts of the world.

A. Phases of the Industrialization Process

Although the process of industrialization has characteristically moved through certain definite phases, both the number and the sequence of these phases have varied in different countries. At the risk of over-simplification we may distinguish two basic models, with the early starters, and particularly England, falling into one pattern and many of the under-developed countries of today fitting into the other.

The industrialization process among these latecomers may be divided into five phases characterized by (1) traditional equilibrium, (2) the rise of

Reprinted from John K. Fairbank, Alexander Eckstein, and L. S. Yang, "Economic Change in Early Modern China," *Economic Development and Cultural Change*, October 1960.

disequilibrating forces, (3) gestation, (4) breakthrough or as some prefer to call it, take-off, and (5) self-sustaining growth. Typical features of these periods may be generalized as follows:

In phase one, minor growth, innovation and technological change may occur but they are not sufficient to break the rigid and inhibiting bonds of the traditional framework of social and economic institutions.

In phase two, disequilibrating forces which arise are typically exogenous, originating outside the society and subjecting it to the shocks of war, invasion, colonial rule or the like.

In phase three, these shocks weaken the traditional forms of political, legal, social and economic organization, while new institutions and modes of production are introduced and clash with the old. Disruption is mingled with construction to produce increasing tension between the technically possible and the institutionally feasible. Gestation is evidenced in the creation of certain external economies (e.g., transport, modern commercial or banking facilities), certain industrial nuclei and technically skilled labor, all prerequisite for a breakthrough.

Phase four sees a rapid spurt in the rate of industrial production based in turn on increased rates of investment. Typically industrial growth tends to be most rapid during the breakthrough or take-off, since it is at this stage that the shifts in the production functions are most marked; for many of these are based on once-for-all economies exemplified by shifts from handicraft to machine methods of production. Usually the active leadership in this process is in one or two sectors—textiles, mining, or foreign trade. Industrial growth is accompanied by continuing changes in agriculture.

In phase five, the new industrial economy eventually enters a stage of self-generating growth which continues at a higher rate than under the old order, although less rapidly than during the period of breakthrough. As the growth of established industries slows down, new industries arise to take the lead in the process, indicating that the economic institutions of the society have now become truly industrial—that is, such factors of production as labor and capital have acquired a high degree of mobility and the institutional obstacles to change have been minimized. Economic change and growth, in short, have become institutionalized.

This model fits the experience of India, China, and most other Far Eastern areas (with the exception of Japan) better than it does the experience of the West European countries. For them, the British model is much more applicable. Professor Rostow's three-stage model outlined in his most stimulating article on "The Take-off into Self-Sustained Growth"[1] applies mainly to this British experience.

The distinguishing feature of the British model is that the traditional preindustrial order itself provided a framework for gestation. The commercial revolution of the mercantile period and the agricultural revolution following it were the necessary precursors of the industrial revolution in England. Endogenous, i.e. internally generated, forces played a dominant role in the rise of disequilibrating forces in the form of new inventions, advances in technology and innovations. Precisely because the disequilibrating forces in the English case arose as the culmination of a long process of preparation, they led directly to a breakthrough, rather than to a prolonged pre-industrial period of tension and gestation as in the Far Eastern case.

In between these two patterns or models are a number of intermediate cases in which intricate interplays of exogenous and endogenous factors produced the disequilibrating forces. For instance, in Japan gestation (in the form of growing commercialization during the late Tokugawa era) evolved endogenously as in Britain; but at the same time, unlike the British case, disequilibrating forces arose exogenously in the shock of foreign contact after Perry "opened" Japan. However, with the period of previous preparation, the Western impact on Japan—unlike that on China—led directly to a breakthrough during the Meiji era.

B. Phases of Industrialization in China

The above scheme can be applied to China by assuming that the Chinese economy of the early nineteenth century was in the first phase, that of traditional equilibrium. The old order had already begun to be disturbed by the population growth of the eighteenth century (the process of domestic decline, which became manifest in rebellion, awaits further appraisal). Meanwhile, the best known agent of change in the nineteenth century was exogenous—the growth of Western trade at Canton, which drew China into the network of expanding world trade. The disequilibrating force of the Opium War of 1840 and the Western political and commercial impact thus coincided with the growth of domestic problems of population pressure and administrative decay typical of a period of dynastic decline. These changes began a century-long process of disintegration, transformation and slow gestation within the traditional Chinese order. During this long period, as we shall see, new institutions grew up side by side with traditional ones, a modern economy was built up on the periphery of the old economy, and there was sporadic and scattered growth in some areas (export trade and railroad-building), paralleled by decline or collapse in other sectors (rural handicrafts, particularly cotton spinning). These developments in the latter part of the nineteenth century began to generate an acute degree of tension, in the minds of proud conservatives and later in the minds of modern patriotic Chinese—a tension between the vision of changes which seemed technologically possible for the growth of national strength and the betterment of Chinese life, and the frustrating realities that prevented national self-realization and industrialization within the institutional structure of the old Chinese society. This tension gradually built up to explosive proportions, until the shackles of the old order were violently broken and the Chinese economy erupted at long last into an industrial take-off under totalitarian control which we are witnessing today.

The vigor and violence of the present breakthrough under Communist auspices seems to have been exacerbated by the unusually prolonged period of gestation. China's remarkable early slowness in responding to the Western economic impact may lie behind her present rapidity of change. The fact that the rise of disequilibrating forces and the period of gestation, according to our model, together occupied at least a century suggests a major problem in the study of Chinese economic history—namely, the institutional stability of the old order, which remained remarkably inert long after the traditional equilibrium had been disturbed.

Two concepts may be suggested to account for China's tardiness of response. One is the view that the traditional Chinese order, within the limitations of its inherited technology and value system, had become over the centuries a strongly integrated society with institutions which, developed over long periods, had attained a high degree of sophistication. The old China was thus a firmly-knit and thoroughly tested society with a culture of great vitality. It was also enormous in size, as well as far removed from the aggressive Atlantic society at the other end of the Eurasian land mass. It could not easily adopt Western ways without a fundamental remaking of the entire social order.

The second concept explains China's slow progress in terms of political institutions: it suggests that China's political tradition inhibited the growth of a nation state. The Middle Kingdom had remained a universal empire in Eastern Asia, subject to the periodic control of non-Chinese dynasties whose alien rule at Peking frustrated the growth of modern nationalism. Hence China lacked both the public sentiment and the political leadership necessary for a Japanese type of rapid Westernization.

However China's slowness may be explained, the modern century of her economic history presents us with a record of retarded development. While this cannot be called a period of "stagnation" in the literal sense of "standing still," it was at least one of far-reaching social and economic disorganization, which may even have resulted in an actual decline of per capita product. Should further research support this hypothesis, such a decline could be viewed as a concomitant of this period of disturbance, representing the price China had to pay for its future growth. Perhaps the disturbance and decline constituted social and economic costs the country had to bear in order to create the preconditions for subsequent economic growth.

II. The Old Order

Before we proceed with an analysis of the Chinese economy of a century ago, certain generalizations are necessary. First, while the old order in China exhibited many characteristics typical of a pre-industrial economy, there were some notable differences between the pre-industrial economies of Europe and China. The Chinese economy existed in an institutional and cultural framework distinctly different from that of Western societies. For example, the single fact of a rice economy based on widespread use of water had far-reaching implications affecting the relationship between land and labor, the density of population, and the forms of village, family and kinship organization. These cultural and institutional differences affected the capacity of the economy to adapt itself to change, to grow and to industrialize.

A second general point is that the economy of early nineteenth-century China approximated rather closely Malthus's and Ricardo's model of a "stationary state," with a population pressing against resources close to the margin of subsistence. The prevailing level of technology remaining more or less static, both the Malthusian population checks and the law of diminishing returns were operative. In sum, the China of the early nineteenth century had a circular-flow economy in which production was absorbed in consumption, with very little if any net saving, so that the economy merely reproduced itself without advancing.

Finally, one basic general factor in China's economic destiny was the rapid population growth in the eighteenth century which led to a doubling, or more, in the mere number of the Chinese people, without much immediate change in the character of their economy, culture and institutions. This demographic growth had been made possible by agricultural expansion in the early Ch'ing period of the seventeenth and early eighteenth centuries, which was facilitated both by the peace and order established under the strong Manchu dynasty after 1644 and its comparatively efficient administration, and by the earlier introduction of new crops like maize, sweet potatoes and peanuts in the period after 1500. The new crops greatly widened the food base by making previously marginal soils productive. By the early nineteenth century, however, the margin or reservoir obtained through the introduction of new crops and varieties was probably exhausted, so that population was pushing against the limit of available resources at the prevailing level of technology. While living standards may have risen in the eighteenth century (on this we lack data), it seems probable that they were forced down in the early nineteenth century. The population expansion had not been accompanied by an agricultural revolution comparable to that of eighteenth century England, while the growth of foreign trade and a money economy during the late Ming and early Ch'ing periods (manifest, for example, in the "single-whip" tax reform) had been contained within the traditional social order.

In effect, the period of the late Ming and early Ch'ing can be characterized as one of extensive, rather than intensive, growth based on expansion of cultivated land area and population. The new crops were not in the category of major technological innovations likely to affect the basic modes of production in either agriculture or processing. While there was some commercialization of the economy, it was not a major or disequilibrating change.

Thus we begin with the general assumption that the Chinese peasantry, through their adaptation to environment, had attained an optimum efficiency in resource use and allocation at a more or less stationary level of technology.

We divide the old Chinese economy of the period 1800–1850 into three levels: (1) the agrarian (rural) level, (2) the commercial level, which is superimposed on the agrarian, and (3) the governmental level which is superimposed on both the agrarian and the commercial.

A. *The Agrarian Level*

The agrarian level was that of the villages where seventy to eighty per cent of the Chinese people lived.

The capital equipment of the economy at this level included a large accumulation of man-made installations which had been inherited over the centuries—for example, paddy fields with their embankments, dikes and sluiceways, as well as terraced fields for dry farming, irrigation canals of all sorts together with the wooden contrivances for lifting water, wells, the usual village and farmstead buildings together with groves of mulberry trees, tea bushes, and other resources for handicraft production. Accumulating over many generations, these installations represented an extensive and long-continued investment of labor and in turn made possible a more efficient application of manpower to the soil. It was noteworthy that among these items of capital equipment such as wooden plows and stone grain-grinding rollers there was a minimum of metal equipment and machinery. Irrigation water might be lifted, for example, by a rather simple foot treadle or, alternatively, by a mere bucket with ropes held by two persons. Technical devices commonly in use were geared to the ready availability of cheap manpower.

The natural resources available to the agrarian economy, combined with the capital installations mentioned above, set the character of economic activity. After the eighteenth century extension of cultivation, the additional resources of water and soil available for an increase of cultivation were not great. Similarly, by that time the destruction of forest cover had proceeded very far while the degree of reforestation was insignificant. Coal deposits, although abundant in the northwest and other areas, were not developed and coal was used only on a small scale for local industries. Among the extractive industries, fisheries were rather well developed, both inland and on the coast. Copper, tin and lead were mined in the southwest but had perhaps reached diminishing returns. Iron mining was comparatively undeveloped. In short, the Chinese peasants' use of natural resources was pretty much at the bamboo and wattle level.

Labor in the village was comparatively plentiful per unit of cultivated area. The population increase, under way since the eighteenth century, had left a high proportion of the people in the younger age brackets. Rice culture in South and Central China and the comparable garden-farming methods of North China created a high seasonal demand for hands, and a corresponding need for handicraft production to absorb farm labor power in the off seasons. Cropping systems, ranging from the double-cropping of rice in the far south to the winter wheat of North China, made use of this farm labor power, but its year-round employment was made possible only by the subsidiary handicraft industries—especially cotton, silk, and tea production. These industries in South China, together with the longer growing season, provided the basis for somewhat higher consumption standards than in North China, where seasonal unemployment and chronic underemployment were more prevalent. The abundance and cheapness of labor fostered and perpetuated the labor-intensive methods of farm production—for example, those used in the tea, silk and cotton industries, in hand or manpower irrigation, in transplanting and harvesting of rice and other crops; and also in the use of manpower for transportation by pole, barrow, chair, or the rowing, sculling or tracking of vessels. In other words, not only agriculture but also transport was labor-intensive.

Farm technology, through an age-long and continuous process of adaptation between land and labor, had come to be based on highly intensive land use with comparatively high yields per unit of land but a low yield per unit of labor. The stability of this technology was posited on the whole economic and institutional structure. The relative abundance of labor tended to minimize the inducement to innovate, while the scarcity of capital impeded the capacity to do so. At the same time, the traditional assumptions of the peasantry and the landlord-gentry militated against rapid technological change.

Land tenure, based on a general freedom to buy and sell land, cannot be called "feudal" in the Western European sense, and there were few legal shackles on the peasantry (such as serfdom or villainage). Yet the hard facts of the population-resource balance, aggravated by the prevailing systems of agricultural taxation, credit and marketing, kept the peasant near the margin of subsistence. As the nineteenth century wore on, owner operators were in increasing danger of having to sell their land to make ends meet in a bad year. Tenants were in similar danger of getting so heavily into debt that absconding into pauperism or banditry was their only way out. The system of land tenure lent itself to an increasing concentration of land holding, tenancy and absentee landlordism in modern times.

The social structure and customs, although they provided a stable matrix for the various factors of farm production, included certain institutions which particularly inhibited an increase in the efficiency of production. For example, the lack of primogeniture and the customary fragmentation of land holdings among all the sons, and the comparatively enormous expenditures expected for marriage and funeral ceremonies, all served to inhibit saving. Above all, the distinction between the literate upper classes of landlords, merchants, officials and city-dwellers on the one hand, and the great mass of the illiterate peasantry on the other hand, set a limit to the latter's capacity for innovation. The difficulties of the ideographic script kept the Chinese peasant at the coolie level, able to use his manpower with certain time-tried techniques and devices, but unable to rise easily into the upper strata of society. Conversely, men of trained intelligence with leisure to innovate would not often be found in the fields or workshops. The Chinese class structure, reinforced by Confucian ideology, made a sharper division between hand-worker and brain-worker than in Western Europe. Thus the philosopher Chu Hsi might make his famous observation that the stones on a mountain-top had once been in the sea, but he was in no position to become a Francis Bacon. None of China's great painters, though *ipso facto* scholars, could become a Leonardo.

Entrepreneurship had little opportunity to develop at this rural level. The manufacture of consumer goods like cloth shoes, cotton textiles for clothing, silk and tea were naturally subordinate to agriculture and were generally geared to supplying a strictly local market by using limited capital resources, except as we shall note below. Extractive industries like mining, fishing and lumbering, while somewhat more specialized for the market, shared the same difficulties of being fragmented, labor-intensive and capital-poor, with little change for expansion of production or of marketing.

B. The Commercial Level

This level of economic life served as a sort of highway or bridge linking the agrarian with the governmental level. It performed the distributive and exchange functions which met the closely related needs of inter-regional trade and rural-urban interchange.

The market structure of old China was extremely complex. The agrarian level of economic life was of course self-sufficient only in a relative sense: the share of the agricultural product entering trade channels was rather small, while the dependence of the rural sector upon non-farm purchases was also only of marginal importance. Broadly speaking, rural self-sufficiency was broken in two ways: (1) through unrequited shipments of tax grain and (2) through an exchange of a variety of special products for salt and similar necessities, the few important staples that had to be purchased, and for a few luxury products. On the other hand, trade in the traditional economy can be considered as the supply system for the Chinese upper classes—that combination of large landowners, scholar literati, officials and merchants who constituted the mobile top strata over the inert peasant mass. These people provided the chief market for luxury products, just as they were also the population groups not directly engaged in the process of agricultural production.

Trading activity took place within a quite complex, inefficient and highly fragmented market organization characterized by a marked proliferation of middlemen. The market structure was inevitably peppered with strong monopolistic and monopsonistic tendencies. Trade in staple commodities, the demand for which was quite inelastic, was mostly subject to government monopoly. However, the system of official regulation and licensing frequently broke down in practice, as illustrated by the operation of the salt monopoly, where as much as half the salt might be distributed through illegal smuggling channels which were not secret so much as connived at by the lower officialdom. Of course, breaches of this type in the power of monopoly, far from leading to invigorated competition, merely involved a change from an official to an extra-legal system of licensing. Within this framework, commodity flows ran through an interlocking maze of local, regional, and to some extent even international markets.

Local trade, to begin with, was part and parcel of rural life, centered on the local market towns with their fairs and periodic (typically, tenth-day) village markets to which merchants regularly brought their wares. This local trading activity had a regularity and rhythm comparable to the other cycles of rural activity which carried the villagers through their daily routines, through the seasons of the year, and through the span of human life in an established context of goals, expectations and techniques. Local trade distributed necessary consumer goods like salt, metal ware and paper to the peasant households, together with items considered to be luxuries, like porcelain, tea or silk. This distribution was effected with an extensive use of barter and personal credit arrangements. In exchange for goods brought in through local trade, the farm surpluses, if any (pigs, fruit, etc.), and special local products like wood oil or opium, were shipped out. Our typical picture of local trade is that it radiated out from the market town or fair about the distance that goods could be transported in one day on a round trip by carrying pole or sampan. This created a cellular pattern of local economy in which a region could survive indefinitely when nature was favorable and similarly might be devastated by natural calamity.

Interregional trade was superimposed on this cellular and interwoven pattern of local trade. Interregional trade was in part merely one aspect of the general urban-rural interchange, i.e., the aforementioned bridge between the agrarian and official levels. However, over and above this, it was a reflection of a certain amount of regional specialization. Among such regionally traded commodities were salt, which was made by a variety of means in some eleven officially established production areas and distributed thence by licensed merchants; tea and silk, which in much of South and Central China were local products of low grade but became goods for regional trade when produced in their highest quality (for example, the teas of Northern Fukien and Kiangsi; and the silk of the Huchow region inland from Shanghai); porcelain, which was specially produced under imperial auspices at Ching-te-chen in Kiangsi; copper, tin and lead which came particularly from Yunnan; or heavy timber such as was brought down the Yangtze.

International trade, against this background, may be viewed as merely a special, and from the point of view of the Chinese economy a rather unimportant, form of interregional trade. Chinese commodities which had gone abroad from ancient times had included the silks which crossed the ancient Central Asian route to Rome; Sung porcelain and copper coins, which went by sea throughout the Indian Ocean region; and brick tea, which was taken from the Wuhan region up the Han River route toward Mongolia and Russia. Over the centuries the balance of trade had generally favored China, where the wide range of latitude from the tropics to Manchuria made for an essentially self-sufficient economy. There had been a general flow of gold and silver bullion from Japan, and especially from

Mexico by way of the Philippines, with some later increments from Europe and India directly. The early Portuguese had facilitated the exchange of Chinese silk for Japanese silver through Macao. Meanwhile the major commercial development of pre-industrial China was carried on over the junk routes. The fleets of Ningpo exchanged a wide range of produce with the Korean peninsula and southern Manchuria. The main southern route centered on Amoy and went around the Southeast Asian coast to the straits of Malacca. Over this route came a variety of woods, spices and edibles, including sugar. However, none of these forms of international trade had dealt in staple consumer goods until the late eighteenth century, when raw cotton began to be imported from India.

The transport network which made possible this regional exchange within China as well as abroad was well developed within the limits of prevailing technology. The paths suitable for carrying-poles or barrows between villages were supplemented in Central and South China by waterways. Where the North China coolie might compete with donkeys and on the northern border with camels, the chief carrier in the Yangtze basin and southward was the sampan powered by human muscle. Large gangs of transport coolies were available for the portages on the water routes—for example, the tea coolies who after 1850 carried shipments from Northern Fukien into the water network of Kiangsi. The water transportation of South and Central China by river, lake and canal served the great bulk of the Chinese population. The accumulated public works of centuries had produced a nexus of canal and sampan routes, fed by the broad continental system of rivers and lakes which were in turn nourished by the heavy precipitation over the hills and mountains of South China. As a result it was possible to move persons and goods by water routes that were continuous or almost continuous from Canton to Peking and from the southeast coast to the borders of Tibet.

The efficiency of Chinese inland water transport was remarked upon by the early Western embassies to China in the late eighteenth century. Both the British Macartney embassy of 1793 and the Amherst embassy of 1816 on their return from Peking used the canal barge route all the way to Canton except for the brief portage of twenty-four miles or so over the Meiling Pass north of Canton. The Dutch embassy of 1794–95 used this route in both directions. These European observers estimated that Chinese rafts could carry twenty tons on one foot of water.

Meanwhile, coastal transport by the seagoing junk fleets, which totaled on the order of 10,000 vessels, also provided a channel of domestic transportation all the way from Hainan Island to Manchuria. Sea transport of the grain supply for Peking by junk fleets around the Shantung promontory provided an alternative to the Grand Canal even before the decline of the latter after 1852. While not capable of the speed of the clipper ships, Chinese junks with their lateen sails were remarkably efficient carriers, especially when using steady seasonal winds on established coastal routes.

All in all, we may regard the complex and pervasive network of Chinese water transport as comparable to the traditional farm economy—that is, highly developed within its technological limitations.

The supply of capital for the operation of this economy was comparatively limited. Savings might be accumulated by the enlarged family in the form of real estate, particularly land, but such savings were not liquid and were seldom available as a basis for credit creation except as security against loans. Rural moneylenders secured high rates of interest but did not become institutionalized as bankers or even as professional moneylenders. The most common kind of rural credit was that granted by landlords to tenants against the security of future crops. Towns and cities naturally had more institutions for capital accumulation. For example, the pawnshops did a lucrative business and were extensively invested in by wealthy officials. Typically, this was a nonproductive type of investment. The hoarded capital of merchant guilds and of licensed merchant-guild members (like the large salt merchant families or the family firms in the Canton Cohong) was sometimes used to finance commercial operations. One of the most rewarding forms of investment was to purchase a licensed position in one of the many monopolies sanctioned by the government—for instance, in the salt gabelle. In other words, money was to be made less by producing goods than by transferring or handling goods or funds, including taxes and fees.

Typical of this situation was the fact that the famous Shansi remittance banks, which were simple partnerships with branches elsewhere in China operating on capital funds on the order of 100,000 or 200,000 taels, were engaged not in deposit banking or lending of funds for productive enterprise but rather in the simple remitting of funds from place to place, mainly for the official class. These banks were developed in the late eighteenth and early nineteenth centuries to replace the more primitive escort agencies (*piaochu*) which had been established to escort and protect the movements of bullion funds from place to place. However, in the course of performing this transfer function in its more sophisticated form—through drafts—they did not become agencies for the creation of credit in the fashion of modern banks. With credit formation thus handicapped, the commercial economy was all the more dependent on the supply of currency, in the form of copper cash or silver bullion. The fluctuations in the rate of exchange between these two media greatly complicated the difficulties of trade in nineteenth-century China, as we shall note below.

The currency and exchange system, like the system of weights and measures generally, was remarkably complex because the major unit of account, the tael (*liang* or ounce) was not uniform but varied from place to place and trade to trade. The classical description of the situation is that of Dr. H. B. Morse, for the city of Chungking:

> Here the standard weight of the tael for silver transactions is 555.6 grains, and this is the standard for all transactions in which the scale is not specified. Frequently, however, a modification of the scale is provided for, depending in some cases upon the place from which the merchant comes or with which he trades, and in others upon the goods in which he deals. A merchant coming from Kwei-chow, or trading with that place, will probably, but not certainly, use a scale on which the tael weighs 548.9 grains; a merchant from Kweifu, a town on the Yangtze a hundred miles below Chungking, will buy and sell with a tael of 562.7 grains; and between these two extremes are at least ten topical weights of tael, all "current" at Chungking. In addition to these twelve topical "currencies", there are others connected with commodities. One of the most important products of Szechwan is salt, and dealings in this are settled by a tael of 556.4 grains, unless it is salt from the Tzeliu well, in which case the standard is 557.7. A transaction in cotton cloth is settled with a tael of 555.0 grains, but for cotton yarn the tael is 556.0 grains and for raw cotton the tael is 547.7 grains.
>
> This seems confusion, but we are not yet at the end. Up to this point we have dealt only with the weight on the scale, but now comes in the question of the fineness of the silver with which the payment is made. At Chungking three qualities of silver are in common use—"fine silver" 1,000 fine current throughout the empire, "old silver" about 995 fine, and "trade silver" between 960 and 970 fine; and payment may be stipulated in any one of these three

qualities. Taking the score of current tael-weights in combination with the three grades of silver, we have at least sixty currencies possible in this one town.

It seems evident that the tael system's complexity suited the interests of exchangers of currency rather than the interests of sellers or buyers of goods; at any rate it favored all of these persons rather than the producer or the ultimate consumer. We must understand it as an institution tied in with the vested interests of the middleman-merchant class and its patrons the official class, rather than with the interests of entrepreneurs seeking to produce goods or to develop new products and markets. Every time goods or funds passed through the commercial network, a percentage was levied for the costs of exchange operations. Half a dozen such levies and operations would not be unusual in an ordinary transaction between one province and another. Furthermore, the complexity of the tael system was so great as to make exchange an esoteric subject, monopolized by specialists and insiders with a knowledge of the system. This facilitated an inefficient proliferation of services, in which the distributive process involved more layers and more manpower than was really necessary. This inevitably must have impeded commodity flows, causing numerous delays, wastage and spoilage. Moreover, the distributive margin between buying and selling prices was thus increased because of the excessive number of persons who derived support from it.

Management and entrepreneurship at this level of the economy were generally inhibited by the subordination of merchants to officialdom. The patronage of the upper stratum of landlords, literati and officials was essential to commercial operations. In theory, the state was expected not only to preempt certain monopolies like salt and iron, but also to regulate commercial and industrial activities by licensing and other means, and in general limit capital accumulation and expenditure by individuals. The merchant had no legal safeguards to protect his property against exactions from the government level, since the officials represented the law. Thus while bureaucratic patronage and protection were essential to commercial operations of all sorts, the official class retained the spirit of tax-gatherers rather than of risk-taking entrepreneurs. Their gentry-landlord background and the scholarly disesteem for the merchant class from ancient times, all imposed strict limits to merchant initiative and innovation. Economic enterprise was carried on within a framework in which the power of officialdom was the final recourse, rather than a system of impersonal law which the merchant might invoke to protect himself. By using official patronage and power, a merchant capitalist could secure certain lucrative opportunities represented by licenses or monopolies, the right to distribute salt, contracts for the transport of grain, or sales orders for the imperial household or official establishments. The merchants' aim was to seek comparatively safe forms of profit-making and therefore to secure an opportunity for levying fees and charges, both official and unofficial, upon one of the great staples of commerce. In each case this opportunity had to be secured on a personal basis and preserved with the support of official power. Thus the whole prevailing structure of incentives was such as to encourage and perpetuate established forms and norms of commerce while at the same time discouraging risk-taking, the seeking out of new markets, or innovation.

C. The Governmental Level

By this we mean the economic activities organized, superintended, or indirectly controlled by the official class on behalf of the imperial government at the capital and in the provinces.

The role of government in the economy was posited on the fact that the official class retained the ultimate power in Chinese society. The government in one sense was rather active in the country's economic life, but in another sense its role was limited and passive. On the one hand, the dead weight of official and quasi-official forms of taxation bore heavily upon the country's economy, as did also the various forms of state monopoly, licensing and the like. All of these, in effect, entailed a negative type of interference. On the other hand, the services performed for the economy by the Chinese state were minimal—largely confined to the maintenance of the waterworks and the stocking of granaries as a safeguard against famine. The active promotion of mercantile activity, the concept of the development of the economy as a whole—i.e., an implicit or explicit concept of economic growth—or the idea of building up the country's economic power as a prerequisite for augmenting state power, all seem to have been minimal in the Chinese tradition. This accords with the fact that the whole notion of international competition and thus of economic nationalism, even in its mercantilist sense, was absent. This can be illustrated by the fact that there was no idea of a protective tariff, and that similar tariff rates were applied to exports and imports. This general attitude was also clearly reflected in fiscal practice.

The Ch'ing fiscal system was pervasive, but highly inefficient. It operated within an imposing facade of regulations including quotas for revenue collections by regions, fixed charges on these collections and allocations of payments, both to the capital and to other provinces by transfer directly. Collections were partly in kind but major revenue collections were in money terms. According to the imperial bookkeeping in the statutes, surplus-revenue provinces regularly paid sums to revenue-deficit provinces and all sums entered were allocated to specific purposes. In actual fact, however, it is plain that much larger sums were handled within each province, if only to maintain the bureaucracy and its activities, without being accounted for to the capital. When under pressure for funds, the officials commonly collected contributions, or in other words, made levies upon merchants or indeed upon anyone known to have money. Since such persons usually had secured their funds in part through official patronage, this system of contributions was perhaps not inequitable. Literary degrees and official titles and, in extreme cases, even official positions were conferred upon the contributors. The sums so levied sometimes reached millions of taels from major monopolists in the salt trade or the foreign trade at Canton. But this form of quasi-taxation was certainly not a type of levy to encourage capital formation.

Land tax and labor service formed the backbone of the fiscal system and were aimed at garnering for the government the surpluses of agricultural products and rural manpower which formed the chief economic resources of traditional China. These taxes had a long and necessarily complex history coming down through more than two millenia. In general, by the nineteenth century they had been combined into a complex system of payments in money terms. Expected receipts were listed as quotas, both for provincial and for local areas at different levels. Statutorily, the local quotas were intended to maintain the official post stations, local public works and the bureaucracy, at the discretion of the local officialdom. Provincial quotas were also set for amounts to be made available to the Board of Revenue at Peking. The actual collection of local taxes, as noted above, was several times the statutory amount of the various quotas listed at Peking. The estimation of the amount of taxation actually levied is one of the more important problems awaiting study by economic historians. In general, officialdom was put somewhat in the position of tax farmers, required to report a minimum to their superiors and expected to collect enough in addition to maintain themselves and their activities.

The efficiency of tax collection depended upon the degree of dynastic vigor at the time. During periods of dynastic strength, official corruption tended to stay within bounds and thus fiscal efficiency could be maintained. This frequently meant a lighter tax burden, more equitably distributed, with a larger proportion of receipts finding their way to Peking and with a better performance of public services. However, in the course of dynastic decline, official corruption tended to be reinforced by the growth of local vested interests, by a decline of morale, and by an increased need for official funds. In such circumstances the efficiency of collection would decline, many large households and favored families would get themselves off the tax registers, and in the end a higher tax total would be collected if possible from a dwindling and impoverished segment of the rural population. The classic result would be rebellion followed by a new dynasty and a beginning of the dynastic cycle.

The grain tribute collected in kind in the Yangtze provinces was a special form of tax to provide the stipendiary food supply of the imperial capital. There was a widespread and intricate administrative network for the transport of this tribute grain to Peking. The grain transport administration had to cope with the problem of maintaining the Grand Canal and the lower reaches of the Yellow River dike system so that grain shipments from the Yangtze delta could traverse the regions normally flooded by the Yellow River system—a major engineering problem as well as an administrative one. The alternative to the Grand Canal was the system of sea transport by junk fleets from the Shanghai area around the Shantung promontory, on a route probably as much subject to shipwreck as the canal route was subject to pilfering or banditry. The grain tribute performed several economic functions: it fed the swollen bureaucracy surrounding the imperial court and the Manchu military garrisons in the north and provided supplies for the maintenance of emergency stocks. At the same time, it played an important role in internal trade and in limiting the self-sufficiency of the rural sector.

The military establishment, with its large stipends to maintain garrisons of Manchu and other bannermen and their families, was one of the great vested interests and administrative problems. The local territorial troops, or constabulary, the so-called Army of the Green Standard, were maintained from local land-tax sources. By the nineteenth century, both the garrisons of bannermen and the constabulary had proved ineffective to quell local rebellion. The eighteenth-century expeditions on China's borders and into neighboring regions like Tibet, Annam or Central Asia had drained funds from the government with questionable economic return. In the ten great campaigns under the Ch'ien-lung Emperor we can see at work the ever-present urge to contain the barbarians, combined with a vested military interest on the part of Manchu commanders who led large forces in border operations and requisitioned even larger sums to support them. It is a question whether the financial profit to be derived from these expeditions was not an important incentive for them. After the White Lotus Rebellion at the turn of the century, however, the traditional military forces had lost their capacity and morale and represented a net drain upon the state economy.

III. Pre-industrial China and Pre-industrial Europe

A comparison of the pre-industrial economies of Europe and China may help us to identify the factors and processes that facilitated growth in the former and retarded it in the latter. Such a comparison yields a number of striking similarities and also some major differences:

A. Similarities

In both societies a primarily agrarian economy supported a small super-structure. It was based on a "natural economy" of local barter with a low degree of commercialization and minimal use of money. Money served more as a standard and store of value than as a medium of exchange and payment. The monetary system was inefficient. The low degree of com-mercialization was also indicated by the extensive barriers to trade in the form of tolls, dues and taxes on the movement of goods; the poor development of roads and communications except for water transport; and the general scarcity of capital as measured by high and usurious rates of interest. As a result, these were essentially what Heckscher has called "storage economies," in which consumption largely depended upon ac-cumulated stocks. Such inventories of grain and other foodstuffs were needed not only to meet inter-harvest requirements, but also to serve as a protection against natural and man-made disasters. Thus a considerable proportion of China's current resources were tied up in an unproductive form of investment. Other similarities to the pre-industrial European scene included the low status of the merchant and money-lender, and the extensive use of guild organization to protect and also control merchant activities.

B. Dissimilarities: Foreign Trade and City Growth

The dissimilarities between China and pre-industrial Europe are perhaps even more notable: for example, in pre-industrial Europe possibly the two most important factors contributing to the process of economic change were the growth of foreign trade and the growth of autonomous cities. Europe's development and expansion overseas after 1492 were marked by a widening in the extent of the market and the commercialization of the economy together with extensive capital accumulation, all facilitated through foreign trade. These developments also depended upon the growth of urban centers, with their legal status as chartered cities or city states and the special privileges extended to the burghers. The growth of the bourgeoisie symbolized the rise of modern Europe.

Neither of these elements had a counterpart in China. Foreign trade in proportion to the total economy, even during the Sung period, never reached the degree of importance which it had in Europe. The reasons for this smaller role of foreign trade in the case of China are many and varied. First, the geographical configuration of the Chinese setting put its centers of ancient population on the broad irrigated plains of the Wei and Yellow Rivers. Only later did dense populations accumulate in delta regions like those of Canton and Shanghai, after China's social institutions had been well established. When seaports eventually developed, their growth was handicapped by China's comparative isolation from other major states. Korea remained an appendage, accessible by land as well as sea. Japan and Annam were comparatively small and peripheral. Chinese expansion was chiefly absorbed in the subcontinent of the modern Chinese area—for example, into the Southwest or into Central Asia. With half a dozen domes—the provinces, each bigger than any accessible foreign state, China's trade remained oriented toward the domestic market and not based upon seafaring. Arab traders from Southeast Asia had taken the lead in developing commercial sea contact with Chinese ports. Only afterward, in the Sung and Yuan periods, had Chinese merchants become principal participants in maritime trade. From the Ming period, the cultural and social institutions of China became still more firmly ethnocentric in character, with little emphasis upon voyaging abroad (as in the European crusades to the Holy Land or later to Asia on the track of Marco Polo).

Against this background, the deliberate government policy of regulating and restricting foreign trade in the Ming and Ch'ing periods is quite understandable. The big Ming expeditions into the Indian Ocean were governmental experiments and were discontinued after the middle of the fifteenth century. The Manchu dynasty came down from the north and controlled South China last. Not until the end of the seventeenth century did it resume the Ming system of tributary trade. Even then it was always ready to sacrifice maritime commerce in the interest of maintaining local order and preventing the influx of subversive foreign influences. China remained largely self-sufficient within her own borders between the tropics and Siberia.

At the same time, the Chinese city was under the domination of officials rather than of merchants. The major urban centers were administrative rather than commercial. The tradition of government monopoly or regulation of all forms of large-scale association and economic activity kept commercial growth subordinate to the political, administrative and military interests of the noncommercial ruling strata.

Lying behind the contrast between China and Western Europe are the differing institutional frameworks and cultural values within which their economies developed. The West, except in Egypt, had little counterpart to the irrigated rice economy which had such far-reaching influence on Chinese life. The Mediterranean Basin facilitated the growth of city-states and sea trade, and Western European geography with its radiating peninsulas later fostered the development of nation-states and overseas explorations. These same factors promoted the introduction and diffusion of new technologies and new ideas. In contrast, the Chinese empire from the beginning was turned in upon itself by the Central Asian land mass and the expanse of the Pacific Ocean. It early developed a bureaucratic empire in which the legal system remained a tool of the official class. Feudalism in China was wiped out at the time of the Ch'in unification. From the Han period on, the bureaucratic network and the ideal of imperial unity militated against the rise of detached and particularistic political-economic areas. In spite of the barbarian inroads after the Han dynasties, the geographical environment and cultural and institutional inheritance of the Chinese people were so strong as to lead to a revival of unified empire. This meant that the pluralistic and multifocal institutional structure of Western Europe, with its struggles and rivalries among the crown, the nobles, the lesser gentry, the cities and burghers, between church and state and between nation and nation within Christendom, had no counterpart in Chinese experience. Where European development out of the chaos of feudalism stimulated dynamic and individualistic innovation and adventure, the Chinese empire remained a bureaucratic colossus bestriding all social life. This was reflected in the legal system which did not protect the individual within the family nor the individual property holder nor, least of all, the merchant; and also in the Confucian ethic, which did not give the individual the same incentive as the Protestant ethic.

It would be a mistake, on the other hand, to regard Chinese society, with its dominant bureaucratic overlay, as the equivalent of a modern centralized state. On the contrary, the old China inculcated the particularism of family-centered kinship relations and village or market-town-centered economic relations. At both of these levels personal relationships remained more important than the universalistic and rational criteria which have developed, rather recently, in modern European society. In short, the different economic growth of Europe and China is symptomatic of the total cultural difference between them.

IV. China's Economic Development, ca. 1760–1914

In essence, the disequilibrating forces and the pattern of disturbance in China were similar to those in most underdeveloped areas. Yet in China economic change followed a different path conditioned by extraterritoriality and the rise of the treaty ports. They served as a means for transplanting not only of Western capital and entrepreneurs, but of Western legal institutions and commercial practices as well. This was possible because the treaty ports were protected from the arbitrary exactions of officialdom and the other impediments to economic activity referred to above. These conditions encouraged the accumulation of capital in the ports, both by Western and by Chinese enterprise.

Therefore, in effect, the prime agents of economic change in nineteenth-century China are comparable to those seen earlier in Europe—foreign trade which provided the impetus, and special city status formalized through extraterritoriality which provided the opportunity. However, unlike Europe, China's new economic growth did not radiate out into, and become diffused throughout, the traditional economy. The institutional barriers in the traditional sector of the economy, and the failure of the government's efforts to achieve an industrial breakthrough under official auspices, seriously impeded factor mobility between the hinterland and the treaty ports; growth did not take root outside the ports, but remained bottled up in them. One part of the economy remained based on the traditional order while another grew up in the coastal and riverine cities. Thus industry was concentrated in the treaty ports in order to secure the institutional advantages of greater legal protection of property and investment. The metropolis of Shanghai and its dominant position in Chinese manufacturing at the end of the treaty century are outstanding examples of this phenomenon, as are also Tientsin and Canton.

In analyzing the pattern of economic change during this century of disturbance, it is useful to distinguish several sub-periods.

A. The Drawing of China into the World Economy, 1760–1842

The domestic economic developments of this period have been little studied but presumably centered about the phenomenal population increase. Under the stimulus of factors operating in the early eighteenth century which need not detain us here, the population more or less doubled in this period. Present estimates give an order of magnitude somewhere around 230 million for 1760 and 430 million for 1842. The economic implications of such growth can be imagined but have not been extensively traced in the record.

Foreign trade in this period centered at Canton as the sole port. It was based on a barter of Chinese tea and silk for Western silver and Indian produce, carried on mainly by the licensed guild known as the Cohong and the British East India Company within a framework of bilateral monopoly. At the Chinese end this trade was conducted on a bargaining basis with a price solution that was necessarily indeterminate. The triangular Chinese-British-Indian trade, balanced by the so-called Country Trade from India, has been studied to some degree. China engaged in a passive trade, in which the foreigner took the initiative by coming to Canton. After arrival, the East India Company vessels had to dispose of their cargoes of British woolens and other products. Very generally, the Hong merchants could take these goods at a loss and consequently had to raise their tea and silk prices to cover this loss. There was an increasing tendency for the Hong merchants to borrow capital from the East India Company. Hong debts and Hong bankruptcies consequently plagued the British company operations. The increasing tea and silk exports which grew in response to the European demand were made possible only by the imports of raw cotton and opium from India. After about 1819 opium eclipsed cotton as the chief means of "laying down funds" in Canton for the continually growing export trade. But while exports passed outward through the established channels of the Hong merchants and the East India Company, the opium import trade was illegal and centered elsewhere, in the hands of the opium merchants both foreign and Chinese. Thus the Canton system with its British East India Company and Cohong monopolists ceased to be the channel for the major import, and was left standing, so to speak, on one leg only. When the tea exports rose to twenty million pounds a year and above, the result was that opium smuggling, administrative collapse, disorder and friction grew proportionately. All of this culminated in the Opium War and the unequal treaties, which led to the abolition of the Canton monopoly and permitted trade expansion.

The repercussions of the opium dispute of the late 1830's on the domestic economy have not been fully analyzed. The growth of the Shansi banks in the early nineteenth century and the simultaneous accumulations of capital by Cantonese Hong merchants and by salt monopolists in the lower Yangtze and other self-producing regions would suggest that there was a general growth of money economy within China during this period. Another indication is in the increased valuation of silver in terms of copper cash—a complex subject of the Opium War period. Chinese officials ascribed the increased cost of silver to its outflow in exchange for opium, overlooking its attendant inflow to pay for tea and silk. Debasement of the copper coinage, the increased demand for silver as the chief medium of exchange in an expanding money economy, hoarding in a period of disorder, to say nothing of population increase, are other factors lying behind this phenomenon.

B. *Economic Disorganization and Decline, 1842–1864*

The treaty system established a new institutional framework for foreign trade. In the treaty ports the lead was taken by commission or agency houses, like Jardine, Matheson and Co., Dent and Co., or Russell and Co., which developed services for trade expansion through chartering ships, insuring cargo and buying and selling on a commission basis for Western merchants at a distance. On the Chinese side, these Western treaty port firms used Chinese compradores, who had formerly been merely buyers of supplies, but who now undertook both to collect export cargoes and to distribute import goods on a commission basis. With the assistance of Cantonese compradores inherited from the earlier period, new trade outlets and trade routes were rapidly developed. They centered particularly on Shanghai, which was closer than Canton to the major centers of tea and silk production. While exports continued to grow, the trade remained handicapped by the small Chinese demand for Western textiles and other manufactured imports. The result was a steady increase of illegal but well organized opium imports.

The impact of this treaty-port trade after 1842 upon the Chinese economy as a whole is still obscure. The domestic living standard recorded in literary references seems to have been characterized by a Confucian austerity and frugality among the ruling strata in the seventeenth century, followed by a more lavish display and consumption of goods in the prosperous eighteenth century. Similar literary references suggest an increasing economic stringency and imperial parsimony in the early nineteenth century. Under the impact of population increase, the decline of the dynasty's administrative competence seems to have been evidenced by an increased incidence of natural calamities, the declining efficiency of the Grand Canal transport route, and the growth of piracy and opium smuggling on the coast. At any rate, the impact of the early foreign trade must be fitted into this larger domestic context more persuasively than has yet been done. The Marxist-Leninist contention that foreign imports depressed native living standards by wiping out rural handicraft production cannot be substantiated for the period before the 1860's. On the contrary, it may be argued that with the phenomenal increase of tea and silk exports, per capita product may have risen in some areas. In any case, such estimates must vary according to the regions considered—the lower Yangtze tea and silk areas may have prospered while the hinterland of Canton may have suffered from the new treaty system.

The Taiping Rebellion of 1851–1864, on balance, must be regarded as a product of domestic causes, with foreign factors playing a minor role. Its impact upon the economy was devastating, though this is another subject that has not been sufficiently explored. The great rebellion and the smaller disorders which accompanied and followed it curbed population growth, and perhaps resulted in an actual decline of population. Key areas of the countryside were ravaged and the channels of trade were disrupted. All of this was made worse by the deterioration of the water control system and consequent flooding of the Yellow River, which changed its course from south to north of the Shantung peninsula after 1852. Thus rice supplies for the capital had to be transported by sea instead of the Grand Canal.

One of the most significant effects of the rebellion was the cutting off of the land tax of South and Central China. In response, the imperial government had recourse to expedients like the issue of paper currency and casting of large copper or iron cash. Its chief recourse, however, was to institute taxes on trade, among which the new Maritime Customs at the treaty ports were most important. Unofficially, new taxes were also levied on opium imports. Most important of all was the new provincial tax on goods in transit, i.e., *likin,* which got started in 1853.

The general result of the rebellion was thus a restructuring of the fiscal system with a shift from direct to indirect forms of taxation. This meant a greater dependence of the imperial government upon foreign trade revenues, at a time when the enforced treaty revisions of 1858 and 1860 made it dependent also on political cooperation with the foreign powers.

C. The Abortive Breakthrough, 1864–1895

This was a crucial period during which Japan succeeded in breaking out of the vicious circle of economic backwardness, while similar attempts to bring about a state-led industrial revolution failed in China, for reasons which we shall try briefly to indicate.

The decade of the active restoration of Confucian government, after the suppression of rebellions, was attended by the use of foreign arms and the setting up of arsenals at Shanghai and Foochow to make guns and gunboats. At the same time, the revised treaties opened the Yangtze River and North China treaty ports to foreign trade, foreign steamships developed these new routes, and China now lay open to complete foreign access by water, along the coast and in the interior. The power of the foreign trade impact was signalized by the growth of such port cities as Shanghai, Tientsin, and Hankow, and the rise of foreign banks, like the Hongkong and Shanghai Banking Corporation formed in 1864.

Foreign trade in this period increased steadily, and the treaty port cities began their economic domination of the commercial hinterland, into which their goods were flowing. The decline in staple exports led to a diversification of trade as reflected in the export growth of a variety of new products—tung oil, dried eggs, bristles, and similar products of the agrarian economy. At the same time, kerosene and tobacco began to develop their mass markets, symbolized later by the wide distribution networks of the Asiatic Petroleum Company and the British-American Tobacco Co.

Technology and training in industry were given some stimulus from translation programs and from the dispatch of students abroad. Yet here again the traditional social structure and cultural values kept the trained men of superior intelligence from pursuing mechanical or even mercantile aims.

Under the impact of all of these developments combined, domestic handicraft production now began to be subjected to the competition of Western textile imports, while at the same time the transplanting of tea plants to India led to serious competition with Chinese tea exports, and the opening of Japan to foreign trade stimulated Japanese competition in silk exports. China suffered in this competition because the standardization of product and organization of marketing and finance were more advanced in India and Japan. It is extremely difficult, however, to get a balanced estimate of the trends of Chinese farm economy and subsidiary handicraft industries of this period. For example, one imponderable factor was the degree of destruction inherited from the period of rebellion. Government efforts to replant mulberry trees for silk production and to revive agriculture generally, and the evidence of widespread destruction in the countryside of the lower Yangtze provinces indicate the magnitude of this factor. In these decades Indian opium imports began to be displaced by steadily rising domestic opium production, so that in the 1880's these imports actually declined.

This is the period which also signalizes the early efforts at industrialization under official sponsorship. Many industries were begun. The China

Merchants' Steam Navigation Company under government auspices and compradore management began to compete with foreign shipping after 1872. The Kaiping Mines were developed north of Tientsin from the late seventies to provide coal for the steamship lines and for Shanghai. Eventually China's first railroad line was built to service these coal exports under central government auspices. The institutional mechanism for these developments in general was that of "official supervision and merchant operation" (*kuan-tu shang-pan*). This in effect was an attempt to make an industrial breakthrough while leaving the institutional framework essentially untouched. The reasons for the failure of this attempt have now been assessed by Dr. Albert Feuerwerker's volume on *China's Early Industrialization*.[2] They will also be clearly illustrated in a forthcoming study by Dr. Kwang-Ching Liu which analyzes the failure of one of the leading enterprises under this system, the China Merchants' Steam Navigation Company. The precursor of this system of "official supervision and merchant operation" had been the traditional Chinese salt administration, a government salt monopoly which was essentially a fiscal institution. The attitudes and practices characteristic of such an institution consequently affected the management of all the enterprises set up under this system. They were viewed by the officials as a source of "squeeze" and personal income; this attitude was typical of all the levels of officialdom, all the way up to the imperial court. At the same time, enterprises operating under this system were used as instruments for broadening the regional power of the different cliques which vied for primacy within the nineteenth-century Chinese state. This attitude then spread to the managers of these enterprises, who viewed them basically as objects of despoliation. Thus both the sponsors and the operators of these would-be-modern enterprises were motivated by a tax-farming rather than an entrepreneurial spirit.

If we may look more closely at the function and the role of official sponsorship under the *kuan-tu shang-pan* system, we see that it first of all provided encouragement and sanction for the founding and initial promotion of the enterprise. This encouragement might take several concrete forms: the granting of certain monopoly rights by the state or its organs to the new company (e.g., shipment of tribute rice); government loans or other types of grants of government capital to the enterprise; and protection of the enterprise by its official sponsors against exactions by other officials. In return the official sponsors would appoint the managers of the enterprise, thereby assuring effective supervision. This inevitably affected the character of management. Managers usually held official rank, and at the same time represented the shareholders. They therefore faced two ways, toward their official sponsors and toward the shareholders. In this situation management tended to be particularistic.

Similarly the investment and financial policies of the company were likely to be characterized by short-term borrowing at high rates of interest, by guaranteed dividend payments, and by inadequate allowances for depreciation. These attitudes and practices were not confined to the late nineteenth century alone, but were widespread in Chinese business and government up to the very advent of the Chinese Communist regime.

Thus the system of "official supervision and merchant operation" was self-defeating. To overcome the dead weight of stagnation in nineteenth century China a massive effort was required, involving large outlays on capital-intensive projects with low prospective rates of return; by raising the marginal productivity of capital such projects could then create a more favorable economic milieu for the growth of private business enterprise. However, an effort of such magnitude could only be mounted by the State and in reality the enterprises fostered by Chinese officials at the time in shipping, mining, communications, etc. were precisely of this type. But because of the very nature of the state and its officialdom, they were doomed to fail.

D. Economic Imperialism and the Beginnings of Industrialization, 1895–1914

The economic repercussions of China's defeat by Japan in 1895 were immediately apparent in the large foreign loans which China had to contract in order to pay the war indemnity. Japan used these funds to develop heavy industry and to build up her monetary reserves prior to a shift to the gold standard, thus forging further ahead of China. The foreign loans were secured on the Maritime Customs revenue and, from this time onward, ate into that reliable and increasing source of central government income. Japan's victory also touched off the scramble for concessions, which were extorted mainly in economic terms. The spheres of interest secured over various regions of China by the imperialist powers included ninety-nine year leases of major ports like Dairen, granted to Russia, or port sites like Tsingtao, granted to Germany. Running inland from these ports were railroads financed by, mortgaged to, and run by, the foreign powers. The Chinese Eastern Railway cutting across Manchuria to Vladivostok, as arranged in 1896, was now joined to the South Manchurian Railway running to Dairen under Russian control. The Germans developed a railroad in Shantung on similar lines. In both cases, mining rights along the railroad right of way were also granted the foreign power. In effect, these concessions permitted the imperialist power to invest in China's industrialization, mainly in the form of transportation and extractive industry. In retrospect it may possibly appear to future students that the imperialist powers on balance invested more than they profited from these arrangements—at least this may be true of Germany in Shantung.

The Japanese treaty had also permitted foreign industrial establishments to be set up in the treaty ports on Chinese soil. Thus the last bar to direct foreign leadership in China's industrialization was removed, but it was a leadership which also meant control over large sectors of the economy. In these same years under government auspices leading officials began official enterprises—for example, the textile mill at Shanghai under Sheng Hsuan-huai or the coal and iron complex at Han-yeh-p'ing in the Wuhan area under Chang Chih-tung.

The Boxer Rebellion of 1900 was another disaster which diverted still more of China's revenue to pay debts to foreigners under the Boxer indemnity. In the decade which followed, the central government reform program created new administrative and economic institutions, such as government banks and a central ministry of commerce and communications. A new army was built up with native and foreign equipment, the provision of which constituted a new industry. Railroad building had its first major decade of accomplishment under Sino-foreign auspices, and there was a considerable degree of economic growth, the extent of which has not yet been estimated. This process involved the rise of new industries and economic institutions and the decline of old ones. For example, the century-old Shansi banks began their final decline, being unsuited to modern banking needs. The new and enterprising merchants of Japan and Germany pushed their distribution networks among the Chinese mercantile communities of the interior and developed their markets with less dependence on China compradores. Groups of provincial gentry, merchants and officials initiated railroad projects in competition with those of the central government, although they usually failed to secure adequate finance and management. A few individual entrepreneurs emerged from the Chinese upper strata, like the top scholar Chang Chien, who developed his own cotton mill and other enterprises in his native place of Nantung, Kiangsu. Remittances from overseas Chinese communities began to flow back to China, playing an increasingly important role in the country's balance of payments. Capital accumulated by overseas Chinese from the Canton and Fukien areas was also flowing back into such investments as department stores in the treaty ports. Naturally there was great regional differentiation in this scattered and sporadic economic growth. It centered undoubtedly in the Canton and Shanghai areas. But there was also, for example, a forward movement under official leadership on the Inner Mongolian frontier, where Chinese agricultural expansion was facilitated by the completion in 1910 of the railroad from Peking through Kalgan to Suiyuan.

Evidences of the continued growth of foreign influence over, if not actual domination of, the Chinese economy can also be seen in the first decade of the twentieth century. Financial development agencies like the Peking Syndicate or the British and Chinese Corporation were formed with funds invested by the Hongkong and Shanghai Banking Corporation and the British firm of Jardine, Matheson and Company. British interests secured control of the Kaiping Mines. British funds were used to build the Shanghai-Nanking railroad and other lines in the lower Yangtze as a British sphere. Negotiations for American financing of Manchurian railroads were prosecuted (to little avail) by Willard Straight and others, and for the Hankow-Canton railroad by an international consortium of bankers. This era of "dollar diplomacy" and projected financial developments under foreign control in various parts of China was climaxed by the collapse of the dynasty in 1911. The foreign bond holders were immediately reassured when the inspector general of Chinese Maritime Customs, Sir Francis Aglen, for the first time took actual receipt of Chinese customs revenues and deposited them for safekeeping in the foreign banks in the treaty ports. This was followed by the Reorganization Loan of 1913 to the new ruler, Yuan Shih-k'ai, from which the United States abstained. The era of financial imperialism was cut short only by the outbreak of the First World War.

As evaluated half a century later, financial imperialism may have seemed more threatening to Chinese patriots in the early twentieth century than it might actually have become in the unfolding of its own operations. Possibly the bark of imperialism was worse than its bite. The fact remains, nevertheless, that from 1896 until the Second World War China's payments abroad on loans and indemnities constituted a sizable and constant financial drain which inevitably impaired her capacity for domestic capital formation, both governmental and private.

E. The Example of Railroads

The various factors facilitating and impeding economic growth may be seen in the history of railroads. In most countries railroads served to widen the extent of the market, stimulate the rapid commercialization of agriculture, the growth of cities and of a money economy, while at the same time the railroad itself provided a market for the iron, steel and engineering industries. But in the crowded countryside of China proper the coming of the iron horse was in no way comparable to its role in the opening, for example, of the American West.

Among many obvious reasons for this, the following may be suggested. First of all, the abundance of water communications in South and Central China, which reached to the capital, serviced by abundant manpower, maintained a severe competition for any railroad enterprise. In the densely populated countryside, land values for a right of way were costly and public opinion on geomantic grounds was superstitiously opposed to railroads. Another factor was the lack of sufficient capital and credit in a society where capital could not easily be mobilized by bond issues or other measures of credit creation. Moreover, the railroad, coming as the tool of the foreigner, met a rising patriotic opposition which was explicitly stated by leading officials: unless and until the Chinese government could build its own railroads and control them, it was preferable to have none. From the beginning it was realized that railroads under foreign control provided strategic means of military as well as economic ingress and invasion.

The railroad pattern which actually emerged was in part a product of the strategy of commercial exploitation through imperialist spheres of influence. Railroads were built under foreign domination from treaty ports inland through the peninsula of southern Manchuria and the peninsula of Shantung, as well as from Shanghai over the Yangtze delta. The Chinese Eastern Railway in the north, for Russia, and the Hanoi-Yunnan Railroad in the south, for France, served as the most obvious strategic spearheads. A similar plan was evident in the Peking-Suiyan line, the first one to be built by China, which facilitated the "secondary imperialism" of China's expansion into Inner Mongolia.

Geography constituted an added barrier to railroad development—first, in the form of mountains which, for example, kept the railroad effectively out of Szechwan until recently. Meanwhile the Yangtze itself is so pre-eminent a highway that, as the geographer George Cressey has noted, the railway lines tend to be at right angles rather than parallel to the river. It is no accident that the Chinese railroad network has been built more extensively in North than in South China. We suggest, in short, that the retardation of railroad development was due to the interplay of a variety of factors, a study of which may serve to demonstrate in microcosm the impediments to China's industrialization.

In sharp contrast, we see an entirely different course of development in Manchuria. In that region the railways assumed the role of "leading sector." They turned out to be highly profitable, almost from the very beginning of their operation. At the same time, unlike the situation in China proper, these profits were largely plowed back into investment, not only in the railroads themselves but in other enterprises as well. Consequently railroad earnings constituted one of the important sources for financing the development of other social overhead facilities and also contributed to the founding of other industries. This railroad development greatly stimulated the commercialization of Manchurian agriculture, drawing it into a world trading network. At the same time the railroads themselves provided an important market for engineering, repair, and machine-building services. Railroad development thus became the center of a broadening pattern of economic growth, which spilled over into agriculture, industry, and trade. Moreover, and again unlike the situation in China proper, this growth did not remain confined to the coastal strip of Manchuria. The example of railroad development illustrates the difference in the course of Manchurian, as opposed to Chinese, economic development in general. This difference may be viewed as the result of three categories of factors: (*a*) the much more favorable population-resource balance in Manchuria; (*b*) the comparative absence of institutional barriers to modernization such as prevailed in China proper; and (*c*) the injection of Japanese control and entrepreneurship coupled with large-scale capital imports into Manchuria.

V. Conclusion: Patterns of Retardation

The preceding survey has touched upon two central questions: (1) what were the active agents of economic change in nineteenth-century China? and (2) what were the chief factors that retarded economic growth? By way of conclusion, let us summarize briefly the roles played by the treaty ports, as principal centers of change, and by certain Chinese institutions as factors of retardation.

The Western impact transmitted through the ports was a multiple challenge, military, political, economic, social, ideological and cultural. The new influences were inevitably subversive of the old order. Thus the Chinese leaders were plunged into a dilemma. They felt the necessity to meet the challenge, but were unable or unwilling to understand that this could not be done without a radical remaking of practices and institutions, even ideas, in every sphere. This was, of course, one of the great differences between nineteenth-century China and Japan.

The transformation of Chinese life was accompanied by an erosion of the traditional economic order which was evidenced, for example, in the decline of handicrafts and later in the displacement of native banks. This decline of the old was paralleled by the creation of a new order in the treaty ports and in Manchuria. The result was a century of growth and decline occuring side by side.

The data now available do not permit the drawing up of a net balance sheet. We cannot measure the rate of growth in the expanding sectors and the rates of decline in the contracting sectors. In our present state of knowledge, we cannot determine whether the Chinese economy as a whole was expanding or contracting during this period. Foreign trade appears to have been the most important disequilibrating force in the economic realm. It performed the role of a "leading sector," generating an almost classic textbook-type process of cumulative economic growth which, however, remained confined to the treaty port segment of the Chinese economy.

The growth process here was interacting and cumulative. The gradual rise of foreign trade in the early nineteenth century stimulated a demand for the development of financial facilities. Up to the middle of the century, foreign trade had to be financed by the trading firms themselves. This necessarily limited the scope of the trade and the number of firms that could enter it. However, the rise of modern banking and insurance companies, particularly between 1858 and 1864, facilitated the entry of smaller merchants into foreign trade. We see here a sequence—the growth of foreign trade giving rise to a demand for banking facilities, which in turn facilitated the further expansion and widening of foreign trade which led to the processing of export products, such as tea and silk, in the treaty ports, and also to the processing of certain import products which were consumed in the treaty ports. The latter involved the growth of such food-processing industries as flour-milling, sugar-refining, and brewing. In turn, the development of the treaty ports, with a growth of foreign trade and of allied industries, necessarily led to population growth in the ports. This stimulated the demand for public utilities such as water, gas, electricity, and local transport. The development of public utilities and of shipping both stimulated the demand for coal. At the same time, there was a need for engineering shops and small works to service all of these enterprises. The expanding population in the treaty ports naturally demanded housing services. This stimulated housing construction, which gave rise to a growing demand for cement and other building materials. Meanwhile as the market for imported textile manufactures widened, it became increasingly profitable for foreign firms to build and operate textile mills in the treaty ports. A similar development occurred with respect to cigarettes and tobacco, canned goods and certain other consumer products.

However, the question still remains as to why this self-generating process of economic growth remained largely bottled up in the treaty port segment of the economy and why the multiplier effect of investment was thus largely confined to the segment. The precise reasons, the factors and variables, that may account for this require further exploration. On the basis of presently available evidence we surmise that there were three types of factors that hindered the spread of economic stimuli from the treaty ports to the Chinese hinterland: (1) institutional as well as physical (transport) barriers to the movement of goods and, even more important, to the movement of factors of production; (2) leakages from the treaty ports to foreign countries through the medium of profit remittances, so that some of the multiplier effects of investment upon income and employment were felt in the home countries of the foreign firms rather than in China itself; (3) the development of public utilities, banking facilities and other "external economies," which raised the marginal productivity of investment and thus reinforced the economic advantages already enjoyed by the treaty ports as compared with the economy of the Chinese hinterland.

On balance, the treaty port performed certain very important historic functions in China's long-run development. First of all, it created the aforementioned "external economies." It built up the modern commercial network, not only external but internal. It fostered the development of railroads and provided a framework within which modern factory production could be initiated, with primary emphasis upon light consumer-goods industries.

Secondly, as a result of this factory and business development, the treaty ports provided a training ground for Chinese technical and managerial personnel and for Chinese entrepreneurship. It is important to bear in mind that the Chinese compradore and his successor, the Chinese merchant and entrepreneur, built up the Chinese portion of the modern economy under the wing of the foreigner's privileges. In fact the treaty ports became jointly administered centers of joint economic growth, from which the Chinese entrepreneurial class was by no means excluded. On the contrary, the ports attracted Chinese talent and capital. Even socially the bifurcation between natives and foreigners became less distinct than in colonial countries.

Through the Chinese merchant and official classes, the ports also served as a means for mobilizing Chinese savings and channeling them either into the modern banking system or into direct investment in treaty port enterprises. To the extent that these enterprises did not remit profits abroad or invest some of their earnings in enterprises abroad, they too created pre-conditions for a later take-off into industrialization.

Thus a more meaningful view of the significance of the treaty ports might see them as the spearheads of a modern Sino-foreign economy, which was encroaching upon the traditional scene. In a physical sense the treaty ports served as entrance points into the traditional network of Chinese water-borne communications. The aim of the foreign merchant from the beginning was to get his goods flowing into this already well-developed distribution system. Western steamers on the Yangtze plying all the way to Szechwan, symbolized this process. It is significant that the British in the late nineteenth century were carrying three-fifths of China's steamer cargo.

This process was similar to that by which the foreigner joined with the Manchu-Chinese official class in such administrative institutions as the Imperial Maritime Customs Service or the Salt Revenue Administration and Post Office. In a comparable fashion the foreign merchant teamed up with his Chinese compradore and the growing Chinese merchant and banker class to dominate the modern sector of the economy, and spread its influence over the hinterland.

To say all this does not resolve that underlying question: Were the treaty ports in the long view a help or a hindrance to China's economic growth? Many considerations must be brought to bear on this thorny question. It involves among other things that difficult task, to prove a might-have-been—that China could have broken out of her traditional order and achieved a modern industrial growth in the absence of a Western impact such as was actually delivered through the treaty ports. We suspect that when another generation has finally gleaned and winnowed all the evidence it will be found that the influence of the treaty ports on Chinese economic life varied markedly over time: that they were a stimulus in the nineteenth century, becoming by degrees more of a hindrance in the twentieth.

Capital accumulation in the age of imperialist domination centered increasingly in the treaty ports for reasons mentioned above. On balance it seems plain that after 1895 a considerable proportion of the capital surplus in the Chinese economy was siphoned off to meet indemnity and loan payments abroad. Such payments must be taken as net withdrawals from China's economic resources, in other words, a tax on the economy. The effect was probably to handicap economic growth.

Yet, without minimizing the evils of imperialism, it would be short-sighted to place the center of China's economic development *outside* of Chinese society. Its retardation, like the long slow process of dynastic collapse, was in large measure a function of the interplay of domestic institutions and conditions. It is these that must be studied to gain further insight into China's economic growth.

If we define "institutions" in the broad sense as long-established patterns of social conduct, we may see their inhibiting influence primarily under the subheads of state activity and the administrative practices of the official class. First of all, the Chinese state failed to provide certain of the minimum pre-conditions essential to economic growth outside the treaty ports. For example, the Chinese authorities singularly failed in the maintenance of peace and order during the whole modern century. They were also unable to create a uniform currency and unified monetary standards. There was no uniform system of weights and measures. There was no stable administrative framework within which an effective market organization could develop. Transport and communications remained poor. Education, health and welfare measures were minimal. The inability of Chinese leaders to create the minimal pre-conditions for economic development was most clearly evidenced in the *kuan-tu shang-pan* system for "official supervision and merchant operation."

Chapter 5

The Economic Heritage

I. Introduction

Comparative View of China and Japan

An informed observer assessing from the vantage point of 1840 the prospects for economic development and modernization in Asia might have considered the vast Chinese empire as the most likely force to successfully repel the challenge from the West.[1] It was much larger and more populous than Japan. It was an independent and sovereign entity, while India was under foreign rule. Moreover, partly because of its vast size, it was much better endowed with mineral resources than Japan.

In terms of social and political institutions, too, China might have appeared in the better position. Unlike India, it had a long history as a unified empire. Feudalism in China had been displaced with the end of the Chou dynasty, in contrast both to Japan and to modern Europe, where the persistence of feudalism was associated with economic retardation. Moreover, as Professor Lockwood has reminded us,

> China alone among the peoples of Asia brought to the modern world a tradition of personal freedom and social mobility, of private property freely bought and sold. . . . If the Chinese remained imbued with the particularist loyalties of the family, and a certain contempt for commerce as a way of life, was this not true of all Asia? Was it not also true of the European elites of yesterday?[2]

Reprinted from *Economic Trends in Communist China,* edited by Alexander Eckstein, Walter Galenson, and T. C. Liu, Aldine Publishing Company, Chicago, 1968.

125

Yet the historical record runs counter to what might have appeared as reasonable expectations a hundred years ago. Between 1840 and 1950 China was in the throes of dynastic decline, political disunity and partial dismemberment. At the same time it was subjected to continuing external pressure, oppression and penetration. All these factors in combination led to disturbance, disequilibrium, and slow and gradual change in the Chinese economy. The economic record of these hundred years is both uncertain and mixed. While the traditional economic order was disturbed and undermined, some growing points did develop in the treaty ports and in Manchuria.[3] However, *modern economic growth* remained confined and bottled up in these peripheral areas.[4] Consequently this was a century of considerable economic growth *in* China but not *of* China.

In retrospect, it would seem that external shocks and stimuli activated the already existing stirrings in Japan, so that within two to three decades these could be transplanted into a national commitment to economic development.[5] In China, on the other hand, the internal stirrings, even under the impact of new influences, crystallized more slowly, taking about a hundred years to reach substantial segments of the society, polity and economy. Thus China's national commitment to industrialization and rising economic strength was correspondingly delayed.

The Sources of Modernization in China

Economic modernization was largely imposed upon China from abroad, principally by foreign enterprises and foreign institutions. This differs markedly from Japan, where modernization became a national undertaking soon after the Meiji Restoration. To cite just one example, a national bank as the sole bank of issue was established in Japan in 1885, while in China this was not seriously attempted until the 1930's.[6] In the meantime a number of foreign banks, notably the Hong Kong and Shanghai Banking Corporation, issued banknotes that served as currency with wide circulation in many parts of China.[7]

In a sense, China was thus caught in a vicious circle. With the commitment to traditionalism came naturally a strong resistance to modernization. Partly because of this resistance, the carriers of modernization had to be largely (though by no means solely) foreigners and foreign institutions. Consequently modernization became identified with foreignism and so was perceived as a threat not only to the traditional order but also to the very integrity of the Chinese state. This fact in turn reinforced the existing resistance to modernization and complicated its spread.

Two fundamental conditions for economic growth were absent in China: the emergence of a modern nation-state, and a technological and institutional transformation in agriculture. Both were delayed despite the efforts of the modernizers in the nineteenth century and the Nationalist government in the twentieth century.

Therefore the *central* government in China played virtually no role in the economic modernization of the mainland until the 1930's. The principal agents of economic change and innovation were: (1) foreign enterprises and their native followers based in the treaty ports; (2) foreign governments and their chosen instruments in Manchuria; (3) a few outstanding Chinese statesmen of the late nineteenth century, whose power base was preponderantly provincial; and (4) the Nationalist government in the 1930's. In this chapter, I intend to show that the efforts of the first, second, and fourth did yield substantial economic growth, while those of the third turned out to be largely abortive. As a result, modern economic growth—i.e., sustained growth in per capita income accompanied by and interrelated with marked structural transformation and technological change—did indeed take place in some areas of the mainland economy. Since in Manchuria this process touched all segments of the economy, it led to economic growth not merely in some enclaves, but in the region as a whole. However, in China Proper, agriculture apparently remained more or less in its traditional state, so that economic growth was largely confined to the nonagricultural sectors in the treaty ports.

The Lag in China's Modern Economic Growth

In the face of these contradictory tendencies, one of the questions that needs to be posed is whether one can legitimately speak of modern economic growth for China as a whole. In one superficial sense it could be regarded merely as a matter of averaging. That is, if there was a sustained rise in per capita income in Manchuria and in the nonagricultural sectors of China proper, while agriculture in China proper was stagnating, then in net terms there would be per capita growth in the economy as a whole. On the other hand, given the massive size of the farm sector in China proper and the comparatively large number of people dependent on it, even a small per capita decline in agriculture could more than out-weigh a sizable rise in industry, transport and trade.

This whole problem is complicated by the fact that our knowledge concerning trends in agricultural development is at best extremely sketchy. Thanks to the surveys of the National Agricultural Research Bureau[8] and of Buck[9] we have a fairly reliable cross-section view of the state of Chinese agriculture in the 1930's.[10] But we know very little about agricultural developments over time. It is uncertain whether yields per acre and product per person employed in agriculture declined, rose, or remained more or less stationary during these hundred years or even during shorter periods (such as 1890 to 1930).[11] Similarly, there are no reliable data concerning trends in farm household income during these decades.

However, even some sustained rise in per capita agricultural income and the resultant net growth *in* the economy as a whole would not necessarily justify a finding of *modern economic growth* of the mainland economy as a whole. Several essential attributes of modern economic growth were missing; most notably, the industrial structure changed but little and the movement of factors out of agriculture and into manufacturing and services was very sluggish. Moreover, assuming that one could show economic growth in each of the three areas—Manchuria, the treaty ports, and the rural hinterland of China proper—one would still have to demonstrate that their developments were functionally and organically related. In more technical terms, one would have to demonstrate structural interdependence or linkages in the process of growth so that new stimuli to which one area might be exposed would reverberate through the national economy.

The fusion of the various parts of the country into one organic whole was seriously impeded both by transport and communications barriers and by political fragmentation. As a result, during certain periods parts of the country such as Shanghai or Manchuria were in some respects more closely integrated with foreign economies than with the Chinese mainland.

One might perhaps characterize this century of economic disturbance and change as one of gestation, during which many of the necessary preconditions for national development and modern economic growth were established. One might also describe it as a very painful and costly century of "creative destruction" during which the traditional economic order was weakened and undermined, new economic institutions were created, an infrastructure was constructed, a modest industrial base was built, an industrial labor force—however limited—was trained and committed, and a small managerial and technical class was raised. Without these institutions, facilities and manpower, the industrialization drive following the Communist take-over would have been inconceivable.

Bearing these hypotheses in mind, in this chapter I will attempt to: (a) characterize briefly the traditional economic order prior to Western impact, (b) explore how this order was disturbed, (c) analyze the economic modernization efforts in nineteenth-century China, (d) contrast the experience of economic growth in Manchuria and China proper, and (e) present a cross-section view of the mainland economy inherited by the Chinese Communists. Since the focus of this whole essay is on the economy as inherited by the Chinese Communists, the analysis will be concerned with the mainland as a whole. For many purposes and from many points of view the economies of Manchuria and China Proper should be analyzed separately. However, both form part of the foundation on which the economy of the People's Republic is built.

II. The Traditional Economic Order Prior to Western Impact

Our knowledge concerning the state of the Chinese economy around 1800 is hazy and imprecise. The understanding we have is largely qualitative, with quantitative indicators virtually absent. While there are some crude estimates for population size and cultivated land area,[12] data on agricultural production, unit yields, and other systematic indicators of land productivity, on output per man, and on income levels are lacking. Of course this situation is not unique to the Chinese economy of that period. Nevertheless our degree of ignorance is undoubtedly significantly greater in this case than for early nineteenth-century Japan or India, not to mention Europe. The sources are scattered and difficult to use, and the data in the sources are fragmentary. Nevertheless, by building on foundations laid by some Chinese and Japanese scholars, it should be possible to reconstruct the situation and the trends in some specific areas. If a more or less representative sample of local data could be assembled, it might provide a more precise view of economic tendencies in the country as a whole.*

---

*Since the publication of this paper Dwight Perkins's study on *Agricultural Development in China, 1368–1968* (Harvard, 1969) has become available. It does to some extent fill the particular gap referred to in this paragraph.

Expansion of the Traditional Economy

The late eighteenth century apparently marked the end of a long period of sustained expansion in the total size of the Chinese economy. Specific evidence for this is the more or less continuous growth in population and in the land area under cultivation. Expansion was also accompanied by an intensification in the patterns of land use. Whether the increases in food production and population also led to a sustained rise in per capita product cannot be determined on the basis of presently available evidence.

It seems, moreover, that expansion was not accompanied by a marked technical transformation in the methods of agricultural production. It rested principally on the introduction of new crops, which pushed the agricultural frontier from the low plains to the more hilly and mountainous regions.[13] Gradual dissemination of early ripening rice (soon after the year 1000) and the development of rice strains with short growing seasons facilitated the spread of double-cropping. A second aspect of agricultural expansion was the spread of dry-land crops such as sorghum, introduced after Mongol conquest, and maize, sweet potatoes, Irish potatoes and peanuts, adopted in the late Ming and early Ch'ing periods.

Finally, population growth was apparently stimulated not only by this expansion of the agricultural base but also by an extended period of peace and order during the seventeenth and eighteenth centuries. All indications thus point to a prolonged period of growth in total national product during the centuries preceding the Treaty of Nanking. This conclusion, based on more recent studies, contradicts the earlier prevalent image of an "unchanging China" with an economy subject to cyclical fluctuations around a more or less stable level, but without any rising trend. Furthermore, it suggests that the concept of a circular flow economy is not applicable to traditional China. The economy did not just reproduce itself; expansion in its total size could not have taken place without some net investment, even if this investment was perhaps not sufficient to permit a sustained growth in per capita product.

The whole pace of economic change in China was apparently accelerated between the eighth and the thirteenth centuries. This was evidenced by a significant increase in internal trade, which permitted a greater regional specialization in crops, with apparently some resultant gains in land productivity.[14] The economy as a whole became much more commercialized. Revenues from government monopolies—particularly those on trade in salt, tea, and wine—and from various commercial taxes increased so rapidly that they outweighed the land tax.

These developments were accompanied and reinforced by a marked rise in overseas trade, with oceanic commerce gradually outbalancing in importance the foreign trade carried on overland.[15] China exported porcelain, fine handicraft products, silks, art objects, some gold, silver, lead and tin, and copper cash. Imports consisted largely of horses, hides, some fine woods and fine cotton textiles. Not unnaturally, this growth in domestic and foreign trade brought with it increasing monetization, marked in part by the increasing use of paper money.[16]

This was a period during which China seems to have been developing much more rapidly than Europe. Because of this, it was also a time when China appeared much more advanced to European travelers. However, with the advent of the Renaissance, the Age of Discovery, and the beginning of the scientific age, change in Europe began to accelerate just at a time when the general pace was slowing down in China.

China did not experience an agricultural revolution in the European sense of that concept. Although some changes in patterns of land use did take place beginning in the eleventh century, these did not lead to a disruption of existing agrarian institutions. To the extent that there was an identifiable commercial revolution in China, its force was largely spent by the fourteenth century. Quite apart from timing, it was much more modest in scope than any comparable European "revolution," and never as disruptive of the traditional order. It is doubtful whether one can find in Chinese history a counterpart to the age of mercantilism, either in the field of policy or theory. It is, of course, true that economic activity in China was surrounded by a maze of regulations, restrictions, and government monopolies reminiscent of mercantilist practices in Europe. But European mercantilism was strongly infused with an economic nationalism coupled with an aggressive foreign trade orientation, which was absent in China. Sustained foreign trade expansion, commitment to a favorable balance of trade, and an active seeking of foreign treasure are mercantilist attributes uncommon in China.

To the contrary, the dominant world view of traditional China, as embodied in the orthodox line of Confucianism, conceived of economic welfare not in terms of economic growth but in terms of subsistence, of satisfaction of the basic minimum needs of the masses. The principal function of the state was the maintenance of social peace and harmony. In this view, a commitment to the pursuit of wealth and power by the state—in particular, the emperor as the embodiment of the state—would in no way differ from the behavior of an official pursuing his own selfish interests.[17] Thus the dominant leitmotif of Chinese statecraft, from at least the fourteenth century up to the self-strengthening movement of the late nineteenth, was *maintenance* rather than *development:* maintenance of minimum subsistance for the peasantry, maintenance of a comfortable though frugal standard for the gentry, maintenance of law and order, maintenance of public works, and protection from barbarian incursions. The accent was on stability—social, political, and economic—rather than on growth. Closely related to this was a looking inward rather than an active seeking of foreign contacts, either friendly or hostile

From this brief sketch of selected aspects of China's economic evolution prior to the nineteenth century, it is clear that at least two fundamental conditions for *modern economic growth* were missing; sustained foreign economic contacts on a significant scale, and the application of technological progress to production processes in agriculture and industry.

The Economy of Early Nineteenth-Century China

As a result, early nineteenth-century China exhibited the typical characteristics of a premodern, preindustrial economy. It was preponderantly agrarian, with the bulk of the population deriving their livelihood from crop production. Given the very high density of population per unit of cultivated area, a pattern of agricultural production had to be evolved to produce the greatest possible energy yield per acre. Consequently, except in the northwest, animal husbandry was purely supplementary and subsidiary to food production. Its high intensity of use probably made land in China, more than anywhere else, "an article manufactured by man." Farm husbandry was characterized by "economy of space, economy of materials, economy of implements, economy of fodder, economy of fuel, economy of waste products, economy of everything except forests and of the labor of human beings whom social habits have made abundant and abundance cheap."[18]

The prevailing system of landholding was based on freehold tenure with the peasant free to buy or sell land. There was no primogeniture, and inheritance was shared equally by all sons. But this system opened the way to fragmentation of landholding. Tenancy was subject to wide regional variation and generally tended to be more prevalent near cities and in the more densely settled farm areas where land values were high.

The peasant household was to a large extent self-sufficient, often processing its own food, spinning its own yarn and weaving its own cloth. At the same time, most households were at least to some extent involved in the local market.[19] As noted earlier, there was some regional specialization in agricultural production; cotton- or tea-producing households and regions had to purchase at least some foods, while grain-producing areas had to import some cotton, wool and tea. Virtually every farm household bought some salt, so that the processing and sale of salt under government license constituted one of the most lucrative trades of traditional China.[20]

The peasant and his family lived close to the margin of subsistence, with their actual net income and standard of living subject to wide variations in different regions and periods. His fortunes depended, of course, not only on the physical environment in his own district, but also on annual fluctuations in rainfall, on the maintenance of public works (i.e., irrigation and flood control), on the extent of tenancy, on tenure practices at any one time in any one area, on the terms on which he could obtain credit and, last but very important, the degree of tax pressure to which he was subjected. Many of these conditions depended on the strength of the imperial center, and the character of the local bureaucracy and the local gentry. Thoroughgoing studies of these variables and their interrelationship in the early nineteenth century are sorely lacking.

Manufacturing was carried on by handicraft and preindustrial methods in both rural and urban areas. There are no output data, and so the possibilities for economic analysis of this period are again limited. Some crude estimates might possibly be attempted through study of consumption patterns in peasant, gentry, and merchant households in the cities and the countryside, and in the imperial household.

The degree of commercialization in the economy also cannot be quantified on the basis of presently available data. But local gazetteers might perhaps be useful in an exploration of the volume of goods moving through local, intermediate, and central markets in different years. Data for even a scattering of years, provided it were for a certain minimum number of markets selected from different regions of the country or from one major region, might provide a suitable sample for analysis. Such an undertaking would be greatly facilitated now because of the availability of

Skinner's path-breaking study,[21] which can in a sense provide the methodological framework for an investigation of this kind.

Despite the lack of data, there is no doubt that the volume of both local and interregional trade was considerable by the nineteenth century. Trade provided the basis for accumulating commercial wealth in traditional China. Although the merchant's status was low, officially lower than that of the peasantry, his links with the gentry and with officialdom were in fact close.[22] What the precise line of dependency was in these relationships is far from clear. Can one accept the rather widely held image of total subordination of merchants to officialdom, or is the relationship one of much greater subtlety and complexity, in which the wealthy merchant is in a position to influence the actions of officials? An equally important question from a long-run development point of view is why these occasional accumulations of merchant wealth did not become growing points for long-run capital accumulation. Why were they not embodied in the growth of reproducible tangible assets? Do the high prestige and security value assigned to investment in land, the traditional outlook and the character of officialdom, and the character of traditional kinship obligations provide an adequate explanation?

There is no doubt that the long cycle of expansion outlined above had largely spent itself by about 1800. As the opportunities for extending the land frontier were more or less exhausted, population growth was slowing down and population was increasingly pressing against available land resources. This process was naturally aggravated by dynastic weakness and its consequences in the field of public administration, taxation, and public works.

In a sense the Chinese economy was now indeed beginning to fall into a more or less circular flow pattern, possibly into a period of decline. It was exhibiting the typical characteristics of a densely populated, underdeveloped economy in which land was limited, capital was short, and labor was abundant. Moreover, it was bound by a value system and based on a social structure that were not conducive to either the exercise of state initiative on behalf of economic development or the encouragement and rise of private entrepreneurship.

Stage of Development in Early Nineteenth-Century China

Against this background, what stage of development did the Chinese economy attain by 1800–1840? Since there are no adequate quantitative indicators for these years, one possible approach is to contrast the state of the Chinese economy in a period for which data are readily available with the economy of early Meiji Japan; and then to use this as a basis for assessing what the mainland situation might have been earlier. This is attempted in Table 1.

Although these data and estimates are subject to sizeable margins of error, they can serve as a fairly adequate basis for comparison. As indicated earlier, we have no long-term trend data for agricultural production or yield per acre in China.* But there are no indications of advances in Chinese agriculture between 1800–1840 and 1930 that could have caused significant increases in rice and wheat yields. We know of no large-scale application of new inputs such as chemical fertilizer, or of greatly improved inputs such as better seeds used on a large scale, or of a technological breakthrough that would greatly increase the efficiency of existing inputs. Therefore we may be justified in concluding that land productivity in early or mid-nineteenth century China was definitely higher than in late Tokugawa or early Meiji Japan.

The problem of cultivated land area per capita is not quite so clearcut. One cannot be certain whether China's population in relation to the cultivated land area has grown, declined, or remained more or less unchanged during this span of approximately 100 years. On balance, however, even allowing for the devastation of the Taiping rebellion (1850–1864) and of the civil wars, the presupposition of some rise in density seems reasonable.† Even if this conclusion were not borne out by subsequent research, a significant decrease in population pressure during this period is improbable. Therefore the quite large differential that Table 1 shows for this indicator would strongly suggest that the degree of population pressure was more acute in Meiji Japan than in early nineteenth-century China.

This fact combined with the yield differentials indicates that the average Chinese had more domestically produced food staples at his disposal than the average Japanese. To some extent the data in Table 1 exaggerate the land productivity differentials, since China's greatest yield advantage is in rice, which is relatively much less important in China's crop production basket and diet than in Japan's. Moreover, given the fact that

---

*This observation no longer holds since Perkins developed his estimates in the excellent study cited above.
†This presupposition is in fact strongly borne out by Perkins's study.

TABLE 1

Selected Indicators of Stages of Economic Development
in Early Meiji Japan and Republican China

Item	Unit of Measure	Early Meiji	China, 1930's
Paddy rice yield	lb/acre	1623	2470[a]–2930[b]
Wheat yield	lb/acre	729	895[b]– 960[c]
Cultivated land per capita	acres	0.298[d]	464
Degree of literacy:			
Male	per cent	43[e]	30.3
Female	per cent	10[e]	1.2
GNP Composition:			
Agriculture	per cent	65	65
Industry	per cent	9	11
Services	per cent	26	24
Share of agricultural produce sold off farms	per cent	25–31	18–34[f]

a. T. C. Liu and K. C. Yeh, *The Economy of the Chinese Mainland: National Income and Economic Development, 1933–1959*, Princeton, 1965, Tables 31 and A–4.

b. Buck as given in Liu-Yeh, *ibid.*, Table 30.

c. National Agricultural Research Bureau data as given in Liu-Yeh, *ibid.*, Table 30.

d. Based on a three-year average for 1880–1882.

e. These are estimates for "the proportion of each age-group who would ever have gotten some kind of schooling at 1868 rates of attendance" as derived by R. P. Dore, *Education in Takugawa Japan*, Berkeley, 1965, p. 321.

f. The lower figure refers to the share of crop output sold off farms as given by J. L. Buck, *Land Utilization in China*, Nanking, 1937, p. 236, while the higher figure adds to this the percentage used for rent. The percentage inclusive of rent overstates the share marketed since it is based on the implicit assumption that none of the rent was retained by the landlords for their own and their household's subsistence, and that therefore all of it is sold. On the other hand, the lower percentage understates the share marketed since it, in turn, is based on the opposite assumption; *i.e.*, that all the rent is retained in agriculture for self-consumption and none of it is sold.

Sources:

Early Meiji: Rice and wheat yields as given in Takekazu Ogura, ed., *Agricultural Development in Modern Japan*, Tokyo, 1963, p. 11; GNP composition and produce sold from Henry Rosovsky, "Japan's Transition to Modern Economic Growth, 1868–1885," in *Industrialization in Two Systems*, Essays in Honor of Alexander Gerschenkron by a Group of His Students, New York, 1966; land per capita from cultivated acreage figures adapted from Supreme Command Allied Powers (SCAP), "Japanese Crop and Livestock Statistics, 1878–1950," SCAP Report No. 143; population from Sadajiro Weda, ed., *Nihon Jinko Mondai Kenkyu*, Vol. 1, 1934, p. 163, and Ryoichi Ishii, *Population Pressure and Economic Life in Japan*, London, 1937, p. 53.

1930's China: Cultivated land from Buck, *op. cit.*, p. 165; Liu-Yeh, *op. cit.*, pp. 171–77; literacy from Buck, *op. cit.*, p. 373; GNP composition from Liu-Yeh, *op. cit.*, Table 8, p. 66.

the overwhelming bulk of the population in both countries lived and worked on the land, one might deduce that the productivity of both land and labor was probably higher in nineteenth-century China than in Meiji Japan.

However, a rather different picture emerges if one examines the "structural" rather than the "absolute level" indicators. In respect to the stock and flow of general basic education, as indicated by the degree of literacy or the share of school age population enrolled (the latter is not given in Table 1), Meiji Japan is well ahead of mainland China in the 1930's, and so must have been even further advanced in relation to nineteenth-century China. The nineteenth-century gap must have been so large that it could not be closed even by allowing for possible margins of error caused by the basic character of the data or possible differences in definition.

Roughly similar conclusions emerge from a comparison of the degree of commercialization in agriculture. One would expect a significant rise in market involvement between 1800–1840 and 1930's for a number of reasons. With the introduction of steamships on the inland waterways and the construction of railways that reached many major market centers, distribution costs were lowered and farm marketing was facilitated and encouraged. This is explicitly confirmed by Skinner's work and by Buck's findings.[23] Therefore one may be justified in concluding that Chinese agriculture of the mid-nineteenth century was almost certainly less involved in the market nexus than its early Meiji counterpart in Japan.

The structure of the two economies seems to have been rather similar, as indicated by the interindustry composition of GNP as shown in Table 1. Bearing in mind the tentativeness of the data and the limited number of comparative indicators available, it would seem that agricultural product per capita and (given the overwhelming weight of agriculture in the economy) perhaps even GNP per capita was higher in nineteenth-century China than in Meiji Japan. However, despite that, one might suggest that the Chinese economy was in a sense less "developed." That is, it was perhaps less prepared for modernization and less capable of absorbing and digesting new influences and external stimuli. This would be the case at least to the extent that one might expect a positive association between modernization and the degree of literacy and commercialization.

The data in Table 1 suggest yet another conclusion. It would seem that the Japanese peasant was even closer to the margin of subsistence than his

Chinese counterpart, yet this did not prevent him from making a significant contribution to financing the economic development of the country through taxation and voluntary saving.[24] This comparison confirms once more the absence of any necessary or automatic relationship between average per capita product or average agricultural product and the capacity to save.

III. Disturbance, Self-Strengthening and the Abortive Breakthrough

China's traditional economic order was disturbed, and eventually permanently displaced, by the interaction of internal weaknesses in a period of dynastic decline and external pressure. There is no need here to repeat the well-documented story of the growth of China's overseas trade in the eighteenth century, the expansion of the triangular trade between Britain, India and China, the increasing opium trade, and the collapse of the Canton system.[25] Nor is this the place to restate the origins of the Taiping rebellion and to trace its course. Both China's defeat in the Opium War and the serious challenge to dynastic survival made by the Taipings were symptoms of internal weakness and of its contributing causes. As such they had a far-reaching effect on the course of economic change in nineteenth-century China.

They affected that course both directly and indirectly. The most direct and immediate effect was on the foreign trade sector which then, through the operation of demand and supply forces, gradually affected internal trade and domestic production as well. The rise of the treaty ports and the associated institutions provided an institutional and geographic base for the development of foreign enterprise and, later, of Chinese enterprise. The Taiping rebellion, on the other hand, wrought great devastation, led to marked depopulation of a number of areas, and contributed greatly to economic decline, particularly in agriculture. At the same time it further undermined and weakened the traditional Chinese state, reducing its capacity for a positive response to the external challenge.

The indirect economic effects flowed from a reactive or defensive nationalism embodied in the self-strengthening movement; led by regional and provincial leaders, rather than by the central government, the movement was a series of more or less abortive modernization efforts and public investment projects. It was clearly an attempt at a creative response to the Western challenge, and coincided roughly in timing with the Meiji Restoration. Bearing these cataclysmic events in mind, in this section I will first outline briefly the immediate trade effects of the Treaty of Nanking, then examine the economic consequences of the rebellion, and finally analyze the economic program of the self-strengtheners.

China's Foreign Trade in the Early Nineteenth Century

The pattern of foreign trade that emerged in the course of the eighteenth century was based on the rapidly growing demand for Chinese tea, primarily in Britain, and to a lesser extent in other parts of Europe. There was at first no corresponding demand for foreign goods in China, so that the balance of trade was consistently unfavorable from a British point of view. By the nineteenth century this situation was "corrected" by the export of opium and raw cotton from India to Canton. As a result, in the first decades of the nineteenth century the trade balance was reversed, as illustrated by the data in Table 2. Although total Canton imports did not rise very rapidly during this period, opium purchases more than doubled in value between 1817 and 1821, and almost quadrupled between 1817 and 1830. As a result, the share of opium in total imports increased from a little over 20 per cent to nearly 60 per cent. This in turn stimulated the expansion of domestic opium production.[26]

On the export side, tea remained the major export item throughout this period, with silk products in second, and raw silk in third place. The first constituted about 55–65 per cent of total sales, while the latter two were about 15 and 10 per cent respectively.

These trading patterns changed gradually after the opening of the ports. Imports of cotton goods were gaining, and in the 1840's they began to exceed the imports of woolens as well as the exports of cotton goods. Silk exports started to rise rapidly after the "opening" of Shanghai in 1843. Thus until about the 1870's, China's exports were virtually confined to tea and silk, while imports were dominated by opium and cotton goods. The total volume of trade, however, was still quite small.

TABLE 2

Canton Trade, 1817–1830

A. Exports, Imports and Trade Balance
(in millions of Spanish silver dollars)

Year	Exports	Imports[a]	Balance[a]
1817	15.57	18.69	−3.12
1821	20.52	21.43	−0.91
1825	22.23	23.27	−1.04
1830	17.60	26.81	−9.21

B. Commodity Composition of Canton Exports
(in per cent)

Year	Tea	Raw Silk	Silk Goods	Other	Total
1817	69	4	6	21	100
1821	57	10	15	18	100
1825	61	10	13	16	100
1830	60	10	13	17	100

C. Commodity Composition of Imports
(in per cent)

Year	Woolen Goods	Metals	Furs	Cotton	Opium[a]	Other	Total
1817	17	3	1	44	22	13	100
1821	15	2	2	24	44	13	100
1825	17	3	2	27	42	9	100
1830	11	3	0.3	21	56	9	100

a. Opium import data are incomplete since they do not include the quantities smuggled in, and it is not certain whether they fully encompass the legally imported amounts.
Source: Computed by author on the basis of data in Y. K. Cheng, *Foreign Trade and Industrial Development of China,* Washington, D.C., 1956, Tables 1A and 1B, p. 6, which are in turn from H. B. Morse, *The Chronicles of East India Company: Trading to China 1635–1834,* Vols. III and IV, Oxford, 1926–29.

As already noted, opium production grew because of rising demand stimulated by imports. One may assume that tea and silk production also rose in response to increasing export demand. It is doubtful that imports of cotton goods had a depressing effect on the handicraft textile industry at the time. Data for the late nineteenth and early twentieth century indicate that handicraft weaving continued to be competitive with imported and domestically manufactured cloth for a long time in mainland China, just as in other countries in the process of industrialization. [27] There are a number of reasons for this, not the least of which is that imported and domestic cloth tended to supply different markets. If this was true in the late nineteenth century when more cotton goods were imported, the resilience of native handicrafts must have been even greater earlier in the century when imports of manufactured cloth were smaller.

For all of these reasons, one might surmise that the initial income effects of foreign trade were positive for the domestic economy. But while foreign trade did stimulate possible increases in production, it also turned the internal terms of trade against agriculture and thus depressed the real income of the peasantry. Which of these effects—the positive or the negative—was more important is impossible to judge from the available evidence. The adverse shift in the internal terms of trade was induced by the rising price of silver. As the foreign trade balance became unfavorable (see Table 2, A), silver flowed out of the country. According to one estimate the flow of specie increased to 11.2 million Chinese dollars by 1841. [28] Since taxes and other contributions were computed in silver, and silver bullion also served as a store of value, an outflow of specie tended to raise its price. Therefore, as the price of silver increased, the speculative demand for it increased as well. However, a rise in the price of silver meant a decline in the value of copper cash expressed in silver. Yet the peasant sold his rice for copper cash while silver remained the standard by which his taxes were computed. Therefore, unless the copper-cash price of rice was adjusted correspondingly, the peasants' real tax burden was bound to increase considerably. [29]

Economic Consequences of the Taiping Rebellion

Whatever the net economic effects of foreign trade expansion may have been, they were overwhelmed by the devastation of the Taiping rebellion (1850–64). It greatly accelerated the process of economic decline which had started in the late eighteenth century. The rebellion reduced the land area under cultivation, thus compressing the tax base at a time when government expenditures were rising. In a sense the economy was caught up in a vicious downward spiral, starting with a decline in farm production because of war devastation, and leading to a decline in government revenues at a time of rising military outlays. As a result, public works and other government services deteriorated while tax pressure on the peasantry increased. These factors in combination contributed to a further curtailment in agricultural production. To finance the constantly rising deficits, the government resorted to a printing of paper notes on the one hand and the introduction of a new tax, *likin,* on the other.

Initially conceived as an ad hoc emergency tax, *likin* became a permanent institution, not abolished until 1931, which had deleterious effects on China's long-term development. It was an ad valorem tax levied either as a transit tax on goods as they passed a *likin* barrier or as a sales tax on the shops where the goods were sold.[30] It was collected by local and provincial officials and was for the most part spent locally. Moreover, unlike the land tax, it was not systematically reported. Because of its very character and the method of administration, *likin* was even more subject to abuses than the traditional taxes. Since a product on its way to final markets might pass by several *likin* stations, it could be subject to multiple taxation. The principal economic effect of this tax was to raise the cost of distribution and erect new economic and institutional barriers to the flow of goods.

In one sense one can view the Taiping rebellion as a symptom of deepseated peasant unrest engendered by the growing population pressure on land resources which by this time were more or less fixed. Chinese agriculture, operating within a context of unchanging technology, was increasingly subject to the law of diminishing returns. A decline in per capita product resulted, which, in the absence of positive policy measures to reverse it, could only be arrested by the Malthusian checks of war and pestilence. Whether or not one takes this view, there is no doubt that one of the consequences of the rebellion was far-reaching depopulation of the lower Yangtze. The following quotation from a statement by a local official of Chekiang may serve to illustrate the extent of the problem:[31]

After the Taiping wars vast areas of agricultural land were laid waste and the various cities and towns reduced to a shambles. Villages far and near are very sparsely populated and ridges and furrows are all covered with thorns and weeds. . . . To rehabilitate this area it is vital that immigrants be attracted.

Therefore it is not surprising that the efforts of the T'ung-chih Restoration were concentrated on rehabilitating agriculture, which in turn provided the fiscal foundations for the traditional Chinese state. Restoration leaders undertook an ambitious colonization program to settle millions of refugees and demobilized soldiers.[32] At the same time, tenant farmers from the mountainous and congested areas were encouraged to settle in some of the best agricultural areas of the country. The Restoration program incorporated all the traditional farm improvement measures, such as repair of old and badly deteriorated waterworks, construction of new water conservation projects, land tax reduction, and more efficient collection arrangements for the land tax levied.

As already indicated, the Taiping rebellion had certain long-run political consequences that had important economic implications. In the course of defeating the rebellion, political power had become much more fragmented. As Peking was cut off from central China, mobilizing armies and carrying on the war effort became increasingly a regional and provincial responsibility. As a result, the Restoration also became, to a considerable extent, a provincially based effort. Fragmentation of the polity, the rise of quasi-fiefs, and the crystallization of local satrapies became a hallmark of the Chinese political scene virtually until the advent of the Chinese Communist regime.

Thus at roughly the same time as Japan was doing away with feudalism and moving in the direction of a unified nation-state, China was moving in an opposite direction. Its lack of political unity not only reinforced economic fragmentation due to transport, communications, and various institutional barriers, but prevented the formulation of comprehensive programs of modernization that could be made effectively applicable to the country as a whole. It precluded the formulation of a national development program based on measures designed both to remove impediments to economic growth and to actively foster it.

Self-Strengthening and the Abortive Industrialization Program

This does not mean that such measures were not attempted. In fact, closely linked to the T'ung-chih Restoration was the "self-strengthening" (*tzu-ch'iang*) movement, which signaled a recognition of China's need for industrialization and the inauguration of projects designed to launch it on that path.[33] The recognition by some came early as evidenced by the following excerpt from a letter by Lin Tse-hsu in 1842:[34]

> . . . . Ships, guns and a water force are absolutely indispensable. Even if the rebellious barbarians had fled and returned beyond the seas, these things would still have to be urgently planned for, in order to work out the permanent defense of our sea frontiers. Moreover unless we have weapons, what other help can we get now to drive away the crocodile and to get rid of the whales?

However, nothing was done about this need for about twenty years, until Tseng Kuo-fan and Li Hung-chang assumed the leadership of the movement. An 1862 entry in Tseng's diary will serve to illustrate his approach to the problem:[35]

> If we wish to find a method of self-strengthening, we should begin by considering the reform of government service and the securing of men of ability as urgent tasks and then regard learning to make explosive shells and steamships and other instruments as the work of first importance. If only we could possess all their superior techniques, then we would have the means to return their favor when they are obedient, and we would also have the means to avenge our grivances when they are disloyal.

This revealing passage illustrates simultaneously the traditional view of China as the universal empire that expects obedience and loyalty from the barbarians; the feeling of deep humiliation produced by the defeats of this empire; and the recognition of the need for acquiring modern techniques of production if the challenge posed by external threats is to be met. These elements of thought and attitude were to run like a leitmotiv through much of China's subsequent history. In effect they represent a crucial element of inheritance that has become a very important part of Chinese Communist cosmology and as such has played a major role in shaping Communist China's economic policy. They also epitomize strivings that were evident in Japan at roughly the same time; these are perhaps most vividly and most succinctly stated by the slogan that played such a major role in the Meiji Restoration—*fukoku kyohei* ("a rich country and a strong army"). Probably Japan perceived the connection between these two elements more clearly than did China; certainly the translation into actual programs and projects was more effective there.

In China, economic modernization efforts in the late nineteenth century proceeded along three parallel paths: government projects; joint public-private undertakings under the aegis of the *kuan-tu-shang-pan* (official supervision-merchant management) system; and private enterprise—Chinese and foreign—mostly operating in the treaty ports. The first two were closely linked to the self-strengthening movement while the last was preponderantly foreign-led.

As Feuerwerker clearly demonstrates, the distribution between the *kuan-pan* and *kuan-tu-shang-pan* forms of organization is an artificial one, partly because some enterprises started in one form and then were converted into the other and vice versa, and more importantly, because both forms had more or less similar practices and methods of operation.[36] Nevertheless there is some point in making a distinction, inasmuch as the strictly government projects were virtually confined to "military industries," i.e., arsenals and shipyards, although an ironworks and railroads fell into this category too.

Several points need to be made about this total effort. First, it marked the beginnings, the first halting steps, of modern industry in China. Second, the total size of the effort was quite modest. It entailed altogether (including both the *kuan-pan* and the *kuan-tu-shang-pan*) about 15 to 20 major undertakings over a thirty year period, starting roughly with the establishment of the Kiangnan arsenal in 1865 and ending with the Treaty of Shimonoseki in 1895.

Third, the different projects in combination do represent a more or less rational economic design, even if that design was not blueprinted in advance. The initial stimulus for the whole undertaking came from the urge to produce weapons and strengthen the defense establishment—thus the arsenals and the Foochow shipyard. It was soon realized that modern transport and communications are essential ingredients of defense, and this led to the organization of the China Merchants' Steam Navigation Company and, somewhat later, the Imperial Telegraph Administration. Then a coal mine was opened to supply fuel for the arsenals and the steamships. This, in turn, made it necessary to provide transportation from the pithead to a suitable port, and so the first railroad line was built. Military requirements also induced the construction of several textile mills to manufacture cloth for the army. Iron and steel works were established to provide the necessary raw materials for the arsenals and to manufacture rails for the new railroads.

Fourth, most of these projects could be regarded as social overhead investments that, because of large initial capital requirements, long gestation periods, and their external economy effects, logically belong within the purview of public or semipublic investments. Moreover, one could argue that precisely because of their social overhead character, they should be established in the early phases of a development program when they can make an important contribution to decreasing costs of manufacturing.

Fifth, this industrialization effort was sponsored by high provincial officials, notably Tseng Kuo fan, Li Hung-Chang and their followers and allies, in the face of either indifference (at best) or active resistance (at worst) by the imperial center. Officials such as Tseng, Li and Chang Chih-tung perceived the need for at least limited modernization and industrialization, although they wished to keep the changes within the bounds of tradition. Their motives were mixed. In part they were anxious to strengthen the defensive capabilities of the country. At the same time these provincial leaders wanted to utilize the new projects as a means of strengthening their own power base. They saw in them an opportunity to tap new sources of potential revenue and political patronage, while at the same time providing a more or less independent industrial base for their armies. Precisely for these reasons, the court and their political rivals both in the central government and in the provinces perceived this industrialization effort as a threat. Moreover, the court apparently showed very little understanding of the need for, and the potential benefits of, industrialization but viewed the new enterprises as prime object for despoliation.[37]

Sixth, this first attempt at modern industrial development in China must be adjudged a failure in several terms. Some projects failed, but this in itself would not have been decisive since the economic history of industrialization in every country is strewn with a record of bankruptcies and unsuccessful experiments. More important despite its superficial economic logic in terms of projects selected and their interdependence, the effort as a whole had very little cumulative impact on China's modern economic growth. As we will see further below, to the extent that China experienced such growth, it came from another quarter.

The reasons for this apparent failure are manifold and complex. One must bear in mind first of all that the total scope and size of the program was quite small in relation to the size of the country and the deadweight of tradition. Furthermore, each project experienced acute difficulties, due to shortages of capital, particularistic business and government practices, and the fact that the risks of such pioneering efforts were so high that to attract private capital, high rates of return had to be guaranteed even if the fortunes of the enterprise did not warrant the payment of large dividends. While all of these enterprises depended to a greater or lesser extent on provincial and central government support in the form of government loans, subsidies, and guaranteed market arrangements, they were constantly exposed to fiscal pressures from these public authorities. Of course, there were other contributing factors closely associated with the country's economic backwardness, such as lack of technical, managerial and organizational skill and the constant scarcity of capital. However, one might venture the view that the more fundamental problems were not economic but ideological and institutional.

Perhaps the fate and character of this early industrialization program is most clearly illustrated by the fortunes of the China Merchants' Steamship Navigation Company.[38] The company did very well by its managers and shareholders, so much so that in 1882 the managers could report that during the nine years of the company's life the shareholders had earned an average rate of annual return of 20 per cent on their investment in the form of guaranteed dividends, special stock dividends and bonuses. In contrast, the company as a steamship enterprise did not prosper. After 1887, at a time when the industry as a whole was expanding, it virtually stopped growing, and in 1914 the size of its fleet, both in number of ships and total tonnage, was almost the same as at the earlier date; and this in spite of rapid expansion in foreign and domestic trade and in the total volume of shipping.

Seventh, despite its apparent failure in one sense, the experiment did in the long run have a lasting impact on the modernization of China. The different projects singly and in combination chipped away at the traditional order and helped to weaken and undermine it. Put in a different way, although the institutional, ideological, political and economic impediments were too strong to permit a breakthrough, the mere attempt—even though not too successful—served to weaken the barriers to modernization and thus open the way for later and more successful attempts. In more positive terms it also served as a training ground for modern entrepreneurship, for the development of modern forms of business organization, and for the training of technical cadres.

Although these different points have been stated rather categorically, they must in many ways still be treated as subject to further verification

and validation. For instance, the relationship between this early industrialization effort and other subsequent efforts requires much closer study. Did
these projects indeed have virtually no impact on stimulating the development of other enterprises? Did the *kuan-tu shang-pan* enterprises have any
external economy or market stimulating effects? Did they have any
learning effects and if so, what kind and to what extent?

The Emerging Pattern of Trade in the Late Nineteenth Century

While these developments were taking place in the traditional economy,
the treaty ports sector was growing very gradually under the impact of
foreign trade expansion and closely associated economic activities. Several
factors combined to stimulate foreign trade growth. A number of new
ports were "opened" to trade. The Suez Canal was opened in 1869, and
the trade route to Europe was markedly shortened. Telegraph communication between London and Shanghai was established in 1871.[39] At the
same time, the demand for foreign goods was slowly increasing in China,
while demand for China's products was rising abroad, with both of these
developments actively promoted by the foreign trading enterprises in the
treaty ports.

As a result, in terms of quantity indices both imports and exports
roughly doubled between 1870 and 1895.[40] Nevertheless, by 1895, imports amounted to no more than U.S. $140 million and exports to U.S.
$115 million.[41] As exports and imports were rising, trade deficits were
also increasing. Between 1868 and 1871 the average annual deficit was
about U.S. $7 million. In the following five-year period this was converted
into an average annual surplus of about the same amount. But after 1877
there was a consistent trade deficit, which by 1890–94 averaged around
U.S. $35 million.[42]

During this period there began a secular decline in the gold value of
silver, amounting in effect to a continuing devaluation of China's foreign
exchange. This is illustrated by the fact that the U.S. dollar value of a
Haikwan *tael* was just about halved, falling from 1.58 in 1871 to 0.80 in
1895. Other things being equal, one would have expected this to encourage exports and discourage imports. In fact the opposite happened, with
imports rising more rapidly than exports, both in terms of current and
constant (1913) prices. The precise reasons for this are not entirely clear.
However, the sustained and rapid rise in the demand for imported goods,

combined with supply inelasticities, must certainly have played an important role. These supply inelasticities in turn were rooted in the difficulties of organizing the silk and tea trade, improving the quality, standardization and internal distribution of these products.

This conclusion is borne out by a closer study of the changing structure of China's exports during this period. In general, Chinese exports became more diversified as the tea trade declined and new products began to be sold. Both India and Japan had begun to compete with China for the world tea trade, with India gaining ascendancy in the United Kingdom market and Japan in trade with the United States. As a result China's tea exports in the 1880's and 1890's began to decline.

Silk and silk exports, on the other hand, continued to increase throughout the period in spite of growing Japanese competition. However, they lost ground in relation both to total world silk exports and to China's total export trade.

Under the impact of these developments the combined export share of tea and silk declined from more than 90 per cent in 1868 to no more than 60 per cent in 1890. By 1890, silk displaced tea as China's leading export product. To these traditional items new export products were now added, such as raw cotton, vegetable oils, hog bristles, skins and hides, eggs and their products, and other agricultural commodities. (See Table 3, A).

Marked changes took place in the structure of imports as well, as shown in Table 3, B. By 1885 cotton goods displaced opium as China's leading import, marking the beginning of a continuing decline in the import of this drug. At first this was due largely to the spread of opium cultivation in China; later on there was also a gradual decline in domestic opium consumption. This decline is illustrated by the fact that while in 1888, 82,000 *piculs* of opium were imported, by 1893 the figure was reduced to 68,000 *piculs,* and by 1898 to 50,000.[43] In the meantime cotton textile imports were gaining steadily in volume and relative importance. This was particularly true for cotton yarn imports, which doubled every few years. The growth in yarn imports was so rapid that by 1898 yarn exceeded in value the manufactured cotton textiles purchased from abroad. We can see here the emergence of a significant industrialization pattern: Imports of manufactured cotton goods find their way into Chinese markets, tapping new sources of demand without displacing handicraft weaving of cloth. To the contrary, handicraft weavers began to use imported cotton yarn which is cheaper than the yarn produced domestically.

TABLE 3

Trend and Commodity Composition of China's Exports and Imports, 1868–1890

(in per cent)

A. Exports

Year	Tea	Silk and Silk Goods	Vegetable Seeds and Oils	Beans	Hides and Skins	Raw Cotton	Wool	Other	Total	Quantum Index (1913 = 100)
1868	53.8	39.7	–	1.0	–	0.9	–	4.6	100	33.7
1880	45.9	38.0	0.1	0.2	0.5	0.2	0.4	14.7	100	47.2
1890	30.6	33.9	0.6	0.4	1.4	3.4	1.6	28.1	100	42.0

B. Imports

Year	Opium	Cotton Goods	Cotton Yarn	Cereals and Wheat Flour	Sugar	Coal	Kerosene	Metals	Ma-chinery	Other	Total	Quantum Index (1913 = 100)
1868	33.1	29.0	2.5	0.8	0.8	2.1	–	4.8	–	26.9	100	25.4
1880	39.3	24.9	4.6	0.1	0.4	1.2	–	5.5	–	24.0	100	36.2
1890	19.5	20.2	15.3	9.6	0.9	1.6	3.2	5.7	0.3	23.7	100	54.8

Source: Y. K. Cheng, *op. cit.*, Tables 3 and 4, pp. 18–19; Appendix I, p. 258.

Another significant change characteristic of this period is the rise in imports of kerosene after the 1880's. In 1887, 12 million gallons were imported, and this amount jumped to 100 million gallons within the next decade.[44] The oil was mostly used for household illumination; its use spread quickly because it gave a better light and yet was cheaper than bean, tea or other vegetable oils. These latter products could now be exported instead of being used for lighting, a case of economic adaptation based on gains from foreign trade.

Foreign Trade Growth and Domestic Economic Development

What was the impact of these changes in foreign trade composition on economic development in the treaty ports and in the domestic economy? In the treaty ports we can see the beginnings of a cumulative development pattern. Foreign trade expansion generated a demand for modern banking services, and so in 1864 the Hongkong and Shanghai Banking Corporation was founded.[45] In turn, the establishment of modern banking facilities contributed to a further growth in foreign trade in a number of ways, not the least of which was that it lowered the capital requirements for a foreign trading firm and thus eased freedom of entry into this business branch. Foreign trade growth stimulated the increase in shipping, which in turn led to the construction of ship repair and shipbuilding yards. Moreover, as foreign trade and its auxiliary services expanded, the number of foreigners resident in the treaty ports grew as well. This foreign population was estimated by Remer to be around 17,000 in 1899.[46]

The demand for urban facilities and public utilities increased rapidly as the total population, particularly the foreign population, of the treaty ports grew. The first electric power generating plant went into operation in Shanghai in 1882 and the first waterworks in 1880. The Shanghai Gas Company was founded in 1863.[47] The provision of social overhead facilities combined with the prospects of profitable business opportunities encouraged the further growth of both the Chinese and the foreign populations in the treaty ports. As a result, the ports themselves became an increasingly important source of import demand.

Foreign trade and other economic activities in the treaty ports were largely dominated by foreign firms. However, by 1895 Chinese merchants were sharing more in this business, either directly through the establishment of Chinese firms or indirectly through the evolution of the comprador system. Not surprisingly, large accumulations of commercial wealth came into the hands of Chinese merchants operating out of the treaty ports. Some of this merchant wealth went into financing the *kuan-tu shang-pan* enterprises discussed above. However, prior to 1895 the bulk of it was apparently channeled into speculative activities in the treaty ports, e.g., in real estate and in inventories, into investment in land, and into usury.

The impact of foreign trade expansion on the domestic economy is much more difficult to assess. Export growth of silk and silk products more than compensated for the decline in tea shipments. Moreover, exports of other farm products rose so that one would expect positive income effects from exports for the farm economy. (This finding may need to be qualified for districts in which tea production was of great importance.)

The situation is much more complicated on the import side. We have already noted the marked rise in cotton yarn imports, and this factory yarn was undoubtedly displacing handspun yarn with quite destructive effects on the position of rural handicrafts in a number of areas. However, it was at the same time augmenting the competitive strength of handicraft weaving against imported piece goods, inasmuch as domestic cloth manufactures could now use the cheaper imported yarn. The import of kerosene probably represented an immediate and direct economic gain, while the wide miscellany of other imports went mostly to the expanding urban market where they were tapping new sources of demand.

IV. The Beginnings of Modern Economic Growth, 1895–1949

On the eve of the Sino-Japanese war there was virtually no modern industry in China. There were fewer than ten cotton textile mills with a total spindlage of about 320,000.[48] In comparison, India had a textile manufacturing establishment of one million spindles by 1876 and Japan attained that size by 1898.[49] As a matter of fact, China was by then importing the largest share of its cotton yarn from India.[50] As noted above, there were a few arsenals and shipyards, some silk filatures laboring under great difficulties, and a small number of shops in various other branches of manufacture.

At the same time, construction of the first railway lines had just begun on the Chinese mainland, with no more than about 200 miles actually completed.[51] Shipping, on the other hand, was more highly developed. Chinese enterprises were running 35 or 40 vessels with a total tonnage of 35- to 40,000.[52] Nevertheless, foreign firms, which had over three-quarters of the carrying capacity, dominated overseas and even coastwise shipping.[53] With foreign trade expansion, the growth of shipping, banking and other services associated with it, the treaty ports, particularly Shanghai, were becoming small islands of economic modernity on the periphery of the Chinese land and population mass.

However, the turning point in China's modern economic growth can be clearly traced back to the Treaty of Shimonoseki (1895) by which the Japanese secured the right to own and operate industrial establishments in the treaty ports. Then all the other powers having "most-favored nation" treaty arrangements with China took advantage of this right, and as a result industrial capacity, railroad mileage, shipping, and foreign trade grew quite rapidly.

In a sense it is surprising that such expansion could take place amid China's political weakness and later chaos. Imperial rule in the last decade or two of its existence was even more debilitated than in the latter half of the nineteenth century. The capacity of the public polity to play a positive role in promoting economic development was further undermined by the reparation burdens and indemnities the Chinese government had to assume, first after their defeat in the Sino-Japanese War, and then following the Boxer Rebellion. The situation was further aggravated by a number of uneconomic foreign loan obligations incurred by the governmental authorities. Between 1911 and 1928, China had no single government that could claim to rule all the country. With the Japanese conquest in 1931, the continuing civil war in the 1930's, the wartime Japanese occupation of north and east China, and the heightened civil war between 1945 and 1949, it would be fair to say that not even the Nationalist government effectively controlled all of the country's provinces.

China's record contrasts sharply with the history of government and of government's role in the economy in Japan. The contrast is so marked that by itself it could account for the different fates of modern economic growth in the two countries. Of course, government itself is not an autonomous factor but a product of a variety of forces and variables, among which the economy undoubtedly played a very significant role.

Whatever economic growth took place in China was accomplished despite, rather than because of, the government's role in the economy. This certainly applied to the Empire which was at best a passive bystander (in regard to modern economic growth) and at worst a seriously retarding influence. During the period of warlordism and civil war (1911–28), government (largely provincial) must have imposed tremendous burdens on the economy. Financing of large military expenditures during the Nanking government period (1928–37) and during the war undoubtedly represented additional heavy burdens. Whether the burdens imposed by the Nanking government were lesser or greater than its direct or indirect contributions to economic growth requires much more study. In fact, the public sector's role in the Chinese economy needs to be explored much more systematically and rigorously than has been done heretofore.

On the basis of presently available evidence it would seem that the bulk of this economic burden was borne by the traditional, rural sector. The government's failure to reform land tenure effectively, organize an agricultural extension service, or institute an effective farm credit system, combined with direct and indirect tax pressure, must have played a crucial role in preventing the technical transformation of agriculture and in perpetuating agricultural stagnation.

The treaty ports, on the other hand, operating within a framework of extraterritoriality, could escape the tax pressure, the exactions, and the devastations of warlordism and civil war. Moreover, they could substitute those attributes of law and order that were lacking in the traditional sector during most of this period. Once the governmental barriers were removed, a number of factors combined to foster modern economic growth in the treaty ports.

The ports as points of entry and exit for the mainland became natural foci for the concentration of foreign trading and shipping activities and all the associated economic services. Extraterritoriality and the foreign concessions attracted foreign residents and foreign firms as well as Chinese firms. This in turn created a demand for modern urban facilities. Once those facilities were installed, they reinforced the attraction of treaty ports as places of residence for both business establishments and households. The presence of social overhead facilities, e.g., electric power, relatively good transportation, communications, and banking services, attracted modern industry after 1895, the first year in which foreign manufacturing firms were permitted to locate in the treaty ports. In addition to these external economies, certain demand factors reinforced the locational advantages of treaty ports as industrial centers. As the population of these ports grew, they necessarily became major market outlets for the manufactured products. These locational advantages are not so clear-cut in the case of raw material supplies for the modern industries. The ports in China proper were in most cases not well situated in relation to the best coal and iron ore reserves. On the other hand, they were close to the sources of agricultural raw material for the consumer goods industries. But it would seem that the external economy effects, broadly interpreted, provided such overwhelming locational advantages as to outweigh any possible increases in costs due to distance from raw material supplies.

These relationships can perhaps best be illustrated by the case of Shanghai, the largest of the ports. Before the opening of China to foreign trade, Hangchow, Soochow and Nanking were larger than Shanghai, but it quickly outstripped them. Though all three were also treaty ports and remained important commercial centers, Shanghai's location at the apex of the Yangtze basin turned out to be decisive. The Yangtze watershed encompasses about half of the land area of China proper, with about 40 per cent of the country's prewar population. The total of inland waterways navigable from Shanghai by junks at all seasons is nearly 30,000 miles. To this must be added an estimated half million miles of canals or artificial waterways in the delta area. It is not surprising, therefore, that between 1865 and 1936, Shanghai handled 45 to 65 per cent of China's total foreign trade.[54]

However, development in the treaty ports was undoubtedly bought at a high social cost, both locally in the ports themselves; and nationally because of the psychological and political impact of the ports as a symbol of imperialism and because of the effect on economic growth in the hinterland. Economic development was based on a foreign-trade orientation that was in part a function of political, institutional and transport barriers within China and in part a function of the circumstances under which foreigners forced open China's door. The treaty ports were naturally favored. At the same time, and perhaps for the same reasons, provinces such as Szechwan remained underdeveloped in spite of their great natural wealth, and the coal resources of Shansi and Shensi were poorly exploited. The inability to develop inland industrial centers of prime importance in China proper may also have contributed to agricultural retardation. Such centers could have undoubtedly served as growing points for modern economic growth, from which modernizing influences could have been transmitted to the surrounding countryside more easily than from the distant treaty ports.

Economic Development in Manchuria

An entirely different set of advantages favored Manchuria as a locus of economic development on the Chinese mainland. Manchuria was an undeveloped frontier, rich in resources but very sparsely settled until the twentieth century. It was legally thrown open to Chinese immigration in 1860, Newchwang was opened as a port for foreign trade in 1861, and by 1903 the Russians had completed the construction of both the main and branch lines of the Chinese Eastern Railway.[55] These developments, combined with the political instability and apparent economic decline in the rural sector of China proper, attracted large-scale immigration, particularly from north China. There must have been sizable movement in the late nineteenth century and again in the 1920's.

Population growth, railroad and harbor development, and land settlement produced a vigorous pattern of cumulative growth. Population growth and land settlement brought with them rapid expansion in farm production, as may be seen from the data in Table 4. Railroad and harbor development encouraged the rise of domestic and foreign trade. Kaoliang emerged as the principal food staple and soybeans as the main commercial crop. Manchurian agriculture became much more market-oriented and more readily responsive to market stimuli than the farm sector in China proper. Foreign trade grew very rapidly. In terms of current prices, expressed in Haikwan *taels,* it increased tenfold in 20 years (1907–27), while for the mainland as a whole it took 56 years (1864–1920) to achieve the same percentage increase.[56]

Agricultural development led to the rise of farm processing industries, i.e., bean-oil pressing, bean-cake milling, flour milling and tobacco manufacture. Population growth combined with railroad and harbor development fostered urbanization, with ports and railroad junctions serving as urban nuclei. Urbanization was further reinforced by industrial development.

During the first few decades of Manchurian development, economic growth was based on the interrelated expansion of population, agriculture, and foreign trade. Only in the 1930's do we witness the beginnings of mining and some heavy industry. However, as may be seen from the data

TABLE 4

Selected Indicators of Economic Development
in Manchuria, 1900–1940

Year	Population (in millions)	Railroad Mileage (in miles)	Total Cereal Production	Soybean Production
			(in thousands of metric tons)	
1900	14	1,500	n.a.	(600)[f]
1907–1915[a]	15–17[b]	2,150[c]	5,700[d]	2,645[e]
1930	34.3	3,700	18,810	5,360
1940	44.5	6,250	21,150	4,390

a. This is not an average, but merely indicates that the different figures in this row refer to individual years within this eight-year interval.
   b. For 1907.
   c. For 1912.
   d. For 1914.
   e. For 1915.
   f. Figures in parentheses are estimates.
Sources: P. T. Ho, *Studies on the Population of China, 1368–1953*, Cambridge, Mass., 1959, pp. 160–63; F. C. Jones, *Manchuria Since 1931*, London, 1949, pp. 4–7 and 101–106; Grover Clark, *Economic Rivalries in China*, New Haven, Conn., 1932, p. 18; Manshikai, *Manshū Kaihatsu Yonjūnenski*, Vol. I, Tokyo, 1964.

in Table 5, industrial development (other than agricultural processing) gathered momentum only after the complete Japanese takeover in 1931. By this time most of the better farm lands were occupied and the force of agricultural expansion was largely spent. In the 1930's and early 1940's, mining and producer goods industries took the place of agriculture as the "leading" sector in the region's economic growth.

The contrast between the course of twentieth-century economic change in Manchuria and in China Proper is marked. At the turn of the century, Manchuria had relatively abundant land and mineral resources and a sparse population. It benefitted greatly from sizable injections of Russian and later Japanese capital and entrepreneurship. Capital imports per capita were undoubtedly much higher than in China Proper. Finally, Manchuria was much less affected by the vicissitudes of civil strife.

Industrial Development on the Chinese Mainland

According to a study by John K. Chang (1965), industrial growth in pre-Communist China was quite rapid. His index, based on 15 series

TABLE 5

Selected Indicators of Industrial Development in Manchuria, 1925–1944

Year	Iron Ore	Pig Iron	Steel Ingots	Coal	Cement	Pulp	Paper (in thousand lbs.)	Electric Power Generation (in million kwh.)
	(production in thousand metric tons)							
1925		137		6,948				239
1927	959	244		9,910	112			341
1928	710	285		9,510	151	6		403
1930	832	349		9,020	194	8		504
1932	993	368		8,830	109	12	22	593
1935	1,362	608	137	12,166	378	14	33	1,084
1940	2,978	1,069	532	21,200	1,035	76	83	2,998
1941	3,703	1,236	561	23,800	1,164	80	117	3,520
1942	4,413	1,341	716	24,169	1,532	95	162	4,086
1943	5,408	1,710	862	25,320	1,503	67	168	4,475
1944	3,758	1,159	439	25,627	1,141	59	101	4,481

Sources:

Iron ore: for 1927–32, South Manchurian Railroad Co. (SMR), Manshu Sangyo Tokei, various years; for 1935, SMR, *Manshu Keizai Nenpo,* Dairen, 1938, Table 1; for 1940–41, SMR, *Manshu Keizai Tokei Kiho,* No. 2, 1942; for 1942–44, E. W. Pauley, *Report on Japanese Assets in Manchuria,* Washington, D.C., 1946, pp. 90–92.

Pig iron: for 1925–35, *The Orient Year Book,* Tokyo, 1942, pp. 603, 607; for 1940–41, SMR, 1942, *op. cit.;* for 1942–44, Pauley, *op. cit.*

Steel: for 1935, Wang Chen-ching, *Tung-pei Chih Ching-chi Tzu-yuan (Economic Resources of Manchuria),* Shanghai, 1947, p. 101; for 1940–44, Manshikai, *op. cit.,* Vol. II, p. 196.

Coal: for 1925–28, *Japan-Manchuokuo Year Book,* Tokyo, 1934, p. 599; for 1930–44, Pauley, *op. cit.,* p. 74.

Cement: for 1927–35, *The Orient Year Book, op. cit.,* p. 686; for 1940, SMR, 1942, *op. cit.;* for 1941–44, Chang Chen-ta, *Tung-pei Ching-chi (Economy of the North East),* Taipei, 1954, p. 196.

Pulp: for 1928–44, Chang Chen-ta, *op. cit.,* pp. 230–31.

Paper: for 1932–44, *Chih Chi Chih Chiang (Paper and Pulp),* Economic Handbook Series on Manchuria, No. 13, Shenyang, 1946, Table 13.

Electric power: for 1925–35, Manshikai, *op. cit.,* Vol. II, p. 537; for 1940–44, State Statistical Bureau (SSB), *Wo-kuo kang-t'ieh, tien-li, mei-t'an, chi-chieh, fang-chih, tsao-chih, kung-yeh, ti chin-hsi,* Peking, 1958, p. 40.

including mining and manufacturing products and electric power (which in 1933 encompassed 40–60 per cent of industrial output value), indicates that industrial production grew between 1912 and 1949 at an average annual rate of 5.5 per cent.[57] As noted earlier, this period was disrupted by civil strife and by the Japanese occupation of east and north China during World War II. The record of industrial performance revealed by the findings of Chang's study (Table 6) therefore seems particularly remarkable.

According to this index, value added in industry grew more or less continuously until 1936 and then declined; but as Manchurian industrialization gained momentum it started expanding again in 1939, exceeding the earlier (1936) record by 1940, and attaining a peak level in 1942. Gross industrial output value followed a similar course with one important exception, that even after its growth was resumed in 1939 it never again exceeded the 1936 level. These differences in the trends of the two value series reflect the rapidly changing composition of industrial product after 1936, with the textile industry declining in China Proper, and the iron and steel, electric power, cement and some other branches of manufacture expanding in Manchuria.

These results must be interpreted with caution. The reliability of the physical production data on which Chang's index is based requires further scrutiny, particularly for the earlier years. As the investigation progresses, specific figures will undoubtedly be revised, so that the rates of growth presented in Table 6 may need to be changed. Nevertheless, it is doubtful

TABLE 6

Average Annual Rates of Industrial Growth in Mainland
China, 1912–1949 and Subperiods[a]

Period	Average Growth Rate per Year
1912–1949	5.5
1912–1920	13.8
1912–1936	9.2
1912–1942	8.2
1923–1936	8.3
1923–1942	7.1
1928–1936	8.4
1928–1942	6.7
1931–1936	9.3
1931–1942	6.7
1936–1942	4.5

a. Based on value added in terms of 1933 prices.
Source: John K. Chang, *Indexes of Industrial Production of Mainland China, 1912–1949* (Ph.D. dissertation, University of Michigan), 1965.

whether these changes will markedly alter the general impression of a pre-industrial economy in which a small industrial sector is rapidly growing.

These trends are the product of a number of mutually contradictory tendencies. The earliest period shows unusually rapid rates of expansion for two principal reasons. First, China's industrial base in 1912 was very small so that any substantial increment would yield rapid rates of increase. Then mainland industry experienced a boom during World War I, when it enjoyed many of the benefits of infant industry protection without a tariff, due to the marked decline of imports as Western nations diverted shipping to military uses.

Not too surprisingly, except in this early period, industrial output increased most rapidly between 1931 and 1936, the period when civil strife was at a minimum, when government policies both in China Proper and in Manchuria were conducive to economic growth, and when the country's tariff autonomy was restored. The reality of a quickly expanding industrial sector is confirmed even if we extend the period so as to encompass the chaotic years of the early 1920's; the average annual rate of growth appears as 8 per cent a year for the 1923 to 1936 period.

It is possible that the result would have been quite different if the omitted industries could have been included in the index. Yet even if we assume that the excluded branches expanded only half as rapidly as those covered, the average annual growth rates for 1923–36 would be reduced from 8 per cent only to 5.6 per cent, depending on whether the index encompasses 40 or 60 per cent of the industrial product.

Other indicators tend to validate this view of rapid industrial growth in mainland China. The pace of expansion for Manchurian industry was noted above and a few selected series are shown in Table 5. The number of cotton yarn spindles in China increased from about 740,000 in 1912 to approximately 2.5 million in 1923 and 5.1 million in 1936, i.e., trebling in the first 11 years and doubling in the next 13. The same impression of expansion is conveyed by the growth in railroad traffic. Total freight miles nearly doubled between 1912 and 1921, and then increased by another 40 per cent between that year and 1936.[58]

What was the composition of this industrial expansion? Growth in industrial output was based first of all on the rather rapid development of the textile industry, which became by far the most important single branch of manufacture in China. It also entailed the growth of food processing (e.g., flour milling and tobacco manufacture) and mining, particularly coal mining. Except for the last, these were preponderantly concentrated in China Proper, especially in the treaty ports. On the other hand, Manchuria dominated iron and steel, electric power generation, oil shale, and cement production. Moreover, as industrial production declined in China Proper under the impact of World War II and the Japanese Occupation, it continued to rise in Manchuria at least until 1942 and possibly until 1944. As a result, mainland industrial output as a whole did not fall as drastically after the outbreak of Sino-Japanese hostilities as one might have expected. In certain areas, both in Free China and in Japanese-held regions, the war led to an expansion of industrial capacity.

As indicated earlier, foreign enterprise led the way in industrial development, but it was gradually displaced by Chinese enterprise. This is most clearly illustrated by the fact that according to the Liu-Yeh estimate, about 67 per cent of industrial gross output value was produced in Chinese-owned factories in 1933, with these factories employing 73 per cent of the industrial labor force.[59] According to Yen Chung-p'ing's compilation, by 1936, Chinese firms produced 71 per cent of the cotton yarn, 36 per cent of the cotton cloth, 42 per cent of the cigarettes, 89 per cent of the matches, 96 per cent of the edible vegetable oils (refers to 1933), 34 per cent of the coal and 45 per cent of the electric power.[60] Whatever the indicator used, Chinese business firms played a significant role in this process of industrial growth and carried a major share of it. This must mean that an industrial labor force was trained and a Chinese managerial and business class was formed. But how large was this industrial sector and how important a role did it play in the economy as a whole?

According to Liu and Yeh, total employment in factory industry, mining and public utilities was no more than 2 million in 1933, or about 4 per cent of the total nonagricultural labor force. At the same time these sectors contributed only 3.4 per cent to national product in terms of 1933 prices, or 6.5 per cent in terms of 1952 prices. If to these industries we add construction, modern transport and communications, and modern trade and finance, we find that the modern sectors generated about 13 per cent of the national product in 1933 prices, or over 20 per cent in 1952 prices.[61]

Therefore, on the basis of a number of different measures it would seem that the modernized sectors of the economy, and most particularly industry, were small in the 1930's despite a fairly long period of quite rapid growth. How can this apparent paradox be reconciled? If GNP in China was growing very slowly between 1912 and 1936, while the industrial output increased tenfold, at the end of the period the share of industry in national income would still be quite small if this rapid growth had started from a tiny base.

It is fundamental to realize that industrial growth remained confined within narrow limits. Within these confines it expanded rapidly but it did not spread and it did not really lead to a structural transformation of the economy as a whole during the pre-Communist period. This conclusion applies only to China proper, not to Manchuria, but because of the relative size of the two it can legitimately be applied to the mainland economy as a whole.

The small size of modern industry necessarily meant that even in the 1930's most of the demand for manufactures continued to be supplied by handicrafts. In fact, all the available studies find that, in terms of aggregate output, handicrafts outweigh modern industry by a sizable margin.[62] The question still unanswered is whether the handicrafts output increased, declined or remained more or less stationary between 1895 and 1936, or between 1912 and 1936. Unfortunately, information on trends in this sector is so poor that one must proceed on the basis of highly fragmentary data. This is a case where a priori reasoning is inclusive and direct evidence is mixed. It should first be noted that there must have been a relative displacement in handicrafts in relation to the manufacturing sector as a whole. Since before 1895 virtually all manufacturing was done by handicrafts establishments, any growth in modern industry would automatically reduce the former's share to some degree. However, the more significant question is whether the handicrafts sector grew, and if so at what rate.

One can almost be certain that if handicrafts expanded, they did so much more slowly than modern industry. It is much less certain whether they expanded faster or more slowly than national product as a whole. At the present state of our knowledge, and for this period, the rate of growth cannot be ascertained.

Disregarding the question of rate, a sifting of at least some of the evidence suggests that there was probably a rise, not a decline, in handicrafts output between 1895 and 1936, or 1912 and 1936. A priori, it is probable, though by no means certain, that there was some population growth in the rural sector of China Proper. This increase may have been more than canceled out by a decline in per capita income and a resulting decline in the aggregate demand of the traditional sector. Moreover, if aggregate demand rose only by, say, 20–30 per cent, such an increase could have been met by the expansion that took place in modern industry. Modern industry would thus have captured a certain share of the traditional market. There is no doubt that in some branches of manufacture this actually happened, the most outstanding case being the displacement of handicraft yarn by manufactured yarn.

In addition to cotton-yarn spinning, at least two other handicrafts branches declined, silk reeling and tea processing. Filature silk gradually displaced hand-reeled silk, while tea production and processing decreased under the impact of shrinking export demand for Chinese tea. On the other hand, the export demand for a wide range of Chinese handicraft products increased continuously, and a number of handicraft branches held their own in the domestic market. According to a recent study published in Communist China, the total export value of 67 handicraft products deflated for price changes increased at an average annual rate of 1.1 per cent between 1912 and 1931.[63]

In indigenous mining, pig iron and iron ore production based on native methods did not decline until 1928–30. Native coal production increased quite rapidly between 1912 and 1923 but decreased thereafter.[64] Reference has been made to the fact that hand weaving was expanding while hand spinning was being displaced. As a matter of fact, some new hand-weaving centers developed using manufactured cotton yarn. This growth in handicraft cloth production continued until at least about 1930. Again, this cloth was principally sold in the rural hinterland, so that it was catering to a more or less different market than imported or domestically manufactured piece goods.

Present indications, some of them sketched above, would suggest that on balance the handicraft sector grew in absolute size between 1895 and 1936 as well as between 1912 and 1936. Within this expansion some branches undoubtedly declined in response to changes in the character of export or domestic demand, and under the impact of increasing competitive pressure from the industrial sector and from imports.

Most of the discussions of Chinese handicrafts have focused on their "ruin," decline, or slow growth. But one could perhaps argue with greater justification that it is surprising that they have grown at all and changed so little. One certainly tends to associate rapid industrialization with marked transformation in the character of handicrafts and small-scale industries.

They do not need to disappear, as the experience of Japan amply illustrates, but they do have to change in terms of their techniques, the character of their products and the kind of economic activities they perform in the interstices of modern industry. Seen in this light, the absence of such marked changes in the handicrafts sector is still another indication of the marginal and superficial character of modern economic growth in pre-Communist China.

This, then, brings us back to a question posed earlier. How can one explain the confining character of modern industrial and economic growth in China? What have been the barriers to the diffusion of modern technology, modern economic institutions and practices? Obviously this is only in part an economic problem.

Changes in the Composition of Foreign Trade

As an intrinsic part of the rapid growth in the modern sectors of the economy, foreign trade expanded markedly during the years following the Treaty of Shimonoseki. As may be seen from the data in Table 7, foreign

TABLE 7

China's Foreign Trade, 1895–1936

			Quantum Indices	
Year	Imports	Exports	Imports	Exports
	(in million Haikwan *taels*)			
1895	171.7	143.3	45.8	66.3
1913	570.2	403.3	100.0	100.0
1928	1,196.0	991.3	131.5	156.1
1929	1,265.8	1,015.7	139.9	149.2
1930	1,309.8	894.8	131.0	131.1
1931	1,443.5	909.5	129.9	136.5
1936	880.7[a]	930.5[a]		

a. Includes Manchuria. Manchurian data are given by Y. K. Cheng in U.S. dollar terms; these were then converted into Haikwan *taels* on the basis of the implicit exchange rates given by Y. K. Cheng in his Appendix I.
Source: Y. K. Cheng, *op. cit.*, Appendix I, pp. 258–59, and Appendix VIII, p. 269.

trade in terms of current prices approximately trebled between 1895 and 1913, with imports rising somewhat faster than exports. In terms of quantity, imports doubled while exports rose by a third. The pace of trade expansion slowed down with the outbreak of World War I, and in general the rate of growth of foreign trade—both imports and exports—was considerably slower after 1913. Exports reached their highest level in 1929 while imports attained their peak in 1931. During the whole period between 1895 and 1936, China maintained an unfavorable balance of trade financed by capital imports in the form of foreign loans and foreign investments.

During World War I, imports valued in constant (1913) prices declined by about a third, largely due to the diversion of Allied shipping to the war zones.[65] The positive impact of this decline on domestic industrial development was noted above. At the same time, wartime shortages in a number of commodity markets raised the demand for Chinese products. Put in another way, shortages, rising prices, and sellers' markets reduced the competitive pressures, and it was easier to find outlets for China's products. As a result, while imports declined, exports (in quantity terms) rose by 40 per cent between 1913 and 1919. They then fell quite rapidly in the postwar years, not exceeding these levels again until 1926.

The slowing down of the rate of foreign trade expansion that accompanied the beginnings of modern industrial development was probably due to both the import-displacing character of Chinese industrialization, and the marked supply inelasticities in Chinese agriculture. As will be shown below, import displacement was particularly marked in the textile industry. At the same time, with limited growth and little transformation in the economy as a whole, the range and variety of products demanded and the level of that demand remained quite limited. Though imports rose rapidly in the first few decades after China was opened, their total value and volume was small. This rate of expansion was then slowed down in the twentieth century as it bumped against the ceiling imposed by the limited effective demand of an economy caught up in the vicious circle of backwardness.

Serious transport and communications barriers, as well as political disunity, contributed to a fragmentation of markets. The resulting imperfections were then reinforced by institutional factors rooted in the character of marketing and farm credit in agrarian China. As already noted earlier, without government encouragement and active support, it was difficult to introduce the quality controls and standardization necessary to maintain and improve the competitive position of China's exports in world markets. The same types of barriers also slowed producer's responses to changing world market conditions, thereby reinforcing supply inelasticities rooted in a traditional peasant society.[66]

However, foreign trade was not unaffected by growth in the modern economic sectors or by increasing commercialization under the impact of railroad development and the expansion of inland shipping. The most apparent change in China's foreign trade in the twentieth century has been growing diversification. While silk and tea accounted for nearly 95 per cent of total exports in 1868 and for 65 per cent in 1890, their share fell to about 25 per cent by 1920, and to 17 per cent by 1930. The most precipitate drop occurred in tea, which declined both in relative and absolute terms. Silk, on the other hand, held its own much longer, declining as a share of total Chinese exports, but maintaining or even somewhat increasing its absolute level of sales until the 1920's. At the same time, however, it was being more and more displaced in world markets by Japanese silk and later by synthetic fibers.

As these two traditional exports shrank in importance, their place was taken by soybeans, soybean oil and bean cake, mostly from Manchuria. Other export products that began to assume some importance after 1900 were vegetable oils, hides and skins, coal, ores, and a wide variety of minor products. The bulk of these exports were agricultural, with mining products also assuming some importance.

The interrelationship between foreign trade and industrial development is shown most clearly in the development of the Chinese textile industry. In the late nineteenth century China was a net exporter of raw cotton while it was importing increasing amounts of piece goods. The volume of net raw cotton exports increased until about 1910, paralleled by rising imports of cotton yarn, which reached record volumes in the first decade of the twentieth century. Then the situation was reversed. By 1920, China was a net importer of raw cotton; imports of cotton yarn were halved, and yarn exports on a modest scale were started. By 1928, China had become a net exporter of cotton yarn, with yarn imports shrinking to negligible proportions by the 1930's.

Before the establishment of a textile industry (i.e., before 1895 or 1900), China exported raw cotton and imported manufactured cloth. Yarn imports were rising in importance in the late 1800's and were displacing handicraft spinning of yarn; they continued to rise as long as the textile industry was small. As the industry grew rapidly during World War I, yarn imports shrank, but raw cotton requirements increased, so that cotton exports had to be curtailed and imports stepped up until China became a net importer of raw cotton. Rising raw cotton consumption then encouraged an expansion in domestic cotton production, and by the 1930's, the exports and imports of the raw material were more or less in balance.

This first sequence was followed by a second. As the demand for cotton cloth increased, it was filled in part by an expansion of the handweaving industry, which relied on domestically manufactured yarn, and in part by the growth of mechanical weaving. As a result, cotton piece goods, which had dominated China's imports since the 1890's, began to decline in relative importance after 1920 and then shrank considerably in absolute terms after 1930. Continuing this long-term historical trend, China became a sizable net exporter of finished cotton textiles in the 1950's.

One could trace yet a third, almost parallel, sequence. As the cotton textile industry grew in China, it relied on imported machinery. However, at a later stage the domestic demand for such machinery encouraged the rise of a textile machinery industry that gradually displaced imports. By the late 1950's and early 1960's, China became a net exporter of textile machinery.

Such neat patterns of backward and forward linkage, at least on this scale, do not appear in the case of other industries and other imports. From the standpoint of China's industrialization, one of the interesting aspects shown by the data in Table 8, A is the very modest scale of machinery imports. If one were to carry the series beyond 1931, the importance of machinery and metals would undoubtedly rise under the impact of Manchurian industrialization.

V. The Inherited Economy

In 1949 the Chinese Communists took over a war-torn and devastated economy suffering from acute and prolonged inflation. However, from the vantage point of this discussion, it might be quite misleading to consider this as the inherited economy. Production capacities in different branches of the pre-1949 economy may provide us with a more appropriate basis for appraising the level and character of Chinese Communist economic

TABLE 8

Commodity Composition of China's Exports and Imports, 1900–1931

(in per cent)

	A. Imports						
Commodity Category	1900	1905	1913	1920	1925	1928	1931
Cotton goods	21.5	25.6	19.3	21.8	16.3	14.2	7.6
Cotton yarn	14.3	15.0	12.7	12.4	4.4	1.6	0.3
Raw cotton			0.5	2.4	7.4	5.7	12.6
Cereals and flour	7.0	2.9	5.2	1.1	8.4	8.3	12.6
Sugar	3.0	5.1	6.4	5.2	9.5	8.3	6.0
Tobacco	0.5	1.4	2.9	4.7	4.1	5.1	4.4
Paper			1.3	1.9	2.0	2.4	3.2
Kerosene	6.6	4.5	4.5	7.1	7.0	5.2	4.5
Liquid fuel				0.4	0.9	1.4	1.8
Transport materials		1.8	0.8	2.6	1.9	2.3	2.3
Chemicals, dyes and pigments			5.6	6.4	5.6	7.5	8.0
Metals	4.7	10.4	5.3	8.3	4.7	5.4	6.2
Machinery	0.7	1.2	1.4	3.2	1.8	1.8	3.1
Coal	3.1	1.6	1.7				
Opium	14.8	7.7	7.4				
Others	23.8	22.8	25.0	24.3	26.0	30.8	27.4
	100.0	100.0	100.0	100.0	100.0	100.0	100.0

Source: Y. K. Cheng, *op. cit.*, Table 4, p. 19 and Table 10, p. 32.

	B. Exports						
Commodity Category	1900	1905	1913	1920	1925	1928	1931
Silk and silk goods	30.4	30.1	25.3	18.6	22.5	18.4	13.3
Tea	16.0	11.2	8.4	8.4	1.6	2.9	3.7
Beans	1.9	3.0					
Beans and bean cake			12.0	13.0	15.9	20.5	21.4
Seeds and oil	2.5	3.4	7.8	9.1	7.9	5.8	8.4
Eggs and egg products		0.9	1.4	4.0	4.3	4.4	4.1
Hides and skins	4.3	6.6	6.0	4.3	4.0	5.4	4.1
Ores and metals			3.3	3.2	2.9	2.1	1.6
Coal			1.6	2.3	2.6	2.9	3.0
Cotton yarn and cotton goods			0.6	1.4	2.0	3.8	4.9
Raw cotton	6.2	5.3	4.1	1.7	3.8	3.4	2.9
Wool	1.9	3.7	2.4				
Other	36.8	35.8	27.1	40.8	31.2	29.6	32.7
	100.0	100.0	100.0	100.0	100.0	100.0	100.0

Source: Y. K. Cheng, *op. cit.*, Table 12, p. 34 and Table 3, p. 19.

performance against the background of a long-term historical perspective. These production capacities, in turn, might perhaps be best approximated by comparing performance since 1949 with peak performance before that year. However, this approach, too, presents certain difficulties since there is no denying that the production capacities themselves were reduced by war, civil war and the Soviet dismantling of plants in Manchuria. The pre-Communist peak production levels overstate the capacity of the inherited economy, while the 1949 output understates it.

Agriculture was probably less affected by these vicissitudes. Therefore one might surmise that the farm sector inherited by the Chinese Communists was not too different from that found by J. L. Buck in the course of his survey. In outlining the principal features of Communist China's agricultural inheritance, I will draw on this body of data relating to 1929–31. For industry we will compare the output of some of the principal products in 1933, in the pre-Communist peak year, in 1949 and in 1952. At the same time, we will examine briefly the structural changes experienced by the economy as a whole between 1933 and 1952.

According to the Liu-Yeh estimates national product increased by 10 to 15 per cent (in terms of 1933 and 1952 prices respectively) between 1933 and 1952. Unfortunately, no really usable estimates are available for any intervening year. Moreover, given the character of the basic data, it would be very difficult indeed to construct meaningful estimates for the period between 1937 and 1952. Therefore we can not be certain whether this growth occurred mostly before or after the advent of the new regime. However, there is no doubt that there was some growth between 1933 and 1936, and very rapid recovery (from a low point) between 1949 and 1952. It is, however, far from clear what path the mainland economy as a whole followed after the start of the Sino-Japanese war. Finally, even the 1933 and 1952 estimates are subject to sizable margins of error, so that the rise in national product may have in fact been more or less than the 10 to 15 per cent indicated. In any case it is almost certain that there was no significant growth in per capita terms, and probably not in total terms, during these two decades.

On the other hand, there is no doubt that the economy experienced some structural change as shown by the estimates in Table 9. Stated most broadly, the importance of agriculture declined, while there was a rise in the national product share of the modern nonagricultural sectors, including government services. Although some of the expansion in government

TABLE 9

Composition of National Product by Industrial Origin,
1933 and 1952*

(in per cent)

| Economic Branch | 1933 National Product | | 1952 National Product | | |
| | | | Liu-Yeh[a] | | Eckstein[b] |
	1933 prices	1952 prices	1933 prices	1952 prices	1952 prices
Agriculture	65.0	56.9	56.6	47.9	47.1
Industry:					
Large-Scale	3.4	6.6	6.2	11.5	9.2
Handicrafts	7.1	7.4	6.6	6.6	13.6[c]
Construction	1.2	1.7	1.9	2.6	2.9
Transport & Communication:					
Modern	1.5	1.8	2.5	2.9	3.0
Traditional	4.1	4.4	3.7	3.7	1.7
Trade	9.4	13.8	8.9	13.5	8.3
Government Administration	2.8	2.4	5.7	4.6	4.9
Other	5.6	4.9	8.0	6.7	9.3

*The sectoral shares indicated in the last column of this table differ from those given in the last column of Table 4 in chapter 6. These discrepancies are due to the fact that the latter were preliminary estimates which were modified as additional information became available. Thus the figures in Table 9 are the final estimates found in my book, Alexander Eckstein, *The National Income of Communist China*, Glencoe, Ill., 1961.

    a. Net domestic product at market prices.

    b. Gross domestic product at factor cost.

    c. Includes farm processing of products consumed within the peasant household.

Sources: Liu-Yeh, *op. cit.*, Table 8, p. 66; Table 20, p. 88; Eckstein, *op. cit.*, Table 10, p. 74.

undoubtedly occurred after 1949, a good part of it must have been a product of war in all areas of the mainland, i.e., in Free China, in occupied China, and in Manchuria.

    The share of modern industry in the national product almost doubled in 1952 as compared with 1933. As noted earlier, it would seem that total industrial output increased until 1942. It then declined, recovered somewhat after the war, and then declined again quite markedly by 1949. As Table 10 shows, except for textiles, industrial production in the early

TABLE 10

Selected Industrial Production Indicators, 1933–1952

Product	Unit of Measurement	1933	1949	1952	Pre-Communist Peak Output	Year
Electric power	billion kwh	2.07	4.31	7.26	5.95	1943
Coal	million MT	28.38	32.43	66.49	64.86	1942
Crude oil	thousand MT	89.00	n.a.	871.00	842.00	1942
Pig iron	thousand MT	609.00	252.00	1,929.00	1,889.00	1943
Steel	thousand MT	negl.	158.00	1,349.00	923.00	1943
Cement	thousand MT	784.00	660.00	2,860.00	2,300.00	1942
Cotton yarn	million bales	2.45	1.80	3.62	2.45	1933
Machine-made paper	thousand MT	45.00	108.00	372.00	165.00	1943

Sources:

Kang Chao, *The Rate and Pattern of Industrial Growth in Communist China*, Ann Arbor, Mich., 1965, Table C–1.

State Statistical Bureau (SSB), *Report on National Economic Development and Fulfillment of State Plan*, Peking, 1956, p. 28.

Additional Sources:

Coal: Ching Chi-pu, Hou-fang Chung-yao Kung-yao Kung-k'uang ch'an-p'ing t'ung-chi, No. 2, Chungking, 1943; and Yen Chung-p'ing, *Chung-kuo chin-tai ching-chi shih t'ung-chi tzu-liao hsuan-chi (Selected statistics in China's modern economic history)*, Peking, 1955, p. 143.

Crude oil: Geological Survey of China, *General Statement on the Mining Industry*, No. 7, Chungking, 1945, p. 85.

Pig iron: Yen Chung-p'ing, *op. cit.*, p. 143; and *Chung-hua Nien-chien (Chung-hua Year Book)*, Vol. II, Shanghai, 1948, p. 1569.

1940's tended to be much higher than in the early 1930's. Clearly, then, a goodly share of the industrial expansion in this 1933–52 period must have taken place before the Communists came to power. Some of this increased productive capacity was dismantled during the Soviet occupation of Manchuria, but the new investment necessary to restore this capacity was less than would have been required for entirely new plants.

This process of expansion was accompanied by changes in the composition of industrial output. After 1936 textile production declined, while electric power generation, iron and steel, and cement producing facilities and output rose. These marked changes in industrial structure antedate the Communist advent to power. They constitute an element of inheritance forced upon the mainland economy by the exigencies of Japanese occupation and war.

In all these respects agriculture presents a sharp contrast. There is no indication of agricultural growth during the years between 1933 and 1952. According to the Liu-Yeh estimates net agricultural product in these two years was about the same. Allowing for the possibility that this finding is due to the assumptions on which their agricultural estimates are based, all other evidence as well points to agricultural stagnation as a reality. As a result, the situation that prevailed in the early 1930's may provide a fairly good basis for assessing the Chinese Communist inheritance in this sector.

Mainland agriculture was characterized by high population density on the land as evidenced by the fact that an average-sized farm had to support 6.2 persons on about 4.2 acres.[67] However, about 60 per cent of the farms had a median size of 2.8 acres or less. Population pressure on arable land resources was greatly aggravated by the pattern of land-holding and tenure. Land fragmentation was a widespread phenomenon with an average of 5.6 parcels per farm. Each of these parcels was less than an acre, the furthest ones being, on the average, 0.7 miles from the farmstead. This naturally led to considerable waste of time and energy, producing a very inefficient pattern of factor use, not only of labor but of livestock and equipment as well.

The situation was aggravated in south China in particular by tenancy combined in some instances with quite adverse terms of tenure. Tenancy data are far from satisfactory and have been the subject of considerable controversy. According to the National Agricultural Research Bureau, nearly one-third of China's farms were tenant-operated in the early 1930's. Buck's data, in contrast, show a tenancy ratio of only 17 per cent. There is a strong probability that in this case sampling errors produced a downward bias in Buck's data.

However the most serious and intractable problem facing Chinese agriculture was not distribution of the product and income inequality, but technological backwardness and resultant low labor productivity. There is no doubt that the Chinese peasant utilized the factors of production at his disposal most intensively at the existing level of technology. Yet according to Buck's estimates, at this level he could produce the equivalent of only 1,400 kilograms of grain per man, compared with the United States, where the corresponding figure was 20,000 kilograms. Another illustration of low labor productivity in agriculture is provided by the Liu-Yeh national income estimates, which show that product per man in farming in 1933 was less than one-fifth of the level prevailing in modern industry.[68]

Acute population pressure was also reflected in the pattern of land use and was in turn partly a function of that pattern. Only 27 per cent of the land area was cultivated, with most of the remainder uncultivable. Of the land in farms, 90 per cent was in crops; of these, close to 70 per cent was in grains. Through a long process of adaptation the Chinese peasant had developed a pattern of farm production to give high energy yields per unit of land. This left very little room for pasture and for livestock raising.

Under the combined impact of all these circumstances, the Chinese peasantry traditionally lived quite close to the margin of subsistence, highly vulnerable to natural or man-made disaster. It is not surprising to find that China's farmers have encountered periodic famines and frequent crop failures short of famine proportions. According to Buck, there had been on the average three famines per *hsien* within the memory of his informants from 146 *hsien*. The causes of the different famines (e.g., floods and droughts) had lasted from ten days to three years, but averaged over ten months in the wheat region and less than four months in the rice region. In addition, there was an average of 16 calamities per locality that resulted in the loss of nearly half of the crop.

Crop failures were most often caused by droughts and floods, with droughts being more common. The effects of adverse harvests were greatly aggravated by the backward state of transport and communications, by grossly inadequate storage and warehousing facilities, and by the poorly developed marketing and credit system. While certain parts of China, particularly in the Yangtze valley, were fairly well provided with inland waterways, the country's total railroad mileage at the end of World War II was only about 15,500, of which approximately 6,500 miles were in Manchuria. For large areas inaccessible by water the cost of transporting farm products was very high, four to six times the railroad charge if carried by animals, and three to eight times as high if transported by men.[69]

This, combined with the institutional impediments cited above and the acute population pressure on farms, necessarily restricted the scope of commercialization. Therefore, depending on whether one includes rent in the marketed portion, only about 15 to 36 per cent of the rice, 25 to 30 per cent of the kaoliang, 29 to 33 per cent of the wheat, and 30 to 34 per cent of the soybeans was sold off farms. As noted in Table 1 of this chapter, an estimated 28 per cent of the total farm output was sold in 1952. One might surmise that this marketed share was probably no higher, and possibly lower, in the 1930's. This would suggest then that the Chinese Communists inherited an agricultural sector that was adapted to sell about 25 to 30 per cent of its output and so was to a limited degree involved in a market and money nexus.

VI. Concluding Comments

When the Chinese Communists came to power in 1949, they inherited an economy which by practically all available measures was near the bottom of the world development scale. GNP per capita was possibly in the neighborhood of $50 as compared with two to three times that level in late seventeenth-century England.[70] As shown in Table 9, about half the GNP was produced in agriculture; all of the modern sectors combined contributed only about 20 per cent.[71] The same pattern is evident in labor force composition, with at most three million workers engaged in modern industry (including mining and public utilities).

Labor productivity was very low in agriculture, which was still operating largely within a traditional technological and institutional framework. This, in turn, was a function of a number of interrelated factors rooted in and epitomized by acute population pressure and a lack of employment opportunities in the nonagricultural sectors.

Modern industrial production was still quite small (contributing about 10 per cent to national product) despite apparently rapid rates of growth in the quarter century preceding the Sino-Japanese war. As indicated in Table 6, the impression of rapid rates of advance remains basically unaltered even if we disregard the early period for which the data are least reliable. However, as pointed out by Deane and Cole, "an index of industrial production for a preindustrial economy is an indicator of developments in a small sector. It tells us nothing about the growth of output as a whole or its relation to changes in the size of the population."[72] In effect, modern industry in mainland China was merely a shallow overlay on a pre-industrial agrarian economy.

Yet as an element of inheritance it was of crucial importance for Communist China. Although narrowly based, both in an economic and geographic sense it provided the new regime with at least a modicum of plant capacity, trained manpower, and management, without which the industrialization drive of the First Five-Year Plan period would not have been possible. However, just as in Republican China, this industrial expansion seems to have been accompanied by agricultural stagnation, which in time arrested industrial growth as well.

Viewed from the vantage point of the mid-1960's, it would seem that at least in a limited sense the pattern of economic development in Communist China bears certain elements of similarity to and continuity with pre-Communist China: i.e., rapid development of a small modern industrial sector in a preindustrial economy without perceptible growth in agriculture. The development drive mounted in the 1950's left the technological base of Chinese agriculture largely untouched, at least up to 1960–61. The Chinese Communists apparently contented themselves with a massive assault on rural institutions and agricultural organization, hoping that institutional transformation might serve as a substitute for technical transformation. It is quite possible that these organizational changes rendered the farm population more receptive to the introduction of innovations and technological change. However, many of these same changes had strong counterincentive effects. If there was any increased receptivity to innovations, it was merely a facilitating or passive factor that only the introduction of a more favorable incentive structure and additional investment in agriculture could transform into an active force.

In analyzing elements of Communist China's economic heritage, its agricultural backwardness, population pressure, and "space friction" stand out as the most critical long-run problems. From a development point of view, population pressure is at least a two-dimensional problem with both the initial stock and the flow playing a very significant role. The Chinese Communists inherited an initial population mass of perhaps 500 to 550 million people. This presented problems not only in terms of population pressure on arable land resources, but in terms of food supply, distribution, and provisioning with other consumer goods as well. However, perhaps even more important are the general scale effects and the sheer implications of size of such a large population. Without dealing with the complex range of factors relating demographic and size variables to economic development, some of the possible effects are outlined below to illustrate their importance in the case of China.

On *ceteris paribus* assumptions concerning per capita income and other variables, the foreign aid requirements per unit of output increment of a large country such as China would be of an entirely different order of magnitude than for, say, Ceylon. This proposition would probably be valid even if one granted that the relationship is not likely to be proportional, and that counteracting factors might tend to reduce the foreign aid requirements of a large country. More generally, the most important consequences of size revolve around barriers to innovation and the introduction of new influences through aid, trade and all other forms of contact. The task of diffusion is rendered much more difficult in a territorially large national unit, preponderantly continental, with a large population and poor transport and communication. The transport requirements themselves are in part conditioned by population size and territorial scope. These factors have undoubtedly been of great importance in mainland China's economic retardation before and since 1949.

For Communist China these handicaps arising from a large initial population stock were seriously aggravated by changes in flow. According to a number of sample investigations conducted in the interwar period, crude birth rates in China may have been around 40± per thousand and crude death rates around 30± per thousand, thus yielding rates of natural increase of 10± per thousand.[73] The advent of the new regime marked the end of a long period of war and civil strife and restoration of law and order on the mainland as a whole. This in itself was bound to lead to a decline in the death rates. However, the new regime instituted a whole series of public health measures that served to reduce infant mortality and led to better control of epidemics, with resultant reductions in deaths of all age groups. Moreover, improvements in distribution have apparently contributed to better control of famines and thus to reduction in the death rate. As a result, rates of natural increase were at least doubled. Such a spurt in the rate of population growth superimposed on a large initial stock has created a host of new problems which have seriously complicated Communist China's development task.

Part IV

Development Patterns and Strategies

Chapter 6

Conditions and Prospects for Economic Growth in Communist China

The Communist conquest of mainland China may be legitimately viewed as the culmination of a century-long interregnum during which the traditional equilibrium of Chinese society was profoundly disturbed by the Western impact, at a time of dynastic decline. The initial impact of the West was in the nature of a shock treatment administered by the Opium War, the subsequent military defeats, the unequal treaties, and the rise of the whole Treaty Ports system. Thus China's first massive contact with the West was associated with humiliation, bewilderment, frustration, and a sense of inequality. In these terms, then, a constant and continuing struggle for equality has been a hallmark of China's development since 1840.

The military and diplomatic defeats suffered by the Chinese made them conscious of the West's technological and industrial superiority. In fact, one of the essential ingredients in China's striving toward equality was economic—expressed in a deep-seated aspiration to catch up, to narrow the gap, and to industrialize. In other words, the Western impact generated "tension between the actual state of economic activities in the country and the existing obstacles to industrial development, on the one hand, and the great promise inherent in such a development, on the other."[1]

Therefore, the Chinese Communist program of industrialization has deep historical and nationalist roots; and it is from its nationalist aspects that the program derives an emotional appeal not only in China, but in

Originally published as a series of three articles in *World Politics,* Oct. 1954, January 1955, and April 1955; a somewhat different version appeared as chapters 12 to 14 in *Prospects for Communist China* by W. W. Rostow in collaboration with Richard W. Hatch, Frank A. Kierman, Jr., and Alexander Eckstein.

Asia as a whole. At the same time, the long-run power aspirations of the regime, important sanctions for tightening economic and political control, and to some extent its very social function and *raison d'etre* are conditioned by industrialization and a sustained process of economic growth.

This is the general context within which the analysis of conditions and prospects for economic growth in Communist China is approached in this chapter. In section I an attempt is made to sketch in broad outline the major characteristics of China's mainland economy prior to the Communist conquest. Section II is devoted to an exploration of economic recovery and structural changes in the economy since 1949. Finally, sections III and IV are focused upon an analysis of factors favoring or impeding economic development under Chinese mainland conditions.

I. The Chinese Economy in 1949

Upon their conquest of the Chinese mainland in 1949, the Communists inherited what was essentially a dual economy. Under the Western impact of the mid- and late-nineteenth century, there had developed in the Treaty Ports a more or less modern commercial economy which was never fused or merged with, but rather grafted upon, the more or less stationary and traditional economy of "earthbound China." Foreign trade, which provided the motive force for a self-generating process of economic growth confined to the Treaty Ports sector, had served to undermine rural handicrafts and thus led to decline rather than expansion in the farm economy.

Viewed in these terms, one of the major long-term economic tasks of the new regime was to find some means of loosening the bonds of the rural economy and of linking it to the modern sector in such a way as to induce a widely diffused and sustained process of economic growth. However, as of 1949, all segments of the Chinese economy (agriculture, industry, transport, and foreign trade) and the institutional framework within which they operated were damaged by war and civil conflict. Therefore, the most urgent short-term tasks of the regime were to restore the basic capacity to produce and to exchange goods and services and to prepare the way for a long-term program of industrialization; joined to these was the task of institutional reform in order to guarantee a maximum degree of detailed Communist authority over the disposition of resources.

In essence, these recovery and institutional targets were attained by 1952, despite Chinese intervention in the Korean War. The existence of large military operations in 1950–1951 cut both ways; it drained off resources from reconstruction, but it also provided a suitable political setting for a drastic transfer of economic powers and resources to the Communist state. Basically, recovery could be rapid only because labor and developed resources were underemployed during this stage. Therefore, the 1949–1952 period provided primarily a test of the new regime's capabilities in the field of economic organization and control, rather than of its capacity to launch successfully and carry through a program of industrialization and economic development. The latter issue began to assume paramount importance in 1953, as resources began to be more or less fully employed and as the regime was increasingly confronted with basic limitations imposed by the interacting forces of physical environment, population pressure, and past inheritance. To understand the character of the Chinese economic development problem, it is necessary to examine briefly these limiting factors.

A. *Agriculture*

The structure of China's mainland economy is typical of a pre-industrial society. Agriculture, accounting for 75 per cent of the population, contributes 40 per cent to national product, while the urban sector, with only 15 per cent of the population, makes roughly the same contribution. At least an additional 10 per cent of China's people live in rural areas, engaged mostly in non-farm tasks and producing about 20 per cent of total national output.[2]

Chinese agriculture is, of course, a classic example of intensive cultivation with high yields per acre, low output per man. The result is a vast population kept at or barely above subsistence level by the most arduous, subtle, personalized cultivation of the soil. The Chinese farmer is caught in a familiar *cul-de-sac* by the self-reinforcing interaction of overpopulation, intensive low per-man yields, illiteracy, and poverty, with practically no margin left for saving and investment.

The pattern of mainland China's population growth constitutes one of the most confusing chapters in the country's long history.* Expanding

---

*Since this paper originally appeared, two major works have been published illuminating China's demographic history. In the light of these later findings this paragraph was slightly revised. See P. T. Ho's *Studies on the Population of China, 1368–1953*, Cambridge, Mass., 1959, and D. H. Perkins, *Agricultural Development in China, 1368–1968*, Chicago, 1967.

food production—brought about by an extension of the cultivated area and by the introduction of corn, sweet potatoes, and peanuts—and a long period of dynastic peace apparently led to a doubling of the population between the seventeenth and nineteenth centuries. As a result, population is believed to have been around 410 million in 1850, rising further thereafter possibly to 450–500 million.[3] (According to the 1953 census results announced by the Chinese Communists, the mainland population was 582 million.) This rapid increase in population outstripped the expansion in acreage.[4]

Inefficiencies inherent in small-sized farms were greatly aggravated by continuous fragmentation of land-holding, resulting from population pressure, lack of non-farm employment opportunities, and China's age-old inheritance practices, which provide for the splitting-up of land among all surviving sons.[5] Surveys conducted in the early thirties indicate that the average-sized farm of about 3.2 to 3.3 acres, or 21 mou, was broken up into close to six distinctly separate parcels with an average distance of 0.4 miles between farmstead and parcel. However, these averages conceal very marked inequalities in farm size, inasmuch as 36 per cent of farms were under 10 mou (1.5 acres) and 25 per cent were between 10 and 20 mou.[6]

The only way these small and highly fragmented holdings can maintain such a densely settled population is by exceedingly intensive land use and double-cropping on nearly two-thirds of the cultivated land area. This practice is particularly widespread in the irrigated rice area of the south, where two or more crops are planted on about three-quarters of the farm area, as compared with only 7 per cent in the wheat region of the north. The very high intensity of land use in China is also illustrated by the fact that in all regions about 90 per cent of the farm area is in crops, while only about 1 per cent is in pastures, as compared with 40 per cent or more in the United States. Yet livestock density per acre is quite high, higher than in Japan or the United States. However, the bulk of farm animals are used for draft power, so that only about one-fourth are available for human consumption or for industrial raw materials. Owing to the small size of farms, parcels, and fields, animal draft power is underemployed. Therefore, some of the livestock on China's farms represent a net drain on food resources.

The same can be said of farm labor. It has been estimated that on China's farms the able-bodied men (15–60) are idle for an average of almost two months a year. Were one to include women in the labor force, this underemployment would be even greater. While much of it is of a seasonal character, there is no question that in China, just as in other underdeveloped agrarian countries, moderate and gradual withdrawals of labor from agriculture (without change in technology) need not affect farm production.

With high intensity of land use and age-old soil conservation and irrigation practices, crop yields per acre are quite high. They are somewhat above the levels attained in Meiji Japan, but lag considerably behind the yields attained in present-day Japan. This would tend to suggest that crop productivity in China has been pushed about as far as traditional practices and methods will permit, so that, just as in Japan, large improvements in farm output can be attained only through the introduction of technology and improved practices from abroad.

All of these factors combined have traditionally pressed the Chinese peasant close to the margin of subsistence. Even allowing for regional differences in topography, climate, and type of agriculture—particularly between the northern wheat region and the southern rice areas—the situation of the peasant probably deteriorated over the disordered century after 1840, mainly in response to the rise in population, but also reflecting civil disturbances and the decay of handicraft industry (notably textiles) in competition with manufactured products. Just as in earlier periods of dynastic decline, the impact of natural disasters such as droughts and floods may also have been aggravated during this period of civil disorder and weak central rule. Thus Buck's investigation show that within the memory of his informants there was an average of close to four famines in the northern wheat region and about 2.5 in the rice areas of the south, caused for the most part by droughts and floods.

During the Nanking government period (1928–1937), considerable efforts were made to reverse this situation by improvement in farm and irrigation practices and in flood control. However, these modest beginnings were interrupted by the Japanese War, which led to a decline in agricultural output, from a peak in 1936 to a low point in 1945. Excepting 1949 itself—a year of acute drought—Chinese agriculture recovered steadily after 1945, roughly achieving the 1936 level in 1952. There was, however, a considerable backlog of repair and maintenance to be done on river control and irrigation installations.

B. Industry

State entrepreneurship provided the initial impetus for the establishment of factory industry in China, confined for the most part to government arsenals and armament works in the 1860's and 1870's. However, the development of modern industry was really launched only in the 1890's, when the Treaty of Shimonoseki opened the way for the construction and operation of foreign-owned factories in the Treaty Ports. This was then coupled with the granting of differential advantages to the Treaty Powers, such as the right of inland water navigation exempt from native charges. As a result, the interest of the imperial powers shifted from trade to railroads, a shift accompanied by a heightening of competition for strategic power in China, as opposed to merely commercial profit.

In the meantime, cotton textile imports increased appreciably with the cheapening of overseas transport and the low-cost production of factory-made cotton-yarn in India. This served to undermine the position of rural handicrafts, particularly the hand-spinning of yarn, and to create a market for manufactured textile products.[7] The growth of this market provided the impetus for the development of a cotton textile industry in China which, as in many other societies, thus took the lead in the process of industrialization. This was followed by the rise of other consumers' goods industries which developed as a by-product of foreign trade, i.e., flour mills, cigarette and match factories, etc. At the same time, power plants and light engineering works, as well as railroads, had to be developed to service these new industries. All of this was accompanied by the institution of other external economies, such as banking and trading facilities.

Industrial expansion was greatly stimulated during World War I, when China was cut off from the world market, so that her infant industries temporarily enjoyed the benefits of protection with but a nominal tariff. These protectionist effects continued to prevail after the war, when the terms of trade moved against China owing to the falling gold price of silver.[8] They were then reinforced by the 1929 tariff. As a result, textile and other industries grew in China proper—with some interruptions—up to 1937. In the latter stages of this development, the initiative passed largely from Western to Japanese and Chinese capital and enterprise. By 1937, not much less than half of China's cotton spindles and looms were under Japanese management; and, of course, Japan controlled virtually all of China's industry at the end of World War II.

Under the impact of this half-century of growth, there developed a modest, largely light consumers' goods industry on the periphery of the Chinese economy. It was confined to the Treaty Ports, where a Western institutional and legal framework, conducive to its growth, was established. This industrial development was essentially an imported and superimposed product—oriented to foreign rather than internal trade—which did not encompass the traditional economy of China and thus did not serve as the base for a sustained process of economic growth.

An entirely different pattern emerged in Manchuria, where the population-resource balance was more favorable and the institutional environment less resistant to industrialization than in China proper. However, the decisive factor was the injection of the Japanese, who from 1931 on were determined to develop Manchuria into a heavy industry and war base. This involved them in a program of comprehensive and planned economic development with an accent upon expansion of communications and producers' goods industries.

The upshot of this complex and erratic evolution was a basic industrial capacity roughly indicated by the following production figures, which combine 1943 Japanese-controlled ouput in Manchuria and the 1936 figures for the rest of China. (See Table 1.) This modern sector, operating at its peak, employed about three million workers, and produced about 7 per cent of national output.*

The Communists did not, however, inherit Chinese industry intact. In 1945, apparently operating on the likelihood that the Kuomintang would reestablish its authority in China, Moscow ordered the dismantling of many key installations in Manchuria and their removal to Russia as Japanese reparations. In addition, there was some important war damage to industrial installations elsewhere in China.

C. Distribution

Primitive, inadequate, and costly transport has been one of the key factors limiting China's economic development. Mainland China (excluding Outer Mongolia and Tibet), with territory roughly the same size as the United

---

*Subsequent studies would suggest that these figures are on the high side. According to T. C. Liu and K. C. Yeh, *The Economy of the Chinese Mainland, 1933–1959,* value added by factory industry, mining and utilities in 1933 is estimated as 6.6 percent and employment in these sectors is estimated as 1.94 million. (Table 11 and Table 19).

186 *China's Economic Development*

TABLE 1

Estimated Pre-1949 Peak Production of Selected Industrial
Products in Mainland China*

Product	Unit	China Proper	Manchuria
Pig Iron	Metric tons	290,640	1,700,000
Crude Steel	"	50,000	843,000
Rolled Steel	"	negl.	485,700
Coal	"	33,000,000[a]	25,630,000
Crude Oil	"	n.a.	214,000
Cement	"	608,000	1,532,000
Paper	"	n.a.	76,000[b]
Flour	"	1,800,000	650,000
Sugar	"	392,000	17,600[c]
Cotton Yarn	bales	2,100,000	n.a.
Cotton Cloth	bolts	30,000,000	n.a.
Cigarettes	billions of sticks	57	25
Electric Power:			
Capacity	thousands of KW	893	1,786
Output	millions of KWH	2,425	4,475

*These figures differ somewhat from those given in Table 10, chapter 5, which is based on additional studies and evidence found since I completed this early essay on "Conditions and Prospects."
[a]Estimates range from 22,000,000 to 40,000,000; the figure used here is based on Woytinski and represents a 1940–1944 average.
[b]1937
[c]1940
Sources: Edwin W. Pauley, *Report on Japanese Assets in Manchuria to the President of the United States,* July 1946; *Report by Kao Kang at the First Conference of Representatives of the Chinese Communist Party in the Northeast,* Mukden, March 13, 1950; *Manchukuo Yearbook,* 1942, pp. 511–70; *Chinese Yearbook,* 1944–1945, pp. 654–55; T. H. Shen, *Agricultural Resources of China,* Ithaca, New York, 1951; *Statistical Yearbook of the League of Nations,* 1942–1944, Geneva, 1945; Kate Mitchell, *Industrialization of the Western Pacific,* New York, 1942; W. S. Woytinski and E. S. Woytinski, *World Population and Production,* New York, 1953.

States, had only 15,000 miles of railway at the time the Communists took over, as compared with approximately 400,000 miles in the United States. With such a small network, only East China and Southern Manchuria were well served, while South and West China were barely touched.

As a result, a very large share of trade was carried by traditional methods, i.e., coastal shipping, inland water transport, pack animals, carts, and the backs of men. Such modes of transport appear cheap per day, but they are expensive per mile, so that farmers seldom take their produce more than thirty miles to market.[9] According to one investigator, the transport cost of grain from Shensi to Shanghai exceeded the total cost of grain imported from the west coast of the United States.[10]

These very high transport costs have been among the principal factors hampering the commercialization of agriculture and narrowing the market for industrial products. However, rural self-sufficiency was not nearly as complete as was frequently supposed. Probably over a quarter of the goods consumed by agricultural families were purchased. In turn, they sold about half of their total output; but the bulk of farm products marketed involved exchange within the same *hsien* (county), and only an estimated 8 per cent was shipped to distant urban markets.[11]

Consequently, China exhibited a highly cellular marketing pattern with varying and fluctuating scarcity relationships and price tendencies in different areas. Frequent local famines were a reflection of this high degree of fragmentation. All of these problems were greatly aggravated by civil strife and a lack of central administrative unity. As the civil war spread between 1945 and 1949, the whole system of distribution and urban-rural interchange was further corroded under the impact of galloping hyperinflation and repeated disruption of railway transport.

D. Foreign Trade

In aggregate terms, foreign trade has never been of major importance for the Chinese economy. Thus, in 1936, for example, per capita imports and exports (including Manchuria) were smaller than in any other country.[12] Moreover, probably at no time did total trade exceed 10 per cent of the national product. At the same time, however, foreign trade played a major role in bringing the closed, traditional economy of China within the purview of the world economy, thereby providing the impetus for the rise of a small modern industry.

Broadly speaking, China's imports and exports evolved along lines typical of a generally underdeveloped and slowly growing economy. This is best illustrated by the course of the cotton textile trade. At first, China was a net exporter of handwoven cotton goods. However, with the opening of the Suez Canal and the decline in overseas transport costs, manufactured cotton textiles began to compete successfully with native cloth. As a result, cotton goods imports grew rapidly until the turn of the century, when they constituted 40 per cent of total imports. During this same period, China was a small net exporter of raw cotton. With an expanding domestic market for manufactured cotton textiles, the development of a cotton textile industry was stimulated, which led to a gradual decline in the import of textile products This change was accompanied by growing net imports of raw cotton; but with expanding domestic cotton production this trend was reversed, so that by the time of the Sino-Japanese War (1937), production had just about caught up with requirements.

A number of other import products, such as cigarettes, matches, and flour, followed a similar course. Thus manufactured and semi-manufactured consumers' goods, which dominated total import figures at the turn of the century, gave way slowly but steadily to industrial equipment and raw materials On the other hand, the rise in urban population, combined with a lag in internal transport development, led to an increasing food import requirement.

Chinese exports, initially confined mainly to silk and tea, broadened out over the years to embrace a wider range of the country's natural resource products: beans and bean products, eggs, hog bristles, hides, soy beans, tungsten, tung oil, and then iron ore and coal for Japan. These structural changes in China's foreign trade and economy were also reflected in her balance of payments. Early in the nineteenth century, China had a favorable balance of trade and a surplus on current account. As trade expanded and opium imports grew, this surplus diminished, while the trade and current account balance became unfavorable.[13] From then on, China's balance of payments, as shown in Table 2, exhibited characteristics typical of most underdeveloped areas.

As China was drawn more and more into the world trading network, its foreign trade expanded rapidly until the 1930's when the country's total exports (including Manchuria) reached about U.S. $1 billion (at 1952 prices). At the same time, the trade deficit and the adverse balance of payment on current account were largely financed by new foreign investment. In this connection, it should be noted that net capital imports and foreign expenditures combined exceeded current outpayments for debt charges and profit remittances. One of the unique features of the whole current account is the great importance of remittances from overseas Chinese.

China's balance of payments followed a rather different pattern during the highly disturbed postwar years. Balance of payment deficits, financed

TABLE 2

Balance of China's International Payments, 1841–1935

(in millions of Chinese dollars)

	1841 (Sargent)	1903 (Morse)	1930 (Remer)	1935[a] (Bank of China)
Current outpayments:				
Merchandise imports	25	492	1,965	1,129
Specie imports	–	58	101	–
Service of foreign loans	–	69	111	108
Chinese expenditures abroad	–	7	13	55
Remittance of foreign enterprises and other profits	–	35	227	55
Total	25	661	2,417	1,347
Current inpayments:				
Merchandise exports	13.3	374	1,476	662
Specie exports	11.2	51	48	357
Foreign expenditures in China	0.5	81	218	150
Overseas remittances	–	114	316	260
Total	25.0	620	2,058	1,429
Capital inpayments:				
New foreign investments in China	–	42	202	140
Unaccounted for	–	–1	157	222

[a]Excluding Manchuria.

Source: Li Choh-ming, "International Trade," in *China, op. cit.,* p. 501.

largely by various forms of foreign aid, were constantly growing, while the flow of private foreign investment declined very appreciably. Trade recovered to about half its peak prewar level by 1948; between 1948 and 1952, the Communist regime roughly reestablished the prewar level. The direction and constitution of foreign trade has, however, been drastically altered as compared with the prewar pattern, with the Soviet bloc countries fulfilling the predominant role formerly held by Japan and the West with respect to both imports and exports.

E. The Institutional Framework

In agriculture the system of organization inherited by the Communists was essentially that of traditional China. Land was privately held but unequally distributed; thus 10 to 15 per cent of the farm population owned 53 to 63 per cent of the land. According to a 1934–1935 Nationalist government survey of 1,545 big landlord families and 752,865 peasant families in 87 districts scattered throughout eleven provinces, landlord holdings ranged from 300 to 20,000 mou and averaged around 2,030 mou, as compared with an average peasant holding of 15.8 mou.[14] This concentration of land ownership was most pronounced in the Yangtze and Pearl river valleys and in recently settled provinces of Manchuria and Inner Mongolia.

In general, outright tenancy was not as prevalent as is generally believed—even though it had increased in recent decades. Thus, in 1947, only about one-third of the farm population were tenants, one-quarter were part-owners, and about 40 to 45 per cent were full owners.[15] Therefore, agrarian unrest in China was primarily compounded of interacting influences generated by the pressure of population and the system, rather than the extent, of tenancy. High population densities—particularly pronounced in South China—led to an intense competition for land. This land hunger of the peasants then opened the way for exploitation and abuse, as illustrated by insecurity of tenure, high rents varying from 40 to 70 per cent of the crop and, for Szechwan at least, collections of rent for years ahead.

The negative features of the tenancy system were greatly aggravated by very onerous terms of credit imposed upon the farmer. In a country like China, the farmer's operational margin is very low even in a normal year; owing to poor communications, a local scarcity can push up food prices and so diminish the real value of a money loan. When to these conditions is added a 30 to 35 per cent rate of interest per annum,[16] the economic forces which tended to pauperize the peasant become clear. The problem was further complicated by the fact that it was the landlords who frequently performed the money-lending and marketing function. Through the complex structure of secret society, clan, and family organizations, they dominated the social life of the villages; and, politically, they remained the villages' chief intermediaries with the central political authorities on the strategic issues of taxation and army recruitment. There had, of course, been changes in the traditional pattern over the first half of the century, as evidenced by a slow spread of peasant cooperatives, institutes to improve cultivation methods, and other government and private efforts to increase the efficiency and equity of life in Chinese agriculture; and, in the north, the Communists had already begun their restructuring of village life by land redistribution and rent reductions in the areas they held. By and large, however, the old system was still in force during the process of Communist takeover in 1948–1949.

The war with Japan and Japanese occupation had broken or seriously damaged the private enterprise structure of Chinese banking, commercial, and industrial life, with its large component of foreign interests. Under the pressures of war and the immediate postwar situation, the Nationalist government assumed an enlarged place in the economy. The scope of government participation in the economy increased, particularly after 1945, when the Nationalist government confiscated as war booty all Japanese-owned and -operated enterprises on the Chinese mainland. As a result, the Communists inherited an almost completely nationalized heavy industry in Manchuria, and a partially nationalized consumers' goods sector in China proper.

The post-1945 Chinese economy was in a state of chronic inflation; and this unstable monetary setting was also part of the Communists' inheritance, posing for them their first major challenge in economic policy. Gaping budget deficits primarily financed by new note issues had been a major source of inflationary pressure in China ever since the beginning of the Sino-Japanese War in 1937. However, this situation was getting progressively worse, with actual expenditures invariably exceeding budgeted amounts. This contributed to further currency depreciation, while, in turn, the very speed of hyperinflation made it even more difficult to balance the budget or to estimate expenditures in advance. In spite of a partial reversion to barter, the fact of inflation bore heavily on the urban population, complicated internal and foreign trade, and transmitted itself as a symbol of the Nationalist government's weakness and inadequacy throughout the country.

II. The Reactivation of Capacity: 1949–1952

The over-all economic objective of the Chinese Communist regime, as defined by Mao Tse-tung in 1950, was to bring about in approximately three years a "fundamental turn for the better" in the torn and disrupted economy of the mainland.[17] Specifically, this involved: (a) capturing the "commanding heights" and thus extending and consolidating the state's control over the economy; (b) attaining fiscal and financial stability;

(c) restoring the country's productive apparatus and output to pre-1949 peak levels; and (d) laying the groundwork for long-range planning.

In broad terms, all of these goals were attained by the end of 1952. This comparatively rapid recovery represents an undeniable achievement which must be appraised against the background of certain favorable factors uniquely operative during the 1949–1952 period.

The Communists, upon gaining control over the Chinese mainland in 1949, inherited an economy in which productive capacity was appreciably curtailed: first by the Sino-Japanese War, and later by Soviet occupation and civil war. Manufacturing capacity was impaired, particularly in Manchuria, where over half of the capital stock in industry was dismantled and carried off by the Soviets in 1945.[18] Industrial capacity was also shrinking in China proper—though to a much lesser extent—owing to depreciation and obsolence and to the flight of some of the movable facilities to Hongkong and Taiwan. The situation was aggravated by a constant shortage of raw materials throughout 1949. This was particularly felt in Shanghai, where many industries depended upon imported materials now cut off by the Nationalist blockade of the port. At the same time, owing to the disruption of internal trade and transport, domestic supply difficulties were multiplied as well. Industrial output was further curtailed by a gradual demoralization of labor under the impact of hyperinflation and a breakdown of plant discipline following the Communist conquest of large cities. Urban labor tended to interpret the Communist victory as a signal for asserting its rights and placing its accumulated grievances and demands before industrial management. Several months elapsed before the new authorities were in a position fully to consolidate their control over the trade unions and disabuse them of their misconceptions.

All of these factors combined to reduce industrial production to 56 per cent of its pre-1949 peak.[19] According to the official index, the production of investment goods had dropped to 30 per cent of peak, while consumers' goods fell only to 70 per cent. The much sharper curtailment in the heavy industries was primarily a reflection of the marked contraction in Manchuria's manufacturing capacity.

On the whole, the rural sector of the economy was much less affected by the vicissitudes of the civil conflict. Actually, civil war brought to the countryside more disorganization and disruption than devastation. Owing to the great importance of the subsistence, non-monetized sector in the rural economy, agriculture could much more easily fall back on its own resources than industry. As a result, food production declined only about 20 to 25 per cent below the pre-1949 peak.[20] Unfavorable weather, particularly floods, rather than civil war, was the most important factor accounting for the drop. According to Chinese Communist sources, in 1949 mainland China had its worst flood since 1931; 120 million mou of land—constituting about 8 per cent of the total cultivated area—were affected.[21] Of course, it must be borne in mind that under more peaceful conditions the same weather would undoubtedly have created less havoc.

A. Recovery in Production

In this situation, the regime set itself the task of restoring industrial and farm production to pre-1949 peak levels by 1952. The extent to which this goal was attained may be gauged by the data in Table 3. This table shows that while recovery in industrial and agricultural production was quite rapid, the degree to which past production records have been surpassed is appreciably less than that commonly claimed by Chinese Communist officials. In reality, contrary to official claims output of pig iron, coal, electric power, sugar, soybeans, and wheat actually lagged behind past peak levels.[22]

The decline in pig iron production reflects, primarily, changed market relationships. Under Japanese tutelage, at least half of Manchuria's pig iron production was exported to Japan. With changed trading conditions, this market was lost, so that current output is governed by rates of domestic steel production. On the other hand, reduction in electric power production may be due to the fact that power-generating capacity dismantled by the Soviets in Manchuria has not yet been fully restored. However, most of this curtailment in production was apparently borne by household consumption, so that industrial power consumption may actually be greater than before.[23]

The lag in coal recovery may be partly accounted for by a marked drop in output of the Kailan mine, the largest in China proper. This seems to be related to obsolescence and lack of replacement of equipment. Strenuous efforts, thus far only partially successful, are being made to compensate for this loss through expansion of the Manchurian deposits. The need to restore and expand coal and power production was assigned a particularly high priority, since failure in these fields limits growth in the other industrial sectors.

TABLE 3

Estimated Production of Selected Commodities in Mainland China*

Product	Unit	Peak	1949	1950	1952
Pig Iron	in 000 MT	2,000	210	827	1,589
Crude Steel	"	900	144	551	1,215
Rolled Steel	"	500	90	259	740
Coal	"	59,000	26,000	35,000	53,000
Crude Oil	"	330	125	207	389
Cement	"	2,140	663	1,412	2,311
Paper	"	120	108	101	264
Flour	"	2,450	1,911	1,200	3,087
Sugar	"	410	164	198	328
Cotton Yarn	in 000 bales	2,400	1,728	2,040	2,784
Cotton Cloth	in 000 bolts	41,000	29,930	3,230	56,580
Cigarettes	in 000,000 sticks	82,000	47,000	54,520	102,500
Electric Power	in 000,000 KWH	6,900	3,600	3,800	5,700
Rice	in 000 MT	48,600	–	46,900	55,890
Wheat	"	24,000	–	19,300	22,800
Soybeans	"	10,000	–	5,890	8,900
Cotton	"	1,115	–	–	1,290

*The same qualifications apply to the figures in this table as were indicated under Table 1 of this chapter.

Compiled by adjusting the indices in the following sources for mutual consistency and then applying them to the data in Table 1: *Communique on Rehabilitation and Development of National Economy, Culture and Education During 1952*, Peking, State Statistical Bureau, September 29, 1953; Chen Chi-ke, "China's Outstanding Financial and Economic Achievements," in *People's China*, October 16, 1951; Ch'en Yun, "Address to the Preparatory Conference of the All-China Federation of Industrial and Commercial Circles," June 24, 1952, in *New China's Economic Achievements, op. cit.*, p. 141; Chia To-fu, "The Advance of China's Industry," in *People's China*, June 1, 1953; Po I-po, "The 1953 State Budget of the People's Republic of China," Supplement to *People's China*, March 16, 1953; Li Fu-chun, "The Restoration and Development of Our Industries in the Past Three Years," October 2, 1952, in *New China's Economic Achievements, op. cit.*, p. 180; Li Fu-chun, "The Present Situation of China's Industries and the Direction of Our Future Work," October 31, 1951, in *ibid.*, p. 124; Ke Chia-lung, "China Builds a New Democracy," in *People's China*, December 16, 1951; Wu K'ang, "Consolidate the Victory, Continue to Advance," *Economic Weekly*, Shanghai, January 3, 1952, in K. C. Chao, ed., *Source Materials from Communist China*, II, Cambridge, Mass., April 1952, p. 14; Huang Yen-pei, "Progress in China's Light Industry," in *People's China*, December 16, 1952; Po I-po, "Three Years of Achievement of the People's Republic of China," in *New China's Economic Achievements, op. cit.*, p. 157.

As against these shortfalls, substantial gains were made in steel, cotton cloth, paper, flour, and cigarette production. An expansion in steel production, despite Soviet removals of equipment in 1945, is not as surprising as it may seem at first. Even at its peak, the Japanese iron and steel industry in Manchuria operated at only about 60 per cent of capacity, so that in order to produce the 1952 output, capacity did not have to be fully restored. To maintain the plant that was left, and to replace as much of the dismantled equipment as was needed to produce the 1952 output, an estimated investment of about U.S. $160 million (in terms of 1952 U.S. investment costs) would have been required.[24] This is an amount which, allowing for competing investment requirements was certainly within Communist China's capacity to invest and import.

Recognizing the crucial role of textiles as barter and incentive goods in the Chinese rural setting, the new regime has placed particular emphasis upon increasing raw cotton and cotton textile production. At the same time, this effort is also motivated by the Chinese Communist drive for self-sufficiency. In both of these respects, the Chinese Communists have had a fair measure of success; they expanded output and by 1953 reduced imports to negligible proportions. However, they have tended to exaggerate their achievements in this field more than in any other. For instance, by using a very low (860,000 MT) prewar peak figure, they can show that 1952 raw cotton production was about 50 per cent above prewar. However, in reality, 1936 output was substantially higher (1,115,000 MT),[25] so that the increase is only 15 per cent. Similarly, increases in cotton cloth production may be more apparent than real. Unlike cotton-spinning, weaving was still preponderantly a handicraft industry before the Sino-Japanese War. Thus the rapid growth in output may represent only a displacement of handicraft by factory cloth, rather than an expansion in total production. The same may be true for flour. While the pace of recovery has been quite rapid, it apparently lagged behind Chinese Communist expectations as evidenced by the fact that 1952 industrial production targets were not met, with the exception of coal and flour. In this respect, as in so many others, the Chinese Communists seem to follow the Soviet and satellite statistical practice of camouflaging failures and exaggerating accomplishments.

Mainland China's economic recovery in all fields was greatly facilitated by a succession of three favorable harvests in 1950, 1951, and 1952. As a result, 1952 farm production seems to have attained, or possibly even exceeded, prewar record levels, despite land redistribution and the subsequent beginnings of the collectivization drive. Actually, it is impossible to ascertain the net effect of land reform upon output. There is no question that during the period of agitation, land redistribution, and transfer of title, there was a great deal of unrest in the areas affected which could not help but disrupt output that year. However, since the process was spread over a three-year period, the total impact upon the country's production as a whole was probably not too significant. This may have been the case despite the fact that land reform seriously disrupted the prevailing system of farm credit. Land redistribution may have had a positive incentive effect upon those farmers who received land; but this effect may be gradually dissipated as the collectivization campaign gathers steam. However, this would not yet have been a major factor during the 1949–1952 period. Thus, on balance, land reform may have had no pronounced impact upon agricultural production. The favorable crop conditions of 1950–1952 must be ascribed to good weather combined with an absence of civil conflict, improved transport and distribution, and efforts to rehabilitate and develop flood control and irrigation facilities.

B. The Nationalization of the Economy

The Chinese Communist economic program has essentially two dimensions. On the one hand, it aims at rapid recovery and growth in production, most particularly industrial production. On the other, it is bent upon bringing an increasing share of this output under government control for political purposes as well as for planning and for specific investment and military use. These objectives require a restructuring of the institutional framework, a task in which nationalization, land, fiscal, monetary, and distribution policies have been blended into an instrument for resource mobilization and allocation.

The Chinese Communists inherited from the Nationalist government a sizeable state enterprise sector which they have consistently enlarged, partly at the expense of the private sector. However, there has been little additional outright nationalization of private trade and industry thus far, although it has been explicitly foreshadowed since the end of October 1953. In this field, Chinese Communist tactics have consisted in a squeezing-out of private enterprise through tax pressures, credit rationing, capital levies, state competition, and union demands, rather than through outright expropriation. In effect, the regime has reduced the private capitalist to performing a bureaucrat's functions without yet assuming the full responsibilities of state ownership. Under the impact of these policies, the government increased its share in industrial production from 44 per cent to 67 per cent between 1949 and 1952.[26] It is officially reported that by October 1952 all the railways, 80 per cent of the heavy and 60 per cent of the light industries, and 60 per cent of the steamships plying in home waters were state-operated. At the same time, the government controlled over 90 per cent of all loans and deposits through the People's Bank, and state trading companies were responsible for about 90 per cent of foreign trade, for about half of wholesale trade, and for about 30 per cent of retail trade.[27] Actually, the area of effective government control was even greater than is indicated by these figures. Through allocations of raw materials and credit, through introduction of "cash and currency control," and through monopoly of trade in key agricultural and industrial commodities, the authorities were in a position to manipulate most of the strategic levers in the economy.[28]

The same general pattern is evident in Chinese Communist land policy, which—through a series of intermediate stages—aims at gradual, step-by-step expropriation of the Chinese peasant's land. The first stage, land reform, was designed to harness land hunger and agrarian unrest into a politically potent weapon and to break the political and economic power of the landlord. While land distribution created a mass of "middle" and "poor" peasants, an effort was begun (but not yet completed by 1952) to supplant the traditional institutions with state-controlled organs: cooperative institutions for moneylending and marketing; mutual-aid teams and producers' cooperatives as the basic production units in agriculture, and Communist-dominated Peasant Associations as the centers of local power.

In the strategy and tactics of Chinese Communism, land reform performed a triple function: it helped to pave the road to power; it helped to extend and consolidate that power at the village level; and it served to transfer the wealth-accumulating function from the landlord to the state. In effect, it provided a vehicle by which the land rent could be appropriated by the state for its own use. Inasmuch as land rent in China was mostly dissipated in consumption—conspicuous and otherwise—in hoarding, and after 1936 also in capital flight, expropriation of this rent furnished a means for raising the level of investment in the economy. In a sense, the outstanding achievement of the regime has been its ability to mobilize and allocate a higher proportion of China's national income to investment and military purposes than has ever been done before.

C. The Quest for Price Stability

As the regime consolidated its control over the mainland, it felt ready to launch a comprehensive attack upon fiscal and financial instability. This attack was based upon the following elements:

(1) Balancing the budget. This involved an initial curtailment (in early 1950) of government expenditure and a reorganization of the tax system based on increased rates of urban taxation. At the same time, fiscal management was greatly centralized, with many local government functions transferred to the central government. After the outbreak of the Korean War, government outlays began to increase once more, but most of this rise was covered by regular income or extraordinary levies and campaigns. The latter served as a means both of raising revenue and of mopping up liquid purchasing power.

(2) Restoring confidence in the monetary medium. In the face of continuing monetary devaluation, the regime decided to guarantee the purchasing power of certain types of transactions. Accordingly, wage and salary payments, bank deposits, some government expenditures, and bond issues were expressed in commodity basket values, termed wage, parity deposit, and victory bond units respectively.[29] This was designed to discourage the flight from money into goods, and foster the accumulation of savings and bank deposits.

(3) Controlling money and credit. In accord with the series of stabilization moves of January to April 1950, the People's Bank began to pursue a tight, deflationary credit policy. In combination with other anti-inflationary devices, the Bank finally succeeded in curbing speculation and black market credit, and in controlling the interest rate. Thus monthly interest rates for loans to Shanghai traders rose from 24–30 per cent in June 1949 to a peak of 70–80 per cent in December, and then declined continuously to 18 per cent in April 1950 and to 3 per cent a year later.[30]

(4) Reactivation of exchange and distribution. The success of the whole stabilization experiment depended upon the government's ability to guarantee the supply of consumers' necessities and the faith of the public in such a guarantee. This was clearly recognized by the Chinese Com-

munists, as illustrated by the following statement of a Bank of China manager:

> The reserve for the issuance of JMP is not gold, but the supplies under the control of the government in the liberated areas . . . The reserve is not kept in the vaults of the bank but is being continuously dumped on the market through the government-run trading companies. The duty of these companies is to stabilize the commodity prices, prevent sudden rises or declines, regulate supply and demand, and prevent speculative activities.[31]

However, the state trading mechanism could perform the function assigned to it only if the volume of goods entering distributive channels could be greatly expanded. In turn, this required not only a recovery in agricultural and industrial production, but also restoration of the badly disrupted transport network. For this reason, rehabilitation and expansion of transport was one of the regime's high priority targets. Thus a high proportion of government investment in 1950 and 1951 was devoted to railroad reconstruction. As a result, while in October 1949 less than half of China's total railway trackage was in operation, all lines were restored by mid-1951 and the intensity of their use was greatly stepped up. At the same time, new railroad construction was vigorously pushed; for instance, the 320-mile-long Chungking-Chengtu railway—the roadbed for which was prepared by the Nationalist government before the war—was completed in 1952, thus bringing the Szechwan rice basin into closer proximity to East and North China.

During this whole recovery period (1949–1952), the regime placed great reliance upon indirect controls and market forces as instruments for stabilization, resource mobilization, and resource allocation. Chinese Communist policy-makers seem to have realized from the very outset that outright price-fixing would not be practicable under mainland conditions. Direct price control would have placed tremendous administrative burdens upon the bureaucratic apparatus, and even then it would have been very difficult to enforce. As a matter of fact, this type of price control had been unsuccessfully attempted by the Nationalist government on several occasions in the 1945–1949 period. As a result, the device as such was in disrepute and an attempt to introduce it might have been viewed by the population as a repetition of the past—an impression the Chinese Communists tried assiduously to avoid. Indirect price control, on the other hand, based upon state trading as a manipulative device in combination with monetary and fiscal tools, was likely to prove more flexible and better suited to China's present stage of economic and bureaucratic development.

On the whole, these policies proved to be rather effective in arresting inflation and in gradually instituting price stability. The inflationary spiral was broken in March 1950; however, under the impact of the rather drastic deflationary policies, a temporary crisis ensued. This unforeseen depression was marked by bank failures, business bankruptcies, accumulation of unsold inventories in the cities, and large-scale urban unemployment. This trend was reversed with the outbreak of the Korean War, after which wholesale prices rose very rapidly once more, so that by the end of 1950 they approached the March Peak. Thus 1950 was a year of violent price fluctuations, during which the regime had only partial control over price formation. This was much less true in 1951, as illustrated by the fact than the average price level rose only by about 20 per cent. However, prices of producers' goods increased much more rapidly under the competing pressures of Korean War requirements and of domestic reconstruction.

By 1952, with virtual price stability attained, open inflation was beginning to be replaced by suppressed inflation—a characteristic of virtually all full-employment economies operating within a framework of economic controls. In China, as elsewhere, comparatively high rates of investment and military expenditure have become a constant source of imbalance between the stream of consumers' income and the supply of consumers' goods. Therefore, occasional bond campaigns or other extraordinary levies have been launched, as in the Soviet Union and the satellites, to mop up liquid purchasing power. Similarly, the regime was forced to introduce rationing for the first time late in 1953, not merely because of an indifferent harvest but because of the pressure of effective money demand.

D. Mobilization and Allocation of Resources

Economic controls developed in Communist China during the 1949–1952 period have not only been used to attain fiscal and financial stability but also to step up the rate of resource mobilization. At the same time that state participation in industry and trade was growing, the nature and scope of the government budget was changing. This budget gradually evolved from a traditional instrument for financing standard government operations into an economic budget of the Soviet type, controlling the contours of the whole economy. In this context, one of the functions of government fiscal operations is to keep consumption in check, both through high taxation and by the maintenance of wide state enterprise profit margins.[32] Price and distribution policy, in particular, serves as a means for raising the level and rate of forced saving. As the volume of domestic trade expands, state revenues are automatically augmented through commodity taxation levied at the wholesale stage. At the same time, state trading companies are encouraged to use their market power to buy "cheap" and sell "dear." Thus, the state appropriates resources through trade in two ways, through the pricing process and through the taxing mechanism.

The growing importance of the budget is clearly illustrated by the data in Table 4. It may also be gauged by an increase in the share of the budget in gross national expenditure from about 15 per cent in 1950 to roughly 27 per cent in 1952.

The annual budget figures given in Table 4 are not comparable from year to year, since they reflect a continuing extension in the scope of government fiscal operations. On the one hand, the government sector has been growing at the expense of the private sector, so that more and more new enterprises and functions are brought within the purview of the government budget. On the other hand, the central government has been adopting more and more of the local government functions every year.

Keeping these qualifications in mind, it is evident from these data that government expenditures rose very rapidly between 1950 and 1952, and particularly between 1950 and 1951.[33] Military expenditures were almost doubled during 1951, in response to increasing Korean War requirements. As the Korean fighting subsided in 1952, growing emphasis was being placed upon modernization of the army, weapons development, and military investment, all of which are probably handled by the Second Ministry of Machine Building. As such, they are in all likelihood entered into the economic construction budgets. For instance, both the 1952 and 1953 investment budgets had an "other" item, which in Soviet budget practice is a cover for hidden military outlays.

The Korean War undoubtedly imposed a serious drain upon the Chinese mainland economy, even though much of the military hardware was

TABLE 4

Chinese Communist Government Budgets, 1950–1952*

(in trillion JMP)

	1950		1951	1952	
	Budget	Actual	Actual	Budget	Actual
Expenditures:					
Military	23.2	28.3	50.6	44.4	42.8
Government administration	12.8	13.1	17.5	22.7	19.3
Economic construction	14.3	17.4	35.1	58.6	73.1
Cultural construction	2.4	7.6	13.4	20.2	22.3
Other	1.4	1.8	2.4	6.8	5.7
Total	54.1	68.2	119.0	152.7	163.2
Revenues:					
Agricultural tax	20.1	19.1	21.7	n.a.	25.6
Industrial and commercial taxes	18.9	29.9	58.5	n.a.	69.0
Other taxes	–	–	1.0	–	1.6
Total taxes	39.0	49.0	81.2	91.7	96.2
Revenue from government enterprises	8.3	8.7	30.5	37.0	46.6
Income from credit and insurance	–	3.3	5.7	4.4	2.5
Total	47.3	61.0	117.4	133.1	145.3
Deficit	6.8	7.2	1.6	19.6	17.9
Proceeds of deficit financing[a]	12.4	8.5	23.3	2.6	20.9
Carry-over	–	–	1.3	23.0	23.0
"Surplus"	5.6	1.3	23.0	6.0	26.0

*The figures for military expenditures and government administration in 1952 differ from those in my *The National Income of Communist China*, which are (in millions of "new yuan") 2,110 for government administration and 4,370 for defense. The latter are based on later and revised official data.
[a]Listed in Chinese Communist sources as "other" revenue.
Source: The data in this table are based on Po I-po's "Report on the 1953 State Budget of the People's Republic of China," *op. cit.*

provided by the Soviet Union on lend-lease terms. The war, particularly in its more active fighting stage, diverted scarce industrial and transport resources from "economic construction," i.e., from investment. This is illustrated by the fact that between 1951 (the year of the most violent military engagement) and 1952, the proportion of total government expenditure channeled into investment rose from about 30 per cent to 45 per cent, while the actual amount was doubled.

Owing to this resource drain, amidst greatly curtailed production, investment may have constituted only about 4 per cent of gross national product in 1950; by 1952 this proportion rose to approximately 12 per cent. While the exact allocation of these investment resources was officially published only for 1953, there is no question but that from the outset industry and transport were accorded the highest priority. Agriculture, on the other hand, was kept on a short investment ration, with major reliance placed on mass applications of seasonally underemployed labor in water conservation.

Chinese Communist budgets differ radically in their scope and character from the budgets of the Nationalist government, to such an extent that they are not comparable. First of all, they are based on a much more tightly knit and centralized system of fiscal management, in which the scope of local government functions is minimized and local government finance is closely integrated with central government fiscal operations. As a matter of fact, in this system, fiscal management provides one of the principal tools for developing a more highly centralized administrative apparatus through which the tentacles of government control reach down to the local levels. Secondly, Chinese Communist budgets include Manchuria, which was excluded from Nationalist government accounts after 1931. Finally, current budgets reflect a much greater government participation in the economy.

One of the salient features of the 1950–1952 budgets are the relatively small deficits;[34] apparently they did not exceed 11 per cent of total expenditure during any one year. This is a reflection of the new regime's much greater fiscal capacity, owing to its larger and more effective arsenal of control and pressure mechanisms. Actually, contrary to earlier Chinese Communist statements, Po I-po's report, on which Table 4 is based, indicates that there have never been any deficits at all, but only surpluses. This extraordinary feat has apparently been accomplished through accounting manipulations. For instance, in Chinese Communist budget practice, proceeds from deficit financing such as bond and note issues, bank overdrafts, and special levies are treated as "other" revenue. Special campaigns were launched every year. In 1950 there was a bond campaign; in 1951 the drive on "counter-revolutionaries" netted important sums by way of confiscation; there was the "donations" drive for guns and planes for Korea that netted about 5 trillion JMP; and in 1952 the "Five-Anti's" Movement (the campaign against "tax evasion, theft of state property, cheating on government contracts, bribery, and stealing of economic information for private speculation") netted a much larger, but unknown, sum. This, of course, would still leave the 1951 and 1952 surpluses unexplained, since it is rather puzzling why there should be such levies if the sums collected were not to be spent. Initially, these so-called "surpluses" may have been unintended, to the extent that they reflected higher proceeds from capital and other levies than were anticipated. Since 1952, however, they seem to be actually budgeted in advance and are serving the function of revolving capital and operating reserve funds for the government apparatus and the state enterprise system.[35]

While government expenditures were rapidly rising between 1950 and 1952, the revenue base was constantly widened. In 1949, the agricultural tax in kind provided the principal source of revenue, but in 1950 it was gradually displaced by industrial and commercial taxes, which grew in importance thereafter. However, it is important to note that by pricing tax grain, throughout, at its 1950 price, which was below the market price, income from agricultural taxation is grossly understated in the budget.

In general terms, taxation in the rural sector is direct, while in the urban sector indirect sales taxes and taxes of the turnover type predominate. Indirect taxes and customs duties have traditionally provided the principal sources of revenue in China. While customs duties are only of minor importance in Communist China, indirect taxes have been constantly gaining, with a gradual approach to the Soviet system of turnover taxation. At the same time, profits of state enterprises have constituted a major and growing source of revenue since 1951. This, in turn, is a reflection of the expanding scope of the state enterprise system and its growing monopolistic and monopsonistic powers.

As the scope of the government budget and the area of economic controls spread, the regime increased its capacity to allocate resources and plan their use. During the 1949–1952 period, the Chinese Communist economy operated within a framework of certain general objectives and partial, rather than comprehensive and integrated, economic plans. These partial plans were mostly confined to individual industries, without a serious effort to interrelate them. On the other hand, in Manchuria, where the regime had been longer in power and where a great deal of experience had been accumulated under the Japanese, planning was in a much more advanced stage. As a matter of fact, this region served as something of a planning laboratory and training ground for the mainland as a whole. It was not surprising therefore that Kao Kang (chairman of the regional government in the northeast) was made chairman of the State Planning Commission formed in late 1952 to prepare the Five-Year Plan.

Generally, the pattern of economic planning in Communist China appears to be broadly analogous to the postwar experience of the Eastern European satellites. In all of these countries, the cessation of hostilities was followed by a somewhat varying period of two to three years during which there was no over-all economic plan. Subsequently, recovery plans, usually of two to three years' duration, were supposed to lay the groundwork for the Five-Year Plans inaugurated in 1949 or 1950.

This timetable of planning was closely tied in with the political situation in the satellite countries. As a rule, the pre-plan period was one of coalition governments, with the Communist Party frequently playing a minority role. The situation began to change rapidly during the recovery plan period, with the Communist parties increasingly asserting their power and gradually pushing out their coalition partners, so that by the time Five-Year plans were inaugurated, all seats of power were monopolized by the Communist Party. This general pattern was also reflected in the character of economic policy. The early period was characterized by a relative absence of direct controls and considerable reliance upon market forces for resource allocation. Concurrently, a rather moderate land policy was pursued. Land reform was the postwar order of the day in all satellites. Upon monopolization of power by the Communist parties, a program of gradual collectivization was launched. It was quite clear from the outset that in this field the satellites would follow the Soviet model without employing the drastic Soviet collectivization methods.

This general pattern seems to be repeating itself in Communist China. Owing to the absence of any clearly crystallized and strong non-Communist political parties at the time of takeover, coalition in China was primarily a facade, designed to gain non-Communist support for the regime. Therefore, satellite stages one and two could be merged, combining the pre-plan and recovery-plan phases into one, with an attempt to go from there directly to long-range development planning of the Five-Year type. Interestingly enough, Yugoslavia was the only East European country which also combined these stages and for the same general reasons.

During this period, credit and price policy served as the principal instruments of planning. Through discriminatory pricing, favorable or unfavorable rates of interest, and credit terms, resources were diverted from industries that had been accorded a low priority to lines of production which the state wished to encourage. Cotton provides a good case in point. In order to encourage an extension in cotton acreage, Chinese Communist planners increased the cotton-grain exchange ratio as shown in Table 5.

D. Changes in Foreign Economic Relations

China traditionally maintained very close economic relations with Britain, the United States, Germany, and Japan. Trade with these countries was based on an exchange of coarse grains, foodstuffs, raw materials of agricultural origin, and minerals, for wheat flour, rice, sugar, tobacco, raw cotton, textiles, other manufactured consumers' goods, mineral oils, chemicals, and capital goods. In contrast, China's contact with Russia and Eastern Europe was of negligible importance.

This pattern has been radically altered since the Chinese Communist capture of the mainland. Western enterprise and economic influences have been gradually pushed out, while intimate ties have been established with the Soviet Union and the Soviet bloc as a whole. On the one hand, this process has been accelerated by free-world trade controls, which compelled mainland China to divert an increasing share of its trade to the Soviet bloc. On the other hand, it may be assumed that, given the "lean-to-one-side" policy, China's trade with the Soviet bloc would have

TABLE 5

Ratio of Exchange for 0.5 Kg of Seven-Eighths Inches
Cotton Lint

	1950	1951	1952
		(in kilograms)	
North China millet	4.0	4.5	4.5
Northwest China wheat	3.5	4.0	4.75
Central South China wheat	3.25	4.0	4.25

Source: "Economic Development in Mainland China, 1949–1953," in United Nations, *Economic Bulletin for Asia and the Far East,* IV, No. 3 (November 1953), p. 22.

expanded in any case, even in the absence of Western trade restrictions, but probably not by as much. This is partly supported by the fact that the impact of trade controls apparently began to be fully felt only in the second half of 1951; while free-world exports to China were at U.S. $314 million in the first half of 1951, they dropped to about $130 million in the second half. The nature of this "push" and "pull" in China's trade orientation is illustrated by the data in Table 6.

Several facts emerge from an examination of this table. Foreign trade recovered very rapidly from its abnormally low 1950 level, so that by 1951 it had more or less attained its prewar peak. Practically all of this expansion was confined to the Soviet bloc, more specifically to the Soviet Union, since trade with Eastern Europe was still very small at that time. In 1952, China's trade with the Soviet bloc increased even further, however; this time most of the expansion was with Eastern Europe rather than with the Soviet Union itself, while total trade actually declined somewhat. It is interesting to note that in her trade with the free world, mainland China maintained an export surplus; this may have been more than counter-balanced by an import surplus with the Soviet bloc, financed out of the net earnings in trade with the West and the Soviet loan of U.S. $60 million per annum.

Close economic relations with the Soviet Union involve not only intimate trade ties but also joint stock companies, credits, and technical assistance. Three Sino-Soviet companies were organized: for civil aviation, and for the exploitation of oil and of non-ferrous mineral resources in Sinkiang. Given their location and scale, these companies do not provide leverage over the economy as a whole equivalent to that exercised by joint companies in Eastern Europe. The character of technical assistance also differs greatly from the role of Soviet advisers in Eastern Europe. All of the available evidence tends to indicate that these advisers do not perform management or control functions in the Chinese setting.[36] However, their influence has been growing, as Chinese Communist planners have begun to run into serious organizational, managerial, planning, and technical bottle-necks. For instance, economic policies of the Soviet type gained in importance during 1952 and 1953, particularly in the fields of fiscal and monetary management. Apart from technical advice, Soviet material assis-tance during this period—exclusive of shipments of war material to Korea—was on a very modest scale, i.e., at a rate of about U.S. $60 million per annum. Actually, it may have been less, since it is more than probable that

TABLE 6

Mainland China's Foreign Trade, 1950–1952*

Year	Trade with the Free World (in million dollars)			As Per Cent of Total Mainland Trade (in per cent)	Estimated Mainland Total (in million dollars)	Estimated Soviet Bloc Trade (in million dollars)		
	Exports	Imports	Total			USSR	Eastern Europe	Total
1950	476	409	885	74	1,200	285	30	315
1951	443	440	873	39	2,240	n.a.	n.a.	1,367
1952	345	257	602	28	2,150	1,148	400	1,548

*The figures given here are inconsistent with the percentages cited for these years in the last three columns of Table 1 in Chapter 11. The data in both of these studies precede the systematic reconstructions of China's foreign trade from the trading partner side. These reconstructions yield the following results (in millions of U.S. dollars) as given in A. Eckstein, ed., *China Trade Prospects and U.S. Policy*, N.Y., 1971:

	1950	1951	1952
Exports	697	977	922
Imports	876	1,025	984
Total	1,583	2,002	1,906

Sources: United Nations, *World Economic Report, 1951–1952*, p. 130; U.S. Foreign Operations Administration, *World-wide Enforcement of Strategic Trade Controls*, Mutual Defense Assistance Control, October 3rd Report to Congress, November 1953; Yeh Chi-chuang, "Three Years of China's Foreign Trade," in *New China's Economic Achievements, op. cit.*, pp. 237–44; Pei Hsiang-yin, "Sino-Soviet Trade," *People's China*, June 16, 1953.

the ruble costs of technical assistance were charged against the annual proceeds of this loan. On the other hand, by combining the proceeds of the Soviet loan with the net foreign exchange earned in her trade with the West, Communist China could maintain an import surplus with the Soviet Union of about U.S. $100–150 million. Since the bulk of Soviet bloc imports, possibly about 75 per cent,[37] consists of capital goods, the Soviet Union in effect helps China to maximize the import of those goods which come within the purview of Western trade controls. Within this context Soviet credits, even though small, have played an important role in the rehabilitation of transport and of Manchurian industry. In effect, the Soviet credit has made it possible to replace some of the equipment dismantled and removed by Moscow in 1945.

The radical shift in mainland China's economic orientation was necessarily accompanied by marked shifts in the commodity composition of foreign trade, particularly in respect to imports. Thus, in line with the economic objectives of the new regime, imports of consumers' goods were drastically curtailed, while capital goods imports were significantly stepped up. More specifically, imports of food and textiles were largely displaced by machinery and metals, mineral oils, chemicals, and industrial raw materials, particularly rubber and raw cotton. The latter constituted close to one-fifth of total import value in 1950. As domestic raw cotton production increased, however, imports declined, so that by 1953 the country was self-sufficient in this commodity.

These shifts in the character of import demand have far-reaching implications for the direction of trade as well. Thus, Japan's prewar trading position in China was to a large extent based upon exports of cotton textiles, so that the disappearance of this market inevitably narrows the potential scope of exchange between the two countries. Communist China would, of course, be interested in replacing these textiles with imports of capital goods. Japan, however, faces a much more acute marketing problem for textiles than for machinery or industrial equipment; and like the United Kingdom, Japan may require a structural shift from textile to engineering exports in order to meet the changing pattern of world demand.

Changes in the structure of exports have been much less marked. Mainland China has continued to base her export trade upon foodstuffs, raw materials of agricultural origin, and mineral products. Most important among these are soybeans, plus other vegetable oils and products, tung oil, hog bristles, and grains. Grains seem to have grown in importance as compared with the prewar period. Mainland China has become a net exporter in recent years; e.g., there have been shipments of 66,000 tons of rice and 450,000 tons of kaoliang to India in 1951, as well as substantial amounts of wheat to the Soviet Far East. These net exports are not as surprising as they might appear at first sight. Known net shipments constituted only about 1 per cent of total mainland grain production and not more than 2 per cent of grain entering market channels. Similarly, prewar net imports were a very small proportion of production and marketings: they were primarily a function of high costs of inland transportation and inefficient domestic distribution. Thus the margin between net grain imports and exports is quite narrow, and therefore depends upon the quality of the harvest in any one year and the efficiency of distribution.[38]

In a static sense, exports are of comparatively small importance for mainland China's economy. For instance, in 1952 they constituted only about 3 per cent of gross national product. But, in dynamic terms, they are very strategic, as illustrated by the fact that the foreign trade component in capital formation was close to 20 per cent in 1952. Viewed in these terms, given its industrialization objective and its limited current capabilities for manufacturing complex capital goods, one of the regime's principal tasks is to find ways and means of translating internal savings (largely in the form of agricultural output) into expanding capital goods imports. The pace of industrialization and the rate of economic growth will in large measure depend upon the extent to which this transformation can be affected.

The conditions and terms on which mainland exports can be transformed into capital goods imports will, however, depend not only upon the extent to which the regime can mobilize agricultural surpluses, but also upon the terms of trade between China and the Soviet bloc. While there is no quantitative information concerning these terms, some of the factors that inevitably affect Sino-Soviet trade relations are quite clear.

In an absolute sense, there is a definite basis for trade between China and the bloc. For most of the commodities exported by China, there is an import demand in the Soviet Union and the bloc as a whole. This is definitely the case with soybeans, oilseeds and its products, tea, tungsten, tin, and antimony, which have been traditional import products for the Soviet Union. Also, under the impact of the post-Stalin policies, Soviet import demand for livestock products has risen considerably—a development that broadens the scope of Sino-Soviet trade. At the same time, the Soviet Union and the satellites undoubtedly have the capacity to provide China with capital goods and industrial raw materials up to the level that she can afford within the limits of her export proceeds and credits. In this connection, it may be worth noting that USSR industrial exports to China may have amounted to 1–2 per cent of Soviet industrial output in 1952.

The relative position, however, is quite different. China's demand for Soviet imports is likely to be much more inelastic than the Soviet demand for Chinese products. On the one hand, China's imports are very strategic from the standpoint of its industrialization program, while Soviet imports of Chinese products are more or less peripheral for the economy of the USSR. On the other hand, owing to free world trade controls, China is completely dependent upon the Soviet bloc for its imports of capital goods and certain industrial raw materials, while the Soviet Union can obtain livestock products, tea, oilseeds, etc., from other countries in exchange for gold or those raw materials that are in surplus in the Soviet Union; that is, she can obtain these products without exporting capital goods at the expense of Soviet bloc development. For all of these reasons, in the Sino-Soviet bilateral trade relationship, the Soviet Union is bound to enjoy superior bargaining powers, at least in economic terms. This may, of course, be altered in either direction on the basis of purely political considerations.

III. Conditions and Prospects for Economic Growth

In general terms, by the end of 1952, mainland China's productive capacity was reactivated and its institutional framework transformed to such an extent that the regime felt the time was ripe for launching an ambitious and comprehensive program of economic development. However, the announcement of a Five-Year Plan for China does not seem to have been preceded by a major debate on issues, methods, and problems of industrialization such as occurred in Russia in the 1920's.* It would appear that

---

*In the light of Red Guard papers and documents released during the Cultural Revolution, this is probably an overstatement. In retrospect it is clear that a rather vigorous debate was carried on behind the scenes prior to Mao's collectivization decision of mid-1955.

Chinese Communist thinking and policy, as it has emerged, is almost completely hypnotized by the Stalinist model of economic development, with Preobrazhenskis and Bukharins absent from the scene.[39]

Proceeding on this basis, the regime envisages a development focused on the rapid expansion of producers' goods and defense industries. This is to be accompanied by a more modest rate of growth in the manufacture of textiles needed for barter with the countryside. Agriculture is to be developed primarily through better organization, rather than through capital investment; specifically, this is to be based upon creation of capital by underemployed labor in mass water conservation and other labor-intensive projects. Finally, this process of industrialization is to be financed, at least in part, through net resource transfers out of agriculture. In order to make sure of this, the peasantry is to be gradually collectivized, but in such a way as not to disrupt output drastically or damage farm capital. Thus, in this respect, Chinese Communist leaders would like to avoid the costly Soviet, one-sweep collectivization experience.

The financing of industrialization through net resource transfers out of agriculture has, of course, been a feature of economic development in many countries, even though in a much less extreme and deliberate form than in the Soviet case. Perhaps the most notable of these, from the Chinese point of view, is the Japanese experience. However, Japan's evolution differs from the Sino-Soviet model in several respects. At the very outset, the Japanese placed great emphasis upon agricultural development. This was attained chiefly through the introduction of Western technology, but most especially through large applications of imported fertilizer.[40] By all indications, Chinese Communist policy-makers are not prepared to sacrifice imports of industrial capital for agricultural requisites, with the possible exception of some imports of seed and livestock for breeding, which absorb only a small share of export proceeds. The impact of these improvements, is however, generally much slower and less dramatic than is the case with commercial fertilizer.

In essence, this is a model which involves industrial development at the expense of agricultural development. Industrialization is accelerated at the outset, by virtue of the very fact that since agriculture is kept on a short investment ration, a larger share of investment resources can be concentrated in industry. This policy, in turn, sets up its own vicious circles; just because agricultural development is sluggish, while the demand for farm products grows—owing to an increasing population, urbanization, and exports—the regime is forced to extract a rising proportion of farm output if this demand is to be met. This very process, however, further interferes with agricultural development, so that the screw must be applied even tighter. Under such circumstances, farm output is sacrificed for control and strong compulsions are set in force which drive the system toward collectivization. Thus, given their economic objectives and the nature of their program, the Chinese Communists are caught in a series of dilemmas, of which the agricultural problem is the most fundamental. These dilemmas, and the ways in which they are likely to affect the character and rate of economic growth within the confines of mainland China's economy, will be analyzed below. However, before proceeding on this path, it may be well to examine where the Chinese economy stands today in relation to Japan, the Soviet Union, and India.

A. Mainland China's Stage of Development on the Eve of the Five-Year Plan

The Chinese economy of 1952 was at a stage of development roughly comparable to Meiji Japan and present-day India. On the other hand, it was much more underdeveloped than the Soviet economy on the eve of its first Five-Year Plan in 1928.

The data in Table 7 show that the Soviet Union embarked upon its drive for industrialization in a much more favorable economic setting than that which confronted the policy-makers of present-day China. Low density per unit of cultivated land and vast and high-quality mineral resources were all factors that facilitated the "take-off." As a result, starting from an aggregate economic and industrial base which in 1928 was not appreciably above that of China today, it was possible to treble Soviet gross national product in twenty-five years.

Over and above this, the Soviet Union launched its program of deliberate industrialization in a much more favorable international setting. The Soviet Union could devote from ten to twelve years of undivided effort to building up its industrial and military potential without involving itself in Korea-like interruptions which would have drained resources away from internal construction and investment. Furthermore, strategic trade con-

TABLE 7

Indicators of Comparative Levels of Development in Mainland China, the Soviet Union, Japan, and India*

Indicator	Units	USSR Approximately 1928 — Amount	Year	USSR Approximately 1950 — Amount	Year	JAPAN Meiji — Amount	Year	JAPAN 1930's — Amount	Year	INDIA — Amount	Year	CHINA — Amount	Year
Gross national product	Billions of 1952 US dollars	$35.00	1928	$100.00[a]	1952	$2.20	1878–82	$22.60[c]	1936	$22.00	1950	$30.00	1952
GNP per head[b]	1952 US dollars	$240.00	1928	$490.00	1952	$65.00	1878–82	$325.00	1936	$60.00	1950	$50.00	1952
Population	Millions	147.00	1926	198.00	1950	35.56	1875	69.25[f]	1935	358.00	1950	582.00	1953
Crude birth rate	per 1,000	43.50[d]	1926	25.00 to 34.00	1950–51	39.00[e]	1885	31.20	1931–37	38.00[g]	1949	40.00	1930–35
Crude death rate	per 1,000	19.90[d]	1926	10.00 to 16.00	1950–51	32.00[e]	1885	17.90	1931–37	24.00[g]	1949	34.00	1930–35
Proportion in agriculture and fishing	per 1,000	76.50[h]	1926	49.00 to 53.00[i]	1950	84.80[j]	1872	42.10[k]	1940	68.00[i]	1931	80.00	1952
Agriculture													
Number of persons dependent on agriculture per acre of cultivated land	Persons per acre	0.20	1926	0.20	1950	2.00	1872	1.60	1936–40	0.60	1931	1.90	1953
Paddy rice yield	Metric quintals per hectare	21.50	1934–38			21.60	1880–84	36.30	1934–38	13.30	1934–38	25.30	1931–37
Wheat yield	Metric quintals per hectare	7.90	1934–38					18.80	1934–38	6.80	1937–39	10.80	1931–37
Industry													
Coal	Total in million metric tons	40.10	1929	281.00	1951	0.60	1875	41.80	1936	34.90	1951	53.00	1952
	Kilograms per capita	273.00	1929	1,419.00	1951	17.00	1875	604.00	1936	97.00	1951	96.00	1952
Pig iron	Total in million metric tons	3.30	1927–28	19.40	1950	0.01	1877	2.00	1936	1.90	1951	1.60	1952
	Kilograms per capita	22.00	1927–28	98.00	1950	0.20	1877	29.00	1936	5.00	1951	2.75	1952
Crude steel	Total in million metric tons	4.30	1927–28	24.80	1950	none				1.50	1951	1.20	1952
	Kilograms per capita	29.00	1927–28	125.00	1950	none				4.00	1951	2.00	1952
Finished steel	Total in million metric tons					none		4.50	1936			0.70	1952
	Kilograms per capita					none		66.00	1936			1.00	1952
Generating capacity of electric power	Total in thousand kilowatts	1,900.00	1928	16,000.00	1949	none		6,777.00	1936	2,409.00	1951	2,850.00	1952
	Kilowatts per capita	0.01	1928	0.08	1949	none		0.10	1936	0.01	1951	0.005	1952
Cotton spindleage in industry	Total in thousands	7,465.00	1929	10,000.00	1949	8.00	1877	11,823.00	1936	10,144.00	1952	5,000.00	1952
	Units per capita	0.05	1929	0.05	1949	negligible		0.17	1936	0.03	1952	0.01	1952
Cement	Total in million metric tons	1.90	1928	10.20	1950	negligible		4.30	1929	3.20	1952	2.30	1952
	Kilograms per capita	13.00	1928	52.00	1950	negligible		63.00	1929	9.00	1951	4.00	1952

*Compiled by the author.

[a] 1950 GNP was $87 billions, or $440 per head.

[b] To nearest $5.

[c] 1938 GNP was $24.6 billions, or $355 per head.

[d] European Russia.

[e] Not official statistics, but based on the interpretation of Irene B. Taeuber and Frank W. Notestein, "The Changing Fertility of the Japanese," Population Studies, I, No. 1, pp. 1–28.

[f] Official statistics (implying some understatement of both).

[g] Estimated from the official returns by applying the Kingsley Davis figures; estimates by Davis for 1931–41 are 45 per 1,000 birth rate and 31.2 per 1,000 death rate. See his book, The Population of India and Pakistan, Princeton, 1951.

[h] Distribution of the male labor force. The figure is 77.6% for the distribution of the population and 81.8% for the distribution of the total labor force.

[i] Distribution of the male labor force. The figure is 53–57% for the 1950 distribution of the total labor force. It was 53.8% for 1939.

[j] Distribution of the total occupied population, including females. Some estimates place the 1872 percentage at 77.1%.

[k] Distribution of the total occupied population, including females. The 1936 figure for the total occupied population, excluding women in agriculture, is 30.1%.

trols were absent from the interwar landscape, so that the Soviet Union could import capital goods, technology, know-how, etc., from the West without any restrictions. However, this was counterbalanced by the fact that the Soviet Union was politically isolated, and had no Communist partner to "lean on." Obviously, this is not the case with China. How concrete a role the Soviet Union is likely to play in mainland China's economic development is left to a later stage of this analysis.

In contrast to the Soviet case, the Japanese experience is much more encouraging from a Chinese Communist point of view. In terms of all major indicators, Meiji Japan was at about the same level or lagged behind present-day China. Thus Japanese per capita product, degree of population pressure, and birth and death rates were just about the same as in China. On the other hand, Japan possessed practically no factory industry and a much poorer mineral resource base. However, Meiji Japan, to an even greater extent than the Soviet Union, launched its "take-off" in a favorable international climate. The world economy was expanding, the volume of international trade was increasing, and the impediments to trade were minimal as compared with the post-World War II era. In this setting, it was relatively easy for Japan to find foreign markets for its products and thus earn foreign exchange with which to import the technology and wherewithal of economic development. As a matter of fact, given the paucity of natural resources, foreign trade was absolutely central and vital to Japan's economic growth. This is probably less the case for China; therefore, export marketing difficulties and trade restrictions may slow down, but will not necessarily frustrate, economic growth in China.

Despite the quite backward state of Meiji Japan's economy, and its poor resource base, gross national product was raised roughly tenfold in about sixty years, between 1880 and 1940.[41] Were China's economy to grow at about the same rate, its gross national product would attain the 1952 Japanese level around 1980, while the 1952 U.S. level would be reached around 2010. Of course, on a per capita basis, China's output would still lag behind current U.S. levels. On the other hand, should China grow at the Soviet rate, current Soviet gross product levels would be attained around 1970, while U.S. output would be approached around 1990.

Several references have been made to the comparative resource endowments of China, the Soviet Union, and Japan. The following data may serve to illustrate these differences:[42]

	Mainland China	Soviet Union	Japan
Coal reserves (millions of MT)	265,000	1,200,000	16,218
Iron ore reserves (millions of MT)	2,504	10,900	38

China is particularly well endowed with coal and non-ferrous metals, but is comparatively poor in iron ore and petroleum.* However, quantitative resource limitations do not present a serious problem at this stage; much more immediate and pressing are the questions of accessibility and quality. Thus, many of the deposits are not reached either by inland water or by railroad transport. At the same time, while aggregate coal reserves are abundant, China is quite short of coking coal, and much of this coal is of inferior quality. Similarly, most of the known iron ore deposits are low in iron content; the principal exceptions to this are the Tayeh mines near Hankow, where one of the new steel mills is to be located, and the high-quality ore of Hainan Island. The latter, owing to its strategically vulnerable location, is apparently not fully exploited at present.

The bulk of the Manchurian ore deposits are lean, with an iron content of less than 40 per cent, so that they have to be concentrated before they can be charged into a blast furnace. Moreover, rich ores are found to occur in veins or dikes and to involve underground mining methods, whereas the lean ores are massive and can be mined by surface and open-cut equipment.[43] All of this, of course, raises investment and current operating costs in the iron and steel industry.

Probably the two most critical bottlenecks and immediately limiting factors in mainland China's economic development are power and transport. While China's current generating capacity exceeds that of the Soviet Union in 1928, this capacity is taxed to the limit. On the other hand, transport is an even more critical factor than it was in the Soviet Union on the eve of the first Five-Year Plan, since the density of the Russian rail network was almost twice as great as that of China today. This is of particular importance, since the Chinese rural economy is much less commercialized and more fragmented than was Russia's in 1928. Given

---

*Since this was written, the Chinese engaged in intensive geological explorations. As a result, new major oilfields have been discovered and there are indications of rich off-shore oil reserves.

China's geographic configuration, she is just as dependent as Russia upon inland railroad transport, while Japan, with her comparatively small inland distances, could rely to a much greater extent upon a more economical form of transport, namely, coastal shipping.

The Chinese Communists have recognized their dependence on inland transport and have devoted a great deal of attention to railroad rehabilitation and development, and they plan to continue this effort in the future. However, while transport is an absolutely essential prerequisite of economic growth in the long run, it draws away resources from industrial investment despite the lavish substitution of labor for capital and thus slows down the process of industrial expansion in the short run. For this reason, the Soviets confined railroad development to rather modest proportions. Obviously, the Chinese cannot afford to do this. The dilemma is aggravated by the fact that the new regime seems to have embarked upon an extensive, rather than intensive, type of railroad development; that is, primary emphasis is placed upon the construction of a railroad line that will eventually run from Chungking to Tihua in Sinkiang, and then connect up with the Trans-Siberian, thus linking West China simultaneously with the Soviet Union and with the rest of China. However, most of this railroad will run through underdeveloped dead space which might eventually be developed, but which can have only long-run economic significance.[44] From a purely developmental point of view, it would have been more logical to extend this network in South China and build feeder lines in other regions of population concentration so as to tap more effectively agricultural resources and output.

This brief review of some of the salient factors facilitating or impeding the "take-off" in China as compared with the Soviet Union and Japan would not be complete without a consideration of China's population dynamics. The data in Table 7 show that population pressure in China is close to the level of Meiji Japan, and exceeds that of modern Japan, India, and the Soviet Union. Thus, mainland China's preponderantly rural population is pressed down close to the bare margin of subsistence, with very little room left for saving and capital formation. However, on the basis of the available evidence—most of it poor and incomplete—rates of natural increase have been low in China.

Chinese birth, death, and infant mortality rates are among the highest in the world.[45] They exhibit characteristics typical of countries in which population movements are close to the biological limit and in which the

Malthusian checks are still more or less fully operative. They also show very large annual fluctuations, in response to famines, floods, epidemics, and civil war.

The character of this whole population dynamics is bound to change with the advent of the Chinese Communist regime. Under this regime, all of mainland China has been administratively unified and more or less pacified, for the first time in decades. Injection of a centralized authority, with its tentacles of control extending down to the village level, and maintenance of political stability as a prerequisite for survival of the regime are factors which are likely to have a direct or indirect impact upon the death rate.

The very termination of civil conflict must have had the most immediate effect upon the death rate. Administrative unity combined with rehabilitation of transport has extended the scope of food distribution so that local famines can be kept within narrower bounds than heretofore. Moreover, the Chinese Communist regime has devoted a great deal of attention to flood control, which, to the extent that it proves successful, is likely to contribute to famine control.

The very character of the regime, its goals, and its commitments to the effective and comprehensive control of all segments of the population, to military prowess, and to industrialization compel it to institute a public health program of some dimensions. Under conditions such as prevail in China, even primitive, rudimentary, and inexpensive measures can go far in checking epidemics and disease. Thus, the regime embarked on a series of nation-wide campaigns for cleanliness and disease control, while the anti-American, bacterial warfare hoax has been effectively utilized to propagate domestic bacteria controls. People were induced to enter fly-catching competitions, with prizes being awarded to those bringing in the largest number of flies.

In view of all of the aforementioned considerations, it is most probable that there has already been some decline in the death rate, and that, barring a civil conflict or external adventures of major proportions, the reduction in death rate is likely to be accelerated. This conclusion is reinforced by the experience of other countries. Thus, the death rate is estimated to have declined by about 30 per cent in India between 1920 and 1940; by 20 per cent in Egypt between 1940 and 1949; by 26 per cent in Mexico between 1940 and 1950; and by 45 per cent in Ceylon between 1939 and 1951.[46]

At the same time, birth rates in all of these countries remained approximately stationary at a very high level. One may expect the same general relationship to prevail in China as well—at least for the decade ahead—since the complex of cultural, social and economic forces which influence the birth rates is much more resistant to change.

Proceeding on the basis of the considerations outlined above, one may expect the death rate to decline appreciably within a decade, thus yielding a rate of natural increase of about 1.0 to 1.5 per cent a year.*[47] This rate would still be substantially below the Soviet rate of the 1920's and would roughly correspond to current Indian rates.

B. The Role of Agriculture in the Economic Development of Mainland China

Chinese agriculture—and, for that matter, agriculture in most underdeveloped areas—is called upon to foster the process of economic growth in three principal ways: it must serve as a reservoir for an expanding labor force; it must provide for food consumption standards (urban and rural) at levels designed to foster an increasing productivity of labor and the maintenance of political stability; and it must produce a surplus for exports.

The first function can be discharged without too much difficulty under Chinese mainland conditions. At this juncture, there is considerable unemployment not only in the rural sector, but in the urban as well. This urban unemployment and underemployment has been aggravated in recent years by what the Chinese Communist press refers to as "blind migration to the cities." While the factors and forces which induce this migration are somewhat obscure, particularly since government policy frowns upon it, it is more than probable that this exodus is primarily propelled by "push" rather than "pull"; that is, it may indicate a deterioration in rural economic conditions under the impact of government extractions, to the point where at least some elements of the rural population seek escape in the cities. It may also be influenced by a general sense that the regime is

---

*In the light of subsequent evidence, this figure seems much too low for the 1950's when the rate of natural increase may have been 2.0 to 2.5; this may have dropped in recent years under the impact of birth control.

concentrating its constructive efforts on the cities and that prospects there are more promising.

This urban unemployment and underemployment, however, may prove to be only a transitory condition which will gradually disappear as industry expands. Should industrialization proceed at the rates projected in the model (see Table 12), the rising demand for labor could be met out of population growth without reducing the size of the rural labor force. In fact, according to Table 12, the rural labor surplus would actually be augmented unless large tracts of new lands were settled and brought under cultivation.

Unlike the problem of labor, the capacity of agriculture to expand output so as to meet a growing demand for its products is one of the most critical questions facing the regime. With this in mind, some of the salient factors affecting the demand for, and supply of, farm products will be explored below.

(1) Demand

Proceeding from the assumptions underlying our model in Table 12, in order to meet domestic consumer requirements, food production in Communist China would have to increase by about 8 per cent in 1957 and 16 per cent in 1962. This is based specifically on the assumption that, while the per capita urban-rural consumption differential will be maintained, per capita consumption within each sector will remain constant. The findings of the National Sample Survey suggest that in India, urban per capita consumption is 1.6 times that of rural consumption. Of course, this does not mean that the real urban content of living is that much higher than the rural, since part of this differential is due to the higher cost of feeding an urban population, particularly in an economy in which, even in the rural areas, food represents the major item in the household budgets, and in which the transport system is still quite undeveloped. For China, there are no adequate household budget data or other reliable indicators of consumption levels and behavior; however, it may be assumed that this differential is at least as great as in India, and, in view of the much lower railway density per square mile in China, probably even greater.

Agriculture, however, will have to provide not only for domestic requirements but also for exports. Before the war, about 70 to 80 per cent of mainland exports consisted of farm products. At the same time, the mainland was a net importer of rice and wheat, and a net exporter of coarse grains. This situation has changed since the Communist conquest;

while agricultural exports have been maintained at roughly the prewar level, food imports have ceased. Moreover, in 1952 about one million tons of grain—mostly coarse grain—were exported, which thus constituted less than 10 per cent of total exports and close to 1 per cent of mainland grain production.

From the model in Table 12, it is possible to calculate certain hypothetical levels of import requirements for the last year of the current Five-Year Plan, 1957, and for 1962. These computations would tend to indicate that to sustain the projected rate of industrial and aggregate growth, imports would have to rise to about U.S. $1.6 billion (1952 imports were roughly around U.S. $1 billion) in 1957, and to about U.S. $2.5 billion by 1962. These estimates are based on the following assumptions:

(*a*) That about 60 percent of total gross investment will be in industry and transport, as indicated by the 1953 and 1954 investment budget allocations (see Table 8).

(*b*) That 25 per cent of this industrial and transport investment will be in electric motors, generators, transformers, machine tools, and complex equipment of varying kinds which cannot be manufactured in China and must thus be imported. This percentage is based on U.S. capital coefficients for 1947[48] with some qualitative adjustments for Chinese conditions.

(*c*) That, *pari-passu,* with increases in industrial production, raw material requirements will rise.

On the basis of these assumptions, capital goods and raw material imports alone would have to be almost U.S. $1.4 billion in 1962. To this must be added imports of military equipment and some consumer goods. However, since there should be some raw material savings owing to expanding domestic production, and since 25 per cent as the import component of capital formation may be too high, a total import estimate of U.S. $1.6 billion and $2.5 billion, respectively, may not be unreasonable.

Obviously, a large share of these imports will have to be paid for with agricultural exports. It is most unlikely that even the increased production of minerals such as coal, iron ore, tungsten, molybdenum, antimony, and others envisaged in Chinese Communist plans would be sufficient not only to maintain, but to raise, the proportion of non-farm exports. Thus, assuming that the ratio of agricultural and non-agricultural exports remains

TABLE 8

Chinese Communist Government Budgets, 1953–1954
(in trillion JMP)

	1953 Budget	1953 Actual	1954 Budget
Expenditures:			
Military	53.3		52.7
Government administration	23.8	95.9	
Other	3.6		46.9
Economic construction:	103.5	86.0	113.2
Industrial enterprises under state budget:	47.6	42.9	54.1
Heavy industry			42.4
Light industry			11.7
Agriculture, forestry, water conservation	11.8	11.3	11.9
Trade	4.4	9.9	12.8
Transport	14.8	12.4	17.6
Other	24.8	9.4	16.7
Cultural construction	34.8	32.0	36.7
Total	218.0	213.9	249.5
Revenues:			
Agricultural tax in kind	27.7[a]	25.7[a]	25.7[a]
Taxes from industry and trade	87.5	92.5	104.4
Receipts from government enterprises	70.0	75.4	83.3
Other	11.9	6.4	4.6
Total	195.1	200.0	218.1
Deficit	22.9	13.8	31.4
Proceeds from special levies, bond issues, note issues, and other types of deficit financing	12.4	30.7	13.8
Carry-over	26.0	26.0	42.8
Cash balance	15.5	42.8	25.2

[a]Since the price of tax grain is not varied from year to year, the constancy of tax revenue indicates that the quantity levied remains unchanged. The differential between the price of tax grain and the market price accrues to the state trading companies and thus appears under "Receipts from government enterprises."

Source: Report of Minister of Finance Teng Hsiao-p'ing on the 1954 State Budget at the 31st Meeting of the Central People's Government Council, held on June 16 and 17, 1954, in *New China News Agency Daily Bulletin,* Supplement No. 204, London, June 24, 1954.

constant, the volume of agricultural exports would have to rise from about U.S. $700 million in 1952 to $1,120 million in 1957, and $1,960 million in 1962; that is, an increase of about 60 per cent and 180 per cent, respectively. Actually, this may be reduced somewhat by Soviet economic assistance; assuming such aid to be equivalent to about U.S. $130 million,[49] farm exports may be projected, under these formal assumptions, as U.S. $1,030 million and $1,800 million, respectively.

The share of cereals in this agricultural export total will depend upon the success attained by the government in increasing the output and collection of grain and upon the availability of other farm products. On the basis of present indications, however, cereals are not likely to play a major role in the export trade.

In order to meet this growing export demand and to maintain per capita food consumption standards in the urban and rural areas, the aggregate net product of agriculture would have to be raised from an estimated U.S. $12 billion in 1952 to $13.3 billion in 1957 and $15.0 billion in 1962.[50] This would mean an increase of approximately 11 per cent and 25 per cent, respectively.

(2) Supply Prospects

The total cultivated area of mainland China may be estimated as 240–250 million acres,[51] which in 1952 yielded an estimated net product of about U.S. $12 billion or U.S. $48 per acre.* This yield is attained with very small inputs of capital and a tremendous expenditure of labor. In this intensive, at times almost garden-type, agriculture, the Chinese peasant has shown admirable ingenuity in maintaining the fertility of the soil. He has accomplished this without a system of crop rotation, and has done this in the south on land which has produced two rice harvests for centuries.[52] Using these age-old practices, he obtains much higher rice and wheat yields than the Indian peasant and, to some extent, even the farmer of Meiji Japan. However, he has probably pushed these practices to the limit, so that further increases in yields will have to depend upon the introduction of modern farm technology.

In the following, an attempt will be made to explore the technical possibilities for increasing farm output, both through extension of the cultivated areas and through increases in per acre productivity, as well as some of the economic and institutional obstacles which may impede or limit the realization of these possibilities.

The most promising areas for new land settlement are found in northern Manchuria, where, according to varying estimates, from 20 to 30 million acres may be brought under cultivation. This is a dry-farming,

---

*In terms of purchasing power equivalents. This is almost certainly a serious understatement.

steppe-like region close to the northern limits of the wheat belt. Thus, methods of cultivation would have to be extensive, and unit yields may be expected to be comparatively low; at the same time, owing to the rigors of the climate, large annual fluctuations in output may be anticipated. The resource costs of reclaiming this land are probably fairly high, particularly if one considers that all external economies—roads, housing, schools, structures for the state apparatus and the party, power and other facilities—would need to be newly constructed. Therefore, it may be considered most unlikely that new land settlement on such a large scale is likely to be undertaken within the next five or ten years. At the same time, however, the new regime has already reclaimed some land in that area, and probably will continue to do so on a modest scale. From the regime's point of view, this not only provides an opportunity for expanding agricultural output, but also for establishing state and collective farms in a setting where institutional resistances are minimal.[53]

There are also some opportunities for increasing the cultivated land area in a few of the old settled regions of China. For instance, it has been estimated that the wheat acreage in northern and central China can be increased by close to 10 million acres, while cotton acreage may be extended in the Yellow and Huai river valleys.[54] Provided that water conservation projects currently in progress actually lead to improved flood control in the future, these acreage extensions could probably be accomplished more easily and at much lower cost than those in Manchuria.

Buck's sample surveys show that almost 25 million acres of farm land are occupied by graves, ancestral shrines, and the like, and that an unknown, but considerable, area is taken up by uncultivated strips separating the small land fragments belonging to different farmers. Of course, the institutional obstacles to bringing this land under cultivation are enormous. It is most doubtful that it could be accomplished without far-reaching collectivization. However, should the Chinese Communists seriously pursue their objective of bringing about one-half of the peasant households into producers' cooperatives by 1957,[55] they will have made considerable progress in consolidating farm holdings and eliminating these uncultivated strips.

On the basis of this brief survey, and assuming that the regime will undertake land development only where this can be accomplished with inputs of underemployed labor and relatively little capital, it may be concluded that possibly about 15 million acres of currently uncultivated land may be brought under the plow within the next five to ten years. This would mean roughly a 6 per cent increase in the land cropped.*

Judging by the Japanese experience, and taking account of the conditions just analyzed, if farm production is to be increased, major reliance will have to be placed upon raising unit yields. It may be interesting to note in this connection that in Japan average rice yields increased by about 20 per cent in the decade between 1880 and 1890. Similarly, the combined unit yield of six major crops rose by about 50 per cent in the four decades between 1880 and 1920.[56] A major part of this rise was accomplished through increasing applications of commercial fertilizer. Thus, by 1936, 3.4 million tons of chemical fertilizer were applied in Japan, on a crop area about 1/16 that of mainland China, as compared with only about 200,000 tons applied to the latter.[57]

The Chinese National Agricultural Research Bureau conducted experiments before the war which indicated that in order to raise unit crop yields by about 25 per cent, applications of 6,500,000 tons of ammonium sulphate, 3,800,000 tons of calcium superphosphate, and 300,000 tons of potassium sulphate would be required. As of 1943–1944, the ammonium sulphate capacity on the mainland was about 320,000 tons, practically all of it concentrated in Manchuria. Most of this was exported to Japan before the war, but is now retained in China, so that, according to official Communist sources, about 350,000 tons were consumed in 1952. However, while this indicates an increase over prewar consumption, it still represents very small applications indeed.

Since domestic fertilizer capacity is so small, practically all of it would have to be imported. Thus, if the experimental increases in yield are to be attained, China will have to spend about U.S. $800 million on imports of ammonium sulphate alone (in 1952 prices); that is, about three-fourths of her total 1952 import value. Obviously, this is beyond the realm of reasonable expectation for a long time to come. At the same time, expansion of domestic productive facilities to anything approaching required levels seems most improbable within five to ten years, in view of high initial capital costs and high electric power requirements in current operations. Raising chemical fertilizer applications to levels where they would significantly affect unit yields would therefore be very expensive,

---

*In fact it would seem that the area cultivated has not increased significantly, if at all, since the early 1950's.

and would force Chinese Communist policy-makers to sacrifice many of their other industrial objectives.*

However, there are other possible ways of increasing unit yields in agriculture, even though these are likely to produce results more slowly. The most notable is, of course, improved water conservation; that is, better flood control, extension of irrigated areas, and better use of water for irrigation. This is a field to which the Communists are devoting most attention, particularly since it can be largely affected through mass applications of labor underemployed in agriculture. These efforts will undoubtedly have some effect on agricultural output within the next five or ten years. For instance, in 1949, a particularly bad year, about 20 million acres were flooded; at the same time, the average annual flooded area of the major river basins may be estimated as about 7 million acres.[58] As was indicated earlier, these floods and droughts have been the major causes of famine throughout Chinese history.

Additional improvements could be expected from other comparatively capital-cheap measures such as better seed selection, introduction of new strains and varieties, plant and animal disease and pest control, grassland and forage crop improvements in the upland areas, and afforestation. However, some of these measures are of a rather long-term character, while all of them require the organization of a capable and efficient network of farm extension services. The Communists are attempting all of these measures to some extent. They are, however, seriously handicapped by an acute shortage of technically qualified cadres.

Therefore, combining the possibilities of expanding acreage and raising yields within the technical and economic limitations discussed above, and abstracting for a moment from possible effects of collectivization, it would seem most unlikely that farm output in China could be raised by more than 10 per cent within five years and a maximum of 20 per cent in a decade.† This means that in terms of purely technical and economic

---

*In fact a substantial expansion in domestic manufacture and imports of chemical fertilizer was attained during the 1960's, so that total chemical fertilizer supply may by 1972 be around 20 to 25 million tons. This means that while rapid growth in fertilizer applications was not achieved in 5 to 10 years, it was attained in twenty years. This could only be done as projected above by shifting industrial priorities in the 1960's as compared to the 1950's.

†In fact grain production rose by 10 to 15 per cent between 1952 and 1957. On the other hand, a 20 per cent rise was not attained until 1964, i.e., twelve years later.

considerations, even within the context of current rates of agricultural investment, it would be difficult for increases in output to keep pace with rising requirements posed by urbanization and exports. In these terms, then, the question of agricultural development will revolve to a large extent upon government price, marketing, and land policies, and the Chinese peasant's reaction to them.

Official Chinese Communist policy is openly and unequivocally based upon collectivization as a definite goal which is to be attained gradually and without the loss of output that accompanied the Soviet experience and the stagnation of output that has occurred in Eastern Europe. With this in mind, the regime has evolved a series of transitional forms of farm organization, each involving a more advanced form of "cooperation." A mutual aid team, the most rudimentary type of agricultural cooperative, is essentially based on a more or less temporary pooling or exchange of labor, with the individual farm operator retaining at least theoretical control over his production, consumption, and sales (after taxes). However, usually at least one member of the mutual aid team belongs to the Communist cadre, the function of which is to show the peasants the advantages of more advanced forms of cooperation. This "education" is combined with economic incentives, disincentives, and pressures so as to induce the peasants to form producers' cooperatives, which are collectives in fact, if not in name. The cooperatives involve pooling not only of labor, but of tools and also call for joint cultivation and planning of production, with distribution of returns based on a complicated system of weights for labor and land input, with high premiums on the former, and low premiums on the latter. Yet, in these producers' cooperatives, the peasant theoretically retains his individual right of ownership of land, and his right to withdraw at any time. In the next stage, the collective, even these theoretical rights are abolished.[59]

In effect, this strategy of collectivization bears a strong family resemblance to the methods tried and used in the East European satellites. The Chinese have, however, contributed to the "storehouse of this strategy" by using the mutual aid team as their point of departure; that is, a form rooted in Chinese tradition, but not generally applied in Eastern Europe.

In appraising the possibilities for collectivization, it should be noted that the Chinese system of farming does not *per se* present any insurmountable or inherent obstacles. There is no question that rice culture presents very serious barriers to mechanization, but collectivization is perfectly feasible without mechanization. Under conditions where there are still large pools of unemployed and underemployed labor, such as in China, its principal function is to give the state more direct access to the farm produce. It was coupled with mechanization in the Soviet Union because industrialization proceeded so rapidly that the demand for urban labor could not be met without introduction of labor-saving technology in agriculture. Thus, the barriers to collectivization in China are not primarily technical but, rather, cultural and institutional.

By 1953, close to half of the peasant households were organized into mutual aid teams and about 273,000 households were organized into 14,000 producers' cooperatives. By 1957, the regime plans to encompass about half of all farm households in such cooperatives.[60]

In the fall of 1953, this stepped-up drive toward collectivization was combined with a complete reorganization of the system of grain collections, and the introduction of rationing.[61] The new system provides for compulsory deliveries of grain to the state—over and above the tax grain—at fixed prices. Thus, it is modeled after the East European system of collections, a system that has plagued the satellites since its inception. Generally, the growing similarities between Chinese and satellite economic policies are striking.

It is therefore quite clear that the regime is not prepared to place primary reliance upon market incentives for expanding agricultural output. This would not only require a diversion of investment resources to consumers' goods production as incentives, but would also commit the regime to accepting a private market economy over the face of agricultural China, with all the relaxation of political control and perpetuation of traditional peasant attitudes that this would entail.

The question still remains, however, as to what is likely to be the impact of these collectivization and collection measures upon the structure of incentives in the countryside, both in and out of the collectives or producers' cooperatives. Will the satellite experience repeat itself, where such serious disincentives were set in motion that despite considerable investments in agriculture, farm output still lags below average prewar levels?[62]

One may also ask oneself whether this problem has any relevance at all in the Chinese cultural setting. Judging by past experience, this question can be answered in the affirmative: Chinese peasants seem definitely responsive to positive price and income inducements. This was demonstrated, for instance, by the effectiveness of some of the Chinese Communist policy measures, such as the raising of the cotton-grain ratio as a means of expanding cotton production. What about disincentives? In this respect, the situation may be much more complex.

For agriculture in the process of gradual and "peaceful" collectivization one might distinguish three effects, which may be termed the expectations effect, the tensions effect, and the disruption effect. Thus, the very fact of vigorous collectivization propaganda, pressure, and targets for organization of producers' cooperatives is likely to set in motion a chain of expectations which will tend to discourage the peasant from making long-term improvements on his farm. Similarly, discriminatory measures directed against "rich peasants" may actually induce the comparatively more capable and prosperous farming elements to curb their output and incomes so as to avoid being placed in this undesirable category.

At the same time, the drive toward collectivization, compulsory grain deliveries, high tax rates, and a constant harassment of the "rich peasants" are almost certainly bound to lead to a state of more or less permanent tension in the countryside. In turn, this state of tension may seriously inhibit that cooperation between farmers and technical cadres (government extension agents) which would be required to introduce better practices and modern technology.

Finally, the very process of collectivization cannot help but entail at least some measure of disruption. The actual degree of disruption would, of course, depend upon the manner and the speed of execution; if it is carried out quite slowly, the disruptive effects may be minimal and transitory.

Thus, the cumulative impact of these three effects upon agricultural production may be considered as negative, in the sense that they all would tend to discourage the farmer from adopting and instituting those measures that might enable him to raise his output. However, in the case of the disruptive effect, the consequences could easily lead to an actual decline in production.

On the other hand, high rates of net resource transfer out of agriculture may, under certain conditions, have just the opposite effect. Thus, a Chinese peasant who lives close to the margin of subsistence will tend to bend every effort to produce enough to meet his own needs and those of his family. In these terms, onerous extractions by the state may actually force him to increase output, to the extent that this is possible within the means at his disposal, so as to satisfy his own demands as well as those of the state.

On balance, this analysis indicates that current and prospective agricultural policies in Communist China may tend to undercut the very measures which would make it possible to raise farm output. Therefore, unless these policies are reversed or relaxed, it is unlikely that agricultural production could be raised by the 10 to 20 per cent projected above on the basis of purely technical and economic considerations. However, if this output lags, then the rising requirements imposed by growth of population, urbanization, and exports could not all be met simultaneously. In such a case, given the over-all character and objectives of Chinese Communist policy, the regime may be expected to bend every effort to transfer the principal burden of this shortfall to the countryside.

Under Soviet or Soviet-type institutional conditions, a lag in agricultural development need not present insurmountable barriers to industrialization and economic growth. For instance, at the height of the collectivization drive in 1930 and 1931, when farmers were slaughtering their cattle and agricultural production was seriously disrupted, the Soviet Union dumped about 5 million tons of grain on the world market. Thus, at a time when grain production was abnormally low, exports from the Soviet Union were higher than during any other interwar year. Since the regime had the will and capacity to enforce a high rate of extraction from the countryside, these grain exports fulfilled a very important function at a critical juncture in the Soviet industrialization program; they enabled the Soviet Union to import the capital goods for the first Five-Year Plan. To be sure, this level of exports could not be maintained indefinitely in the face of declining production. However, this example serves to illustrate the principle—perhaps in its most extreme form—that in a Communist society high rates of resource transfer out of agriculture can be maintained in the face of stagnating production and, in the short run, even in the face of declining production. Actually, at any given level of output, the rate of net resource transfer out of agriculture is largely limited by the administrative capacity, degree of ruthlessness, and political stability of the regime.

(3) The Five-Year Plan

It is a curious fact that despite the official announcement of a Five-Year Plan in 1953, the plan itself has not been published thus far.[63] The launching of the plan was followed only by the publication of annual targets for the first year, i.e., 1953,[64] and by the definition of certain general goals in an article in Pravda published in Moscow on September 28, 1953.

Actually, it is rather doubtful that China's mainland economy is operating within the framework of a comprehensive and total economic plan of the Soviet type. It is more likely that annual targets are being fixed in terms of a broad set of five-year objectives, but without an attempt at detailed planning. Thus, these plans may be viewed—to use Stalin's terminology—as "prognosis, guess-plans which bind nobody,"[65] rather than plans based on a system of "balanced estimates" or definite inter-industry relationships.

Within this context, one must view the planning process in Communist China as evolving gradually from a series of loosely coordinated plans into a national plan. This process is paralleled by a gradual shift from primary reliance upon indirect controls to increasingly direct controls. In a country such as China, with only a partially monetized rural sector, and with an underdeveloped bureaucratic and economic control apparatus, the task of planning resource use and resource allocation is seriously handicapped and greatly complicated. It is for this reason that, as the scope of planning is widened and deepened, technical and administrative bottlenecks are becoming more serious, bottlenecks which Soviet advisers are called upon to resolve.

In the early days of their rule, when their principal task consisted of organizing the state apparatus and the economy, the Chinese Communists drew on their own past experience, instituting policies of their own making. However, this began to change as they gradually entered into the development and industrialization phase of their program, when they faced problems which were unfamiliar and therefore required Soviet technical assistance in planning and execution.

Viewed in these terms, 1953 may be considered as an experimental and preparatory year in mainland China. For instance, production targets were revised three times during the year; at first they were sharply curtailed, but toward the end of the year many of the cuts were partially restored.[66] One generally gets the impression of a considerable measure of groping, uncertainty, and confusion during this first planning year. This may have been a function of inadequate organization, lack of planning experience and skills, and, most important of all, of a failure to come to an economic aid agreement with the USSR until the middle of the year.

Once the regime knew what it could expect from the Soviet Union, it apparently felt ready to embark upon a new phase of "austerity" and "bitter struggle." This phase was marked by a general acceleration in the tempo of nationalization and collectivization within the framework of the new "general line of the state."[67] In the course of this new drive, the rate of resource mobilization is being stepped up, as illustrated by the new compulsory grain delivery scheme and the launching of another bond drive.[68]

Inadequate planning and failure to attain overambitious goals are also reflected in the government expenditure pattern, as shown in Table 8. Thus, total 1953 outlay was somewhat lower than budgeted, and while investment fell almost 20 per cent short of the goal, military expenditures substantially exceeded budgeted amounts. In appraising the level of military expenditures, it is important to note that these may be financed partly through long-term lend-lease arrangements between the Soviet Union and Communist China, over and above the economic assistance rendered.

After a series of protracted negotiations that lasted almost a year, a Sino-Soviet economic aid agreement was finally announced in September 1953. The announcements referred only to 141 "enterprises"—50 of which were already under way—that were to be rehabilitated or newly constructed with Soviet aid. The bulk of these "enterprises" are in the field of electric power generation, mining, chemicals, and producers' goods industries, particularly metals and engineering; however, they also include some fertilizer and textile plants.[69]

On the other hand, information on the total value of aid is withheld. This is particularly strange in view of the fact that no secret was made of Soviet and Communist Chinese aid to North Korea and of the 1950 Sino-Soviet aid agreement. On the contrary, the U.S. $300 million granted to China over a five-year period was hailed as an act of great generosity. These circumstances, combined with the protracted nature of the negotiations, would tend to suggest that the level of aid projected may not be very high.

There have been unconfirmed reports that the agreement provides for a ten-year aid program totaling U.S. $1 billion.[70] According to this version, the agreement is retroactive to 1950 and thus includes the 300 million dollars originally granted. If this is correct, then the annual level of aid for the 1954–1959 period can be estimated as U.S. $117 million, i.e., an amount which, while representing close to a doubling of the 1950–1953 rate of aid, is still very modest by United States standards. Over and above this, the Soviet Union advanced an additional 520 million rubles within the context of more recent Sino-Soviet arrangements concluded in October 1954.[71] While it is not quite clear for what period this new loan is granted, the general context of agreements would suggest that it also may run through 1959. This would involve an annual level of additional aid of about U.S. $25 million, at the official rate of exchange. On this basis then, Soviet economic assistance to China may be currently estimated at a maximum of U.S. $142 million; however, allowing for gross overvaluation of the ruble, it probably is actually less than that.

According to the aforementioned *PRAVDA* article, part of this Soviet aid will be used to achieve the production targets given in Table 9.

Should these targets be met, mainland China's crude steel capacity would exceed the current output of Canada, Belgium, and the other small countries of Europe, but would still lag considerably behind the levels attained in Japan during the 1930's. At the same time, the projected levels of steel output would be roughly equivalent to that of the Soviet Union in 1928.[72]

On the basis of United States and Latin American investment costs, to expand mainland China's crude and finished steel output to the levels

TABLE 9

Selected Industrial Production Targets for Communist China*

Product	Units	Output 1952	Target Output[a]	Index 1952 = 100
Crude steel	thousand MT	1,215	4,860	400
Rolled steel	thousand MT	740	1,850	250
Coal	thousand MT	53,000	84,800	160
Electric power	million KWH	5,700	11,000	200
Mining equipment	n.a.	n.a.	n.a.	200
Metal-cutting machinery	n.a.	n.a.	n.a.	350

*These figures given here for 1952 output are appreciably lower than those in Table 10, chapter 5. Since the data shown here are based on much more limited information available in the early years and is drawn from *PRAVDA*, where it appeared in a context designed to show the strides that will be made, the later figures of Table 10, chapter 5, should be used.
[a]No exact date is given; reference is made either to the last year of the plan, 1957, or to the year when the current aid agreement expires, i.e., 1959.
Source: PRAVDA, September 28, 1953, Table III.

planned would call for an aggregate investment of about U.S. $600 to $900 million, depending upon the size of the newly built mills.[73] However, construction labor costs would undoubtedly be lower in China than in the United States, but this may be counterbalanced, at least to some extent, by lower productivity.

A similar calculus for electric power plants would indicate that to expand generating capacity up to the planned levels would involve a total investment of about U.S. $340 million. This is based on U.S. investment cost per kw of installed thermal capacity of U.S. $120.[74]

It should be clearly borne in mind that all of these estimates can represent no more than the crudest of approximations to the actual investment costs in China. This is even more true in the case of power than of steel, since the former does not take account of the vastly different investment cost structure in hydroelectric power construction.

Thus, the total capital cost of new steel mill and power plant production may be estimated as about U.S. $1 billion. According to the stated plans, these projects are to be completed before 1959; in that case, they would absorb about 10 per cent of total industrial investment resources projected in Table 12 for 1953–1958. It may be assumed that about one-third of this total investment would have to be imported from the Soviet Union,[75] which would mean that about half of the estimated Soviet economic aid for this period would be channeled into expansion of power and steel production.

On the basis of these calculations and assumptions, this rate of growth would not seem to lie beyond the resource capabilities of the Chinese economy.

The only specific Five-Year production target disclosed by official Chinese Communist sources is that which calls for a 30 per cent increase in annual grain output between 1953 and 1957. Unlike the industrial goals analyzed above, this target appears to be quite unrealistic, particularly if it is appraised against the background of agricultural investment, marketing, and land policies discussed in Section B above. A 30 per cent increase in crop production over a huge land area such as mainland China, where the opportunities for bringing new areas under cultivation are very narrowly circumscribed, and where the possibilities for raising fertilizer consumption are also quite limited, would be most extraordinary indeed. As was indicated in Section B, it is most unlikely that given favorable farmer incentive conditions, crop production could be raised by more than 10 per cent within five years. However, in the face of current and prospective agricultural policies, the disincentives may become strong enough to block or seriously impede any increase in farm output.

IV. Prospects for Economic Growth: A Model

Regardless of whether a detailed Five-Year Plan is in operation or not, there is in Communist China every indication of a determined, relentless, and massive effort to pursue a program of industrial expansion. The rapid rate of recovery, the restructuring of the institutional framework, the possession of an industrial base in Manchuria, the termination of hostilities in Korea, and, above all, the application of political and social power to the mobilization of resources in the hands of the state are all factors that have enabled the regime to raise the rate and level of investment considerably above that of the past. At the same time, the regime is mobilizing not only capital, but technique and entrepreneurship as well. In essence, the Chinese economy—after being more or less stationary for centuries, with only erratic and partial spurts of growth in recent decades—seems to be entering a self-sustaining growth process.

Barring another world war or a major agricultural crisis in China, the long-run question before us is not whether the Chinese economy will grow at all, but whether the rate of growth will be sufficiently rapid so that the forces of the industrial revolution will be in a position to defeat the Malthusian counterrevolution. Given the previously discussed conditions and limitations, how rapidly may industrialization be expected to proceed? Obviously, these questions can only be answered conditionally and hypothetically. However, before approaching this problem, it may be well to take a schematic look at the "size" and "structure" of the Chinese mainland economy in 1952, which may be considered as the point of departure for the upward climb.

The data in Table 10 are based on some quite tentative and crude calculations and are, therefore, intended merely as indications of approximate orders of magnitude rather than as actual estimates.

In many respects, this is a pattern that is fairly typical for many underdeveloped areas. However, it exhibits several unique characteristics, the most outstanding of which is the large share mobilized by the government and appropriated for its own use. This is, of course, but another indication of the degree to which the Chinese economy had been nationalized by 1952. As a result, this share is higher than in any other country

TABLE 10

Gross National Product and Its Composition in 1952*

By Sector	Product (in per cent)	By Use	Expenditure (in per cent)
Agriculture	40	Consumption of households	73
Small-scale and rural		Communal services	4
industry	15	Government administration	4
Factory industry and			
mining	7	Military outlays	7
Trade and transport	24	Investment	12
Dwelling service	4		
Government and other			
services	10		
Total: in per cent	100		100
in billions of			
U.S. dollars	30.0		30.0

*The shares given in this table differ from those presented in Table 9 of chapter 5. The figures given on this page are based on my early studies of the Chinese economy. They represent crude orders of magnitude, antedate the research and systematic compilation of national income estimates, and are based on very limited information available in the early 1950's. These early figures understate the weight of agriculture and overstate the share of transport and trade. Similar discrepancies arise on the expenditure side with household consumption somewhat overstated and investment understated.

in Asia. Even more important in this context is the high rate of investment as compared with that in other underdeveloped countries. For example, the rate of investment in India was estimated at about 8 per cent in 1949–1950.[76]

The investment share given above is based on government budget figures in Table 8. Thus, it leaves private investment out of account. By 1952, such investment was probably negligible in the urban sector; but in the rural sector there was undoubtedly some non-monetary investment. Owing to the very character of government budgeting and accounting, an extremely broad concept of investment is used in Communist China. As a matter of fact, the term officially applied is expenditures on "economic construction"; these include outlays both on fixed and on working capital, including, for instance, raw material and fertilizer credits.*

---

*This statement was based on a misunderstanding of these concepts as used in Chinese national accounting practice at the time. We now know that the Chinese term for investment is "capital construction," while "economic construction" refers to all budgetary outlays on the economy.

According to aforementioned budget figures, investment resources were allocated as shown in Table 11.

Assuming that the Chinese follow Soviet budget practice, one may legitimately surmise that the non-specified projects are partly military in character; however, they may also include investments in government overhead, social and cultural services, and a wide miscellany of small projects. On a more general plane, it is interesting to note the striking similarities in the Soviet and Chinese patterns of investment allocation, with the marked emphasis upon, and high priority accorded to, producers' goods industries in both cases. Thus, while 45 to 50 per cent of total investment was allocated to industry in both countries, the bulk of this—slightly over 80 per cent in the USSR, and somewhat under 80 per cent in China— was devoted to the expansion of the producers' goods branches. At the same time, it seems that agriculture in China is kept on an even shorter investment ration than in the Soviet Union, with only 10 to 13 per cent of the investment allocated to the former as compared with 19 per cent in the latter. This, however, may be largely due to the fact that rapid collectivization, accompanied by a large loss of livestock, forced a speedy substitution of machines for animals and labor in Soviet agriculture.[77]

TABLE 11

Allocation of Investment Resources, 1953–1954*

(in per cent)

	1953		1954
	Budget	Actual	Budget
Industry, including mining, manufacturing, and electric power	46.0	49.9	47.8
Agriculture, forestry, and water conservation	11.4	13.2	10.5
Railway and communications	14.3	14.5	15.5
Trade and banking	4.3	11.5	11.3
Non-specified projects	24.0	10.9	14.9

*The 1953 data given here diverge from those shown in Table 1 of chapter 8. The coverage of the latter are more comprehensive so that these two sets of figures are not fully comparable. Moreover, chapter 8 is based on more detailed and complete information.

Heretofore our analysis of the dynamics of economic growth in Communist China has been confined to an examination of prospects in terms of specific factors and sectors, such as resource endowments, agricultural policies, planning practices, and investment patterns. On the other hand, the model in Table 12 attempts to combine these interrelated elements into a projection of the potentialities for aggregate and industrial growth in mainland China. Proceeding from the 1952 estimates of population, gross national product and expenditure, and published government budget data on levels and patterns of investment, a hypothetical growth model was constructed as follows:

(1) Increments in national product and industrial output were treated as a function of aggregate and industrial investment, respectively. It was thus assumed that for every 3.5 units of net investment made during one year, national product would increase by one unit during the following year (i.e., that the incremental capital-output ratio would be 3.5:1 with a one-year investment lag). Similarly, it was assumed that for every unit increase in industrial output, four units of investment would be required; and that the currently prevailing investment share for industry—about 45 per cent—would be maintained throughout the decade.

(2) Personal consumption was treated as a function of population growth and urbanization; specifically, it was assumed that (*a*) population would grow at a rate of 1.25 per annum; (*b*) urbanization would be a function of the rate of industrial growth, with urban population expanding at one-quarter of the industrial rate; and (*c*) starting with a 1952 per capita rural-urban consumption ratio of 1:1.8 per capita consumption levels in each sector would remain constant.

(3) Government consumption was projected on the assumption that the share of gross national product devoted to military expenditure and social overhead for administration and for community services would remain constant.

(4) Investment was derived as a residual, after deducting personal and government consumption from national product.

The choice of an incremental capital-output ratio is a most complex problem, particularly for a country such as China, where there is no sustained development experience to draw upon. At best, the capital-output ratio is a more or less rough-and-ready average which is a product of a host of counteracting tendencies and policies at work in the economy.[78] For purposes of the model in Table 12, this choice was based on

TABLE 12

Model of Economic Growth in Communist China

(in billions of 1952 U.S. Dollars)

Year	Gross Natl. Product Dollars	Gross Natl. Product Index	National Income	Consumption Pers.	Consumption Mil.	Consumption Other Gov't	Consumption Total	Aggregate Investment Gross	Aggregate Investment Net	Industrial Investment Gross	Industrial Investment Net	Industrial Investment Dollars	Industrial Output Index	Population Total	Population Urban	Population Rural (in millions)	Personal Consumption Urban	Personal Consumption Rural	Total Capital Stock at Beginning of Year Old Cap. Remaining	Total Capital Stock at Beginning of Year New Cap. Remaining	Total Capital Stock at Beginning of Year Total	Industrial Capital Stock at Beginning of Year Old Cap. Remaining	Industrial Capital Stock at Beginning of Year New Cap. Remaining	Industrial Capital Stock at Beginning of Year Total
1952	30.0	100.0	28.4	21.9	2.1	2.4	26.4	3.6	2.0	1.6	1.2	2.1	100.0	580	116	464	6.8	15.1	40.0	—	40.0	6.0	—	6.0
1953	30.5	101.7	29.0	22.2	2.1	2.4	26.8	3.7	2.2	1.7	1.3	2.4	114.3	587	120	467	7.0	15.2	38.4	3.6	42.0	5.6	1.6	7.2
1954	31.1	103.7	29.6	22.5	2.2	2.5	27.2	3.9	2.4	1.7	1.4	2.7	128.6	594	124	470	7.3	15.3	36.9	7.3	44.2	5.2	3.3	8.5
1955	31.7	105.7	30.3	22.9	2.2	2.5	27.6	4.0	2.6	1.8	1.5	3.1	147.6	602	128	474	7.5	15.4	35.4	11.2	46.6	4.8	5.0	9.8
1956	32.4	108.0	31.0	23.2	2.3	2.6	28.1	4.3	2.9	1.9	1.6	3.4	161.9	610	132	478	7.7	15.5	34.0	15.2	49.2	4.5	6.9	11.4
1957	33.2	110.7	31.9	23.6	2.3	2.6	28.6	4.6	3.3	2.1	1.8	3.8	180.9	617	136	481	7.9	15.6	32.6	19.5	52.1	4.2	8.8	13.0
1958	34.6	115.3	32.8	24.0	2.4	2.7	29.2	5.4	3.7	2.4	1.8	4.2	200.0	625	140	486	8.2	15.8	31.3	24.1	55.4	3.9	10.9	14.2
1959	35.7	119.0	33.9	24.3	2.5	2.8	29.6	6.0	4.2	2.7	2.0	4.7	223.8	633	144	489	8.4	15.9	30.0	29.5	59.5	3.6	13.3	16.9
1960	36.9	123.0	35.1	24.7	2.6	2.9	30.2	6.7	4.9	3.0	2.2	5.2	247.6	641	148	493	8.7	16.0	28.8	35.5	64.3	3.4	16.0	19.4
1961	38.4	128.0	36.5	25.1	2.7	3.1	30.8	7.6	5.7	3.4	2.5	5.7	271.4	648	151	497	8.9	16.2	27.7	42.2	69.9	3.1	19.0	22.1
1962	40.2	134.0	38.1	25.4	2.8	3.2	31.4	8.7	6.7	3.9	2.9	6.4	304.8	656	155	501	9.1	16.3	26.6	49.8	76.4	2.9	22.4	25.3

an analysis of the Soviet and Japanese growth experience, on the one hand, and on current economic realities and policies in Communist China, on the other. Moreover, our selection was based on the hypothesis that the capital-output ratio is ultimately determined by the resource-population balance, the pattern of investment, and the level of technology and entrepreneurship available in the economy. In other words, the more favorable the population-resource balance, the more advanced the technology and the entrepreneurial skills, and the lower the relative investment share of social overhead and other sectors in which the capital coefficient is high, the lower will tend to be the aggregate incremental ratio.

On the basis of our current state of knowledge concerning national product and capital formation in the USSR between 1928 and 1937, it would seem that the incremental capital-output ratio for that decade was no higher, and possibly lower, than 3.[79] For Japan, there are studies in progress that definitely indicate that Colin Clark's ratios are too high. While there are as yet no reliable estimates of the ratios as such, recently published national product estimates for 1878–1942 show that the rates of growth for 1880–1900 were close to 5 per cent per annum as compared with Clark's estimates of less than 2 per cent.[80] If one accepts the 5 per cent rate, then it is most doubtful that the incremental capital-output ratio could possibly have been higher than 4, or maybe even 3, since this would require a net rate of investment of from 15 to 20 per cent. A 20 per cent rate of investment would seem extraordinary indeed for an economy at that stage of development.

In terms of the factors discussed above, one could expect the incremental capital-output ratio in Communist China to be possibly lower than in Meiji Japan, but higher than in the Soviet Union. The resource-population balance was undoubtedly more favorable in the USSR of 1928, but less propitious in Meiji Japan. The poor quality of Chinese coking coal and iron ore, coupled with the fact that frequently the distance between deposits of these two key raw materials is quite considerable, would tend to raise the capital-output ratio. This may be counterbalanced to some extent by the fact that there may be greater opportunities for utilizing underemployed rural labor for capital formation in China than in the Soviet Union. So far as the level of technology and entrepreneurship is concerned, Communist China may again assume an intermediate position between the two countries; in this respect, China probably has a considerable advantage over Meiji Japan, since it is starting with a relatively larger industrial base and from a more advanced stage of world technological development. On the other hand, the Russia of 1928 was technically and educationally much more advanced than the China of 1952. The rate of literacy, the number of technicians and skilled workers, and the general state of the arts were all higher.

A comparison of the pattern of investment in the three countries yields a less clear-cut conclusion as to the relative magnitudes of the capital-output ratios. China, with a much more underdeveloped transport system than the USSR, seems to be allocating a smaller share of its total invest-ment resources to this sector than the Soviet Union did during 1928–1937. However, the bulk of this railroad development in China is concen-trated in sparsely populated, remote areas where transport returns are bound to be low, and the sectoral capital-output ratios quite high. Owing to its geographic configuration, Japan was less dependent upon highly capital-intensive railroad development. On the other side of the balance sheet, the Soviet Union had to pay relatively more attention than China to the expansion of its electric power facilities, in view of its very small generating capacity in 1928. Housing—another sector with a high incre-mental capital-output ratio—was notoriously neglected in the USSR, and China may be expected to follow suit. It must be noted, however, that opportunities for economizing on housing space through overcrowding may be much more limited in China than they were in Russia. Moreover, while the initial cost of residential construction is undoubtedly lower in China, relative costs of replacement and maintenance may be much higher. However, differences between the patterns of investment allocation in the three countries are not confined to the social overhead sectors. Thus, Meiji Japan concentrated its efforts upon the development of agriculture and of the textile industry, with the latter based to a considerable extent upon small-scale, cottage-type manufacture.[81] In contrast, both the Soviet Union and Communist China seem to accord a considerably lower priority to agricultural development and a much higher priority to the expansion of producers' goods industries. These, of course, would be factors making for a comparatively lower capital-output ratio in Meiji Japan.

On the basis of all of these considerations combined, an aggregate incremental capital-output ratio of 3.5 and an industrial ratio of 4.0 were selected as most reasonable for this first decade of deliberate industrializa-tion in China. The ratios applied in the model were based on net, rather than gross, investment. For this purpose, aggregate and industrial capital stock was estimated for 1952, with net additions to this stock computed on the basis of the following capital consumption allowances:

	1952 Stock	New Stock[a]
	(in per cent per year)	
Aggregate	4.0	2.0
Industrial	7.0	3.5

[a]These rates applied only after 1957, on the assumption that even some of the new capital will have to begin to be replaced after a few years.

The 1952 aggregate capital stock figure is strictly arbitrary, based on an assumed average capital-output ratio of 1.33. However, the industrial stock figure is based on a pre-war estimate for China proper and a 1945 estimate for Manchuria, both converted into 1952 prices.[82]

As was indicated above, the model in Table 12 is based on the assumption that population will grow at an aggregate rate of 1.25 per cent a year. However, owing to rural-urban migration under the impact of industrial and other closely related demands for labor, urban population will grow at a much more rapid rate than rural. An examination of Japanese and Soviet rates of urbanization,[83] indicates that, in the first case, roughly a trebling in industrial output was accompanied by a doubling in the urban population; in the second case, a doubling in urban population was paralleled by a quadrupling in industrial production. Given the respective character of Japanese and Soviet economic development, this is not at all surprising. The much greater capital intensity of the Soviet process of economic growth, with its heavy emphasis upon expansion of producers' goods industries, naturally meant that the urban demand for labor per unit of output was lower than in Japan, where textiles and other light industries played a much greater role. On the basis of these considerations, it was assumed that urbanization in China would proceed at a rate that would be closer to the Soviet than the Japanese tempo. This assumption is based on the fact that the Chinese Communist regime seems to place much greater emphasis upon the development of heavy industry than the Japanese did in the first decades following the Meiji restoration. Recent evidence seems to indicate that Chinese Communist planners are allocating roughly the same share of investment resources to the expansion of heavy industry as the Soviet Union did during the period of its first two Five-Year Plans.[84]

The level of aggregate consumption will be in part a function of this urbanization, since available evidence would tend to indicate that standards of consumption are higher in the cities than in the countryside. To this must be added the fact that in a largely pre-industrial society the resource costs of maintaining a person in the city are higher than in the countryside. Therefore, proceeding from Indian data on rural-urban consumption ratios and allowing for differences in transport costs and direction of net resource flows in the two countries, it was assumed that urban consumption in China would be 1.8 times the rural average.

Moreover, it was assumed that government consumption would increase at a more rapid rate than personal consumption, i.e., it would expand at the same rate as gross national product. This assumption is based on the hypothesis that maintenance and expansion of the state apparatus to assure the degree of control desired and required by the regime for resource mobilization and allocation and for non-economic ends will necessarily involve increasing unit costs. Moreover, with the high priorities assigned to modernizing and reequipping the army, unit costs of maintaining a large standing army are also likely to rise.

In appraising the computations in Table 12, it should be noted that this type of model is highly sensitive, so that even a comparatively small change in assumptions may yield vastly different results. Thus, should all variables such as population growth, the rate of urbanization, the rural-urban consumption differential, and the incremental capital-output ratio be higher, the rate of growth would of course be greatly reduced. On the other hand, should some or all of these variables be lower, significantly higher rates of growth than those postulated would result. Our analysis is focused on what may be considered as the intermediate model, based on assumptions which, in terms of current Chinese realities, evaluated against the background of Japanese and Soviet experience, seemed to be the most plausible ones. One of the most serious limitations of this model is that the assumptions on which it is based are not changed. As a result, the model tends to become less and less applicable as the projections are carried further into the future.

Bearing these limitations in mind, on the basis of these assumptions the Chinese Communist economy may be expected to grow at a rate of less than 2 per cent a year at the beginning, a rate which under the cumulative impact of the growth process would be stepped up to almost 5 per cent a year by the end of the decade. Thus, toward the latter half of this period, the Chinese economy would be expanding at a rate roughly corresponding to that of Meiji Japan, but lagging appreciably behind the Soviet tempo of

1928–1937.*[85] Industrial output in China would, however, be growing so rapidly that it would be trebled during the decade, and its share in gross national product would be doubled. This rapid pace of industrial growth would be due to the large additions of new plant and equipment to a very modest industrial base. However, precisely because such a large share of investment is devoted to industry while industry's share in gross national product is small (7 per cent in 1952), the aggregate rate of growth would be relatively slow during the first years, despite the rapid tempo of industrial expansion. This situation changes only in later years, as industry begins to have a greater weight in the economy as a whole.

One of the central elements in this process of growth is a rapidly rising productivity of labor under the impact of complex and interrelated forces. On the basis of all of the data available, it would seem that the more underdeveloped an economy, the greater tend to be the differentials between the labor products of the economic sectors. Under such conditions, the very shift of labor out of agriculture—a low productivity sector—into urban, factory industry—a high productivity sector—is reflected in rising per capita product in the economy. Under modern conditions of development this is reinforced by the advantages of delayed industrialization inasmuch as the process of industrial expansion in a country such as China is accompanied by discrete leaps in technology. Within this context, even the postwar dismantling of Manchurian plants by the Soviets may be considered a blessing in disguise, from the Chinese point of view. Plant installations built by the Japanese that were removed in 1945 have by now largely been replaced by more up-to-date Soviet equipment. The same applies to plants newly built; for instance, on the basis of eye-witness and other accounts, a flax mill located near Harbin and completed in 1952 seems to incorporate the advances of modern technology. Similarly, it may be assumed that the two new steel mills to be built in China by Soviet engineers with Soviet equipment will be based on modern Russian methods of steel-making—methods which do not seem to lag far behind those applied in the United States.

---

*In retrospect this projection turned out to be too pessimistic for the 1950's, i.e., for the first six to seven years, but not too far from reality for the two decades (1952–1972) as a whole, as pointed out in chapter 1. The slower economic growth projected in this model as compared to the actual growth between 1952 and 1960 or 1952 and 1972 is to a considerable extent due to differences in population growth. That is, the rate of population growth assumed in the model was lower than that actually experienced in China.

The same may be put differently—i.e., high rates of investment in an economy in which the capital base is small will necessarily lead to rapid transformations in the age-composition of capital. Thus, in our model, aggregate stock would be almost doubled, while industrial capital would be quadrupled, during the ten-year period. By 1962, practically all of the industrial capital will have been installed during the preceding decade, while for the economy as a whole only one-third of the stock will still be old.

Of course, this process of rejuvenation accelerates economic growth not only through its technological effects, but also by virtue of the fact that as new capital displaces old, the share of replacement allowances in the investment total declines. This tendency is reinforced in countries such as China, which concentrate upon the development of producers' goods industries with a longer life-span for equipment and therefore relatively lower rates of capital consumption.

In working with aggregate models of this type, the problems of structural adjustments are frequently overlooked. In the Chinese case, three types of bottlenecks may be ultimately limiting: the rate of net resource transfer out of agriculture, the terms and conditions under which China can import the wherewithal of economic development, and the level of technological and entrepreneurial skill available in the economy.

As was pointed out earlier, in order to satisfy the rising demand for farm products implicit in Table 12, agricultural output would have to increase by about 26 per cent within the decade. It was also concluded that even if such an increase were technically feasible within the narrow limits of current agricultural investment levels, it is rather doubtful, in the face of prevailing Chinese Communist farm policies, that such increases can be attained. Actually, given the general character of the regime, its policies, and its objectives, it may be expected to bend every effort to maintain the level of net resource transfers out of agriculture even with stagnating or declining agricultural production. The extent to which this can be accomplished without seriously undermining the stability of the regime is necessarily one of the most critical variables affecting the rate of growth.

Similar limitations to growth and industrial development may be imposed by restrictions upon Communist China's ability to import raw materials and capital goods. It was previously indicated that in 1952 Communist China's imports from the Soviet Union constituted about 1 to

2 per cent of Soviet industrial and mining production. Assuming that there is no relaxation in free-world trade controls, that China continues to obtain about half her imports from the USSR, and that economic growth in China proceeds at the rate projected in our model, while in the USSR it continues at an estimated rate of from 6 to 7 per cent a year, this percentage may have to be maintained. Such a close dependence upon the Soviet Union and the Soviet bloc not only may yield terms of trade unfavorable to China, but is almost certainly bound to result in specific bottlenecks in deliveries of capital goods—that is, goods for which the demand is high in the bloc itself. On the other hand, should trade controls be lifted or significantly relaxed, China's import position would be greatly relieved.

A highly centralized administration of an economic development program in a vast country such as China requires a huge bureaucratic apparatus with a wide variety of skills. There is need for engineers, technicians, foremen, skilled workers, technical and economic planners, statisticians, cadres to administer the economic controls, rural extension agents, managers of plants and vast state enterprises, etc. While some of the gap in trained manpower is to be filled through Soviet technical assistance and through greatly expanded domestic training facilities at the secondary school rather than the advanced university level, shortages are likely to remain acute throughout the decade. This, in turn, will tend to exercise a depressing effect upon growth, through inefficiencies, errors in economic and industrial management, and low productivity.

While recognizing the fundamental impact of these structural bottlenecks upon the prospects for economic growth in Communist China, it is essential not to overemphasize them. These bottlenecks present no absolute barriers, but only additional roadblocks. This means that in order to maintain a high rate of growth (e.g., from 3 to 4 per cent) under such circumstances, the rate of resource mobilization must be raised above the levels that would be required in the absence of such bottlenecks. It may be said on a priori grounds that a regime which is capable of channeling 20 to 30 per cent of national expenditure through the government budget is likely to be able to sustain a comparatively rapid tempo of economic and industrial expansion—somewhat more rapid in the absence of serious structural problems and less rapid in the face of such problems—unless all or most of these resources are dissipated in current military expenditures and in the costs of administering the controls required to mobilize this share of current output. Finally, in appraising the plausibility of a 3 to 4 per cent a year rate of growth for Communist China, the Japanese experience may be most relevant. Meiji Japan, starting from roughly the same stage of backwardness as mainland China on the eve of its first Five-Year Plan (1952), and with a resource base that was certainly no more favorable, moved ahead at an estimated rate of from 4 to 5 per cent between 1880 and 1900.[86]

While a number of factors seem to point to comparatively rapid rates of prospective growth in Communist China, per capita gross product in 1962 would still be only around U.S. $60, in spite of the pace of expansion envisaged in our model.* However, the share of industrial production in total national product would rise from 7 to 16 per cent. The economy of mainland China would thus attain a stage of development which would still definitely rank it among the underdeveloped areas of the world. In the context of Asia, however, growth at such speed would constitute a most impressive performance. Depending on the course of events elsewhere in Asia, a development of this kind in Communist China could significantly affect the regional political and power balance.

---

*This turned out to be an underestimate for, let us say, 1960 or any other non-depression year in the late 1950's or mid-1960's. It so happens that in 1962 China was still in the throes of an agricultural crisis so that the $60 figure may not be too far off the mark for that particular year. For more detailed estimates and an analysis of this problem see Table 6 in chapter 1 and the discussion relating to it.

Chapter 7

Collectivization and the Prospects
for Economic Growth in
Mainland China

I

About three years have passed now since my study of China's growth prospects was completed. The work was done before the Chinese mainland authorities published any detailed statistics, so that in many cases even the most elementary production series had to be estimated on the basis of "peak" performance data in combination with published index numbers which at times were mutually inconsistent. Beyond these statistical difficulties, it is always hazardous to attempt growth projections for economies which are in the process of particularly speedy transformation so that the parameters themselves are subject to continuous and rapid change.

Since 1953, China has become more deeply immersed in comprehensive and long-range planning, she has launched and almost completed a full-blown collectivization program in agriculture, and has proceeded a long way towards completing the socialization of industry and trade through the device of the joint private-public enterprises. At the same time, as the system of statistical reporting and organization improved, more and more data began to be published. Therefore on both of these accounts, one's perspective in examining economic growth and assessing prospects for future development in China is naturally different as of mid-1957 than of mid-1954. Yet the essential outlines of the analysis in chapters 12 to 14 of *The Prospects for Communist China* seem to me to be still valid with one notable exception, i.e., the collectivization experience and its economic effects.

Reprinted from *Keizai Kenkyu* (The Economic Review), July 1957, published by the Institute of Economic Research, Hitotsubashi University, under the title "Conditions and Prospects for Economic Growth in Mainland China; Some Comments."

248

Against this background and in view of the fact that a Japanese translation of the *Prospects* was recently published, I would like to (*a*) examine some of the economic implications of this collectivization experience, and (*b*) discuss the methodological or theoretical structure of my growth model in the light of some of the criticisms advanced by Japanese economists working in this field.[1]

II

From an economic point of view, collectivization can be viewed as a means of enforcing a high rate of involuntary saving in agriculture. Or to put it another way, it is a mechanism which facilitates the extraction of an unrequited export surplus out of agriculture. This export surplus is obtained in two general ways through the taxing system and through the price mechanism; that is through direct agricultural taxation in kind and through manipulation of price relations in such a way as to turn the terms of trade against agriculture. To accomplish the latter, the state trading organs and their local agents—the marketing and supplying cooperatives—use their monopolistic and monopsonistic market power to buy "cheap" and sell "dear." This provides the basis for the accumulation of large "excess" profits by the state enterprises, both in industry and trade. Thus high profits of socialized enterprises in effect amount to a quasi tax, the principal—but not the sole—burden of which is borne by the agricultural sector of the economy.

While it is easy to visualize this process in theoretical terms, it is very difficult to test it empirically owing to a lack of adequate and sufficiently detailed data.[2] Even measurements of the direct tax burden present many difficulties. For instance, we do not know precisely in what prices are farm tax collections accounted for in China; are they valued at, above, or probably below state purchase prices? Moreover, as far as I am aware of, no data have been published on the quantity and/or value of each farm commodity collected for tax and its aggregate value. "Grains," however, comprise a wide variety of commodities from rice to potatoes, so that the annual incidence of the tax burden will depend upon the product mix of the tax-take in a particular year in relation to the product mix of the total farm crop output.

Even greater difficulties confront the investigator who attempts to measure shifts in the price and/or income terms of trade facing Chinese agriculture. Ideally, we would need to have data on the pattern of farm consumption in kind, farm household expenditure patterns, the quantities and prices of each non-farm product purchased. Obviously, this is the kind of information that is difficult to obtain even for economically and statistically more highly developed areas than Mainland China.

While it may be hard, if not impossible, to measure accurately changes over time in rural-urban price relations, one can be fairly certain on a strictly a priori basis that: (*a*) in any one year actual rural-urban price relations do not adequately reflect the "true" scarcity relationship prevailing in the Chinese economy, and (*b*) this divergence between the actual and the hypothetically true exhibits a systematic bias against agriculture although the extent of this bias is not measureable.

What is the link between all this and collectivization? After all, agricultural taxes were levied and monopolistic market power was applied by state trading companies prior to the large-scale collectivization campaign of 1955. However, administration and control of an agricultural collection system is much more complex and difficult in a system of small-scale peasant agriculture as compared to a collectivized system. It is much easier for a vast number of small units to evade taxes and it requires a much larger apparatus to collect them. At the same time, the enforcement of compulsory purchase schemes at fixed prices becomes very difficult, since there always looms the danger of a "scissors" crisis. The range within which the rural-urban terms of trade can be manipulated is likely to be much narrower in a private peasant agriculture, so that in such a system greater reliance needs to be placed upon market incentives as a means of collecting the marketable surplus. This in turn, means that more manufactured consumers' goods are required to pay for the marketed share, with the net effect that rural and aggregate consumption is higher, and conversely the supply of saving is lower, than would otherwise be the case. In effect then, one of the prime functions of collectivization is to institutionalize the process of—what Marx termed—"primitive accumulation."

These are some of the crucial issues that must have confronted Mainland Chinese planners when they instituted rationing and compulsory purchase programs and then greatly accelerated the pace of collectivization. This rapid pace and its apparent success probably constitutes one of the most significant developments in China since the advent of the Communist regime—a development of far-reaching economic consequence. On the basis of present indications, the collectivization process in Chinese mainland agriculture will have been basically completed during this year. Thus, it would seem that collectivization in China is proceeding even more rapidly than it did in the Soviet Union, and—on the basis of all available evidence—at much lower human and resource cost. This is a development which could not be foreseen and certainly runs counter to the expectations of most observers.

These differences in pace may be illustrated by the following figures:

Proportion of Farm Households Collectivized

Year July 1	Soviet Union in per cent	Year end of year	Mainland China in per cent
1927	0.8	1954	0.0001
1928	1.7	1955	3.9
1929	3.9	1956	83.0 approx.
1930	23.6		
1932	61.5		
1937	93.0		

Sources: Norodnoe Khozyastvo S. S. S. R., Statisticheskii Sbornik (National Economy of the U.S.S.R., Statistical Handbook), p. 99. *Tsu Kuo Weekly* of February 18, 1957, quoting *Kung-jen jih-pao* of December 30, 1956.

Therefore, it would seem that a process, the consummation of which took about seven years in the Soviet Union is being completed in China in about two.

The implications of these differences become even clearer if we pause briefly to examine some of the costs of Soviet collectivization. Lorimer in a throughgoing and careful study of Soviet population comes to the tentative conclusion that during the inter-census period of December 17, 1926 to January 17, 1939, there may have been an "excess mortality" of some five million; i.e., excess in the sense of deaths over and above that normally expected. While he concedes that this estimate may involve a certain margin of error, there seems to be little question that the excess was appreciable and that in part at least it reflects direct and indirect losses due to collectivization.[3] Of even greater importance from an economic point of view is the curtailment in farm output and livestock numbers during the first Five-Year Plan period. While here too the data are far from perfect, it would seem that between 1927 and 1932 grain output dropped by about 10 per cent, while total farm product is estimated to have decreased by about 20 per cent. A large share of this contraction was due to a 40 to 50 per cent decline in meat production induced by the aforementioned slaughter of livestock. The following figures will serve to illustrate the percentage drop in the livestock population of the Soviet Union between 1928 and 1934–35.[4]

Horses	50%
Cattle	40%
Hogs	33%
Sheep and goats	65%

As pointed out above, thus far at any rate, there is no evidence to indicate that mainland Chinese collectivization involves such disruption and contraction in agricultural output. This does not necessarily mean that collectivization is proceeding smoothly, without any strains and stresses, but only that they are not of devastating proportions. While noting this, it must also be admitted that collectivization in China is so recent that we lack a historical perspective and that it is really too early to judge its outcome. However, assuming that current trends can be considered as indicative, it may be worthwhile to explore what are some of the factors that might account for a different collectivization outcome in Communist China as compared to the Soviet Union.

The roots of this difference may possibly be found in the relations between the regime and the peasantry in the Soviet Union. In both cases, land redistribution was the first item on the agenda of the agrarian program. However, the Chinese Communists came to power after a prolonged period of civil war, while in the Russian case the civil war came after the revolution. Thus, while the Chinese were able to carry through their land reform program undisturbed and in a systematic manner, the Bolsheviks were plagued by very acute food supply problems during the period of "war communism," and were thus compelled to resort to forced confiscation of grain and other agricultural produce. This served to alienate the peasantry from the regime, almost from the beginning, and at the same time it turned out to be counter-productive from a procurement standpoint, since it created an atmosphere in which the peasants would hide their grain, feed it to livestock, and consume it themselves, rather than surrender it to the authorities. At the same time, peasants reduced their plantings to meet only their own consumption needs.

In view of this situation, the Soviet regime found it necessary to beat a tactical retreat and to institute the New Economic Policy. One of the essential features of NEP was a considerable reliance upon market incentives as a means of expanding and procuring the marketable share. But, this inevitably brought with it a strengthening of the economic and political power of the kulaks. This was actually explicitly recognized by Lenin in his statement that "We must not shut our eyes to the fact that the replacement of requisitioning by the tax in kind means that the kulak element under this system will grow far more hitherto. It will grow in places where it could not grow before."[5] Within this context, the "scissors crisis" of the 20's was but a reflection of the dilemma facing the Soviet regime during the NEP period. It committed itself to reliance upon market incentives, but it was reluctant to pay the price in terms of reduced savings and investments. Collectivization was to point the way out of this dilemma. However, given the power of the kulaks this course was bound to meet with strong resistance, so that if the process was to be consummated rapidly it necessarily meant a resort to violent means.

Yet, while this solution represented a short run remedy, in the long run it turned out to be but the first link in a vicious circle which has plagued Russian planners throughout Soviet history. As indicated above, one of the central purposes of collectivization was to institutionalize a high rate of saving in the economy. However because of the curtailment in farm output and livestock numbers, the high rate of saving had to be imposed upon a shrunken farm product and income. This in turn, not only reduced rural standards of living, but undermined peasant incentives even in the collectives, and thus greatly hampered agricultural recovery. At the same time, capital had to be diverted to replace the animal draft power lost in the process. The more agricultural recovery was hampered the greater had to be the pressure on agriculture. This situation was greatly aggravated by the sharp setback in agricultural recovery owing to World War II. As a result, it would seem that per capita gross agricultural product and grain output was at about the same level in 1954 as in 1928.[6] At the same time livestock numbers, as well as average productivity per animal was still at or below the precollectivization levels, which means that the per capita output of livestock products was appreciably below it. This is truly a pattern of industrialization at the expense of agriculture to the point where unless the Soviets are willing to place a much greater reliance upon foreign trade in general, and food imports in particular—the lag in agricultural development has become a seriously limiting factor in Soviet economic growth.

In contrast, land reform in China went so far that very few "rich peasants" were left. At the same time, by launching the collectivization campaign as soon as the land redistribution program was completed, the Chinese Communists proceed with the more advanced stages of their agrarian program before the new and old owner-operators could consolidate their economic position, extend their landholding through purchase or renting, and accumulate wealth. Thus the potential development of a "rich peasant" or kulak class was nipped in the bud so that both the incentive and the power to resist collectivization was minimized. This was reinforced by the reliance apparently placed upon persuasion, economic incentive and disincentive, rather than force.

What are the implications of all this upon Mainland China's economic growth prospects? Unless the pattern sketched above is reversed, this could mean that—unlike the Soviet Union—Mainland China may be in a position to pursue its industrialization objectives and at the same time attain at least modest increases in farm output per capita. One could argue on an a priori basis that even though Soviet agriculture was kept on a rather short investment ration—with the bulk of investment being labor and livestock displacing, rather than yield increasing—and was subjected to an unfavorable incentive structure, barring the setbacks of collectivization and World War II, farm output would have expanded appreciably. In these terms then, one might expect that unless the Chinese suffer such setbacks, they may be able to pursue the Soviet development model without being compelled to apply the same degree of pressure on agriculture and on the consumer sector in general. This in turn could mean that, *ceteris paribus*, the Chinese could place greater reliance upon incentives, even in agriculture, than the Soviet were able to do. In effect then, it may turn out that Chinese Communist agricultural policy will bear as much family resemblance to the Japanese as to the Soviet experience.

III

On the basis of these assumptions agricultural supply prospects may be expected to be more favorable than could be anticipated some years ago.

If there really turns out to be a minimum disruption in agriculture, it is quite possible that through better organization and capital-cheap inputs, modest increases in yields may be attained. What about the demand side of the equation? Would this output be expanding at a rate adequate to meet rising requirements owing to population growth, urbanization, and export demand? While it would be beyond the scope of this article to attempt an answer to this problem, it may perhaps be appropriate to examine briefly the more general theoretical question as to what are the factors or variables that determine the level of consumer demand in a comprehensively planned economy. More specifically, need changes in national income and household consumption, or the food component thereof, be necessarily related functionally?

It would seem to me that the answer would have to be in the negative. Given the short and intermediate-term development objectives in Soviet type economies, functionally related increases in national income and levels of household consumption can be viewed as representing failures in the efficacy of planning. To the extent that food consumption actually increased in 1953 as a result of Mainland China's economic recovery, this represented an undesired development from the planners point of view— i.e., development that called for countermeasures as evidenced by the introduction of the compulsory grain purchase schemes and rationing in the fall of 1953. Thus, one of the very purposes of centralized national planning under these conditions is to break the functional link between increases in national income and consumer demand in order to raise the marginal propensity to save. Or to put it another way, in the predominantly non-market economies of the Soviet type, government demand provides a guaranteed outlet for a wide range and assortment of investment and military goods, so that national product can rise independent of any changes in personal household consumption. Similarly increases in national product need not be reflected in rising levels of consumption. Should there turn out to be a gap—either *ex ante* or *ex post*—between flows of money income and consumer goods availabilities, these can always be bridged through rationing, other direct controls and/or raising prices.

This is not intended to suggest that in practice this works out smoothly, in fact these adjustments are usually characterized by lags, and there are all the usual limitations due to imperfect knowledge, lack of foresight, administrative and other types of frictions, etc.

However, there is one important respect in which even in a Soviet type system the nexus between Y and C prevails; that is the one based upon the interrelationship between growing national product and rural-urban population shifts. One of the concomitants of rapid economic growth and industrialization is urbanization. Therefore, to the extent that the resource cost of maintaining a person at a comparable standard of living is higher in the city than in the village,[7] rural-urban population shifts will be reflected in increases in average per-capita consumption even if urban per-capita consumption levels remain unchanged. In fact, depending upon what the scarcity relationships in the labor market are at any one time, wages and consumption standards may or may not be raised in order to recruit labor for an expanding urban industry. That is, if there are large pools of unemployed and underemployed labor both in the city and the country, the existing rural-urban consumption differential may be sufficient to insure a continuous supply of urban labor over a five to ten years period. Only as shortages of labor begin to be felt may it become necessary to widen the rural-urban consumption gap so as to attract more labor from the countryside and at the same time also augment the incentives of those workers who are already in the city.

Actually, Mainland China on the eve of its first Five-Year Plan was apparently in a position of pronounced urban and rural labor surplus. This combined with the considerations outlined above seems to me to justify the assumption of stable rural and urban per capita consumption in a theoretical growth model intended to apply to a Soviet type economy.

IV

Another problem of considerable importance that has been raised concerns the basic character of the growth model used in The Prospects. Of particular significance for general development theory is the question whether Harrod-Domar type dynamic models—essentially built around capital inputs as the strategic variable—are applicable to processes of economic growth in underdeveloped areas. Do not these models leave out of account growth effects due to institutional changes, improvements in the efficiency of organization and management, and to leaps in technology, which are such important aspects of the development process?

It would seem to me the answer to this set of questions would very much depend upon how the particular model is constructed and what considerations have entered into the choice of parameters. One of the virtues of the Harrod model is precisely its simplicity and high level of generality. Essentially it provides a framework which can easily be modified by fitting additional variables into it. Thus in our case, the model was based on eight parameters: capital-output ratio—aggregate and industrial, share of government consumption in GNP, rate of population growth, ratio between the rate of industrial growth and the rate of urban population growth, share of industrial investment in the investment total, per capita rural consumption, and rate of growth in per capita urban consumption. Given these constants and the assumption of a one year investment-output lag, national and industrial product, aggregate and industrial investment, rate of urbanization, and level of consumption (rural, urban and governmental) can be derived.

In what way does such a model take into account institutional variables? It certainly does not do so explicitly, but institutional factors play a very important role in the choice of assumptions on which the model is based. For instance, as was shown earlier, the assumption concerning stability of per capita rural and urban consumption is based on an analysis of the nature of the system and the character of planners' preferences. The analysis may not be valid and it may be open to challenge on its own terms, but the problem has not been ignored.

A similar problem arises in connection with organizational and technological improvements. The model is basically built around rising factor inputs rather than increases in productivity and changing production functions. It is actually very doubtful that with the data and the theoretical apparatus at our disposal now, there is any meaningful or operationally relevant method by which organizational changes could be introduced as inputs the growth effects of which could be clearly separated and identified. Yet this does not mean that they cannot be taken into account. On the contrary, they may, for instance, be introduced indirectly through the choice of criteria in terms of which the magnitudes for the capital-output ratios are fixed.

Thus, given the resource and transport constraints under which China's mainland economy operates and the supply inelasticities resulting therefrom, one might *a priori* be justified in using a high capital-output ratio for growth projections. Yet our particular model is based on the assumption that during this initial industrialization decade marked improvements in organization and management will tend to bring the capital-output ratio down to an average level of 3, which in terms of the historical experience of other countries more favorably placed in respect to resource and factor endowments, would appear to be low.

Our model exhibits another characteristic that may bear mention in this context, i.e., the assumed constancy of the capital-output ratio. Obviously, it would be extremely unrealistic to expect that the ratio will actually be constant during this initial big industrialization spurt. However, this is beside the point. The model was never intended to plot the precise expansion path of Mainland China's economic growth during the period of the first two Five-Year Plans. Its purpose was more modest, i.e., to explore the direction of economic change, the stage of development that was likely to be attained at the end of the period on the basis of the stated assumptions, and the character of interrelationships of some of the variables that were considered as most strategic at the aggregative level of analysis. In these terms then the capital-output ratio is viewed as an average over the decade as a whole based on a hypothetical backward look from the vantage point of the end of the model period. In effect then, it is intended as a hypothetical *ex-post* average, which disregards short-run fluctuations around this average-fluctuations that may be quite marked owing to annual changes in the degree of capacity utilization, harvest fluctuations, etc.

Chapter 8

Economic Development Strategies in China

I. Introduction

There is a frequent tendency to view the economy of China as a carbon copy of the Soviet model. This view neglects the fact that China is an underdeveloped Soviet-type economy with the accent on underdeveloped. There are obviously vast differences in the factor endowments of Russia and China which is most dramatically illustrated by the differences in population dynamics. Thus, while the population of the Soviet Union has been growing at an average annual rate of 0.6 per cent since 1913, China's population has expanded during the past decade at about a 2 per cent a year rate. Even if we abstract from war influences and take only so-called normal periods, Soviet population grew only at about a 1 to 1.5 per cent rate. This divergence in population patterns becomes even more highlighted if we consider the vastly different states of population pressure on arable land resources in the Russia of 1928 and the China of 1952.

In these terms, Chinese conditions are clearly much more applicable to those encountered in other overpopulated underdeveloped economies than would be the case for the Soviet Union. However, the same can be said of Chinese development experience only if it can be shown that Chinese planners and policy makers have themselves recognized these differences and have evolved a strategy adopted to their own conditions. Therefore, this paper will attempt to examine first what are the general ingredients or

This chapter is based on a paper read at the 13th Annual Meeting of the Association for Asian Studies, March 28, 1961; it is combined with an article entitled "Strategy of Economic Development in Communist China," published in the *American Economic Review, Papers and Proceedings,* May 1961.

requirements of a development strategy; second, to what extent and how are these requirements met in the Soviet model; third, whether and in what ways does the Chinese model depart from the Soviet example; and fourth, what are the implications of this for other underdeveloped areas.

The central thesis of this paper is that during the first five-year plan period (1953–57) Chinese Communist policy-makers pursued a Stalinist strategy of economic development with local adaptations. However, given the vastly different factor endowments of Mainland China in the fifties as compared to the Soviet Union of the twenties, Chinese planners were forced to modify significantly their original approach. They thus evolved a new strategy for the second five-year plan (1958–62), based on intensive utilization of underemployed labor combined with promotion of technological dualism, as a means of maximizing the rate of economic growth. In effect, then, building on Stalinist foundations, they adopted an essentially Nurkse *cum* Eckaus model of economic development.

II. Elements of a Development Strategy

Ideally a development strategy should be based on a clearly articulated set of objectives—both economic and non-economic—and an arsenal of instruments, means, clearly designed to attain them. The means, in turn, could be categorized under three headings: ideology, institutions, and patterns of resource allocation.

For the strategy to be fully successful the objectives must be mutually consistent and complementary, rather than competitive, and the three categories of instruments must be woven into a functionally interrelated and integrated pattern. Thus, a rationally designed plan can not attempt to maximize a number of objectives simultaneously such as for instance military prowess and standards of living, or quantity (measured in physical units) and quality of goods produced.

It would probably be possible—though beyond our scope—to rank ideologies according to their degree of totalism. Societies committed to raise standards of national power or standards of living higher, faster, and with less to work with than the countries they are emulating, will naturally require a more comprehensive and all-embracing ideology of zealotry in the name of which, and for the sake of which, large sacrifices can be demanded or commanded—sacrifices necessary to yield the desired rate of economic growth. From this point of view, the Protestant Ethic, nationalism alone, and finally nationalism combined with communism, may be considered as progressively more potent ideologies.

There is obviously an intimate relationship between ideology and institutions. Certain ideologies are compatible with private property relations or decentralized decision-making as exemplified by the market mechanism, while others clearly are not. Similarly, certain institutions are either consciously designed or at least unwittingly suited to accomplish maximal objectives, while others may be altogether incompatible with economic development. Systems of land tenure, the character of the banking system, or of capital markets provide good cases in point.

Thus traditional landlord or communal systems of land tenure have tended to hamper economic development in most countries. They have done so in two principal ways, by serving as obstacles to raising agricultural productivity and by channeling their surplus into consumption credit, speculative land purchase, or conspicuous consumption. It is not surprising therefore that it is difficult to think of cases of successful industrialization that were not preceded or accompanied by an agrarian transformation.

One of the most critical institutional means are those related to mobilizing actual or potential savings. In this respect, too, alternative mechanisms could be ranged along a spectrum extending from minimal to maximal, exemplified perhaps by small individual postal savings on to credit creation through the banking system and finally by involuntary savings institutionalized through turnover taxation or forced extraction from a highly collectivized agriculture.

Patterns of resource allocation will inevitably be interrelated with institutional mechanisms. Highly decentralized decision-making will necessarily be preponderantly based on consumers' preferences and will thus yield a rather different resource mix than a highly centralized pattern. It is true that theoretically one could conceive of central planning consciously based on consumers' preferences, but in practice this is most unlikely.

To sum up this phase of our analysis, one could say that the function of ideology is to provide the rationale for carrying out the objectives which are actually implemented through the institutional framework and then translated by the prevailing pattern of resource allocation into the production and distribution of goods and services implicitly or explicitly postulated by the objectives.

III. Schematic Outline of the Soviet Model

Applying this framework of analysis to the Soviet model and concentrating first on objectives, it can be clearly shown that this model falls short of the ideal requirements of a development strategy. While it would be difficult to pinpoint precisely what really the basic long-term objectives of Soviet policy-makers are, it may be fair to say that the central operational *leitmotiv* of Soviet planning has been to catch up and overtake the West in industrial and economic power as soon as possible. Concretely this has meant maximizing the rate of economic growth year in, year out.

However, Soviet planning is often based on a multiplicity of mutually inconsistent goals. They would like to maximize several objectives simultaneously, e.g. collectivize while raising agricultural production, overfulfill production targets and improve quality of product, increase production without additional inputs of capital, labor and raw material. These inconsistencies are then resolved by an implicit or explicit ordering of priorities, with some objectives becoming more maximal than others.

Ideology need not detain us for long in this context since its implications are fairly obvious. One need only underline the fact that this is a maximal ideology in the sense used above, that is, it is a most potent ideology which harnesses the forces of nationalism and communism into a combined religion ideally suited to command great sacrifices.

The institutional framework is in turn designed to provide maximum control over all of the social, political and economic levers and thus provide the channels for centralized direction and resource allocation. Public ownership of the means of production, collectivization of agriculture, the whole banking mechanism, the tax system, the primary reliance on planning through administrative *fiat* rather than through the price mechanism, are all examples of this.

This institutional framework was then used to shape the pattern of resource allocation. In its Stalinist phase in particular, high rates of saving and investment institutionalized through agricultural collectivization, preponderant emphasis on the development of industries producing raw materials and investment goods, reliance on large-scale and capital-intensive technology in industry—and to a considerable extent in agriculture coupled with relative neglect of yield-increasing rather than labor-displacing investment and in social overhead may be said to represent the principal features of the resource allocation pattern in the Soviet Union. In effect, it is a pattern of economic development which is bound to lead to rapid rates of industrial expansion at the expense of agriculture, i.e., both agricultural productivity and rural standards of living.

IV. Chinese Development Strategy

Comparing Soviet and Chinese development strategies in the context of the elements outlined above, one finds no essential differences in objectives, in ideology, or even in institutional framework broadly conceived, with the single exception of the communes about which more will be said later. Of course, there are some differences in degree and in tactics. Thus, the objectives of the Chinese Communist leadership are even more ambitious than those of their Soviet counterparts. They would like to go even further, with much greater speed, and with much less to work with. This ambitiousness is then not too surprisingly coupled with greater ideological militancy, both in its communist and nationalist aspects.

The extent to which Chinese planners adopted the Soviet model as their own may be illustrated by a comparison of the rate and structure of investment during the first Soviet and Chinese Five-Year Plan periods as shown in Table 1. These data must naturally be interpreted with considerable caution. First of all, the national income and investment estimates are necessarily more tentative for China than for Russia. Second, the sectoral definitions are not quite the same in the two cases. Moreover, the data for the inter-industry allocation of investment refer only to investments by the state. To the extent that the importance of non-state investments is not the same in the different sectors of the two countries, Table 1 could present a misleading picture.

Subject to these qualifications, the data in Table 1 suggest that in some respects the Stalinist features were even more pronounced in the Chinese than in the Soviet case. While rates of investment were lower in China, the difference between the two does not appear to be very great. Actually, considering how low Chinese per capita product is relative to the Soviet level of 1928, it is surprising indeed that such a high rate of saving could have been attained. However, the Stalinist tendencies appear most clearly in the investment allocation pattern as evidenced by the fact that the Chinese channeled a significantly larger share of investment resources into industry and most particularly into heavy industry. At the same time, both

TABLE 1

Rates and Patterns of Investment in the Soviet Union (1928–1937)
and in China (1953–1957)

(in per cent)

	China		Soviet Union	
	1953	1957	1928	1937
Rate of Investment	16.0*	20.0*	21–33†	19–23†

Rate of Investment	Planned		Realized	
	China	Soviet Union	China	Soviet Union
Sector				
Industry	61.8	40.7	56.0	49.0
Of which heavy industry		31.3	49.0	42.1
Agriculture	6.2	15.3	8.2	19.1
Transport	17.1	21.1	18.7	17.6
Communications	7.2	0.6		1.1
Trade and procurement				1.8
Social-cultural services and administration	7.7	22.3	17.1	11.0

*Gross investment as a ratio of gross national product.
†The lower rates represent gross investment as a ratio of gross national product at established market prices, while the higher rates are in terms of adjusted factor costs.
Sources: For China: A. Eckstein, *The National Income of Communist China,* Glencoe, Ill., 1961, Table 15; W. W. Hollister, *China's Gross National Product and Social Accounts, 1959–57,* Glencoe, Ill., 1958; C. M. Li, *Economic Development of Communist China,* Berkeley, 1959, Table 1, p. 9; State Statistical Bureau, *Communique on Fulfillment and Overfulfillment of China's First Five-Year Plan,* Peking, April 13, 1959.
For the Soviet Union: A. Bergson, *Soviet National Income and Product in 1937,* New York, 1953, Table 8, p. 75 and Appendix, Table 3, pp. 136–37; O. Hoeffding, *Soviet National Income and Product in 1928,* New York, 1954, Table 6, p. 46; N. M. Kaplan, *Capital Investment in the Soviet Union, 1924–51,* Santa Monica, RM735, 28 Nov., 1951, Appendix Table 1, p. 80.

at the planning and at the realization stage, Chinese Communist policy-makers paid correspondingly less attention than their Soviet counterparts to agriculture and to social overhead.

The essentially similar approaches to industrialization which character-ized the initial five-year plans of China and Russia produced a rather different outcome in the two settings. As shown in Table 2, industrial production expanded very rapidly in both countries, but while farm output grew—however modestly—in China, it declined markedly in Russia under the impact of forced collectivization.

As indicated in Table 2, for the most part these are official data and as such they are subject to an upward bias. However, the fact that the degree of bias cannot be assumed to be the same for China and the Soviet Union impairs the comparability of the figures for the two countries. The availability of a number of studies such as those of Hodgman and Johnson enable us to correct the bias for the Soviet Union. Unfortunately, such adjustments are as yet not possible for China due to the absence of independently derived indices of industrial and agricultural production.

Professor Li's paper clearly demonstrates the inadequacy of Chinese agricultural statistics in particular. There is no question that the apparent rise in farm output between 1953 and 1957 is at least in part statistical rather than real, largely due to improvements in the system of crop reporting and concomitant expansion in statistical coverage. Nevertheless, all of the available evidence suggests that there was some rise in farm production, although less marked than shown by the figures in Table 2.

If this is indeed the case, how can the differing trends in Soviet and Chinese agricultural production be explained? The answer to this question must be sought in the less violent course of agrarian transformation in China. Thus, while collectivization proceeded just about as swiftly as in the Soviet Union—being consummated between 1953 and 1956—it did not provoke the peasantry to active resistance. Therefore it did not, as in the Soviet Union, lead to drastic disruption of farm organization with consequent declines in agricultural production accompanied by mass slaughter of livestock.[1]

The different course of collectivization and agricultural production in China as compared to Russia had a far-reaching impact upon all sectors of the economy; i.e., the rate of involuntary farm saving, trends in industrial real wages and labor productivity, the pattern of rural-urban migration, and the structure of investment.

The drastic curtailment of Soviet farm output under the impact of collectivization, just at a time when agriculture was called upon to supply an expanded industrial labor force and to provide in addition an export surplus for financing capital goods imports, meant that a growing share of a shrinking agricultural product had to be saved. This in turn produced a vicious circle: the more farm output declined, the more the rate of involuntary saving had to be raised in agriculture. However, increases in

TABLE 2

Chinese and Soviet Rates of Growth in Industry, Agriculture
and Population During Their Respective First Five-Year-Plan Periods

	China*		Soviet Union	
1. Averate annual rate of growth in industrial production in per cent: Official				
Industry	16.5		19.0	
Industry and handi- crafts	16.0			
Hodgman, large-scale industry			15.0	
2. Average annual rate of growth in farm production in per cent:				
Official	4.5		–4.0	
Johnson			–5.0	
3. Average annual rate of population growth in per cent:				
Total	2.2		1.3	
Urban	5.0		6.0†	
Rural	1.8		–0.4†	
4. Cultivated land per capita (in hectares):	1953	1956	1926–28	1938–39
Total population	.187	.180	.738	.720
Rural population	.216	.209	.936	1.195

*The figures for China are based on official data.
†These are average rates for the 1926–39 period as a whole since urban-rural breakdowns are available only for 1926 and 1939.
Sources: For the Soviet Union: D. R. Hodgman, *Soviet Industrial Production, 1928–1951,* Cambridge, Mass., 1965, Table 1, p. 2 and Table 15, p. 89; Harry Schwartz, *Russia's Soviet Economy,* New York, 1954, Table 8, p. 127; D. G. Johnson and Arcadius Kahan, "Soviet Agriculture: Structure and Growth," in *Comparisons of the U.S. and Soviet Economies,* Joint Eco. Comm., 86th Cong., 1st Sess., Part I, pp. 204–05; Frank Lorimer, *The Population of the Soviet Union, History and Prospects,* Geneva, 1946, Table 26, p. 67; Table 43, p. 110; Table 44, p. 113; p. 150 and Table 64, p. 159.
For China: Helen Yin and Y. C. Yin, *Economic Statistics of Mainland China, 1949–57,* Cambridge, Mass., 1960, pp. 4, 25, 26, 42 and 43.

the rate of involuntary saving only served to reinforce peasant disincentives, thereby contributing to further reductions in agricultural production.

In spite of increasing extractions forced out of agriculture, the Soviets encountered serious difficulty in provisioning the cities. This, in turn, set up another vicious circle. Urban shortages of foodstuffs and other consumer goods led to a drop in real wages with consequent disincentive effects reflected in declines of labor productivity. Therefore, if rates of industrial growth were to be raised or even maintained, more workers had to be imported from the countryside. However, growth of the urban labor force depressed industrial labor productivity only further, both because it aggravated the supply problems and thus led to another round of real wage decreases and also because it brought more and more unskilled labor into industry.

In China, we observe a rather different pattern. With no comparable curtailment in agricultural production, there was no marked disruption in food supply and distribution to the cities. At the same time, as imperfect as the evidence is, it strongly suggests a rising trend in real wages and industrial labor productivity. As a result, greater reliance could be placed upon increases in labor productivity as a means of obtaining high rates of industrial growth. Moreover, there was considerable room for expanding the industrial labor force just by stepping up the rate of urban labor utilization, first by absorbing the unemployed and then by increasing the labor participation rate. Due to all of these factors combined, a pace of industrial expansion that was not too far behind that attained in the Soviet Union could be achieved with relatively slower rates of urbanization.

Given the differential natural rates of increase in the populations of Russia and China as shown in Table 2, rates of rural-urban migration must have been significantly lower in China. This trend is also reflected in the fact that while rural population declined slightly in the Soviet Union, it continued to grow quite rapidly throughout the first five-year plan period in China.

These differences in the course of collectivization and urbanization account, at least in part, for the lower investment share allotted by the Chinese to agriculture and to social overhead as noted earlier in Table 1. Unlike the Soviets, they did not have to mechanize agriculture just to replace slaughtered animal draft power. At the same time, with a slower pace of urbanization in China, pressure on public utilities and municipal facilities was not as acute as in the Soviet Union. Another consequence of the slower rural exodus was the increasing damming of population in the Chinese countryside as evidenced by a decline in cultivated land per capita between 1953 and 1957.

Therefore, Chinese policy-makers by carefully avoiding the Soviet collectivization debacle in effect faced a new set of dilemmas in the field of population control. Apart from doctrinaire incantations against Malthusianism, up to 1955 the Chinese leadership apparently paid little attention to the population problem. However, rising rates of natural increase, primarily due to a reduction in mortality rates, forced a re-evaluation in population policy. As a result, some birth control measures were instituted between 1955 and 1957.[2] Yet, this new population policy was only half-heartedly pursued, since the leadership could not make up its mind whether to follow its doctrinaire bias and treat population as a productive resource, as a source of labor supply, or whether to stress its role as an actual and potential impediment to increasing saving and investment.

In spite of five to eight years of rapid industrial growth accompanied by relatively nonviolent collectivization, Chinese Communist policymakers approached the end of their first Five-Year Plan with some serious unresolved problems on their hands. Within this context, they began to grope for a new development strategy, one that would provide a way out of the dilemmas facing them. The most intractable issue confronting them was agricultural stagnation. Farm production grew only slowly, possibly just sufficiently to keep pace with population growth. Unless this trend could be reversed, agriculture would increasingly retard the pace of industrialization in a more or less closed economy. Therefore, Chinese planners were seeking a strategy which would promote growth in farm production without significant diversion of investment funds from industry to agriculture.

The problem was aggravated by the rising rate of population growth and the increasing pressure of population on arable land resources as shown earlier. The frantic search for an escape from the "low-level equilibrium trap" was thereby only accelerated.[3] All of these problems converged in the course of 1957, when the pressure on domestic saving was also rising, due to the approaching exhaustion of Soviet credits to China.

The essence of the problem facing China's planners was most succinctly defined by Eckaus in the following terms:

Suppose that the respective demands for output are such that a large part of the available capital is drawn into the capital-intensive and fixed coefficient sector. The amount of labor which can be absorbed in these sectors is dependent on the amount of capital available. Since capital is a scarce factor, labor employment opportunities in this sector are limited by its availability rather than by demand for output. The relatively plentiful labor supply is then pushed into the variable-coefficient sector and absorbed there as long as the marginal value productivity of labor is higher than the wages it received.[4]

It is against this background that a new development strategy began to crystallize in 1958—one better suited to China's factor endowments on the one hand and her planners' scale of preferences on the other hand. At its core, this strategy involves mass mobilization of underemployed rural labor on a scale not attempted before, even in China.

This additional labor is to be largely used locally for three purposes: (1) labor intensive investment projects such as irrigation and water reclamation, (2) more intensive methods of agricultural production based on greater applications of labor designed to increase unit yields through closer planting, more careful weeding, etc., and (3) development of small-scale industry. Moreover, all of this is to be accomplished by preventing leakages into consumption, thus capturing all of the increase in marginal product at zero marginal cost. In effect, then, this represents an application of the Nurkse model of capital formation in its purest form.[5]

Of course, none of these were entirely new measures. Mass labor projects are based on an ancient tradition in China and have only been perfected and rationalized by the new Communist regime. However, rural labor mobilization prior to 1958 was much less comprehensive and systematic than since.

One of the interesting by-products of this new strategy was a shift in Chinese population policy. As was noted above, between 1955 and 1957 there was considerable—although somewhat equivocating—concern about the rapid rate of population growth and its implications for economic growth.[6] With the new emphasis on labor as a productive resource, population again was viewed as an asset rather than a liability. This is most clearly illustrated by the following quote from Liu Shao-ch'i:

All they see is that men are consumers and that the greater the population, the bigger the consumption. They fail to see that men are first of all producers and when there is a large population there is also the possibility of greater production and accumulation.[7]

It was already indicated that the development of small-scale industry was one of the uses to which the rural underemployed were to be put. While small-scale industry has been traditionally a subsidiary occupation for the Chinese farm population, it was mostly confined to weaving of textile cloth and other handicrafts. Within the context of the new strategy, Chinese Communist planners view it as one of the principal means for increasing the rate of industrial growth. In effect, they concentrate on the simultaneous development of two distinct industrial sectors: a modern, large-scale capital-intensive sector based on fixed factor proportions and a small-scale labor-intensive sector based on variable factor proportions. In pursuit of this policy of technological dualism, or "walking on two legs" as it is officially termed in Chinese Communist writings and pronouncements, the expansion of small-scale industry is promoted in a number of sectors such as iron and steel, machine shops, fertilizer production, power generation, coal extraction, in addition to the more traditional textile and food processing industries.[8]

The strategy of dualism is, however, not confined to its purely technological and factor proportions aspect. On the contrary, it seems that the model is extended to incorporate the notion of rapid development of a national economy, but based on two almost separate economies within it, only loosely linked through interregional and rural-urban trade. According to this concept, the state would concentrate the preponderant bulk of its investment resources on the development of the modern sector. This is a sector with a high reinvestment quotient, with practically all of this reinvestment to be channeled into continuing growth of itself. At the same time, the diversion of output from the modern to the rural sector is to be minimized. Therefore, the expansion of the rural sector should be a function of its own output and investment.

Small-scale industry is to be developed by using simple equipment manufactured locally, local labor, and local raw materials. The output of these industries would then be used to satisfy the rural demand for manufactured consumer goods and agricultural requirements for production inputs. The rural sector is thus pushed into involuntary and partial autarky—partial, in the sense that while the rural sector should not import from the modern sector, it would be expected to provide a large unrequited export surplus to it. Thus the rural sector would need to save enough of its current income to finance its own development while contributing to the growth of the modern sector.

How literally and with what results has this new strategy been implemented in China? Attempts to apply it in its purest form were most pronounced in 1958—particularly in the second half of that year. As the strategy evolved, the policy-makers were clearly groping for an institutional instrument suited to mass mobilization of rural labor along lines outlined above, since the existing institutional framework of agriculture was not adapted to an effective implementation of the model.

By the end of 1956, practically all of Chinese agriculture was encompassed by small collectives (officially termed "producers' cooperatives of the advanced type") of 35 to 100 households each. Management, supervision, and control of such a vast number of small units placed a considerable strain upon the administrative and party apparatus. Moreover, their proliferation and small size made them ill-suited as units of mass labor mobilization and utilization. Therefore, during 1958 a number of such small collectives were merged to form communes. These new units were sufficiently large to harness major labor-intensive projects beyond the resources of the collectives and integrate agricultural production with the mass labor projects on the one hand and the development of small-scale industry on the other. At the same time, the communes served not only as an instrument for the better utilization of the existing labor force, but also for augmenting the labor force with women released from housework. Last, but not least, the task of managing consumption controls and preventing leakages must have appeared easier with a smaller number of large units.

In its first year (i.e., 1958) the application of the new strategy, coupled with the organization of communes, was characterized by improvisation, lack of realism, misstarts, and a great deal of waste. This was perhaps most pronounced in the mass movement to produce iron and steel in the backyard. As is well known by now, the quality of the resulting product was so defective that much of it had to be scrapped. Yet it would be erroneous to base one's judgment of the success or failure of the strategy as a whole on this single example.

First of all, there are definite indications that the mass applications of labor in 1958 led to a considerable extension of the irrigated area and to significant increases in unit yields resulting therefrom. While there is no question that in this field particularly the official claims are exaggerated, I suspect that when careful studies of China's agricultural production now in process are completed, they will show a discreet leap in agricultural production in 1958, although much below the official claim.

Second, in respect to small-scale industry growth, Chinese Communist planners seem to have learned from their failures in 1958. Realizing that they overreached themselves, they continue to push vigorously for the development of these industries but on a more modest and rational basis. In the course of 1959 and 1960, considerations of technical feasibility received more attention. At the same time, it was recognized that the rural sector could not be thrown back on just its own resources; if it was to grow, it had to receive technical assistance as well as some investment goods from the modern sector. Thus in the course of its adaptation to reality, this model—like all others—lost some of its purity.

V. Implications for Underdeveloped Areas

What are the implications of all this for other underdeveloped areas? Are any elements of the Soviet or Chinese Communist strategy applicable to underdeveloped countries pursuing different objectives, based on a different ideological orientation?

It could perhaps be said that both communist and non-communist societies are dedicated to the same long-range objectives, namely raising standards of national power and standards of living more or less simultaneously. But as was pointed out earlier, these two objectives are, at least in the short or intermediate run, mutually inconsistent. The contradiction tends to be resolved in Soviet-type economies by assigning a high priority to power and downgrading welfare. Other underdeveloped areas, however, tend to follow the opposite course to varying degrees.

There is no question that a Soviet-type strategy, other things being equal, can always attain a much higher rate of savings and capital formation. But will this necessarily guarantee higher rates of economic growth under a wide variety of conditions?

In this context it should perhaps be noted that the Soviet and Chinese Communist strategies are peculiarly well suited to large countries with vast and varied natural and human resources. These strategies are essentially autarkic in character and to this extent at least, much less well adapted to small countries for which the actual or potential advantages of international specialization are much greater; and for which the penalties of an autarkic policy are much greater too. This proposition seems to be borne out by the postwar experience of Eastern Europe where the imposition of the Soviet model has met with much less success than in its own habitat. In effect, a part of savings may have been dissipated through significant diseconomies due to attempts to pursue a domestically based pattern of "balanced" growth. Under these conditions high rates of capital formation were at times accompanied by low rates of economic growth.

What this suggests is that even countries which are prepared to sacrifice present for future consumption, and to disregard social costs and the surrender of individual liberties, may not necessarily reap the high rates of growth which could be expected on the basis of the Soviet experience.

What about the welfare aspect of the problem? Assuming that Soviet-type strategies are adopted in countries to which they are most suited and granted that they sacrifice present consumption, do they not provide the optimal path for maximizing future consumption? Unfortunately, this is not a testable proposition since one would be hard put to find two countries with exactly the same factor endowments. Therefore, in comparing two situations we would have no way of determining the extent to which the results obtained were a function of the strategy or of resource endowments.

In the case of the Soviet Union, it took roughly thirty-five years for the benefits of industrialization to be translated into rising levels of household consumption. One might expect that given the much higher population pressure and more rapid rates of population growth, it would take longer in China. It would thus be really impossible to say whether, let us say fifty years from now, standards of living are likely to be higher in China or in a country such as India.

Turning finally to the specifically Chinese elements of the strategy, let us briefly explore their applicability to other underdeveloped areas.

Employment of the underemployed in mass labor projects at zero or quite low marginal cost, that is, the Nurkse aspect of the strategy, requires elements of coercion and control of such vast magnitude that they are probably incompatible with non-totalitarian forms of political structure. Moreover, as was indicated above, it is far from clear that these projects really succeeded in raising agricultural productivity in China. It is more than likely that masses of labor working without practically any equipment can build only simple and small earth dams which may be incapable of halting major floods. Similarly, depending on the terrain, irrigation works using no, or only primitive, pumps may perhaps be not too useful.

The question may of course be posed whether the Nurkse model could not still be relevant if it is applied in a less radical form, that is by combining mass labor with some equipment and by not holding the marginal wage cost down to zero. This of course is possible, but under these constraints the model becomes quite blurred and its solution indeterminate. If one introduces these qualifications one must be able to show that the value added (i.e., the margin of social benefits over the costs incurred) will be greater in this than in other types of projects. Whether this in fact is likely to be the case, particularly if one takes account of all indirect costs as well, may be doubtful.

Technological dualism, on the other hand, may be of much greater importance and relevance for all underdeveloped countries suffering from heavy population pressure and experiencing rapid rates of population growth. In such a case, however rapidly modern industry is growing, it can not possibly absorb at the same time both the existing stock of under-employed rural labor and the continuous large additions to the labor force. In this connection, it is worth while to note that, as shown in a number of studies, the degree of population pressure in pre-industrial Asia was much greater than in pre-industrial Europe. Therefore, in this respect the industrialization experience of 19th century Europe provides an inadequate guide.

Faced with a population and employment problem of such major proportions, it could be argued that a strategy of technological dualism may represent an optimal pattern for developing countries. In effect, it permits the husbanding of scarce capital in those industries in which the gains accruing from economies of scale are greatest and which are most subject to decreasing costs. However, the capacity of these industries to absorb labor is most limited so that this task is left to industries or to certain processes of production within an industry which can operate much more easily on the basis of constant costs.

Japanese development experience may serve as a classic example of a historical and unplanned adaptation to a set of factor endowments which produced a clear-cut pattern of dualism running through all aspects of the country's economic life. This pattern is evident in the dual structure of the labor market in Japan coupled with a dual wage structure. It is evident in industrial technology, in a bi-modal distribution of factor proportions in industry, and consequently in a bi-modal distribution of scale of plant. It is also quite evident in the structure of Japanese foreign trade which is based on a dual standard of comparative advantage—one in labor—intensive products in the markets of highly developed countries and another in more capital-intensive products in the markets of underdeveloped countries.

The Japanese example combined with the much shorter Chinese and Indian experience suggests that this dual pattern may become even more pronounced in the course of economic development in Asia. To the extent that this turns out to be the case, we may witness a new and perhaps paradoxical situation in which Asian countries will possess large industrial complexes well before they are industrialized in the usual sense of the term. That is while their industrial production may be quite large, the bulk of their population may continue to be tied down in agriculture and the rural sector for a long time to come.

This has certainly happened in Japan, which may provide us with another portent of the future. At the present time and for roughly another five years Japan will be in the midst of a labor force bulge due to the entrance of age cohorts into the labor force that were born in a period characterized by high birth rates. But, since the war, Japan has experienced a drastic decline in the birth rates, which means that the rate of growth in the labor force will begin to decline within a decade. At that point we may witness the beginning of the end of dualism in Japan. Barring a major and prolonged depression, labor shortages are bound to be felt, leading to competition in the labor market, narrowing of the dual wage structure and a more rapid rural exodus.

On this basis then one could speculate that Chinese and Indian economic development may be dominated by technical dualism until such time as industrialization begins to yield a restructuring of attitudes and outlook with an attendant decline in birth rates resulting therefrom.

In the Chinese case this may also mean continuingly rapid industrialization amidst chronic agricultural stagnation with the economy as a whole advancing by spurts and halts under the impact of marked harvest fluctuations. From this point of view, the current agricultural crisis and the attendant slowing down in the rate of economic growth may be regarded as more or less temporary. It may be expected to last until another favorable harvest widens the regime's room for maneuver once more and enables it to mount another push forward.

Part V

Economic Fluctuations

Chapter 9

The Economic Crisis
in Communist China

I

Communist China's drive for major power status—an urge to narrow the gap between herself and the two superpowers—has been one of the key objectives of her campaign for economic development. In pursuit of this goal, Chinese planners have concentrated on expanding as rapidly as possible the country's capacity to produce capital goods and military material. For this purpose, a mechanism for institutionalizing a high rate of involuntary saving and for channeling it into the desired lines of investment had to be fashioned.

Concretely, this meant that the different segments of the economy had to be brought under the immediate control of the planners and policy-makers, so as to enable them to mobilize and allocate resources at great speed and with maximum flexibility. Agrarian transformation, nationalization of banking, transport, industry and trade, centralization of fiscal administration, rationing, price and wage control, and a variety of other regulations were all intertwined and designed to assure this goal.

During its first ten years the Chinese Communist regime was singularly successful. It rapidly captured "the commanding heights" in the economy, restored it to working order and launched an industrialization program of vast proportions. Manufacturing plant capacity was expanded at a very fast pace and industrial production rose about 14 to 18 per cent annually between 1952 and 1959. As a result, the output of steel increased about tenfold, electric power almost sixfold, coal fivefold and cement fourfold.

Reprinted from *Foreign Affairs*, July 1964, under the title "On the Economic Crisis in Communist China."

In contrast, manufactured consumer goods, such as cotton yarn, grew much less rapidly—that is, about two to two-and-a-half times between 1952 and 1959, still a very respectable rate.

This rapid advance was dramatically reversed in the aftermath of the Great Leap. The marked decline of agricultural production in 1959 was soon followed by stagnation and contraction in industry. Thus economic development was brought to a standstill and since 1960 Communist China has been in the throes of a depression. How can this dramatic reversal be explained? What are its background and economic history?

II

In spite of eight years of rapid industrial growth accompanied by relatively non-violent collectivization, Chinese Communist policy-makers approached the end of their first Five-Year Plan with some serious unresolved problems on their hands. They needed a development strategy that would provide a way out of the dilemmas posed by agricultural stagnation. Farm production was growing only slowly, possibly just sufficiently to keep pace with population growth. Moreover, the harvest was subject to sharp fluctuations in response to changing weather conditions. This in turn led to marked annual fluctuations in the rate of industrial growth.

Agriculture was clearly becoming the critical bottleneck in the further development of industry. A poor harvest would inevitably lead to domestic food shortages reflected either in rising prices or in tighter rations. This could, of course, be alleviated by imports of food; but such imports would have to be at the expense of capital goods needed for expansion of industry. In the absence of these imports, food shortages were bound to interfere with the provisioning of an expanding urban labor force. This was brought home forcefully by the fact that while urban population grew by about 30 percent between 1952 and 1957 (rural population increased by only 9 per cent), total government collections of grain did not rise correspondingly throughout this period. Thus collectivization, which was primarily designed to fortify official control over farm output and its disposal, apparently did not bring with it marked increases in what was collected from the farm. Contrary to the planners' scale of preferences, farm consumption probably increased while urban consumption declined.

Under Chinese conditions, agricultural stagnation and poor harvests have an almost immediate impact on industrial production as well. Inasmuch as the bulk of Mainland China's exports were in the past agricultural, shortfalls in farm production thereby reduced the country's capacity to import capital goods for industrialization. At the same time these shortfalls cut into the domestic supplies of raw materials available for textile manufacture and food processing. Thus unless agricultural output could be raised, the growth of industrial capacity would be curtailed, and existing plants would be forced to operate below capacity. To these difficulties were added a rise in the rate of population growth and increasing pressure of population on the available land.

The pressures on agriculture were further aggravated by the fact that Soviet credits were largely exhausted and repayment of the accumulated debt had to begin in 1954–55. Previously, China had imported more from the Soviet Union than she exported—the deficit being financed by credits— but now the situation was reversed. In order to amortize the debt, an export surplus had to be maintained, which in turn meant stepped-up deliveries of agricultural products.

All of these problems converged in the course of 1957, in part due to a succession of two mediocre harvests (in 1956 and 1957) and in part due to strains, shortages and bottlenecks engendered by a sudden and marked increase in the level of investment and the quickening in the pace of collectivization between 1955 and 1956. The Chinese leadership now faced a disconcerting dilemma: to find a strategy which would permit and foster the simultaneous development of agriculture and industry, or to push one at the inevitable expense of the other. Yet it was unthinkable to divert investment resources from industry to agriculture with a consequent decline in the rate of industrial growth.

It was against this background that a new development strategy was evolved during 1958. In its reluctance to divert investment resources from industry to agriculture, it still resembled the Soviet model, but in other respects, and in its implementation, it represented not only a sharp departure from that model, but also from its specifically Chinese variant as incorporated in the first Five-Year Plan.

As shown in the preceding chapter, the new strategy involved mass mobilization of underemployed rural labor on a scale not attempted before, even in China. The same can be said for the development of small-scale industry, which has traditionally been a subsidiary occupation for the Chinese farmer, though mostly confined to weaving of textile cloth and other handicrafts. Now the Chinese planners viewed it as one of the principal means of increasing the rate of industrial growth. In effect, they decided upon the simultaneous development of two distinct industrial sectors: a modern, large-scale, capital-intensive sector and a small-scale, labor-intensive sector. In pursuit of this policy of technological dualism, or "walking on two legs," as it was officially termed, the expansion of small-scale industry was promoted in such fields as iron and steel, machine shops, fertilizer production, power generation and coal extraction, in addition to the more traditional textile and food-processing industries.

The success of this strategy was critically dependent upon the degree to which underemployed labor could in fact be mobilized; if so, whether this could be done without curtailing farm production on the one hand and raising farm consumption on the other; and finally, whether earthen dams or canals, built almost entirely by raw labor without equipment, would be adequate to cope with major floods or droughts. Available evidence suggests that the Chinese leadership genuinely believed that these problems could be overcome through institutional reforms combined with a far-reaching change in the attitudes of cadres and of the peasantry at large.

As to the first, it became clear by early 1958 that the collectives (officially referred to as agricultural producers' cooperatives of the advanced type) were too small in size and too large in number to serve as adequate instruments for administering and controlling vast labor projects; there were then about 740,000 collectives averaging less than 200 households each. Communes, representing an amalgamation of close to 30 collectives with an average membership of about 4,330 households, proved much better suited to this purpose.

As for the need for changed attitudes, the Chinese policy-makers understood that better control and administration had to be coupled with adequate incentives. But reliance on material incentives was precluded if increases in farm production were to be set aside for financing investment in industry. The leaders therefore managed to convince themselves that psychic income would replace increases in real income, provided the attitudes of the rural cadres and particularly of the peasantry could be changed.

The attitude of the party leadership was epitomized by the key slogan of 1958: "Politics takes command." Beginning in late 1957, the impression was conveyed that policy-makers had adopted the principle of "where there's a will there's a way." They appeared to feel that during the period 1955–57 they had overestimated difficulties and underestimated the possible impact of ideological remolding on the economy.

In a sense what the Chinese policy-makers were saying was that ultimately economic development is a function of organization and attitudes as molded by ideology. No doubt these are important and within limits may compensate for lack of physical resources, capital, and backward technology. However, part of the difficulty in late 1957 and in 1958 was that the Chinese leaders talked and acted as if the limitations on their resources were completely irrelevant. In doing so, the party was apparently strongly influenced by its perception of the lessons learned from the collectivization, the "hundred flowers" and the "rectification" campaigns.

Before mid-1955 the official approach to collectivization had been cautious and gradualist. There is considerable evidence of a debate within party councils at the time between those who wanted to maintain this go-slow approach and those who wanted to accelerate the pace. When Mao decisively sided with the latter group, the die was cast and collectivization was completed within a year and a half. Looked at from the vantage point of 1957, collectivization turned out to be surprisingly successful. Contrary to expectations, it encountered no active resistance from the peasantry, was carried out relatively smoothly and without the dire consequences *at the time* that were associated with collectivization in the Soviet Union. This experience no doubt greatly emboldened many elements of the leadership and the party as a whole; it led them to conclude that they had overestimated peasant resistance to change and had given too much weight to the counsel of the technicians and experts who constantly called attention to the constraints, obstacles and difficulties.

As a result, the expert was downgraded—a move reinforced by the discovery during the "hundred flowers" campaign that many intellectuals and professional groups were hostile and ideologically unreliable. This, in turn, prompted the party to embark upon the all-out "rectification" campaign, which stressed the need for greater reliance on the "masses" and on politically tested elements, even if these were technically less competent.

It is within this framework that the ambitious targets of the Great Leap were formulated and that maximum pressure was exerted on the cadres to fulfill and overfulfill them. These pressures, propelled by the notion that nothing was impossible, and coupled with the subordination of economic administration to local party control and the general downgrading of the expert, removed all of the independent checks previously built into the system of economic planning and management. Thus in 1958 the door was opened wide to self-generated delusion concerning production accomplishments in agriculture and industry.

To understand how these errors in judgment were made, one must perhaps reach back into Chinese Communist Party history. It seems quite possible—though it cannot be explicitly documented—that decisions at this time were strongly influenced by experience during the long civil war extending from 1927 to 1949. On many occasions in these years, small guerilla groups were isolated and had to shift for themselves with little or no contact with the Party Center. Under these circumstances, the leaders of these groups had to be given wide latitude and they, in turn, had to exercise initiative and judgment, which they did with notable success. Would not a similar approach be worth trying in 1958 to accomplish somewhat different tasks? And would not the fact that the regime was now at the seat of power, not in the wilderness, facilitate rather than hinder the effort?

Often Chinese Communist writings and major policy speeches suggest that Mao and his closest associates viewed the process of economic development as if it were a series of military campaigns; in their eyes economic development entailed a conquest of successive obstacles and fixed positions. After all, these leaders spent a major part of their life in guerrilla warfare which must have left its mark on their modes and habits of thought. Therefore in formulating economic objectives or policies they looked for ingredients and inputs which were essential for military success; they showed little understanding or appreciation of the measures necessary for economic growth.

III

On top of this came unfavorable weather. While officially all of the blame for the current agricultural crisis is placed on nature, it is clear even from the regime's own pronouncements that the prolonged neglect of agriculture*—inadequate investment, poor production incentives, perpetual re-

---

*This observation pertains primarily to the 1950's. Under the impact of the crisis examined in this paper, agriculture was accorded much higher priority so that this finding would not apply to the 1960's and the early 1970's.

organization and disorganization of agrarian institutions, and a host of specific planning errors—was bound to have an effect sooner or later even if the weather had been favorable. In order to understand the dimensions and the impact of this crisis it is necessary to examine its character in greater detail.

The State Statistical Bureau stopped publishing annual production results in January 1960, after releasing the annual communique on plan fulfillment for the previous year. As a result, for 1960, 1961, and 1962 we do not even have official production claims. However, it has been officially admitted that production declined in recent years, with some statements hinting that it has dropped to 1957 or 1955 levels. Because of all this statistical confusion and secrecy, the last more or less reliable set of agricultural statistics is for 1957; since then, most of our information is based on qualitative and circumstantial evidence. Table 1 represents an attempt to translate these indications into quantitative terms.

As far as hard information is concerned, data on population are perhaps just as scarce and unreliable as for farm production. If one accepts the official figures, population must have grown between 2 and 2.5 percent a

TABLE 1

Total and Per Capita Food Crop Production Trends, 1957–1962

Year	Food Crop Production Index	Population Growth Index, Assuming an Annual Rate of Population Growth of:			Domestically Produced Food Crop Availability Per Capita Based on Assumed Annual Population Growth Rate of:		
		1.5%	2.0%	2.5%	1.5%	2.0%	2.5%
1957	100	100.0	100.0	100.0	100.0	100.0	100.0
1958	115	101.5	102.0	102.5	112.9	112.3	111.8
1959	91	103.0	104.0	105.1	87.9	87.9	86.2
1960	86	104.6	106.1	107.7	82.4	81.2	80.0
1961	90	106.1	108.2	110.4	84.8	83.2	81.5
1962	98	107.7	110.4	113.1	91.4	89.2	87.1

Sources: Food Crop Production Index based on production estimates of the United States agricultural attache in Hong Kong. These series were subsequently revised (see the CONGEN column in Table 1 of chapter 1). The figures in Table 1 of chapter 1, based either on the official or CONGEN series yield a slower rise in 1958 as compared to 1957 and a somewhat slower recovery after the low point reached in 1959. However, these differences are small.

year between 1952 and 1958. Given the depressed food situation and the resulting nutritional deficiencies since 1959, it certainly could not have grown at a higher rate and probably expanded more slowly than that.

Reliable information concerning the precise magnitude of the food crisis is not available. What evidence we have is based on reports of refugees in Hong Kong, of foreign visitors to China, some scattered reports in the Chinese press and the incontrovertible fact that China is importing grain from Canada, Australia, and other countries.

The indices in the table suggest that food crop production reached its low point in 1960, when per capita availability of domestically produced grain declined by close to 20 per cent as compared to 1957—and has been slowly recovering since. Apparently, food production in 1960 dropped even below 1959 levels not only because of another poor harvest, but also because hog-raising and vegetable-growing had been collectivized with bad results.

In retrospect it is clear that the acute food crisis of recent years was brought about by a decline in the quality as well as the quantity of food. As might be expected, the incidence of nutritional diseases increased and apparently reached a peak in 1961. What effect this had on the death rate we do not know. The most that one can say is that, while the food crisis has been serious, there have been no indications of mass famine on a nationwide scale. Nevertheless, the situation in the winter of 1960–61 was so acute that even military rations had to be cut. Partly on this account and partly because the soldiers saw adversity all around them, affecting their relatives and friends as well as themselves, army morale and discipline seem to have been seriously undermined at that time. All this also led to considerable demoralization of local party cadres and of the local militia so that in some areas there were peasant uprisings accompanied by an almost complete disintegration of local administration and authority.

IV

Chinese agriculture was in a state of constant instability between 1949 and 1956. Following three years of turmoil accompanying land reform, the transformation from private landholding to almost complete collectivization was compressed into four short years extending from 1953 to 1956. Yet collectivization did not mark the end of this process. The introduction of the communes—at first slowly and cautiously at the end of 1957, and then at an unusually rapid pace in 1958—spelled not only instability, but upheaval in the countryside.

The precise origin of the communes, in conception and in practice, is rather obscure; but there is no question that they constitute an integral and essential element of the Great Leap. Central to it was the notion of the "mass line," release of the "spontaneous initiative of the masses," mass mobilization of labor and of the total energies of the people as a whole. In implementing this strategy, economic management was decentralized and the communes emerged as instruments of local control and decision-making. In effect, then, centralization at the top was replaced by centralization at the bottom.

What seems to have been intended was a far-reaching and completely revolutionary change in the forms of agricultural production and in the pattern of rural life—not far from the *agrogorods* advocated by Khrushchev at one time. Both in a sense strove for the creation of agricultural cities in which the peasantry would be uprooted from the land and, in effect, proletarianized. Such measures, if successful, would not only greatly facilitate state control over the countryside, but could (it was hoped) lead to a restructuring of peasant attitudes, rendering them more pliable and amenable to the regime's objectives.

Many regulations for these early model communes were not implemented. For instance, dismantling of villages did not get very far. Other measures were not instituted to the same degree everywhere. Many difficulties were encountered in 1958, primarily those revolving around the problems of incentives and of shifting resources (including labor) from place to place.

In this early phase, differentiated and incentive rewards were more and more replaced by an egalitarian wage system based on "each according to his need." This created a great deal of friction, and soon proved to have a negative effect on labor productivity. At the same time, the shifting of labor led to considerable disruption of agricultural production, so that by the end of 1958 and early 1959 the leadership was forced to begin its retreat from the early concept of the commune.

As the agricultural crisis deepened in the course of 1960, mass labor mobilization schemes were abandoned and the construction and special production units that had proliferated during the Great Leap were discontinued. The commune was further decentralized so that gradually the production team, composed of about 40 households, became the basic unit for the allocation of resources and other economic decisions. As part and parcel of this reversal, peasants were again allowed private garden plots where they might raise livestock and vegetables. In many cases even the communal mess halls were abandoned. By the end of 1961, the agrarian transformation of the Great Leap had run full circle. The commune had become little more than a unit of local planning and government, so that in essence the forms of agricultural production, consumption and distribution were back to the collectivization stage of 1955–56.

The uncertainties caused by these experiments and constant shifting back and forth were bound to have a negative effect on incentives; indeed they may have been more damaging than the ills which each change was designed to cure. These constant changes, which have characterized Chinese agricultural policy since 1949, are a symptom of a continuous groping for an incentive system which would allow the regime to have stable consumption with steadily rising production. But, in fact, food supply per capita barely rose—if at all—during the first Five-Year Plan.

Having been relatively successful in their drive to collectivize, and now desperate to break out of the vise of agricultural stagnation, the Chinese were apparently emboldened in 1958 to go beyond tested forms of agricultural and economic organization under socialism. Thus they began to innovate (through communes, through decentralization and through mass mobilization), and in the process departed from the Russian model.

Consequently, while the Chinese carefully avoided the Soviet collectivization debacle up to 1957, they fell after that into the same trap as their Soviet predecessors. But, while a sharp decline in Russian crop and livestock production between 1928 and 1932 did not arrest industrial growth, in China it led to an industrial standstill after 1959. Except during World War II, when vast areas of European Russia were overrun by German armies, the Soviets never experienced industrial stagnation of comparable proportions at any time after 1928. Finally, the Soviets were never forced to reverse radically and completely their order of planning priorities as the Chinese had to do in early 1962.

V

As one surveys Communist China's brief economic history, one is struck time and again by how much harvest fluctuations and trends affect the level of economic activity in general. This relationship became particularly clear when in 1959 the sharp downturn in agricultural output, followed by a succession of several bad crops, led to a cumulative decline in industrial production and in national product as a whole. As the leadership became fully conscious of the depth of the agricultural and economic crisis, it finally closed the books on the Great Leap and the development strategy associated with it. This was coupled with a sober re-assessment and the enunciation of a new economic policy at the Ninth Plenary Session of the Eighth Central Committee in January 1961, when the food supply crisis was at its worst. The policy crystallized in the course of 1961 and was articulated as doctrine by Chou En-lai in his Report on Government Work at the National People's Congress in the spring of 1962.

The new line is based on the slogan that "agriculture is the foundation for the development of the national economy." This is coupled with a policy of "readjusting, consolidating, filling out and raising standards" in industry and all of the non-agricultural sectors. In concrete terms this has meant a complete turnabout in planning priorities, with agricultural development accorded highest rank, and heavy industry relegated below the manufacture of consumer goods. As a result, the level of investment was curtailed and its composition was markedly altered.

The new policy also brought with it an upgrading of technical considerations and a greater reliance on material incentives in all segments of the economy. In industry this meant that greater attention was paid to quality, plant maintenance and costs.

Unfortunately, reliable and precise information on trends in industrial production, investment and employment is not available for recent years. Therefore, we do not know the rates of change in industry between 1960 and 1963. Nevertheless, from official statements and the reports of travelers and refugees, it is possible to determine the direction of movement even if its extent cannot be accurately measured.

It is clear that the pace of industrial advance began to slow down significantly in 1960. At first this decline was confined to the food-processing and textile industries which had to cut back production because of the shortage of raw materials (e.g., cotton, tobacco) resulting from the agricultural crisis. It would appear that in 1960 the level of investment was still increasing although the rate (in relation to national product) probably declined. However, this situation changed markedly when the Great Leap was officially abandoned in 1961; thereafter there was a marked drop in production in most, if not all, branches of industry: in consumer goods industries because of continuing shortages of agricultural raw materials, and in producer goods industries because of shortages in demand engendered by investment cutbacks resulting from the agricultural crisis. The decline in heavy industry was also accelerated by the exodus of Soviet technicians in the fall of 1960, which delayed the completion of a number of plants. Also, some existing plants were closed, creating significant pockets of urban unemployment.

The net result of this stagnation is that much of the ground gained by industry during the Great Leap has been lost in the past three years. On the basis of qualitative indications, it would appear that for a number of industrial products, output fell back to 1958—and in quite a few cases even to 1957—levels. The principal exceptions to this are crude-oil extraction, which apparently continued to expand throughout all of these years, and certain branches of the chemical industry, particularly fertilizer production, which of course is closely tied to the "agriculture first" policy. More recently there has also been a growing emphasis on the manufacture of synthetic fibers in a gradual attempt to render the country's textile industry less dependent on agricultural raw materials.

In effect, then, since 1960 the Chinese economy has exhibited many of the classical symptoms of a deep economic depression, quite uncharacteristic of Soviet-type economies. The Great Leap had induced a sharp rise in urban employment and migration to the cities; in the depression that followed, this swollen and partially unemployed population in turn complicated the problem of urban food supply at a time of falling agricultural production. A more or less forced backward migration to the villages was then called for, apparently with the thought not only of easing the urban food problem, but also of reducing the burden of collecting food in the countryside. By relying to a considerable extent upon grain imports to feed the remaining urban population, the regime could preserve—at least for the time being—its more favorable incentive system. The net effect of these measures is that in the last three years, China has in some respects reverted to a prewar pattern of agricultural trade. She has once more become a net importer of grain, using these imports to feed the cities and thus relieve the burden imposed on the peasant.

It now appears that the 1960–61 consumption year marked the low point of the depression. Since the 1962 harvest, there has been a significant improvement in the supply of food and agricultural raw materials, as well as some signs of a general economic recovery. Whether this recovery will continue and provide the basis for a comulative upturn, it is too early to say. As always in China, the quality of the harvest in the next few years will be one of the decisive factors.

Is China's present economic stagnation temporary or is it a more chronic condition reflecting intractable problems? In attempting an answer, we should remember that the Chinese Communists mounted a program of economic development which carried them forward with a strong momentum for "ten great years," 1949–59. The rapid rate of economic growth attained justified itself and spurred on the party, the cadres and the people to increasing effort and sacrifice. To be sure, during the first half of that decade, economic expansion was speeded to a considerable extent by rehabilitation of war-devastated or disrupted plants, so that relatively modest inputs yielded sizeable increments in output. Another favorable factor was the availability of Soviet credits until 1957 and of Soviet technical assistance until mid-1960.

In recent years, on the other hand, some uniquely unfavorable factors have been at work. In addition to a succession of three bad growing seasons, the sudden withdrawal of Soviet technicians in 1960 and the near cessation of complete plant deliveries following on its heels contributed greatly to the sharp curtailment and disruption of industrial production. These special conditions aside, the failure of the Great Leap itself seriously damaged morale and organization. The setback destroyed the image of invincibility and infallibility in which the regime had enveloped itself; the cadres were left confused and disillusioned and the people's confidence in the leadership was shaken. At the same time the institutional framework of the economy was weakened. This of course applies particularly to agricultural organization, patterns of land use and the whole incentive structure in agriculture. Last but not least, statistical services were profoundly disorganized and technical considerations were thrown to the wind.

These tendencies have, of course, been reversed since 1961–62, but the question remains how rapidly the damage can be repaired. If the leadership continues to pursue an "agriculture first" policy, if it can curb its ambitions for rapid industrialization, if it keeps the rate of investment at modest levels, and if it carefully nurtures a favorable incentive system in the countryside, it may gradually repair the damage done and bring the economy to the point where rapid industrialization is again feasible. It may be that the Chinese Communist leadership has set aside the third Five-Year Plan period (1963–67) for this purpose.

Chapter 10

On China's Descending Spiral

Mr. Alsop in his most interesting article advances four basic propositions:

1. There are limits to the hardships which any government can safely inflict upon the governed. These limits will vary from society to society depending upon a host of factors such as climate, historical conditioning, customary standard of living, etc.
2. Communist China is caught in a remorselessly descending spiral, which if not reversed will drive the system to the breaking point.
3. This breaking point seems to be near and may in fact be reached if this year's harvest also turns out to be poor.
4. The break may lead to three alternative types of development: a New Economic Policy—somewhat along the lines followed by Lenin in the early twenties—a new type of Communist regime perhaps emulating the Polish example, or a total collapse under the pressure of an elemental peasant rebellion in the tradition of Chinese rebellions of the past. Of these three alternatives, the first seems least likely, while the chances for the last would increase in proportion with a worsening food situation.

I find myself in rather complete agreement with the first and the last proposition, but have serious reservations concerning parts of the intervening analysis. Similarly, while the discussion of factors that contributed to the food crisis is based on relatively firm ground, including the differ-

Reprinted from *The China Quarterly,* October-December 1962, under the title "Is There a Descending Spiral in China?" This brief essay was written in response to an article published by Joseph Alsop in *The China Quarterly* forecasting a collapse of the Chinese Communist regime under the then prevailing agricultural crisis.

ences in the Chinese and Soviet pre-collectivization situations, considerable doubts are raised by the analysis of the dimensions of the food crisis itself.

In approaching this problem it is essential to bear in mind that our information concerning the general economic situation in China and the trends in industrial and agricultural production is quite poor since 1957, and most particularly since 1959. None of us, and probably not even the Chinese authorities, know how much food was actually produced on the Mainland in 1958–62. Therefore it may be well to approach the study of China's economic development since 1958, and especially since 1960, with caution and considerable humility, rather than with absolute certitude.

This is not intended to suggest that we are completely at sea. There is no doubt that the food situation in China has been serious since 1959 or 1960, but the question is how serious. What has been the actual level of food consumption? Has it declined continuously year by year? And what is the nature of the evidence available to us concerning these issues?

One incontrovertible item of evidence is the far-reaching restructuring of China's foreign trade for which we have good and rather complete statistics from the trading partners' side. Thus it is clear that China's exports declined by one third between 1959 and 1961, largely due to the country's inability to maintain agricultural exports at its former levels. The seriousness of the agricultural crisis was even further underlined by large scale grain imports from Canada and Australia, beginning in 1961. As a result, the whole commodity composition of foreign trade has been radically altered. The shift is most striking on the import side, where foodstuffs constituted less than 1 per cent of the total in 1959 and about 40 per cent in 1961.

Another incontestable indication of the food crisis is its explicit recognition in a number of Chinese Communist statements and official policy pronouncements. This was most clearly dramatized by Chou En-lai's speech before the last session of the National People's Congress, in which the order of planning priorities was radically reversed, with agriculture being elevated to the position of the "leading sector." However, none of these straws in the wind provide an adequate basis for estimating the *extent* to which household food consumption has declined. For this we must rely on refugee reports. But, how reliable are these?

Theoretically, if a large number of refugees were to flow into Hongkong from all parts of China, it should be possible to construct a carefully designed sample representative of the total mainland population. In order to be representative, the sample would have to be carefully stratified in terms of rural or urban origin, regional background, occupation, etc. In fact, none of the Hongkong refugee reports on which our information concerning food consumption levels is based satisfies these conditions. The overwhelming bulk of refugees come from one province, Kwangtung, and even more particularly from one part of that province with only a thin scattering from other parts of China. Therefore, at best they can provide relatively reliable reports of the trends in food consumption in one province which *may*, but *need not*, be indicative of the trends in the country as a whole.

Quite apart from the problem of representativeness, how reliable are these refugee reports, and therefore how warranted is the judgment that the food consumption figures obtained from them are "unchallengeable except by those experts who think they know more about the Chinese diet than the people who have recently been eating it?" The latter statement takes it for granted that people are fully aware of what kinds of food, and in precisely what quantities, they consume daily. One cannot help but wonder whether such complete confidence in human memory is justified. It might perhaps be safe to assume that refugee information concerning the size and composition of the food rations would be more or less reliable. The same could hardly be said of the non-rationed items obtained in the free market, the black market, or from food parcels sent by overseas Chinese. Admittedly, the rationed foods represent a very significant proportion of the total, yet the remainder is sufficiently large so that a substantial margin of error just in the non-rationed portion could significantly affect the estimated level of total calorie intake.

The problem at hand is further complicated by the fact that, precisely because of these methodological difficulties, a number of different food consumption estimates have been published relating to the same period and all based on refugee reports. Most of these indicate a daily food consumption level of 1,600–1,700 calories for the past winter, rather than 1,300–1,600.

Therefore, for all of the reasons cited above, it is most doubtful that we can derive a reliable estimate of food consumption levels in China today. On the other hand, it may be possible to determine the direction of change. Has the food situation continuously deteriorated since 1958, has it fluctuated up and down at random, or has it entered a descending spiral up to a point which then was reversed? This question can be illuminated by (*a*) a careful scrutiny of mainland press reports concerning weather conditions, floods, droughts, rations, and food consumption trends, (*b*) travellers' reports concerning crop and food conditions, and (*c*) refugee reports.

A careful analysis of this evidence does not support the vision of a spiral ever descending up to the present day. The situation is rather more complex and mixed, defying black and white characterization with broad brush strokes. A study of the aforementioned sources suggests that the food crisis in China reached its low point in the Spring of 1961 for several reasons. By all indications the 1960 harvest was the poorest since 1958. In spite of this, food exports were maintained at a high level, although somewhat reduced as compared to the preceding year. Whatever food stocks were accumulated after the 1958 harvest were dissipated by that time so that reserves must have reached a critical point. It is against this background that the regime was finally forced to resort to large-scale imports of grain. As a result, under the double impact of a slightly better harvest in 1961 and growing grain imports, the food situation seems to have improved in 1961–62 as compared to 1960–61. Thus the descending spiral in food consumption seems to have been arrested, at least for the time being. This tendency was reinforced by a relatively favorable winter crop this year.

At the same time, the declining trend in industrial production seems to lag behind agriculture. The limited information that is available indicates that industrial production started to decrease in 1960, i.e., a year later than farm output. This decrease seems to be continuing up to the present time under the combined impact of agricultural raw materials shortages for consumer goods industries (e.g., textiles and food processing) on the one hand, and a marked curtailment in the demand for investment goods on the other. The latter is, of course, also traceable to the agricultural crisis which has forced a reallocation of resources from saving and investment into consumption to provide the necessary incentives to the peasantry for the recovery of farm production. As a result, industry is at present operating well below capacity levels and there is apparently considerable unemployment.

What are the implications of all this for political stability? Does this imply that the regime is near the breaking point so that it is apt to collapse under the weight of a peasant or mass rebellion of some kind, or is it likely to be transformed from within it? Obviously these questions cannot be answered without much more information about popular attitudes and the

Chinese Communist leadership structure. In the absence of such information we can only speculate and perhaps delineate the kinds of conditions
that may be expected to lead to one rather than another outcome.

Granting the general proposition that a constantly deteriorating food
situation is bound to threaten political stability at some point, the question arises at what point? This is not only a matter of trends in calorie
levels, but also in attitudes, psychological predispositions, strength of
political organization, etc. Thus would one expect unrest to be most
widespread and most active when food consumption levels are so low that
people begin to feel seriously debilitated, weak and apathetic? Or, would
the critical point be reached well before then, when people still feel quite
vigorous? With the same average levels of per capita food consumption, is
it immaterial as to how the total food supply is distributed among the
different groups of the population? Given a limited food supply, which
pattern of distribution is likely to assure greater political stability: spread-
ing availabilities evenly so that everyone is assured a bare minimum or less,
or providing a fully adequate diet to those who hold the levers of
power—i.e., the army, security organs, and the Party cadres—and distribut-
ing the rest perhaps evenly? Another very difficult problem in this context
is duration. That is, whatever the critical food consumption minimum may
be, for what period of time would the people be willing to endure a diet
which is below this level? Would it be one month, one year, five years, or
ten years?

Just raising these questions clearly indicates how many imponderables
enter into this equation, and therefore how insoluble the equation may be
if it is formulated in this particular way. It is rather doubtful therefore as
to how operational or fruitful the concept of a specific breaking point may
be even if one admits that logically there must be some such point
somewhere. Perhaps a comparison of past Chinese and Japanese food
consumption levels may help to place this problem in perspective. Average
per capita food consumption in prewar China (1931–37) was estimated by
FAO at 2,220 calories daily. For prewar Japan (1934–38), for which the
figures are incidentally much more reliable, the corresponding estimate is
2,175 calories. On this basis, it would seem that the two levels were very
close. This comparison is reinforced by the fact that the composition of
the diet was similar too, i.e., in both cases about 77 percent of the total
was derived from cereals and tubers. During the war, Japanese food intake
declined to an estimated 1,990 calories daily.[1] In 1946, shortly after

surrender, the situation deteriorated rapidly so that Japan was facing a critical food shortage. Food available from domestic sources could provide no more than 1,435 calories. It was assumed that this total supply was, however, very unevenly distributed, with the rural population consuming an estimated 2,000 to 2,200 calories daily, leaving only 925 to 1,060 calories for the urban population. This was considered to be well below the 1,550 calories defined by the occupation forces as the minimum required to avoid serious disturbances.[2]

The 1,550 calorie figure is of interest primarily because it represents a conscious attempt to translate the concept of a breaking point into quantitative terms in a dietary setting that is similar to the Chinese. Unfortunately, however, the political setting of Communist China today is so vastly different from that of postwar Japan that given the imponderables referred to above, this figure could hardly be used in the Chinese context.

All of this suggests the need for alternative approaches to the study of conditions conducive to political stability or breakdown in Communist China. Given the instruments of terror at the disposal of the authorities and barring a much more serious deterioration in economic conditions than is presently in sight—say a further decline in food consumption by 20 to 30 per cent—the regime is much more likely to be threatened from groups within the power elite than from the masses.

Given the commitment to rapid industrialization and the rising national power of mainland China closely associated with it, prolonged stagnation could deprive the regime of its principal ideological sanction, particularly in the eyes of the Party and its cadres. This is perhaps the central reason why it must regain its momentum if it is to survive in the long run.

What are the chances for this occurring? As in the past this depends to a large extent on weather and the policies of the regime. The strategic variable here is how soon will there be a good harvest and what will the regime do with it. The agricultural crisis has gone beyond the point where the planners can afford to skim off once more the surplus gained in one good harvest for raising the rate of investment and channelling the bulk of it into the development of investment goods industries, all at the expense of agriculture. If this is attempted, the agricultural situation is bound to deteriorate even further. That is, attempts to pursue either the First Five-Year Plan or the Great Leap strategy are likely to prove abortive until agriculture is well under way to recovery. Therefore, if the regime is to regain its momentum, it must utilize a good harvest as a basis for launching a new Five-Year Plan which would accord first priority to agricultural development with everything that this implies.*

To be effective, such a strategy would need to be based on a lower rate of saving and investment so as to leave enough room for the full operation of incentives in the countryside. At the same time, a significantly larger share of the total investment basket would have to be allotted to agriculture. If such a program is carried out wholeheartedly and the necessary institutional adjustments are made, domestically produced food supply per capita might perhaps be restored to 1957 levels in about five years. It may be roughly estimated that China's population has grown by about 8 per cent since the end of 1957, while farm production has remained stationary. Thus, assuming an average rate of population growth of 2 per cent over the next few years, for per capita food supply to be restored to 1957 levels, farm production would have to grow at 4 per cent a year over the next five years. This would be a significantly higher rate than was actually attained during the First Five-Year Plan, but given adequate incentives, proper organization and adequate investment, it may not be beyond the country's reach.

Agricultural recovery based on some such allocation pattern would naturally have favorable repercussions upon industrial recovery as well. However, after plants reached full capacity again, industrial development would probably be proceeding at a significantly slower pace than during the First Five-Year Plan. In effect, the planners would be trading agricultural recovery for a substantial rate of industrial growth, but one that would be lower than that of the past.

None of this is intended to imply a forecast that this will indeed be done, but merely that it could be done under certain specified conditions. How feasible would such a program be in political terms? Is it reasonable to expect that the present regime would adopt such a strategy of economic development? In a sense, a program very much along these lines seems to have been promulgated at the National People's Congress this Spring and is apparently being implemented at the present time. This could of course be easily reversed in case of a good harvest. Therefore, ultimately one's judgment on this problem will depend upon what assumptions one makes

---

*It is interesting to note that this approach has in fact been pursued since this paper was published.

about the structure and rationality of the top leadership. Certainly, the possibility of factionalism, sharp conflicts, a struggle for power, and a realignment within the leadership, under the stresses and strains of economic stagnation cannot be ruled out. Similarly, it could be that the policy makers will once more indulge in wishful thinking and become prisoners of their own dogma and propaganda as appears to have been the case in 1958–59. On the other hand, the cohesive tradition and force within the leadership were quite strong and durable in the past. Furthermore, Chinese Communist history, both before and after 1949—with the single but most important exception of the Great Leap period—is characterized by a clear recognition of where the Party's self-interest lay and by a calculated assessment of what policies are best suited to accomplish the Party's objectives.

Chapter 11

Economic Fluctuations in Communist China's Domestic Development

Definition of the Issues

Business cycles and endogenously generated economic fluctuations have generally been considered as peculiar characteristics of market-oriented free enterprise economies.[1] In effect, they have been considered as a hallmark of the capitalist order and of economic development under capitalism. This view has been commonly held by virtually all of the various schools of Marxism and the different wings of the socialist movement have been united in this belief. Recurring crises and alternating movements of expansion and contraction with their dire social consequences in the nineteenth century constituted one of the principal elements of Marx's indictment of the capitalist order. By the same token, implicitly and explicitly socialist systems of economic organization were assumed to be free of these economic fluctuations.

This view is also widely, if not uniformly, held by many professional economists. However, postwar developments in the socialist economies of Europe and Asia suggest a need for a re-examination of this assumption. It is perhaps an interesting paradox that just at the time when questions are being raised as to whether the business cycle is obsolete in so-called capitalist economies, economic fluctuations seem to appear with a certain degree of regularity in socialist economies. The possible presence of fluctuations in the economies of Eastern Europe and the Soviet Union was first noted by the present writer in 1958.[2] Since then a growing interest in this problem has developed among economists and an international conference on business cycles and economic fluctuations held in the spring of

Reprinted from Ping-ti Ho and Tang Tsou, eds., *China in Crisis*, vol. I, bk. 2, University of Chicago Press, Chicago, 1968.

1967 had a special session set aside for an analysis and discussion of this phenomenon in socialist economies.[3]

Assuming that further empirical research validates the hypothesis that economic fluctuations can be endemic to socialist as well as to capitalist economies, one may presuppose a priori that no single theory could be equally applicable to all these different types of economies. Thus a theory of economic fluctuations for socialist economies may need to incorporate a different set of variables than those that would be considered relevant for a private business economy. Given the much larger role of central management and planning, a theory of economic fluctuations applicable to socialist economies would have to give much greater weight, or would have to pay much more attention, to the economic behavior of the central planners and policy makers than would need to be the case for the business economy. It is also doubtful that a single theory can serve as an adequate explanation for economic fluctuations even in various types of socialist economies. Thus one would imagine that a rather different type of theory would be required for a preponderantly foreign-trade-oriented socialist economy as compared to a much more inward-oriented system. Similarly one would expect a rather different pattern of cyclical behavior in a preponderantly industrialized, commercialized, and monetized system as compared to a predominantly agricultural economy.

Bearing these general considerations in mind I will attempt to develop a tentative theory of economic fluctuations applicable to China. I will then attempt to subject this theory to some empirical tests by analyzing the actual course of economic policy behavior in China and the behavior of a number of important economic indicators. All references to economic fluctuations in this paper will be to changes in the rates of growth rather than changes in the absolute levels of economic activity. In a sense, one might view level cycles merely as special cases of growth cycles. Generally, in this paper economic fluctuations, unless otherwise specified, will not refer to business cycles in the conventional sense of that term. Obviously, by definition, we could not identify *business* cycles in socialist economies such as that of China, since we are not dealing with a business system; we are not dealing with private enterprises and private businessmen as important actors in the system, as independent actors that affect levels of economic activity and patterns of resource allocation.[4]

In most general terms, fluctuations in rates of economic growth in Communist China can be viewed as resulting from a confrontation between Mao's vision of development possibilities in the Chinese economy and society and the country's economic backwardness—particularly as evidenced by a high degree of population pressure, rapid population growth, a technically backward agriculture, and a low per capita food supply resulting therefrom. The essence of the theory to be developed further below is that the constant interplay between these two sets of forces creates a perpetual conflict between the goal structure of the policy makers and the economic capabilities of the system. This conflict and attempts to resolve it leads to a dialectic process which provides both the basic engine of growth and the sources of cyclical fluctuation in Communist China.

Some Key Concepts

Before proceeding with an outline of the theoretical framework on which this analysis is based, it is necessary to define a few standard concepts in the theory of economic fluctuations. First of all I am using the term *economic fluctuations* rather than *business cycles* advisedly, since the former is a more comprehensive concept while, obviously, the latter is more restrictive; the former can be applied both to economies based on private business organization as well as to other forms of economic organization.[5] Second, for our purpose, fluctuations may best be defined as recurring alternations of expansion and contraction in rates of growth in economic activity.[6]

These economic fluctuations bear certain definite characteristics. They tend to be cumulative and self-reinforcing so that a change in a given direction generates further change in the same direction. Thus, in a sense, movement in one direction tends to feed on itself; once begun it persists until endogenous forces accumulate to reverse the direction. Moreover these fluctuations tend to be pervasive in their effects. They affect virtually all sectors of the economy but not necessarily simultaneously, that is, not necessarily at the same time, or in the same way and at the same rate. There is no evidence that these fluctuations recur over and over again in precisely the same form, that they are precisely of the same duration, or that the amplitude of movement is the same in each case. Analyses of business cycles in capitalist economies suggest that the duration of a cycle may vary anywhere from two to ten years. Business cycle history for the United States suggests a range of duration from 28 to 99 months.

For purposes of analysis, we can distinguish four phases in these movements: the upper turning point, the downswing or contraction, the lower turning point, and the upswing or expansion. In measuring duration, we usually consider the lapse of time between two consecutive upper or lower turning points. A theory of economic fluctuations must meet certain minimum requirements in order to have adequate explanatory value. First, it must distinguish between endogenous and exogenous variables, that is, variables which are endemic to the economic system and to the character of economic activity as compared to variables which lie outside the economic system or outside the explanatory model. Second, the theory must incorporate an explanation and a set of hypotheses about the turning points and a set of hypotheses about the character of the downswing and the upswing. Moreover it must indicate and explain how the ingredients and characteristics of one phase endogenously generate the next phase.

In proposing a theory of economic fluctuations, there is no presumption that all changes in levels and/or rates of growth in economic activity, or all disturbances in these, are endogenously generated or necessarily take the form of cyclical fluctuations. Any economic system may be, and is in fact, subject to random disturbances which necessarily interact with the cycle and may affect the particular characteristics of a single cycle or, in some cases, even several cycles. Another factor to be considered is that fluctuations are closely intertwined with long-term secular changes and secular movements in the economy. These secular changes and movements revolve around the operation of such variables as population growth, labor force participation rates, changes in technology and labor productivity, changes in the quality of the labor force, changes in tastes, and long-term changes in economic organization and institutions. In a sense, economic change, economic growth and decline, and the whole economic process represent a continuous interaction between cycles and trends, both of which mutually interact and mutually shape each other. In the Chinese case, the period we are dealing with is really too short to permit too many generalizations about trends and secular movements, although as we will try to show below there are definite indications that these have affected fluctuations in certain ways. However, the period does not seem to be too short—18 years since 1949—to reveal the presence of several successive cycles.

Finally, the predictive value of the model developed in some detail below is necessarily more limited than its explanatory value. The theoretical framework on which the model is based rests on certain givens, namely the character of Mao's cosmology, the prevailing system of economic organization, a low per capita agricultural product, and a critical dependence of the non-farm sectors on agricultural output changes. The first of these characteristics may perhaps be the most ephemeral of the four and to the extent that Maoism should not survive Mao, the model may need to be modified accordingly. However, unless Mao's death leads to sudden and drastic alterations in official ideology and in economic institutions, the behavioral characteristics of the system may be expected to change rather slowly and gradually. In time, as these changes lead to significant departures from presently prevailing features of the system, both the explanatory and the predictive value of the model is bound to be reduced.

The Theoretical Framework

As indicated, mainland China's economic history since 1949 could be viewed as a perpetual confrontation between Mao's cosmology, Mao's vision, the vision of the Chinese Communist Party (CCP), on the one hand, and the realities of the country's economic and technical backwardness, on the other. It is the conflict between these two sets of forces and continuous attempts to resolve and reconcile this conflict that ultimately produces cyclical behavior in patterns of economic growth. The core of the hypothesis to be further developed below is that these fluctuations are generated by the interactions of a harvest cycle and a policy cycle. The harvest cycle is in part weather-induced and in part policy-induced. On the other hand the policy cycle revolves around a *vision*-induced pursuit of industrialization which leads to resource mobilization measures with attendant input augmentation effects, but at the cost of disincentives and inefficiencies in the utilization of these added inputs. Therefore, before proceeding further, it will be necessary to define the elements of the *vision* and the elements of Chinese economic backwardness.

Mao's Vision

An analysis of Mao's writings, speeches, articles, editorials, as well as those of his close associates, reveals his ideal of a Communist man and of the possibilities open for development and transformation of society and economy made possible by the particular characteristics of Communist man. Similarly they reveal Mao's *vision* of a future industrialized socialist society.

Possibly one of the most interesting characteristics of Maoism is its overwhelming stress on man. Man is the most precious thing. "Of all the things in the world, *people are the most precious.* As long as there are people, every kind of miracle can be performed under the leadership of the Communist Party."[7] Actually what Mao means is that man is *potentially* most precious or, more specifically, that man being malleable, he can be energized and committed and his potential mobilized provided that he is properly organized and indoctrinated by the CCP.[8] Coupled with this stress on man is an almost messianic quality, a conviction that almost all men may be saved, although salvation is enormously difficult and back-sliding is an ever-present danger. This danger can only be countered by vigilance, continuous indoctrination, and periodic "rectification" movements.

This Communist man, once properly imbued, indoctrinated, and committed, can become a fountain of tremendous energy and consciousness which can conquer nature and overcome virtually all obstacles. "The more it is possible for men to carry out a conscious revolution in their own social relationships, the more they increase their power in the combat with nature, the more they can really command as by magic the latent productive forces, making them appear everywhere and develop rapidly."[9] The same theme was reiterated by Mao in 1955 when he said, ". . . people consider impossible things which could be done if they exerted themselves."[10]

Another outstanding characteristic of Communist man, or perhaps one should say of model Communist man, is his capacity for total self-denial. For instance A. S. Chen in an analysis of 48 stories published in China during the first half of 1960 found in them two preoccupations about work: first, the sacrifice of sleep for the sake of work, particularly for carrying out scientific experiments and pursuing inventions, and second, a complete imperviousness to weather conditions. Thus these stories in effect tended to glorify man's dedication to work and his ability and willingness to overcome natural limitations and to subordinate his bodily needs and personal comforts to the tasks of socialist construction.[11] The same theme of self-denial is stressed much more explicitly and repeatedly in one of the basic party documents drafted by Liu Shao-ch'i "On the Training of a Communist Party Member." In it Liu stresses that "the individual interests of the Party member are subordinate to the interests of the Party, which means subordinate to the interests of class and national liberation, of Communism and of social progress. The test of a Communist Party member's loyalty to the Party and to the task of the revolution and Communism is his ability, regardless of the situation, to subordinate his individual interests unconditionally and absolutely to those of the Party." This is given added emphasis in Ch'en Yun's directive on "How to Be a Communist Party Member." He points out that "every Communist Party member should not only have an unwavering faith in the realization of Communism, but also be resolved to fight to the very end, undaunted by either sacrifices or hardships, for the liberation of the working class, the Chinese nation, and the Chinese people." At the same time "Communist Party members are fighters for a Communist *mission* under a leadership of the Party. Thus the interests of a Party member are identical with those of the nation, the people, and the Party. Every party member should give his unlimited devotion to the nation, to the revolution, to our class, and to the Party, *subordinating individual interests* to those of the nation, the revolution, our class, and the Party."[12]

Another essential ingredient of Communist man is his initiative and inventiveness, his willingness to experiment, to innovate, to try out new things. This is another one of the very important themes found by Mrs. Chen in her studies of the Chinese stories published in the early 1960's. These stories convey the impression that an ordinary factory worker or young technician without research training and sometimes even without much formal scientific education can, by sheer determination and long hours of persistent work and study, come up with inventions which can make an immediate contribution to production. Similarly in agriculture, innovative efforts can overcome limitations imposed by weather, soil conditions, water supply, etc.

Very significant operational and policy consequences follow from this vision of Communist man possessed with these particular attributes of self-denial, total commitment, energy, struggle, initiative, and inventiveness. The stress on "men over machines" or "men over weapons" or "better red than expert" logically follows from the above vision of Communist man. This does not mean that Mao necessarily believes that man in Chinese Communist society actually conforms to this ideal. It merely means that he is convinced that, given certain conditions, man *can* approximate the ideal and the model spelled out above. Furthermore, a careful analysis of the writings and directives of the fifties and sixties will show that at least as far as the top leadership is concerned, "red" and "expert," "men" and "machines," and "men" and "weapons" are not as sharp dichotomies and dualities as they are at times interpreted to be in different writings on Chinese Communist ideology, polity, society, and economy. In the short run, these are viewed by the leadership as possible substitutes. Under certain conditions, and most pronouncedly during the Great Leap, ideological commitment, mass mobilization, and organization were viewed as possible substitutes for expertness, professionalism, and the availability of capital equipment.

However, it was all along recognized that in the longer run professionalism, technological progress, advanced weapons, and complex machinery were necessary for continuing economic growth. In this longer run, expertness was, and probably still is, viewed as an integral part of redness; that is, part of being "red" is to be inventive and innovative, and to seek scientific training and education sufficient to enable one to carry out innovations either of a simple or of a more complex character, depending on one's role in the economy. Conversely, even a scientist or an expert who has all the necessary qualifications will not be innovative and inventive unless he is imbued with a spirit of boldness, zeal, and ideological commitment.

In Mao's and the Chinese Communist's view all of these qualities combined are necessary to realize the vision of a powerful industrialized China which is beginning to catch up in terms of economic progress and in terms of growing national power with the Soviet Union and with the countries of the West.

The accent on man, on consciousness, on the human will, on the role of policy and organization, and the primacy of politics represent Leninist elements in Maoism. However, these elements have been given much greater emphasis by Mao and seem to play a much more central role in his cosmology as compared to Lenin's. This strong streak of voluntarism can be viewed as an outgrowth of China's backwardness and lack of the classical Marxist-type preconditions for revolution. It reflects a recognition that revolutions must be willed and organized rather than expected to arise more or less spontaneously out of conditions of economic and social disintegration or crisis.

In this cosmology, industrialization plays a double role and is derived from two different wellsprings: Marxism and nationalism. On the one hand, the revolution re-creates the Marxist evolutionary path through rapid industrialization. Thus, through rapid industrialization a proletariat is developed and strengthened so that the end result of the process conforms to the Marxist schema of a proletarian dictatorship. On the other hand, industrialization serves as a prime means and as a necessary condition for attaining military and economic power. It provides the only road to great-power status in the modern world.

The Realities of China's Backwardness

The salient elements of China's economic backwardness are relatively well known and need not detain us too long. It may be sufficient just to sketch them out briefly.[13] For our purposes, the most essential fact about the Chinese mainland economy is its preponderantly agricultural character. While population and labor force data are unsatisfactory, and the same applies to agricultural production statistics, there is a wide degree of consensus that 70–80 per cent of the country's labor force is tied down in agriculture and about 40 per cent of the national product is generated in the farming sector. This is a preponderantly pre-modern agriculture based on highly labor-intensive methods of cultivation within a framework of traditional and pre-modern technology. Given the high degree of population pressure on the land, labor productivity is low, per capita product is low, and total food supply availabilities per person are consequently quite low as well. Given the prevailing pattern of land use combined with agricultural backwardness, production has traditionally been subject to more or less marked harvest fluctuations. With a low average per capita agricultural product, the farmer and his family necessarily live close to the subsistence margin, agricultural surpluses have tended to be relatively small, and the bulk of the agricultural product has been generally consumed within the farming sector itself. In such a preponderantly agricultural economy, aggregate levels of economic activity are necessarily closely dependent upon the fates of the farming sector. The production of goods and services in the non-agricultural industries is directly or indirectly dependent to a greater or lesser degree upon agriculture.

What is the character of this interdependence? First of all agriculture serves as a potential source of labor supply for the non-farm sector. Given a high degree of population pressure on arable land resources, rapid rates of population growth, and no opportunities—or at best only limited opportunities—for new land settlement, labor surpluses are likely to be generated in agriculture. Second, it is the principal supplier of wage goods to the non-agricultural labor force. Thus, fluctuations in farm output will not only affect the availability of food supplies, but of clothing as well, with the latter largely dependent upon the production of cotton and wool. In turn, the state of wage good supplies not only conditions the consumption levels of the non-agricultural labor force, but also affects industrial labor productivity both through its effect on incentives and on nutritional standards. Third, as indicated above, agriculture is a major supplier of raw materials to the consumer goods industries, most particularly to the various branches of food processing and textiles.

Fourth, levels of investment activity are also closely intertwined with levels of agricultural activity. However, these investment linkages are most indirect. As noted before, fluctuations in farm output and changes in raw materials supplies resulting therefrom tend to have a marked effect on the output of consumer goods industries. This, in turn, will necessarily have an effect on the investment good demand of the consumer goods industries. In socialist systems, fluctuations in investment goods demand by the consumer goods industries could—at least theoretically—be made up by counterbalancing movements in investment goods demand by the investment goods industries themselves and by industries producing the inputs for these branches of manufacture.

Let us examine this proposition. Suppose that agricultural output declines and that as a result consumer goods industries are faced with raw materials shortages. ("Declines" as used here is intended to refer to declines both in rates of growth and in levels. The inter-relationships traced here would hold under *ceteris paribus* assumptions for both, although one would expect the effects to be milder for rate declines than for level declines.) A decline in agricultural output will necessarily lead to a decline in the output of manufactured consumer goods, which then will affect investment goods demand by these industries. Why should this affect total investment in a centrally planned and managed economy? As noted above, a decline in agricultural production will lead to a decline in the supply of wage goods. This, in turn, may be expected to produce strong dis-incentive effects with a negative impact on industrial labor productivity. Should real stringencies in wage goods supplies develop, these might affect the physical health and strength of the workers, thus leading to very sharp declines in labor productivity. Such effects would not be confined to consumer goods industries but may be expected to encompass all branches of mining and manufacturing, leading to a possible decline in output or at least to sharply rising real costs per unit.

Quite apart from these effects, investment goods output is likely to be curtailed amidst declining farm production due to the large import component in China's capital goods output. At this stage of development, China's exports must necessarily be largely agricultural. More specifically, the bulk of these exports consist of foodstuffs, raw materials of agricultural origin, and processed products and manufactures dependent upon agricultural raw materials such as cotton textiles. Therefore a decline in farm production will necessarily depress exports and, thus, the capacity to finance imports. To the extent that China's investment goods industries have been critically dependent on imported components, a curtailment in capital goods imports can in and of itself produce serious bottlenecks in the investment goods industries. Moreover, the more serious the downturn in farm production, the more acute will be the effect on capital goods imports, and thus on capital goods output.

It is apparent therefore that the international sector constitutes a fifth link between agriculture and the non-farm branches of the economy. Theoretically, the constraints imposed by agriculture on food supply, raw materials for consumer goods industries, and the supply of wage goods could be relieved through imports. The only problem is that these same constraints affect exports, and thus the capacity to import. As a result, just when the constraints are most severe it is also most difficult to relieve all of them simultaneously via the import route. That is, one set of supply bottlenecks can be relieved either at the expense of leaving another set untouched or possibly even aggravating it.

One might presuppose that in a centrally managed economy with far-reaching political controls the link between fluctuations in farm production and urban food supplies could be broken. This indeed was the case in the Soviet Union when grain exports were rising while farm production was markedly shrinking under the impact of collectivization in the early thirties. However, in China it was apparently not possible to duplicate this Stalinist "feat." It is not entirely clear to what extent this was due to the fact that the Chinese peasantry lives much closer to the subsistence margin than its Russian counterparts, or to the reluctance of the mainland regime to apply brute force in the same or in greater measure as that used by Stalin. As a result, the constraints imposed by agriculture on the economy as a whole are necessarily more severe in China than they were in Russia during the period of the First Soviet Five-Year Plan.

The Policy Cycle

The central economic objective of the Chinese Communist regime, as stated on many occasions, is rapid industrialization. This in turn requires large-scale mobilization of resources—most particularly capital, labor, and technical, scientific, and managerial manpower—and its allocation to desired ends. For these reasons—as well as for a host of non-economic reasons—soon upon attaining power the regime embarked on a process of collectivization in agriculture and socialization in other sectors of the economy.

Given the pattern of its implementation, socialization was not a cyclical but an irreversible and once-for-all phenomenon which, however, proceeded in an unstable and jerky, rapid-advance—consolidation—rapid-advance fashion. The jerkiness and instability of this socialization trend was occasioned by several factors. Major institutional changes—for example, collectivization, nationalization of industry—were carried out in the form of large-scale campaigns which taxed to the limit the organizational and bureaucratic capacities of the regime. At the same time, to the extent that they disrupted prevailing forms of economic organization, they contributed to disruptions in the production process, gave rise to disproportionalities, strains, and supply bottlenecks. These factors in combination forced slowdowns in the pace of the campaigns and a period of consolidation before embarking on another. This particular phenomenon is, of course, not unique to Communist China; it seems to be a significant feature of all command economies.

Of primary interest for purposes of this paper is what may be termed the *pure policy cycle*. The hypothesis to be developed is that cyclical fluctuations in economic policy have characterized the Chinese Communist system from its inception. However, during the period when the socialization process was being consummated, these fluctuations were closely intertwined with it. Beyond it, the policy cycle acquired, in a sense, a life of its own, independent of the socialization trend. The essence of the policy cycle revolves around the resource mobilization—production nexus on the one hand, and the dichotomy between model Communist Man and Economic Man on the other. Consequently, the dilemma facing the regime is that precisely the kind of measures imposed to mobilize resources tend to (a) produce strong disincentive effects, and (b) lead to losses in productive efficiency.

Actually, these two effects are closely interrelated inasmuch as losses in productive efficiency are in part due to disincentive effects occasioned, for instance, by measures designed to keep consumption in check and raise the savings rate. However, certain mobilization measures may affect production more directly. Thus, agricultural changes such as periodic reductions in the size of private farm plots, or movements of labor from locality to locality or task to task, may have profoundly disruptive effects on production processes, most particularly if these measures are carried out with great speed. Similarly, sharp increases in investment and large-scale expansion of plants in many different locations simultaneously tends to produce acute imbalances, strains, disproportionalities, and serious supply bottlenecks.

In effect, then, resource mobilization measures enlarge the bundle of inputs placed at the disposal of the production process. In its early stages a mobilization phase may proceed without substantial losses in incentives or efficiency. However, beyond a certain point disincentive effects and inefficiencies are likely to cancel out some of the gains due to increased mobilization of inputs. This then leads to a decline in the rate of growth. If in spite of this slowdown, mobilization measures continue to be enforced, a point may be reached when the negative incentive and efficiency effects outweigh the positive input expansion effects with an attendant level decline in output. In a centrally managed economy such as the Chinese, one would expect the planners to step in and adjust mobilization policies so as to check the slowdowns—provided they are recognized— before they degenerate into an absolute level decline. This is one of the principal reasons then that economic fluctuations in an economy such as the Chinese usually take the form of movements in rates of growth rather than in absolute levels.

The disincentive effects accompanying mobilization measures may be viewed as due to a clash in the scales of preference, particularly time preference, of planners and households. The conflict could, of course, be resolved either if man could be remolded into the model Communist Man of Mao's vision, who would internalize the preference scales of planners and policy-makers, or by giving more or less free play to market incentives and the motivations of Economic Man. Unfortunately, remolding proved to be a most intractable task on a mass scale and surrendering to Economic Man was a most unpalatable alternative because of its undesired allocative and political control effects.

To sum up, the roots of the policy cycle are to be found in the regime's commitment to the Maoist vision. This commitment leads to the adoption of economic mobilization measures. Collectivization of agriculture and socialization of the non-farm sectors is carried out to augment the regime's mobilization capacity. Both the mobilization measures accompanying the collectivization and socialization process and those following its consummation tend to produce a pattern of economic fluctuation in rates of growth, even though the socialization process as such is a terminal, once-for-all trend phenomenon. The fluctuations arise from the fact that each new wave of mobilization tends to be carried to the point at which it (*a*) begins to tax the organizational and bureaucratic capacities of the regime; (*b*) leads to disruptions in the production process due to disruptions in economic organization; (*c*) leads to disproportionalities, strains, and supply bottlenecks in the production process; and (*d*) produces unfavorable incentive effects. Therefore the initial phase of a mobilization wave tends to be characterized by an acceleration in the rate of growth until the disincentive and inefficiency effects begin to cancel out the input augmentation effects. When the resulting slowdowns in rates of growth are recognized they lead to policy adjustments, dampening of the mobilization pace, or the suspension of mobilization measures altogether. This may then lead to a reversal in the rates of growth as incentive and efficiency effects are more fully taken into account. However, as these effects are given freer play and market incentive policies are pursued, a point may be reached beyond which another slowdown occurs due to the fact that savings rates may be reduced. Thus, while capital and other factors may be more efficiently utilized, the total inputs applied may be reduced so much that the incentive and/or efficiency gains are at least partially canceled out. Once this is recognized by the planners and policy-makers, another input mobilization phase tends to be instituted, and so the pattern repeats itself.

The Cyclical Process

According to the theoretical framework developed here, economic fluctuations are generated by the interactions of this policy cycle and a harvest cycle. One might distinguish a *pure harvest cycle* which is exclusively induced by periodic weather fluctuations of an exogenous character, and the harvest cycle of our model which is in part weather-induced but in part policy-induced. Correspondingly, the *pure policy cycle* outlined above is modified by the harvest cycle.

The character of this cyclical process will be outlined below in terms of four phases which are generally used in the theory of economic fluctuations, that is, the upswing, the upper turning point, the downswing, and the lower turning point. I will attempt to sketch the dynamics of each and the transition from one stage to the next. In the theoretical framework used here, the points of departure, the givens, or the independent variables are the elements of Mao's vision outlined above, on the one hand, and the elements of China's economic backwardness, on the other. Most specifically, as far as the latter is concerned, the crucial factors to be considered as givens are the low per capita agricultural product and the dependence of the non-farm sectors on agricultural output in the various ways indicated in the preceding section.

The upswing. Given a low per capita product in agriculture and in the economy as a whole, a good harvest provides a much larger surplus potentially available either to the farm population and/or to the economy as a whole. A good harvest can mean either higher food consumption by the peasantry and/or larger marketings of agricultural products, and thus more availability of farm produce for the urban labor force, for stock-piling, and for export. In either case, it provides much greater room for maneuver, more policy choices, and the opportunity for new policy ventures or an intensification and renewal of old ventures. In the case of Communist China, favorable harvest prospects or a high realized harvest out-turn has invariably led to attempts to step up the rate of fixed capital investment, and the rate of growth in heavy industry in particular and in all non-agricultural sectors in general. In pursuit of this objective, the rate of resource mobilization in the economy tends to be stepped up. This may take a variety of forms, depending on what period in Communist China's economic history we are considering. This may be reflected in an acceleration of collectivization and communization policies in the countryside, in circumscribing the scope of the private plot, in narrowing the scope of the rural market, raising the tax pressure, raising the collection pressure, and in general pursuing policies which are designed to raise the level of extraction from the countryside. Similar policies are pursued in the non-agricultural sectors with curtailment of the scope of private industry and commerce, or whatever is left of it, a general lessening of the reliance on material incentives both in agriculture and industry, and placing greater reliance on normative, exhortative, ideological, and to some extent even coercive appeals for increasing effort and commitment by the peasantry and the non-agricultural labor force.

The upswing is generated and gains cumulative strength from two interrelated sources. On the one hand, the good harvest provides more agricultural raw materials for industry. It also provides more foodstuffs for the industrial labor force, and it supplies more produce for export. As a result, the rate of industrial growth can be, and in fact is, greatly accelerated: in consumer goods industries because of the much larger raw material supply, in all industries because of the possibility to supply an increased labor force with the necessities of life, that is, with wage goods. Investment goods industries expand due to both of the reasons just cited and also by virtue of the fact that with higher export levels it becomes possible to finance an increased volume of imports, particularly of capital goods, which constitute an important component of domestic investment goods production as well as a significant component of capital formation at home. However, these more or less automatic results of a good harvest are greatly reinforced by the policies which are initiated following improvements in agricultural production. These policies provide the second source for the cumulative impact of the upswing. The particular policies are of course the mobilization and accumulation measures referred to above, with a shift from remunerative to normative appeals designed to raise not only the level but the rate of capital accumulation.[14] To the extent that these policies succeed, they tend to reinforce the upswing—at least in the short run. However, these very policies tend to be self-destructive in the same sense that they contribute to the gradual negation of the upswing.

The upper turning point. After a certain point these mobilization, capital accumulation, and high investment rate policies are necessarily brought to a halt by the simple fact that they cannot be pushed any further. After a certain point it becomes increasingly difficult, if not impossible, to increase state procurement of produce in the countryside and to raise the rate of extraction from the agricultural sector. Attempts to increase procurements beyond a certain point are bound to bump up against a minimum subsistence ceiling.

Moreover, tightening socialization and collection policies tend to have strong disincentive effects on the peasantry. This is aggravated by the fact that very frequently, if not invariably, these policies are accompanied by the introduction of some new institutional forms in agriculture such as the collectivization drive following the good 1955 harvest and the communization drive and the Great Leap policies following the 1958 harvest. They not only produce disincentive effects, but are in and of themselves quite disruptive, with negative consequences for agricultural production flowing therefrom. The disincentive effects, of course, arise in large part from the fact that the Chinese peasantry and the realities of its motivations and behavior do not accord with the Maoist vision of ideal Communist man. As noted earlier the cosmology of Mao and the Chinese Communist leadership does not necessarily presuppose that the Chinese peasantry in fact behaves like the model Communist man. But it does presuppose that if properly led, properly indoctrinated, and properly organized and mobilized, it can be imbued with the kind of values that would yield a pattern of behavior more or less approximating that of the ideal vision. However, actual experience thus far would suggest that this does not seem to be generally the case even for the masses of the poorer peasants upon whom the regime places its principal reliance for attaining its objectives and for ideological remolding. Normative appeals based on Chinese Communist ideology, patriotic and nationalist appeals, and appeals to the self-interest of the poorer peasantry, can have an effect up to a point and on some occasions. However, appeals to self-interest can be repeated only if the earlier appeals did in fact lead to significant improvements in the lot of the poorer peasants. Normative appeals also lose in force as they are repeated again and again, even though the slogans might be slightly different, or the appeal might be couched in slightly different terms.

Therefore, the upswing is brought to a halt basically for two kinds of reasons. First, because mobilization and accumulation policies sooner or later are bound to bump up against some real subsistence and organizational ceilings. Second, because these same policies tend to produce strong disincentive effects, partly because of the organizational disruption that may result from them, partly because they usually increase the pressure on the peasant. This pressure may take the form of increased collections or manipulation of the terms of trade in ways which are adverse to agriculture, or through a series of other measures which are directly or indirectly designed to raise the extraction ratio from agriculture.

The downswing. Sooner or later, the kind of policies just referred to will lead to a decline in agricultural production, that is, a slowing down in the rate of growth of agricultural output or, under some circumstances, even an absolute decline. This may come about not only because of disincentives and disruptions in the production process engendered by the policies outlined above, but may also result from certain resource allocative effects engendered by these same policies. For instance, during periods of "socialist upsurge," labor tends to be diverted from the private plot to the collective or to the commune, from agricultural production per se to mass labor projects, with negative consequences for livestock production in the first case, and with adverse effects on crop production in the second case. Similarly, these policies can lead to large-scale diversion of organic fertilizer, from the private plots where they are produced to the collective or to the commune, to the point that fruit and vegetable production on the private plot suffers. Moreover, this fertilizer production itself may be undercut by the declines in livestock production which may result from the re-allocation of labor from the private plot to the collective.[15] The effects of a harvest downturn (either absolute or relative) then tend to spread throughout the economy, generating a cumulative downswing or contraction. The factors operative in this cumulative downswing are very much the same as in the upswing except that they have the reverse effect and work in the reverse direction, that is, a poor harvest can and does force a contraction all along the line throughout the economy. A fall in agricultural output leads to shortages of industrial raw materials, to shortages of export supplies, and to food-supply shortages both for the rural sector and for the expanding industrial labor force.

The cumulative downswing forces the regime to shift its policy mix and to place primary emphasis on measures which are congruent with the peasantry's own scale of preferences. This means that for a relentless pursuit of the Maoist vision there must be substituted a more realistic recognition of peasant motivations and the incentive structure as it actually is, rather than as the regime would like it to be. Concretely, this means a shift from policies based preponderantly on normative and even coercive appeals to those relying much more heavily on remunerative appeals.

Such a shift in the policy mix could then be reflected in a general easing of the pressure on the peasantry, that is, more favorable prices, more favorable terms of trade, easing of the collection pressures, greater scope for the private plots, greater scope for the free rural markets, and less control over labor allocation and degree of labor mobilization.

Lower turning point. These policies then tend to lead to the development of what the Chinese Communists refer to as "capitalist tendencies" in the countryside. Increased reliance on material rewards and greater scope for the exercise of material and financial incentives will necessarily mean less control over the daily activities, the daily lives, and the day-to-day pattern of resource allocation in the villages, on the farms, and in the countryside at large. This type of a policy will also encourage those peasants, those households, and those collectives that are most involved in the market nexus, that are most responsive to financial incentives, and that are most enterprising. Correspondingly, policies of this type will tend to encourage better effort, more careful husbandry, growth in livestock production, and growth in crop production, but at the same time they will also tend to encourage greater income inequalities within villages and between villages.

The new policy mix leads to at least three kinds of consequences: first, it tends to undermine the economic and political control system in the countryside; second, it interferes with the regime's economic and political power goals; and third, as already indicated, it does tend to have positive effects on agricultural production to the extent that the new policies do, in fact, lead to an improvement in agricultural production. They then provide once more new room for maneuver following a good harvest. At the same time, because of the negative economic and political-power effects emanating from these policies, strong inducements are built up for the suppression of the "capitalist tendencies" in the countryside and the re-imposition of controls.

The cumulative downswing then forces the regime to change its policies. This policy shift tends to encourage agricultural production. But it also has adverse power consequences as far as the regime is concerned. Therefore, to the extent that the new policies sooner or later contribute to a good harvest, following such a harvest strong inducements are generated for a new policy shift to suppress capitalist tendencies, to raise the rate of investment, and to increase the socialization and accumulation pressures all along the line. This policy shift is in turn made possible by the increased room for maneuver gained by the good harvest. This very harvest then enables the system to turn the corner and once more embark on a process of expansion reinforced by high rates of investment which are in part engendered by the new policies.

Learning Effects

As indicated above, one of the crucial ingredients of these economic fluctuations is a policy cycle. The question may legitimately be posed as to why this cycle keeps recurring. Are there no learning effects? How is it that the experience and the lessons that could be drawn from one cycle are not utilized for preventing or obviating the next? Do not these lessons and experiences affect the behavior of policy-makers in ways which could lead to systematic attempts to pursue counter-cyclical policies—policies designed to reduce the amplitude of the fluctuations at the least? Actually, the evidence would suggest that there are some learning effects, although different segments of the leadership and the bureaucracy may be learning different and, at times, contradictory lessons. Thus the absence of apparent learning effects on Mao and some of his associates can probably be explained by the particular characteristics of their vision and image of the model Communist man. Needless to say, this vision or cosmology is not a fixed, static, or unchanging entity, but it travels in certain definite directions and is based on certain clearly crystallized biases and preferences.[16] To put it more precisely, it is not that no lessons are drawn from experience by Mao and some of his associates; rather, it is that the learning effects are likely to be of a character that might tend to aggravate instead of diminish the force of the cycle.

From a Maoist point of view, optimal policies are those designed to inculcate the masses with the values of Communist man. Ideally and hopefully, these values could and would be internalized by the peasantry, workers, and the intelligentsia. However, to achieve this aim, the CCP must be well organized and the cadres must be imbued with the right ideological posture, a proper ideological zeal and commitment, and strong leadership qualities. Therefore, if the pursuit of the Maoist vision—and policies based on it—leads to strong disincentive effects, on the one hand, and the rise of "capitalist tendencies," on the other, the fault is to be found in policy implementation, in cadre leadership, or in inadequate organization, rather than in the basic policy guidelines. This then does not call for major changes in policy direction but for measures designed to insure tighter organization and an ideologically purer posture by the cadres.

On the other hand, a host of indications would suggest that at least some elements of the leadership were quite conscious of the fluctuations in rates of economic growth.[17] It is, however, unclear whether they regarded this as a necessity or a virtue. Some students of Communist China's economic growth go as far as to suggest that this may even be based on a deliberate development strategy.[18] While this possibility can not be totally ruled out, it is very doubtful that the economic strains of 1956 or of 1959 for instance were allowed for or anticipated in advance. At the same time, one can be quite certain that the crisis of 1960–62 was not at all foreseen.

Nevertheless, it would seem that the leadership groups which were conscious of the reality of cyclical fluctuations also recognized the crucial role of agriculture in imposing severe constraints upon the economy. The rise of an "agriculture first" strategy after the onset of the economic crisis, and strenuous attempts to keep the Cultural Revolution contained, to prevent it from spilling over into the economy, may be considered as possible symptoms of such learning effects. This conclusion would also seem to be borne out by the fact that economic fluctuations have been milder since the Great Crisis of 1961.

On balance, the issue of learning effects and its impact on economic policy is unresolved and is likely to remain in this state as long as the current policy and power struggle remains unresolved. Should Maoist influences prevail, the learning effects may be such that they would not only continue to push the system into recurring policy cycles but also further away from the economic realities of the Chinese mainland. On the other hand, should the Maoist vision become less influential, one could begin to see a different set of learning effects at work, which might reduce the amplitude of the policy cycle.

Qualifications

The first qualification to be noted refers to weather effects. In outlining the cyclical process, I have focused explicitly on the interplay of policy and harvest. However, the quality of the harvest is necessarily also affected by weather changes. In the absence of detailed data, it is really very difficult to determine the extent to which the quality of any one harvest is affected by weather, on the one hand, and by policy, on the other. One can very clearly test the quality of the harvests themselves and the ebb and flow of policy, but at this stage it is impossible to determine the extent to which harvest fluctuations are caused either by the policy cycle or the weather factor alone, or the two in some particular combinations. To put it differently, the empirical evidence will show that certain policies tend to follow certain types of harvests. They will also show that certain types of behavior by the actors in the system follow from these policies. Whether these policies and this behavior then produce the good or bad harvests in and of themselves is very difficult to state categorically. Relevant weather information is potentially available, but to collect and correlate these data would constitute a major undertaking well beyond the scope of this study.

There are other factors besides weather and policy that might affect harvest fluctuations, and economic fluctuations in general, in this type of an economic system. I am referring particularly to a phenomenon which could be labeled as a communications cycle, implementation cycle, or perhaps a bureaucratic-error cycle. This type of a cycle may be generated by the particular leadership structure and the particular character of the party and administrative bureaucracy permeating a system such as the one we are dealing with here.

This type of a cycle might arise from the particular way in which programs and new policies are enunciated, on the one hand, and the way in which they are communicated from the top to the lower level organs, and finally the way they are implemented at the various levels. Very frequently the specific goal structure articulated in a new campaign or new program tends to be ambiguous or very delicately balanced. For instance, its general spirit might be "collectivize but do not disrupt agricultural production" or "push ahead with measures to promote agricultural production without slowing down collectivization." This type of directive confronts the cadres with a number of problems and difficulties. First, they are not sure how to read it, since to some extent the directive is mutually contradictory. They know that collectivization cannot help but have a disruptive effect and a negative impact on agricultural production, at least in the short run. Similarly, they are conscious of the fact that if

they are to promote improvements in agricultural production, collectivization may need to be slowed down. Therefore, they tend to read the first
type of directive as meaning, "collectivize even if you do have to disrupt
agricultural production," and interpret the second type of directive as
meaning "place major emphasis on improving farm output even if you
have to slow down collectivization."

A second type of difficulty may arise from the fact that even if the
directive, the message, is less ambiguously formulated, it may get more or
less distorted in the process of communicating it from the top down; that
is, the communications channels themselves may distort the message. For
both of these reasons, ambiguity and distortion, there tends to be a
considerable gap between the outcome of certain policies and the intent of
the policy-makers at the time they formulated the new directive. To the
extent that this happens and there is a bureaucratic deviation from the
policy intent, and an implementation error in terms of the policy intent,
to correct it a new directive will have to be issued. The new directive,
however, may itself be in turn distorted in the process of transmission and
may lead to an overcorrection of the errors resulting from the earlier
directive. As a result, there may be a deviation in the opposite direction
which now again needs to be corrected.

These problems may produce "secondary" waves around the "primary"
waves outlined earlier in the section on "The Cyclical Process." Needless
to say, none of these cyclical effects work themselves out simultaneously.
Thus it takes time for the effects of the harvest cycle to permeate
throughout the system. Similarly, changes in policies are implemented not
instantaneously but over a period of time, so that the impact of new
policies on the economy may also be more or less delayed. The same, of
course, holds for the bureaucratic cycle. Therefore, these different cycles
are likely to intersect and their effects may be expected to operate with
lags.

In terms of the model presented in the preceding sections, the policy
and harvest cycles reinforce each other. Whether the distortion-correction-
distortion oscillations of the "secondary" waves would tend to reinforce
or dampen the "primary" waves cannot be determined since the bureaucratic-error cycle does not constitute an integral part of our model. It was
introduced here as an element which could modify the model, but one
that could not be taken into account since it is not yet clearly enough
understood.

The Empirical Evidence

The Statistical Indicators

The Character of the Statistical Series. In the preceding sections I have advanced certain reasons as to why one might expect to find cyclical fluctuations in rates of economic progress and expansion in Communist China. In this section I will attempt to test this proposition in terms of certain statistical indicators of levels and rates of change in economic activity between 1949 and 1965.

A host of statistical complications stand in the way of testing these hypotheses thoroughly and rigorously. Communist China has been enshrouded in a virtual statistical blackout since 1960. Prior to 1960 many of the official data are poor and of limited reliability. Some of the statistical indicators are better than others and, similarly, the quality of the data is better for some periods than for others.[19] Furthermore, in order to test more accurately the presence of economic fluctuations and the relationships and behavior of different economic sectors and different economic components during the cycle, we would really need quarterly data. With two harvests in China, and the major one in the fall, quarterly data could give us a much more precise view of the timing of the fluctuations and their duration. Also, such data would enable us to pinpoint better the turning points and to measure the leads and lags in the relations between the different sectors and components. Most particularly, it would give us a better idea of the lag with which the quality of the harvest impacts on the various nonagricultural sectors of the economy. As it is, we have to be satisfied with annual data.

In spite of these statistical shortcomings, the data in Table 1 are based on official series for several reasons. Many of the independent estimates— due to the assumptions used in their derivation and due to the methods on which they are based—do not lend themselves readily for short-run analysis. This applies particularly to the national income and agricultural output estimates of T. C. Liu and K. C. Yeh. They assume a stable per capita consumption of foodstuffs for 1952 to 1957 and this assumption is a critical building block in their agricultural product estimate. Therefore this estimate by definition cannot take account of year-to-year harvest fluctuations. For a number of series and components we do not have as yet

TABLE 1

Selected Economic Indicators, Year-to-Year Percentage
Changes, 1949–1959

Year	Grain Production Tonnage (1)	Gross Value of Agricultural Production (2)	Gross Industrial Production Value (3)	Railroad Freight Turnover Tonnage (4)	Total Value of Retail Sales (5)	Economic Construction Outlays (6)	Total State Investment Outlays (7)	National Income (8)	Export Value (9)	Import Value (10)	Total Trade Values (11)
1949–50	15.0	17.7	36.3	78.6	n.a.	n.a.	n.a.	18.6	n.a.	n.a.	n.a.
1950–51	8.0	9.3	37.8	11.0	37.3	101.1	108.0	17.0	25.0	89.8	56.6
1951–52	14.0	15.8	30.2	19.2	18.1	117.3	85.5	22.3	12.9	-8.4	-0.3
1952–53	1.6	3.0	30.2	22.0	25.5	13.3	83.4	14.0	19.2	24.3	21.7
1953–54	2.1	3.4	16.2	19.5	9.5	42.8	13.3	5.7	7.7	13.8	10.8
1954–55	9.0	7.5	5.6	0.4	2.9	11.3	2.5	6.5	20.1	4.8	12.0
1955–56	4.4	5.0	28.2	26.9	17.5	15.6	60.0	14.0	19.1	10.9	48.9
1956–57	1.3	3.4	11.4	11.4	2.8	-6.3	-6.7	4.6	0.1	-5.1	-2.4
1957–58	10.7	25.0	67.9	39.0	15.5	76.2	93.0	34.0	18.3	34.0	25.6
1958–59	-16.7	...	40.0	...	16.4	22.4	18.7	22.0	16.2	7.9	12.0

Sources: Year-to-year percentage changes calculated by the author. Except for 1958 and 1959 grain production figures, all data in columns 1–10 are based on official series; they were obtained from Dwight Perkins, *Market Control and Planning in Communist China*, Cambridge, Mass., Harvard University Press, 1966; T. C. Liu and K. C. Yeh, *The Economy of the Chinese Mainland*, Princeton, N.J., Princeton University Press, 1965; A. Eckstein, *Communist China's Economic Growth and Foreign Trade*, New York, McGraw-Hill, 1966; State Statistical Bureau, *Ten Great Years*, Peking, Foreign Languages Press, 1960. Foreign trade data are based on A. Eckstein, *Communist China's Economic Growth and Foreign Trade* and on *Communist China's Balance of Payments 1950–1965*, CIA/RR ER 66-17, August, 1967; 1958 and 1959 grain production figures obtained from E. F. Jones, "The Emerging Pattern of China's Economic Revolution," in *An Economic Profile of Mainland China*, Washington, D.C., Joint Economic Committee of Congress, 1967, 1:93.

independent estimates. Finally, the official data even with all of their shortcomings may serve our purposes reasonably well. To test short-run changes in rates of economic growth, the indicated absolute levels and absolute values are of less importance than the rates of change. The official data undoubtedly contain an upward bias due to statistical improvements over time and also due to changes in coverage over time. These problems are probably less serious for the period after 1955 than before that date. However this may be, for purposes of a crude and preliminary statistical test, these data may serve reasonably well, inasmuch as they undoubtedly reflect the actual direction of change and reflect acceleration and deceleration in annual rates of change. This probably is the case even though the particular annual percentage changes may be overstated. None of these observations applies to the three trade series, since these are derived independently for the whole period, 1950–65, on the basis of trading partner statistics. Since publication of official statistical series virtually ceased in 1959 and 1960, we had to rely on a different set of indicators for the 1960–65 period. These are given in Table 2. They are necessarily very tentative and conjectural estimates based on fragmentary data. However, they probably reflect reasonably well the direction of change year by year, and they are consistent with a host of qualitative indicators culled from the Chinese press, official Chinese publications, and official statements.

The Trend of Economic Activity, 1949–65

The Chinese mainland economy was carried forward by an unusually strong momentum between 1949 and 1959. During the early part of the period, this momentum was reinforced by a strong recovery trend and by a number of once-for-all changes in the economy and the society. The reunification of China under a strong and highly centralized polity, the introduction of law and order, and the restoration of nationwide transport and distribution were factors which in and of themselves would have led to rapid expansion even without additional investment. Over and above this, however, a host of institutional changes made possible significant increases in the rate of capital accumulation and thus an acceleration in the rate of expansion for the period of the fifties as a whole. In effect, the decade between 1949 and 1959 was characterized by a continuous and strong

TABLE 2

Selected Economic Indicators, Year-to-Year Percentage Changes, 1959–1965

Year	Grain Production Tonnage (1)	Industrial Production Index (2)	Value Added by All Modern Sectors Except Government (3)	Net Domestic Product (4)	Net Domestic Product Adjusted (5)	Export Value (6)	Import Value (7)	Total Trade Values (8)
1959–60	−5.9	+3.8	−11.3	−8.1	−8.2	−9.5	−5.0	−7.3
1960–61	+6.2	−34.0	−8.2	−3.9	−1.2	−21.9	−26.1	−23.9
1961–62	+5.8	−12.0	−7.6	+2.0	+2.6	+1.6	−19.6	−8.4
1962–63	+2.8	+10.1	+8.2	+4.3	+5.0	+2.0	+4.9	+3.0
1963–64	+5.4	+11.7	+10.2	+6.2	+6.5	+11.2	+22.1	+15.9
1964–65	0.0	+9.4	+8.2	+3.7	+5.0	+20.2	+21.2	+21.2

Sources: Calculated by the author based on the following: col. 1: E. F. Jones, "The Emerging Pattern of China's Economic Revolution," in *An Economic Profile of Mainland China*, Washington, D.C., Joint Economic Committee of Congress 1967, 1:93; col. 2: R. M. Field, "Chinese Communist Industrial Production," Table 1, in *An Economic Profile of Mainland China*; cols. 3 and 4: T. C. Liu, "Quantitative Trends in the Economy of the Chinese Mainland, 1952–64," Table 24, in *Economic Trends in Communist China*; col. 5: This is based on T. C. Liu's estimate as adjusted by the author. The difference revolves around the agricultural estimates. Liu's are based on a grain series presented by R. F. Emery in an article on "Recent Economic Development in Communist China," *Asian Survey*, June, 1966, p. 303. Mine are based on a series developed by O. L. Dawson and published by E. F. Jones in "The Emerging Pattern of China's Economic Revolution." Foreign trade data (cols. 6 and 7) from sources cited in Table 1.

upward trend which was broken by the acute and sharp economic crisis of 1960–62. This crisis not only slowed down the rate of economic growth, but resulted in an actual absolute decline in the levels of economic activity—and a sharp decline at that. As a result this crisis had many of the attributes of a classical-type great depression, with considerable under-utilization of plant capacity and large-scale industrial unemployment. Since 1962 we have witnessed a continuing and steady economic recovery, as a result of which by 1965 agricultural production may have more or less approximated 1958 (the previous peak) levels, while total national product probably exceeded the former peak levels of 1958–59. Therefore, in a sense the recovery may be considered to have been more or less completed by 1965.

Evidence of Cyclical Fluctuations

The data presented in Tables 1 and 2 and Figures 1, 2, 3, and 4, strongly suggest the presence of cyclical fluctuations in rates of growth and eco-nomic expansion since the Communists came to power in 1949. These data seem to indicate the presence of four to five short cycles.

The first three of these occurred before 1959 and were conditioned by three very good harvests, one in 1952, another in 1955, and a third in 1958. Each of these was then reflected in an accelerated rate of expansion in total retail sales, investment outlays and total budgetary outlays on the economy, rates of growth in industrial production, and national income. These cycles seem to have been of two to three years duration. However, several qualifications are in order. The first cycle, peaking in the early fifties, is quite blurred because it is still overwhelmed by the strong recovery trend from the very low levels of economic activity in 1949 and 1950. It is also blurred by the very marked institutional transformation of the economy resulting from socialization of the non-agricultural sectors and broadening of the scope of the government budget, both of which are clearly reflected in the very high rates of growth in economic construction and total state investment outlays for the early years. The recovery element similarly shows up in the very high rates of expansion in industrial production. This strong recovery trend probably also accounts for the fact that in 1952 acceleration in the rate of national income growth shows up in the same year as acceleration in the rate of growth in agricultural production.

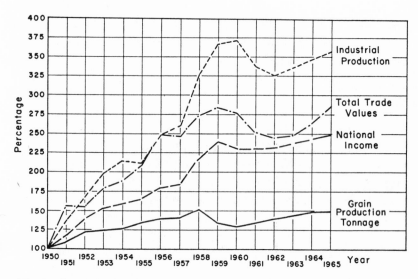

Fig. 1.–Cumulative Percentage Change of National Income, Industrial and Grain Production, and Total Trade Values

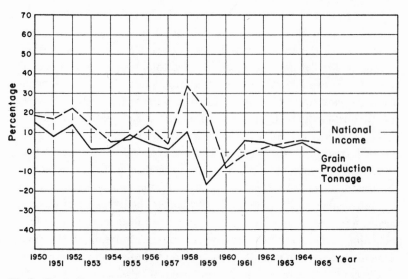

Fig. 2.–Yearly Percentage Change, National Income and Grain Production

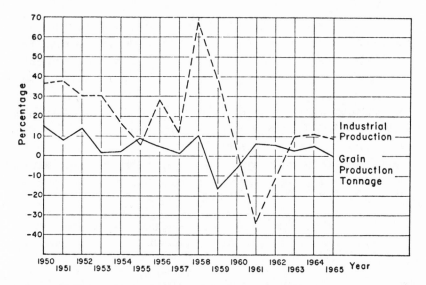

Fig. 3.–Yearly Percentage Change, Industrial and Grain Production

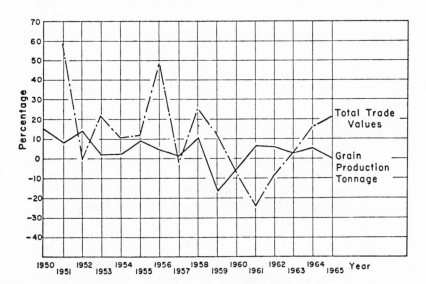

Fig. 4.–Yearly Percentage Change, Grain Production and Total Trade Values

Notes for Figures 1, 2, 3, and 4: The grain production and total trade series are continuous and comparable for the periods preceding

On the other hand, following the good 1955 harvest, all of the non-agricultural indicators show a marked acceleration and peaking with a one year delay. However, in 1958 these same indicators show an acceleration at the same time as the harvest. The absence of a one year lag in this case can be explained by certain special factors. Mass labor mobilization and accumulation measures were beginning to be stepped up in late 1957 and early 1958. However, the pace of mobilization was quickened after the exceptionally favorable summer harvest of 1958. In this case, the autonomous force of the policy cycle was so strong that the harvest almost played a secondary role. Therefore, the evidence for the first decade seems

---

and following the Great Leap. Therefore, the series as presented in Tables 1 and 2 could be used for graphing. The same, however, cannot be said of industrial production and national income.

For the industrial production series Chao's and Field's indices were combined (Chao Kang, "Policies and Performance in Industry," in *Economic Trends in Communist China*, ed. Alexander Eckstein, Walter Galenson, and T. C. Liu, Chicago, Aldine Publishing Co., 1968, and R. M. Field, "Chinese Communist Industrial Production"). Both of these are partially value-added indices. Since they are not methodologically fully comparable, the relevant curve in Fig. 1, is broken for the period since 1959, that is, the period for which the Field series were used.

For the national product series, Hollister's data were used for the period up to 1957 (W. W. Hollister, *China's Gross National Product and Social Account, 1950—57*, Glencoe, Ill., Free Press, 1958), and Liu's estimates ("Quantitative Trends in the Economy of the Chinese Mainland, 1952—1965," in *Economic Trends in Communist China*, Table 24) as adjusted by the author for the years beginning in 1958 (see col. 5, Table 2). The two sets of estimates are not strictly comparable. Hollister's is for gross national product, while Liu's is for net domestic product. Otherwise, too, the two differ in their estimating methods and approach. We could not use the Liu series throughout, because for the 1952—57 period their derivation is crucially dependent on the assumption that food consumption per capita was stable year by year. Hollister's estimate suffers from other methodological flaws. Therefore, the linking of these series represents at best an unsatisfactory expedient. These flaws undoubtedly affect the amplitude of the annual rates of change. However, there is very little doubt that even if these methodological shortcomings were obviated, the shape and character of the national product curve in Fig. 1 would not be markedly altered.

to suggest the presence of cyclical fluctuations which in some cases show up in the non-agricultural sectors with a one year lag following a good or bad harvest, while in some other cases, due to special policy, trend, or random factors, they appear at the same time as the harvest.

In general terms then it would seem that, looked at from the standpoint of the agricultural sector, the first upswing took place between 1949 and 1952 with the upper turning point coming in 1952. The downswing phase then lasted until 1955 when there is a new upswing and an upper turning point, with the next downswing in 1956 and 1957 and the following upswing in 1958. Seen from the vantage point of national income the upper turning points came in 1952, 1956 and 1958. The latter two years were also upper turning points for all of the other sectors.

The harvest impact also affected quite clearly exports and imports, with a one year delay following the good 1952 harvest, but without any delay in 1958. In the case of the 1955 harvest the impact on exports seems to have occurred the same year, while imports were only affected the following year. Of course the relationship between exports and agricultural output is quite direct, while that between agricultural output and imports is only indirect. Given the character of China's export markets, exports may be considered largely a function of supply availabilities, while imports are a function of domestic demand. To the extent that a favorable harvest accelerates rates of growth in the rest of the economy, this expansion in the non-agricultural sectors then tends to lead to a rise in import demand, and this mechanism seems to have been operative in 1953, 1956, and 1958.

The rate of economic growth began to decline again after 1958, but in this case a downswing which started as a decline in the pace of development was converted into a sharp absolute level decline. The role of Mao's vision and its concrete policy concomitants in producing economic fluctuations came most clearly to the fore during this fourth cycle. It was at this time, during the Great Leap of 1958–59, that these policies were pushed to their extreme and achieved full crystallization. This did indeed lead to a marked acceleration in the rate of economic growth, but at the cost of being self-destructive. It was self-destructive in several senses, but most particularly in that the Great Leap policies played a very crucial role in sharply reducing the level of agricultural output beginning in 1959 and then again in 1960. This marked downturn in the agricultural sector spread throughout the rest of the economy with a one- to two-year lag. Thus, industrial production turned down sharply in 1961 and again in 1962. The output of all modern sectors (modern industry, trade, transport, and banking) was beginning to be markedly curtailed in 1960 and the same applies to total domestic product and to foreign trade. In effect, industrial production was slowed down one year following a poor harvest, but was still expanding to some extent, while all of the other non-agricultural sectors experienced a level decline within a year after the poor harvest and continued to do so for one or two more years.

The sharp decline in agricultural output, and in levels of economic activity in general, forced a major re-assessment in planning priorities and in general economic policies. As a result, beginning in 1961 agricultural policies were markedly revised. The communes were decentralized with the production team gradually re-acquiring its responsibilities as the basic accounting and resource allocation unit. Private plots were re-instituted and were given much greater scope. Free rural markets were re-instituted; price terms of trade for agriculture were improved, and this sector was accorded a significantly higher investment priority. This, in turn, made possible a gradual improvement in the agricultural situation, with the 1962 harvest initiating the recovery from the crisis. The agricultural improvement was then reflected in a one year lag in all of the other sectors of the economy as shown by the indicators in Table 2.

The downswing phase of this fourth cycle was extended over a period of about three years, 1959 to 1962, thus lasting longer than any of the previous recessions. This was but another symptom of a deep depression, of an acute economic crisis, rather than just a slowdown in the rate of growth. The lower turning point of this crisis can be dated as about the last quarter of 1962, with the upswing getting under way in 1963. The upper turning point may possibly be placed in 1964, in which case the mainland Chinese economy might now be in the throes of a fifth cycle. On the other hand, it is possible that as of this writing (mid-1967) the economy is still in the upswing following the crisis and that the upper turning point is yet to come.

The Policy Cycle

In the preceding section, I tried to test the presence of harvest fluctuations and to show how these were related to cyclical fluctuations in the rest of the economy. The presence of short-run fluctuations seems to be fairly clearly borne out by the data in the tables and in the figures. Prior to 1952, as noted earlier, the economic scene was dominated by a marked institutional transformation and by a rapid recovery trend. On the other hand, since 1962 the economy has once more been in the process of recovery from a deep-seated crisis.

Against this background, I would now like to trace briefly the ebb and flow of economic policies and most particularly agricultural policies in Communist China. I will try to explore whether a distinct policy cycle can be detected and then functionally related to the behavior of the economic indicators presented in the preceding section. Given limitations of time and space in this paper, these policy fluctuations can be presented only in an outline fashion and therefore only in a tentative and preliminary way.

The annual rate of growth of investment outlays probably provides us with a fairly sensitive index of the Chinese Communist regime's short-run economic policy direction, ambitions, commitments, targets, and expectations. The investment series in Table 1 show a sharp percentage rise in 1953, 1956, and 1958. Correspondingly they indicate a marked decline in 1954 and 1955, in 1957—when the decline was not only relative but absolute as well—and then again in 1959. Unfortunately for the period since 1960, we have no reliable investment data and therefore cannot use this index. In each case, the sharp upturn in investment followed a good harvest, except in 1958 when it accompanied or, in a sense, even anticipated such a harvest. In 1958 there was a bumper summer crop; this was coupled with the expectation of a record autumn harvest which then encouraged policy-makers to forge ahead with increasing rates of investment even without waiting for the actual production results. On the other hand, mediocre harvests were followed by relative, and in the 1957 case by absolute, cutbacks in investment. The year 1959 represents an exception to this rule, inasmuch as the decline in the rate of growth of investment accompanied, rather than followed, a mediocre crop. This was in part due to the record rise in investment in the preceding year, which would have made an equal or higher rise in the following year as well most difficult, if not impossible.

Good harvests tend to stimulate investment, of course, not only by setting up strong inducements for accelerating the rate of economic progress, of rising optimism and a more ambitious outlook, but also by improving the capabilities of the economic system to support higher levels of investment. Undoubtedly both of these elements were important in accounting for the prevailing pattern of investment behavior in China.

Quite apart from the rhythm of harvest-induced investment cycles, there is very little doubt that each good crop signaled the beginning of a new economic policy phase, except for the initial land-reform phase which was launched as soon as Chinese Communist authority was established in particular areas. Thus, after the good 1952 harvest, not only is investment stepped up, but the first Five-Year Plan is launched in 1953, and compulsory grain-purchase quotas are introduced late that year. After 1955 we witness a sharp acceleration in the collectivization drive, a similar acceleration in the socialization of trade and the remnants of private enterprise, the launching of a very ambitious twelve-year agricultural plan in January, 1956, a step-up in investment in 1956, and a very significant rise in the production targets for that year. Similarly, after the bumper summer harvest of 1958, communization is officially launched, and the full crystallization of Great Leap measures and policies unfolds.

The cyclical character of these economic policies is particularly pronounced since 1955 and will therefore be traced in somewhat greater detail. Under the impact of the collectivization and socialization campaigns of 1955–56, the private plots in agriculture began to be encroached upon. As a result, while official regulations provided that these private plots could occupy a maximum of 5 percent of the arable land in a village, in fact on the average they encompassed a considerably smaller land area.[20] In some areas, private plots were abolished altogether during the collectivization campaign. At the same time trees, implements, and livestock (including poultry) were forcibly collectivized, in some cases without any compensation or at low prices. Moreover, the use of labor on private plots was restricted. The collectivization campaign also led to marked centralization in agricultural planning, with the assumption of resource allocative powers by the collective itself rather than by the production brigades or teams. This was coupled with the setting of very high agricultural production targets to be fulfilled in too little time with too few means. It was also accompanied by the closing of rural fairs and markets.

The combination of these measures naturally had negative consequences for agricultural production. They were reflected in large-scale slaughter of livestock (in part also due to fodder shortages), in a general decline in private plot production, a fall in the output and sales of subsidiary products, such as vegetables, fruit, and meat, and a concomitant decline in farm-household income, particularly cash income. The decline in livestock numbers then led to a fall in the production of organic fertilizer and to a reduction in draft animal numbers. Both of these developments had a negative effect on the collectivized sector of agriculture as well, with shortages of draft animals and organic fertilizer exercising a depressing effect on grain production.

These consequences were clearly visible by the time of the Eighth Chinese Communist Party Congress in September, 1956. They were, of course, accentuated by a mediocre 1956 harvest. It is not surprising, therefore, to see that the Eighth Congress marked the beginning of a relatively liberal phase in economic policy. In agriculture this involved improving the incentives for the collectivized sector, through gradual decentralization of allocative responsibilities within the collective, through better prices for pigs and industrial crops, and through a system of incomes and rewards which were more closely linked to production.[21] The collectives were also ordered to pay a fair price for the fertilizer produced on the private plot. Free markets were re-opened in September, 1956,[22] and cadres in the collectives were directed to implement faithfully the regulations permitting the operation of the private plots. These liberalizing tendencies in agriculture were strongly reinforced by the statement of Teng Tzu-hui (Director of the Central Committee's Rural Work Department) in May, 1957, confirming and elaborating on these policies, calling for the return of livestock to the private plots, and raising the permissible limit for them to 10 per cent of the arable land per capita in a village. This new limit was then given the sanction of an official directive by the standing committee of the National People's Congress in June, 1957.[23]

These policies did lead then to a gradual revival of subsidiary food production and particularly to a rapid increase in hog production in 1957. However, the possible benefits flowing from this revival were seriously marred from the regime's point of view for two reasons: on the one hand, lack of substantial progress in the collectivized sector as reflected in another mediocre grain harvest in 1957, and on the other hand, the revival of "capitalist" forces and tendencies in the countryside. The latter was reflected in a fairly rapid erosion of certain distinguishing features of the collectives, such erosion being directly traceable to the liberalization policies. From the regime's point of view, the advantages of collectivization were considered to be economies of scale, collectivized ownership of land so that no rent had to be paid to members, collectivized ownership of draft animals, thus providing important control over one of the strategic inputs in agriculture, and the possibility of increasing the rate of investment.

In the face of these corrosive tendencies, the government closed the free market once more in August, 1957.[24] Thereafter, the private sector began to be gradually curtailed. Later in the year additional measures were adopted which signaled the radicalization of economic policies all along the line. They gradually fed into the Great Leap concepts and measures and most particularly the communes, which swallowed up the private plots altogether. This was followed by the collectivization of all livestock, a high degree of centralization of authority in communes, centralized labor allocation, and a further separation of work from reward as evidenced by the introduction of the part wage, part supply system. The high degree of centralization then led to numerous technical blunders in irrigation and reclamation projects and to a host of planning errors. One of the consequences of centralized labor allocation was marked labor shortages in crop and livestock production. These measures, aggravated by a whole host of other dysfunctional policies, then produced a disastrous effect on farm output in 1959, 1960, and 1961. However, the shape, proportions, and consequences of the Great Leap are too well known by now to detain us further here.[25]

Signs of serious food and raw material supply difficulties became increasingly visible in 1959 without yet leading to a full recognition of crisis by the regime. The information and statistical gap resulting from the virtual dismemberment of the State Statistical Bureau obscured the full dimensions of the crisis so that the response in terms of policy shifts came more slowly than was the case in earlier agricultural downturns. However, in response to growing food shortages, rural markets were re-opened in September, 1959. By the summer of 1960, the regime began to encourage the restoration of small private plots. By 1961, the decentralization process in the commune had gone a long way, with production brigades being designated as basic ownership units. By early 1962, this was carried a step further with the production team becoming the basic ownership and allocative unit. At the same time, hog raising was once more restored largely to the private plots. Gradually, all vestiges of the part wage, part supply system had disappeared to be replaced by the pre-commune system of rewards based on the quantity and quality of labor input.[26] Therefore, by 1962 the system of agricultural organization, resource allocation, and incentives prevailing in early 1957 was restored in fact, even if not in name.

In a sense, this whole process of policy reversal and retreat, which started in late 1959, was most clearly epitomized by the marked change in planning priorities, probably decided upon at the Ninth Plenum of the Central Committee in January, 1961, and made public at the May, 1961 session of the National People's Congress. In keeping with these decisions, agriculture seems to have been assigned highest priority. The combination of new policies and measures was then reflected in gradual recovery of agricultural production beginning in 1962, affecting both grain and the output of subsidiary products. However, the price of this recovery was the kind of erosion of the collectivized sector that had occurred before during periods of liberalization. Most particularly in a number of areas "individual farming" began to rear its ugly head. Not too infrequently communes, through the production teams, would subcontract specific production tasks to individual farm households. For instance, in some cases the cultivation of dry lands would be assigned to individual farm households with an obligation to deliver certain quotas to the production team. In other cases the early ripening crop may be assigned to the farm household.[27] To counteract and curb the spread of these "capitalist tendencies," the "socialist education campaign" was launched once more in the countryside, first on a more modest basis in 1963 and then, after the relatively good 1964 harvest, pursued with much greater vigor and on a national scale. However, up to 1965 this had not yet resulted in a reversal of rural policies.

In terms of the theoretical framework outlined in this paper, we are dealing with two separate but closely interrelated movements—a policy cycle and a harvest cycle. However, if and when the forces propelling the policy cycle are particularly strong, they can overwhelm the influence of harvest fluctuations. This happened to some extent in late 1957 and early 1958, when radicalization in economic policy followed a mediocre and preceded a bumper harvest.

Correspondingly one would not expect a reversal of agricultural policies in the sixties until there is again a bumper harvest, that is, one that provides higher than 1957 levels of per capita grain output, unless the policy cycle moves again with such force as to swamp the effects flowing from changes in farm production. Thus the Cultural Revolution could, for instance, lead to a radicalization in economic policy without the benefit of a spectacular harvest.

Concluding Comments

At the outset I suggested that the cyclical fluctuations in Communist China's economic policy and in the rates of economic expansion on the mainland could be viewed as a function of a deep-seated conflict between the Maoist vision and the realities of the country's economic and technical backwardness. The realities of this backwardness could not be changed very rapidly even under the most optimistic assumptions. Thus it will necessarily take China a long time to modernize its agriculture and to attain high levels of industrialization. But what about the Maoist vision? Will it survive Mao? Assuming no radical systemic change emanating from the Cultural Revolution, Mao may be expected to leave a fairly durable legacy in terms of world outlook, values, and attitudes. Nevertheless, if the successors should turn out to be in some sense "pragmatists," one would expect an alleviation in the cyclical character of economic policy. The successors might draw different lessons from the recent past than Mao did; they could conclude that the agricultural failures were not just failures in implementation by the cadres but also failures in policy formulation and conception. They might also be less optimistic concerning the possibilities of remolding Chinese man to approximate the ideal Communist model than Mao was. However, even under these presuppositions, it is not too likely that the policy cycles will disappear altogether since they are deeply rooted in the very structure of the Chinese Communist decision-making and value system.

Part VI

Epilogue

Chapter 12

The Chinese Economy:
Some Firsthand Impressions

The purpose of this chapter is twofold. On the one hand, I want to explore the extent to which the findings, analysis, conclusions, and generalizations concerning the Chinese economy developed in this book of essays are borne out by direct observation in China itself. To put it differently, to what extent has our view of the Chinese economy been distorted by our lack of direct access in the past? Therefore, to what extent, if any, does firsthand observation force one to modify perceptions, findings, and interpretations?

Another and closely related question bears on the research value of such a trip. What kinds of information and data can one gather on a one month's visit to China? Is this merely tourism, or can one classify it as research? Or even if it is not research, is it of research value, and if so, how and why?

Surprisingly, after a very rich month of intensive interviews, briefings, and visits to many different kinds of installations, I came to the conclusion that on the whole what we saw in China did not seem totally unfamiliar or radically counter to my previous image or to the research findings of the community of China scholars. This is, of course, in some respects comforting and reassuring. It indicated that as scant and uncertain as the materials at our disposal are, our use of these materials and our research methods do not appear to be too far off base. However, this does not mean that my understanding of certain aspects of economic organization, systemic characteristics, and resource allocation processes has not been refined, and even somewhat modified, as will become evident in the course of this chapter. On the other hand, lest one become too complacent, this conclusion must necessarily be coupled by the recognition that there are vast areas of Chinese reality which we cannot encompass without having direct access to China. Unfortunately, most of these areas would require extensive field work, coupled with stays ranging from several months to at least a year, which currently is not yet feasible.

What kind of observation, then, is possible during a brief tour of China, typically of a month's duration? One certainly cannot get macroeconomic data; that is, attempts to seek quantitative information on macroeconomic magnitudes such as GNP, rate of saving and investment, rates of growth, an index of industrial or agricultural production or other aggregative measures, will very rarely evoke a positive response. These data are not readily available outside China, and they cannot be readily obtained inside. They must necessarily be pieced together painstakingly and with vast areas of uncertainty by researchers who are unlikely to be able to check, confirm, or validate their quantitative findings on a visit of this kind.

On the other hand, a month of direct observation does enable one to do many other kinds of things. To an analyst who has never been to China, the economy and society must necessarily be something of an abstraction. He cannot quite visualize it; it is a skeleton without flesh. A trip of this kind brings the whole thing alive, makes it concrete and specific. Beyond that, it is possible to gain considerable insight into processes of decision-making, policies, institutions and institutional relationships, and more generally, all aspects that illuminate the character and functioning of the economic system. In addition, it is possible to collect a fair amount of microeconomic data; for instance, one can get information on wages and salaries and on a wide range of retail prices in markets and department stores. It is also possible to gather production data for some of the factories and communes one visits. Sometimes one can get cost data as well as certain kinds of information about tax rates, income distribution policies and mechanisms in the countryside, management practices in industry, as well as some insights into economic planning processes.

At the same time, it is essential that the observer be acutely aware of the limitations under which he has to operate. These limitations are by no means only externally imposed by the environment; on the contrary, much of what one sees is in the eyes of the beholder. One's perceptions are very much a function of one's attitudes, background, and depth of knowledge. Clearly, a person deeply steeped in Chinese history who has lived in China in the past will approach what he sees differently than, let us say, an economist specializing on China who has never been there before. Correspondingly, a Soviet specialist, be he an economist or a political scientist, will yet bring a different perspective and will probably be looking for other things than the China historian. In this context, it was fascinating to me that our group of fourteen, the majority China scholars from different disciplines, seeing the same thing, perceived it differently and drew varying conclusions from it.

Another crucial factor in observing China is the time perspective. It makes a great deal of difference at what point in time one encounters this society. Correspondingly perceptions and attitudes are necessarily affected by the circumstances of one's own society and the mood of the times at home. One would form quite different impressions of China if one visited it for the first time during the Cultural Revolution, or in a period when things were returning to "normalcy," such as the time of our visit (December 1972), or alternatively, mid-year 1974, when there appears to be some reversion to Cultural Revolution practices. Economic policies in China have been subject to marked shifts and fluctuations, and therefore, what one sees at one point in time may not necessarily be valid for all time.

Another type of limitation results from the fact that during a period of three to four weeks, even if one keeps going from morning to night, the sample of observation will necessarily have to be limited. It would be physically impossible to systematically investigate a representative sample of, let us say, factories and farms in such a limited period. Perhaps this could be done if one concentrated on one narrowly defined focus during a month's visit. But even then, one would be circumscribed by the fact that the sample is selected for you, perhaps according to criteria that may be different from those you would apply. For these reasons, one can never be certain how far to generalize on the basis of what one has seen.

One of the ways in which both the limitations and the research payoffs of such a visit can be best understood is to describe the itinerary and the range of observation of a group such as ours. I visited China from December 11, 1972, to January 6, 1973, with a delegation sponsored by the National Committee on United States-China Relations. The majority of this group of fourteen were China specialists, most of them political scientists.

We were the guests of the Chinese People's Institute for Foreign Affairs. The primary purpose of our visit was to discuss and plan for cultural exchanges between our organization and our Chinese counterparts. We were received very warmly and were extended the most cordial possible treatment. Our hosts were eager not only to provide for our comfort but to make sure that we learn and see as much as possible in the limited amount of time.

We traveled from Canton to Peking to Shenyang (known as Mukden during the period of Japanese dominance), Anshan, back to Peking, Nanking, Shanghai, Hangchow and back to Canton for departure to Hongkong. We traveled mostly by air, at times by train such as from Peking to Shenyang and back, and also from Nanking to Shanghai. Shorter distances, such as visits to communes in the vicinity of major cities, were covered by car.

During this period of twenty-six or twenty-seven days, we visited factories, communes, a number of small scale rural industries in communes, a city neighborhood organization, factories in a city neighborhood, a number of universities, middle schools, and a variety of other institutions and facilities. In addition, we had quite extensive briefings and interviews with government officials at varying levels. We met with the Deputy Foreign Minister and other leading officials of the Foreign Ministry, foreign trade officials from the China Council for the Promotion of International Trade, the Director of the Budget Bureau of the Ministry of Finance, the most senior officials of the Science and Education Group of the State Council, and members of provincial and municipal revolutionary committees in all of the cities we visited. We also had a long session with some members of the Institute of Economics of the Chinese Academy of Sciences, a briefing from the Vice-President of the Academy, a long discussion with the corporate planning officials of the Anshan Iron and Steel Corporation and a number of others. We were thus able to gather a fair amount of information on Chinese foreign policy, educational policy and practice, social and health policies, and a number of other topics, but in this chapter, I will confine myself largely to those observations which relate to the Chinese economy.

I. Social Control

One of the most overwhelming impressions I carried away from our visit to China relates to the comprehensive extent of social control over the population maintained by the regime. In many respects, this control appears all-pervasive and quite effective, at least as long as the leadership is capable of providing clear direction. Naturally, when the leadership flies apart, as happened during the Cultural Revolution, then social control falls apart too. If this impression of extensive social control is valid, it necessarily has far-reaching implications for the operation of the whole system, including the economic system. In a sense, this social control exercised through the interaction of ideology and organization provides for informal, non-bureaucratic channels of communication. These then can become partial substitutes for formal, administrative, bureaucratic channels of command and communication. In effect, social control can reduce the rigidities in the system and diminish its bureaucratization. It may act as a lubricant which may facilitate flexibility in economic planning and resource allocation while permitting a considerable degree of centralized control over this process.

An example may be provided by the operation of the service sector in China, at least those parts of it that a foreign visitor is in a position to observe. I am referring primarily to the operation of all retail outlets which come in contact with the public, such as markets, specialty food shops, department stores, shops of various kinds, restaurants, and so forth. These sectors constitute, in many respects, a disaster area in the Soviet economy. One can hear many accounts of poor, inefficient and desperately slow service in all of these establishments in Russia. This does not seem to be true in China. Why should this be the case?

I do not presume to have an answer to this question. However, the material incentive structure and the pattern of remuneration is not vastly different in this respect in China as compared to Russia. If anything, the role of material incentives is downgraded in the former as compared to the latter. This leads me to hypothesize that the whole attitude of personnel engaged in the service sectors in China must be much more positive. There seems to be more of a spirit of service, and the notion of "serving the people" may indeed have taken hold, at least to some extent. This may then in part be attributable to differences in internalized values. In turn, these values must have become internalized partly through spontaneous adherence and partly through systematic indoctrination.

In either case, ideology and organization working in combination must be the crucial ingredients and avenues through which these attitudes are being inculcated. All students of Chinese society will testify to the high degree of organization in this system. This is true both in urban and rural areas. In urban areas, operating through a network of neighborhood, street, lane, and block committees—all the way down to a small group—each household is encompassed by such a unit of organization and control. Similarly, in rural areas, operating through communes, production brigades, production teams, and work groups, the same pattern is replicated. These organizations and small groups can exert enormous pressures for conformity, using a variety of positive, patriotic, and ideological appeals combined with psychological pressures bordering on negative sanctions of varying kinds. It seems to me that these pressures for conformity serve to induce the actors in the system to behave in ways expected of them. To the extent that these inducements are effective, they can contribute to the efficiency of management and resource allocation at the various levels of government as well as within the enterprise.

The extent of social control is perhaps most dramatically exemplified in the field of birth planning. As part and parcel of their maternal, child health, and family planning program, a new approach to birth control was gradually crystallized. The lowest level organizational unit—the small group—be it in the city or countryside serves as the focus of birth planning. The women of child-bearing age meet periodically to discuss their family situations and more or less decide who will have the next child.

The desired norm is two children in the city and three in the countryside spaced five years apart. Therefore, a newly married couple will not be expected to practice birth control. But as soon as they have a child, they are expected to wait out their next turn. If a woman becomes pregnant before her turn comes, she is expected to terminate her pregnancy so that someone else in the group, who either does not have a child or had her last child more than five years ago, can go ahead. Obviously, this process of group planning of births, rather than individual planning, presupposes far-reaching social consensus and control.

II. Wage and Salary Structure

One of the most striking characteristics of Chinese society as seen by virtually any visitor is its apparently egalitarian character. As one travels around China, be it in the city or in the countryside, one sees poverty but very rarely abject misery or degradation, so frequently associated with the extremes of deprivation. One certainly has the impression that the Chinese have succeeded in placing a floor on real incomes. This observation is confirmed by first hand visual impression, since people seem well fed, adequately clothed—at times with patched clothing but never in tatters—and with a relatively narrow band of differentiation in quality of dress, be it man or woman.

This impression is reinforced by the fact that one very rarely is exposed to extremes of luxury and high living. It is also particularly striking if one has been to India or some other parts of Asia. For instance, I recall my first visit to Hongkong in December, 1952, when I saw many people homeless, sleeping in the streets or inhabiting miserable squatters' settlements on the outskirts of Kowloon. (This, of course, no longer applies to Hongkong today). Similar impressions, only even worse, could be gathered on a visit to Calcutta or some other parts of India in 1966. I saw nothing even remotely corresponding to these symptoms in any part of China we visited.

In this respect, the impressions I carried with me before going there were greatly reinforced. At the same time, however, and paradoxically, they were also seriously qualified. After a while, it became clear that there certainly is a role and status differentiation, however subtle. If one entered a room for a reception or dinner, one could almost invariably pick out the senior officials by their bearing and the quality of their dress.

More tangibly, however, we were able to collect wage and salary data in every factory, local industry, school, university or organization we visited. Gradually, certain patterns emerged. It became clear that the wage span of industrial workers in factories varied from about 3:1 to 5:1. Based on an eight grade classification, typically, industrial wages would range from 30 yuan to about 100 or 120 yuan a month. Wages for apprentices would be even lower, ranging usually from 17 to 20 yuan a month to which must be added certain payments in kind. Similar data were gathered by earlier visitors and can also be confirmed from fragmentary evidence in Chinese documentary sources. Interestingly enough, this range of wage differentials is quite typical for industries in many other countries, both developed and underdeveloped.

For instance, in Guatemala the ratio of average hourly earnings of electrical fitters to laborers was 7:1 in the early 1960's. The ratio of carpenters' wages to unskilled laborers in construction was 5:1. In Singapore, the ratios between government skilled and unskilled rates was 2.5:1. In Egypt, average weekly earnings of semiskilled workers in all industries were more than three times as high as unskilled earnings in 1960. [1]

In the United States and in Europe the wage spread within industry seems to be typically around 3:1. All these examples would suggest that the Chinese industrial wage structure is not significantly more egalitarian than that of other countries. Yet this conclusion must be treated with caution since many of these wage data are not fully comparable.

For technical and engineering personnel, the salaries would usually start at about 50 to 80 yuan and go up to 150 to 200 yuan a month. For instance, a chief engineer would frequently be in this top range. However, for very senior management, technical and professional personnel, including senior full professors, salaries of 300 to 400 yuan were quoted to us. This would suggest that a wage and salary span of 10:1 i.e., ranging from 20 yuan for an apprentice to 200 yuan for a chief engineer is not too uncommon in China. Moreover, differentials of 20:1 can also be encountered. There is no doubt that the number of people in these top ranges must be very small. At the same time, there almost certainly are at least some senior government ministers, artists and others who perhaps are above these top ranges.

What would this mean in terms of United States equivalents? According to the *Handbook of Labor Statistics,* the average farm wage rate in the United States in 1972 was about $360 per month.[2] The lowest union wages quoted in the same *Handbook* were $2.11 per hour for truckers' helpers in Birmingham, Alabama. Translated very crudely to an annual rate, this would mean roughly $4,000 to $4,500 a year. Let us say, starting with a base of $4,000, ten to one would call for an income of $40,000 a year and twenty to one for an income of $80,000 a year. Since there is no income tax in China, these would have to be net spendable incomes, which according to recent United States tax rates for a family with two children would be equivalent to gross salaries of about $160,000 a year. Of course there are some very few chief executives in the United States who are earning salaries and bonuses (exclusive of property incomes) of perhaps as much as $200,000 to $300,000 a year, net of tax payments.

Therefore at these very extremes the United States wage and salary span may go as high as 50:1 or even 75:1. In most African countries, where the disparities tend to be largest, the ratio between the usual starting salary of a university graduate in the civil service and an unskilled laborer in the capital city was between 8:1 and 11:1 in 1963. In India, the comparable ratio was 5:1 in 1958. However if we take the top of the scale reached by the numerous graduate cadres and compare it to unskilled labor rates, the differential is much more striking–about 30:1 in Africa and roughly the same in India. In fact, a young university graduate may be paid 10 times more than an unskilled worker, a permanent secretary (the top career rank in the civil service) 30 times more, and an industrial manager in the private sector 80 times more.[3]

All of this would suggest that at the extremes the wage and salary spread in the United States and in many underdeveloped countries is much wider than in China. Of course, if property incomes are added, then the spread becomes even wider. At the same time, the spread in China is significantly greater than one would presuppose on the basis of visual observation alone. Of course, wage and salary data in and of themselves do not tell us much about distribution, since we do not know how many people are encompassed by each income earning class. Beyond that, wage and salary spreads of 10:1 or 20:1 may represent very differing degrees of real income differential in China as compared to the United States, India, or other underdeveloped countries. One would expect this to be true for a number of reasons. Housing rentals are nominal in China, very rarely exceeding 2 to 4 percent of monthly income. Health services for all factory workers are free and for workers' dependents provided at nominal rates. Moreover, prices are fixed in such a way that all necessities are priced very low, while luxury goods are priced very high. As a result, the price structure itself has built into it certain elements of progressivity which tends to narrow the real purchasing power differential between the top and the bottom of the income scale in China. This is further reinforced by the fact that the range and quantity of luxury goods obtainable at any price is quite limited in China. Finally, luxury consumption is frowned upon, particularly since the Cultural Revolution, so that even if the luxury goods are available and people can afford them, they are discouraged from buying them.

Therefore income differentials both in money terms and in real terms are almost certainly higher in the United States or in India than in China. This is of course what one would expect. The purpose of the comparison is not to suggest that the two spans or distributions are comparable, but merely to illustrate that the degree of inequality in China is probably significantly greater than visual impression would suggest. This then also implies that the Chinese clearly must be relying to a much greater extent on material incentives as a means of motivating workers, technicians, managers and professionals than is often sanctioned by official pronouncements. At the same time, in the face of this reality, it is not surprising that Mao and many of his associates see the need for periodic campaigns designed to inculcate egalitarian values as a means of countering inegalitarian trends built into the wage and salary structure.

III. The Purchasing Power of Wages

It is always very difficult to attach significant meaning to wage and salary figures for other countries unless these can be combined with some household budget and price data. From these we can then gain some insights concerning the purchasing power of these incomes and possibly the prevailing standard of living.

Fortunately during our trip it was possible to obtain retail price quotations in markets, department stores and other shops. These were combined with prices collected by a Yale group of economists who went to China in the early Fall of 1973.[4] As a result, a total of about 210 price quotations were gathered for 110 different items. In a number of cases prices for several different varieties or qualities and from several different cities were obtained. In addition, Bruce Reynolds of the Yale group pieced together a household budget for an industrial worker's family in Shanghai, the basic data having been obtained from interviews with the worker and members of his family.

This was a family of five consisting of a mother and father in their late thirties, two children aged nine and eleven, and the father's mother, aged sixty. The father worked in a machine-building plant, earning 72 yuan a month—that is, an above average industrial wage. His wife worked in a textile mill, earning 60 yuan a month; the mother had been employed in the bus company, where her peak wage was 48 yuan a month. She is now retired and draws a pension of 34 yuan a month. Therefore the total family income was 166 yuan a month or 1,992 yuan a year. At the official exchange rate this would be approximately $83 a month or $1,000 a year. Clearly this income may be expected to buy much more at Chinese prices than would be the case at United States prices, at least as far as necessities are concerned. Therefore, in and of itself it is not a very meaningful figure.

A monthly household income of 166 yuan is almost certainly well above the average for urban families. By national standards, given that rural household incomes are significantly below those in the cities, this must be considered a quite prosperous household. Given this family's expenditure pattern, Bruce Reynolds calculated what the cost of such a consumption basket would be, based on United States prices. It would come to $422 a month instead of $83 based on the exchange rate.

However, there are many problems with this figure as well. Many expenditure items were not explicitly furnished to Mr. Reynolds but had to be reconstructed by him. Moreover many items may not be comparable, for instance, housing. Therefore these measures are subject to considerable margins of error.

The United States value of a Chinese expenditure basket derived this way may overstate the standard of living in China as compared to the United States for several reasons. By evaluating a Chinese bundle of goods at United States prices, we have in effect forced a hypothetical United States family with a $5,000 annual income to consume those commodities which the Chinese are most efficient at producing—principally food and simple housing, which are relatively expensive in the United States. At the same time we have prevented that family from consuming any of the goods which the United States produces most efficiently, i.e., consumer durables such as refrigerators, television sets, and cars, all of which are prohibitively expensive or unavailable in China.

Finally, average urban household income in China may be assumed to be significantly less than 166 yuan a month, and the rural average, where the bulk of the population lives, is considered by Chinese sources to be half of the average city incomes. Therefore the national average household income may well be one third of our "model" family's level. This would, not surprisingly, place it well below the poverty level in the United States.

Given these conceptual and statistical difficulties it may be useful to find another way of gauging the comparative living standards in China and the United States and in effect to gain some sense of how large is the purchasing power gap of an average industrial wage in the two countries. The results of this second approach are presented in Table 1. In making this comparison, it must be borne in mind that the average industrial wage represents a far higher position in China's total income distribution than would be the case for the corresponding United States wage in our income distribution.

The Chinese goods for which we had price data were first matched by United States equivalents in terms of size, weight, quality, etc. Only consumer items for which reasonably close equivalents could be found

TABLE 1

The Relative Purchasing Power of an Average Industrial
Wage Over a Sample of Consumer Goods
in China and the United States

	Amounts the Average Wage Can Purchase		
Category	In China	In the United States	Ratio (rounded)
Foodstuffs in pounds	*per hour*		
Rice (long grain)	2.0	14.2	7:1
Wheat flour	1.8	23.9	12:1
Irish potatoes	4.8	30.5	6:1
Carrots	4.8	12.4	25:1
Cucumber	5.5	10.9	2:1
Chicken	0.26	6.9	26:1
Beef	0.48	2.0	4:1
Pork	0.34	2.7	8:1
White sugar	0.44	20.4	46:1
Fabrics, clothing and footwear	*per week*		
Cotton prints (square meter)	7.0	129.2	18:1
Corduroy fabrics (square meter)	2.7	81.9	30:1
Unpadded cotton cloth jackets	1.6	6.4	4:1
Cotton work pants	2.1	26.9	13:1
Corduroy jacket	1.6	5.6	3.5:1
Corduroy trousers	2.3	19.2	8:1
Cloth coats with lining	0.2	2.9	14:1
Blue cotton work shirts			
Good quality	3.2	19.2	6:1
Poorer quality	5.0	33.6	7:1
Cotton flannel colored Western-style shirts	2.5	44.6	18:1
Light wool sweaters	0.7	10.7	15:1
Men's cotton socks (pairs)	11.3	206.7	18:1
Tennis shoes			
Basic quality	3.1	33.8	11:1
Sturdier	1.5	21.3	14:1
Cloth shoes with rubber or synthetic soles	2.3	48.8	21:1

TABLE 1 (*cont.*)

Category	Amounts the Average Wage Can Purchase		
	In China	In the United States	Ratio (rounded)
Miscellaneous Consumer Manufactures		*per week*	
Three gallon pots	1.2	29.8	25:1
Drinking glasses	49.4	1,344.0	27:1
Simple alarm clocks	1.0	16.8	17:1
Very simple bedside lamps	1.3	29.8	23:1
Metal folding chairs	0.7	22.4	32:1
Wooden straightback chairs	1.5	12.2	8:1
Umbrellas	1.7	26.8	16:1
Ballpoint pens	13.8	149.3	11:1
Plastic four-ounce baby bottles with nipple cap	34.6	336.0	9:1
Durable Consumer Goods		*per month*	
Bicycles	0.4	9.1	23:1
12-inch TV sets	0.14	6.5	47:1
Small transistor radios	1.6	84.4	53:1
Watches			
Swiss	0.11	5.9	53:1
Domestic	0.54	32.8	60:1

Sources: The figures in this table were derived by the author based on price data for China and the United States. For China these data were collected by Professor Robert Scalapino during a visit in December, 1972, and by Bruce Reynolds on a visit in the fall of 1973. For the United States, they are average 1972 prices based on *Retail Food Prices* (monthly), published by the U.S. Bureau of Labor Statistics; non-food prices were obtained from Sears Roebuck and J. C. Penney's catalogues.

were used. Then the United States retail prices for these were compiled. These two steps reduced the number of items from 110 to 38–9 entries for foodstuffs, 15 for fabrics, clothing and footwear, 9 for miscellaneous manufactured consumer goods, and 5 for durable consumer goods.

For foodstuffs the purchasing power ratios range from 2:1 for cucumbers to 46:1 for white sugar. For the staples, the largest consumption items in China, the ratios range from 6:1 for potatoes to 12:1 for wheat flour. For meats the range is 4:1 for beef to 26:1 for chicken, with pork—an important consumer item in China—8:1. The median ratio for all foods is 7:1.

For fabrics, clothing and footwear the range is from 3.5:1 for corduroy jackets or 4:1 for unpadded cotton cloth jackets to 30:1 for corduroy fabrics. However, cotton cloth prints were 18:1 and so were several other items. The median was 11:1. In the miscellaneous manufactures category, wooden straightback chairs were relatively cheapest with a 8:1 ratio, while metal folding chairs were relatively dearest at 32:1. The median of these nine items was 17:1.

The purchasing power gap was greatest for durable consumer goods which ranged from 23:1 for bicycles to 60:1 for domestic watches. The median was 53:1. Ideally one would want to have a much larger sample of observations for each category. Thus undoubtedly the small number of comparable items reduces the validity of any generalizations one would wish to make. Nevertheless the data exhibit a consistent pattern.

The purchasing power of the American industrial wage is a multiple of the Chinese for all items and sizeable multiple for most. The differential is relatively narrowest for foods and widest for durable consumer goods, with fabrics, clothing and footwear and miscellaneous manufactures between these two in the order cited. This is precisely what one would expect *a priori* on the basis of international cross section comparisons of consumption patterns.

Of course, from these data we can not derive a single index or derive a single measure of the relative purchasing power of the two wages in their own price settings. However, one is strongly tempted to conclude that the purchasing power gap is likely to be at least 7:1 since this is the median for foods and since this is the ratio for rice. Almost certainly this is on the low side in the light of the data in the table. One might speculate that based on Chinese tastes, habits and consumption expenditure patterns, a United States wage in manufacturing might buy ten times the quantity that could be obtained in China. However, based on United States tastes and patterns, the purchasing power multiple could go as high as 20:1 or higher.

All calculations in Table 1 are based on an average monthly wage in Chinese industry of 60 yuan. Since there are no income taxes, this is a net wage. Average weekly earnings of production and non-supervisory workers was $154.69 in the United States in 1972. However this is gross income. At the same time the *Handbook of Labor Statistics* gives the gross weekly earnings of production and non-supervisory workers on private agricultural payrolls as $135.78 in 1972. The corresponding net spendable income for a wage earner with three dependents was $120.79 net of taxes. This 88 percent ratio was applied to the $154.69 figure to obtain a net average weekly wage in United States manufacturing of $134.40. This is equivalent to $2.84 per hour, assuming a 40 hour week, and $591.00 a month. If one were to convert the monthly Chinese wage into dollars at the exchange rate prevailing in late 1972, it would be about $24. On this basis the American worker would be earning almost 25 times more than his Chinese counterpart. As may be seen from Table 1 this probably overstates the purchasing power gap, while the Reynolds calculus of household budgets almost certainly understates it.

IV. Decentralization of Economic Management

The Chinese economy is frequently referred to as a decentralized command system. It is generally believed that following the Great Leap and then again in the aftermath of the Cultural Revolution, a vast array of economic management functions were transferred from the central to the provincial and local governments. Many analysts of the Chinese economy are convinced that in the last ten or fifteen years, there has been a very significant process of decentralization in economic management to the point that one could legitimately describe China as a cellular economy. This view is buttressed by a similar image projected in many of the Chinese sources.

In contrast to this view, I came away from China with the very distinct impression that decentralization has been much less far-reaching than is often believed. Correspondingly, the central authorities have continued to maintain a vast degree of control over resource allocation. This conclusion is based on evidence gathered during our trip, principally from briefings and discussions with the Director of the Budget Bureau in the Ministry of Finance, the planning officials of the Shanghai municipal government, representatives of the planning group of the Anshan Iron and Steel Corporation, and planning officials from several other provinces. These discussions helped to illuminate the character of the budgetary process and certain aspects of resource planning.

The Budgetary Process

Information concerning the character of the budgetary process was obtained principally in a long interview with Mr. Fu Tse-hao, the Director of the Budget Bureau in the Ministry of Finance, and also in a meeting with two economists from the Academy of Sciences Institute of Economics. Certain points were further confirmed in later briefings and meetings with provincial planning officials.

The picture that emerges is that of a highly centralized system of budgetary control and budget administration. Central control over the budgetary process is maintained both at the stage of budget plan formulation and later at the stage of actual expenditure control. All local and central government budgets are based on a unified, consolidated and integrated national budget plan. The process starts when the Ministry of Finance provides certain informal briefings and guidance to central governmental organs and to provincial governments. These then serve as the basis for their formulation of preliminary draft budget plans. However, provincial governments, before undertaking these first drafts, will turn to municipal and county governments, requiring their first drafts, based on guidance provided by the Provincial Finance Bureau. On the basis of these first drafts, the provincial authorities will formulate a preliminary, consolidated budget plan which is sent up to the Ministry of Finance. The latter, upon receipt of these first drafts as well as those submitted by the central ministries and other central governmental organs, will work up a preliminary consolidated national budget plan. This will then be discussed at national budget conferences, where a process of bargaining, adjustment and balancing takes place, following which the national budget plan may be finalized.

This process does not seem very different from that prevailing during the First Five-Year Plan period, which is usually associated with a high degree of centralization in economic management in China. However, it is possible that local governments now have a greater voice in the process of plan formulation than was true in the 1950's.

Once the plans are finalized, local governments have very little discretionary power to change them. In general, budget outlays are divided into two categories: productive and nonproductive expenditures. Small reallocations within each of these two major categories are permitted during the budget year, but no changes in the size of each expenditure category or transfer from one to the other is permitted without the approval of higher level organs. Local governments have certain limited, discretionary powers over funds which result from unplanned surpluses. That is, if actual expenditures fall short of those planned, the surplus thus obtained can be retained and spent locally. Similarly, if actual revenue collections exceed the revenue plan, the surplus resulting therefrom may be divided according to certain ratios between the central government and the local government. This retained surplus can then also be spent at the discretion of the local authorities. However, even these discretionary powers are subject to considerable constraints. That is, surpluses can be spent freely, provided that such expenditure does not require adding workers and employees and provided that all of the materials purchased by this source of discretionary finance can be locally obtained. Otherwise, the approval of higher level planning organs is required.

Therefore, the net effect of the presently prevailing budgetary system would seem to be perhaps some decentralization in revenue collection coupled with a high degree of centralization of control over expenditures. The decentralization in revenue collection is in turn a reflection of the fact that during and following the Great Leap, a large number of enterprises were transferred from central to local jurisdictions, so that enterprise profits and taxes constituting the bulk of government revenue are in the first instance collected by local governments. However, this does not mean that they are retained by these governments; on the contrary, about 80 percent of this is remitted to the central Ministry of Finance, and the remaining 20 percent is also subject to expenditure control within the confines of the national budget plan.

In evaluating all of this information, one must necessarily allow for the possibility of error. That is, in a briefing or discussion, particularly carried on through interpreters, there is always an opportunity for misunderstanding. It is therefore possible that my notes on which this discussion is based may be faulty or that I may have interpreted certain things that were said erroneously. Therefore, this analysis should be treated with caution until it can be more fully confirmed by other sources or by documentary forms of evidence.

Economic Planning and Resource Allocation

Centralization or decentralization are necessarily vague concepts unless they are more closely and more operationally defined. The view of the process is crucially dependent on the vantage point from which it is approached. For instance, a transfer of a vast array of resource allocation and economic control functions from the central to the provincial governments would represent a considerable degree of decentralization as seen from the vantage point of the central authorities. On the other hand, from the standpoint of a county or other units of governments below the provincial level, this may evolve no change or conceivably even a greater degree of centralization than existed before. This would certainly be the case if the provincial government claimed for itself certain discretionary powers left earlier to lower level jurisdictions. The same may apply in the relationships between a county and a commune, or the municipal government and the factory enterprise. That is, there may be a high degree of delegation from the center to the lowest levels of local government without any increase in the autonomy of a factory enterprise. On the other hand, under some conditions, decentralization could go so far that it would allow some greater exercise of autonomy by the enterprise.

The prevalent view in recent years has been that economic planning and resource allocation has become much more decentralized in China. However, very rarely do these discussions face up to the question of, decentralized in what sense and from what vantage point? Thus, it is far from clear whether a transfer of responsibility from the center to lower level governments—assuming it did in fact occur—necessarily meant a gain in enterprise autonomy.

The evidence gathered on this subject during our trip was less firm and clear than on the budget. To gain a clear picture would require a much larger sample of observations than our time permitted. Therefore, my impressions on this aspect of decentralization are more uncertain. Nevertheless, in this respect too, I came away with the impression that decentralization was by no means carried as far as is generally believed—both in the sense of transfer of responsibilities from the center to lower levels, and in the sense of significant gains in enterprise autonomy. However, it probably was carried further than in the field of budget administration.

In most general terms, enterprises in China today are under three alternative forms of control or "leadership" (the term generally used by Chinese officials): central, dual and local. The bulk of large-scale industries and certainly all those of any economic or military importance would be either under central or dual leadership. Dual in this context refers to joint and concurrent supervision by two different jurisdictions, e.g., central and provincial, central and municipal, provincial and municipal. Typically, enterprises under dual leadership will be centrally controlled for purposes of planning but locally administered. Specifically, this means that capital for investment and basic materials subject to national supply distribution will be allocated centrally. Net revenues generated by the enterprises, both on profits and on tax account are remitted to the central Ministry of Finance with a small portion (the frequently mentioned figure was 20 percent) retained locally. At the same time, it is not entirely clear where the locus of manpower allocation lies and what role central versus local governments play in controlling the wage bill and the labor force of the enterprise.

As indicated above, administrative and political supervision for enterprises under dual leadership is provided locally. This means that the appointment of key personnel such as chairmen and vice-chairmen of enterprise revolutionary committees would have to be approved by the local government. Similarly, party activities and party committees in the factory would be guided by local party authorities. To the extent that during the First Five-Year Plan period, these enterprises were for all purposes under central jurisdiction, one can legitimately speak of a certain measure of decentralization in comparison with those years. This conclusion is reinforced by an impression that a certain number of centrally governed enterprises have now been completely transferred to local governments. On balance, it would seem that the administration of enterprises has been decentralized, but the central government has continued to maintain significant control over economic planning and resource allocation.

It is quite apparent from what has been said that much more detailed and intensive study would be required before one could arrive at some definitive conclusion on this very complex problem. It may, however, be useful to consider a few specific aspects of planning on which we were able to gather some evidence and see what light they throw on the matters discussed above.

Officially, the Chinese planning process is no longer based on control figures issued by the central planning authorities. On the contrary, the process is supposed to start from below, at the shop floor and enterprise level. But except for the two handicraft plants, in all the other factories we visited we were told in response to our probing that indeed, before the planning process starts in the factory, officials from the Ministry or from the Planning Commission come down and provide some preliminary guidance concerning their hopes and expectations for this particular industry or this particular plant for the coming year. This would suggest that to some extent at least the planning process still starts from the top down. Proceeding on this basis, a process of discussion is started in each shop to explore the implications of this guidance and to begin the formulation of preliminary draft plans. This may represent some change in comparison with First Five-Year Plan practice and also in comparison with Soviet practice, in that the workers themselves seem to be more involved and may perhaps have a greater sense of participation in detailed plan elaboration.

The same factory visits and discussions with planning officials at provincial, municipal and corporation levels also indicated that the key and highest priority *success indicator* for an enterprise is *production quantity of principal products expressed in physical terms.* This certainly is a type of target that would tend to leave the minimum of discretion to an enterprise. Enterprise objectives formulated either in gross value terms or in profit terms clearly permit greater autonomy for the enterprise management. This would tend to suggest that at least from the standpoint of the enterprise, there has not been much decentralization.

A third aspect of enterprise operations on which we were able to gain some impressions relates to the degree of tautness in planning. A study of Chinese documentary sources during the 1950's as well as the testimony of Russian technicians, Japanese engineers, and others who had occasion to visit Chinese enterprises at that time would suggest that Chinese plans were never as tightly drawn as those for the Soviet Union or some of the East European countries at an earlier stage. Chinese managers probably were never under the same degree of pressure to fulfill and over-fulfill the plan as their counterparts in Stalinist Russia. Over-fulfillment did not command large managerial bonuses in China, nor did under-fulfillment result in the kind of brutal or negative sanctions that many factory managers were exposed to in the Soviet Union in the 1930's. Nevertheless, what evidence we have for the 1950's would suggest that Chinese plans were fairly ambitious and that considerable pressure was put on the enterprise to fulfill them. It would seem that this is much less the case now. There would appear to be a considerable slack in Chinese planning and enterprise operations. For instance, when we visited the Number 1 Machine Tool Plant in Shenyang in the third week of December, quite a few machines were idle. In response to questions, the explanation given was that the plan had been fulfilled by October and therefore an opportunity was afforded to repair and overhaul some of the machinery. It was not made clear why the time was not utilized to over-fulfill the production plan.

The principle of slackness was made quite explicit in our interview with the planning officials of the Anshan Iron and Steel Corporation. We were told that it was explicit policy not to fix targets too tightly; on the contrary, targets are set so that the plan can be overfulfilled and enough room left for "the exercise of initiative by the masses." It was indicated to us that the state tends to provide enough raw material and fuel to over-fulfill the production plan by 5 percent. On occasion, the state provides less of the basic materials than requested by the corporation, and in that case, the enterprise cannot be held responsible for a shortfall in the production plan. There was no indication given as to whether this was standard practice for all Chinese industries or whether it applied only to such highly strategic and unusually important enterprises as the Anshan Iron and Steel Corporation.

An essential feature of planning in China, just as in other socialist countries, is supply planning of all basic materials. In China this sytem became crystallized during the period of the First Five-Year Plan. Just as in other centrally planned economies, it involved a system of rationing and licensing in the distribution of basic industrial materials. At the outset, in 1952, 28 commodities were subject to this type of planned distribution. The number rose to 96 in 1953 and to 235 in 1956. It was generally thought that the number may have been reduced under the impact of decentralization. However, we did not know for certain what this number has been in recent years. Shanghai planning officials told us that "over 100" commodities were subject to planned distribution, presumably in 1972. It should be added that we found repeatedly that expressions "over" or "under" could incorporate a very wide range, so that over 100, for example, could mean 150, 175. However that may be, it would seem that there indeed was some reduction in this number since 1956.

Judging from the briefings by officials of the Shanghai Planning Group, the system of materials allocation does not seem to have changed substantially. These basic materials were being distributed on a priority basis so that high priority industries were generally accorded more generous allowances than low priority ones. On the whole, low priority sectors had to operate on the basis of tighter norms and were expected to achieve this tightening through "improvements in management and technology." We were told that for instance, virtually all enterprises had some reserves of coal, and therefore, when basic materials were particularly scarce and norms had to be tightened, low priority sectors were expected to draw on their coal reserves.

In the same briefing as well as in some others, Barry Richman's findings concerning a peculiar Chinese planning and allocative device were confirmed.[5] I am referring to the so-called *National Order* or *National Supply and Sales Conferences.* These are most often convened in December and June. They are usually convened for a particular industry with raw material suppliers, representatives of each major enterprise in the industry and their principal customers participating. At the December conferences, final plan adjustments and reconciliations at the inter-enterprise level could take place involving enterprises from sectors which are mostly closely linked. The June Conferences in turn provide an opportunity for reviewing how the plan is working, based on the experiences of the first half year, and then making the necessary adjustments for the second half. In effect, these Conferences could be considered as quasi-trade fairs or quasi-exchanges, serving as partial substitutes for a market. They provide a means for introducing a measure of flexibility into the planning process while maintaining central control.

V. Labor Allocation

Before my visit, I was under the impression that a mixed system of labor allocation prevailed in China, that is, a system which combined direct command, administrative allocation of all scientific, engineering, managerial and skilled manpower with market allocation of unskilled labor. It was always clear to me that university graduates and all individuals with highly specialized and scarce skills were subject to assignment by government authorities. However, I thought that unskilled workers could move from job to job, only subject to general constraints on mobility.

There always was a concern about "blind migration to the cities" and a desire to stem the exodus from the countryside, associated with the process of industrialization. Irrespective of this, movement was difficult because it required the permission of the authorities for a ration card to be transferred from one locality to another. Moreover, housing had to be obtained in a new place. However, I was surprised to find that even beyond these restrictions, all labor—be it skilled or unskilled—is subject to administrative allocation and to direct job assignments. This probably has been prevailing practice since the Cultural Revolution. Whether it was also true before to the same degree is unclear.

The process of labor recruitment and labor assignment was explained to us in several factories and schools. For example, when the Heavy Steel Rolling Mill in Anshan needs additional workers, it will make a request to the Labor and Wages Division of the Anshan Iron and Steel Corporation. If they approve, then the Corporation will seek the permission of the Provincial Labor Department and the Central Planning Commission. Both of these have to be involved in the decision because the Anshan Iron and Steel Corporation is under dual leadership. If and when the request is approved, the Anshan Municipal Labor Bureau will recruit the necessary number of workers for the Rolling Mill. Generally speaking, once workers are assigned to an enterprise or an organization, they are not likely to be dismissed except if they are "bad elements." As a result, there is probably very little open unemployment in China. However, there is clearly visible underemployment. Superficially at least, one gains the impression that there may be more workers assigned to a particular task and more workers in a factory than perhaps is absolutely required. This again is a symptom of a certain slack in the planning and production system.

When an enterprise expands or when new enterprises are established, the additional labor required is recruited from three sources: school graduates, surplus labor drawn from the countryside and surplus labor drawn from other factories. Moreover, before a new factory starts its operations, it is assigned a nucleus labor force composed of some management, engineering and technical personnel and some experienced workers. This nucleus then trains the newly recruited unskilled workers.

One of the most dramatic and well-known features of manpower allocation in China is represented by the *hsia-fang* movement. It involves the mass migration of large numbers from the city to the countryside, reversing the flow one normally associates with the process of industrialization. In terms of character and scope, this movement has no precedent in the economic history of any other country since the Industrial Revolution. This point was perhaps most clearly driven home to us in Shanghai. Based on briefings and a conversation with one of the most senior officials in the Shanghai municipal government, it would seem that 1.7 million workers have been sent from Shanghai to the countryside since liberation. About half a million of these were skilled workers mobilized to help industries in the interior. Others were university or college graduates, graduates of professional schools and of middle schools. Since the Cultural Revolution, i.e., since 1968 or 1969, 900,000 young people were sent to the rural areas.

In effect, through this movement Shanghai has become a major and key supplier of technical, professional and managerial manpower to the rest of China. We were told that the motivation for this movement is severalfold. It is designed to help the development of industry in the interior. It is also designed to help bring culture and education to the rural areas so as to elevate the cultural level of the peasantry. Perhaps last but not least, it is hoped that it will simplify the problems of administering a large city. For instance, the host at our farewell dinner in Shanghai (senior official in charge of administering Shanghai City proper) indicated that in his view, it would be most desirable to reduce the city's present size from 5.7 million to 2 or 3 million. However, he admitted that this would be impractical and difficult to do. He felt that reducing the population would ease the strain of food supply in a large center of this type, and this certainly was one of the factors motivating the forced urban exodus since 1968. By way of illustrating the point, he told us that the registered population of Shanghai was larger than the actual population and that this problem was due to the rationing system; rationing created an incentive for over-reporting population.

VI. Rural Development and Commune Organization

The Role of Rural Electrification

According to Chinese figures, grain production was 185 million tons in 1957; it dropped during the crisis years, recovered to 183 million tons by

1963 and then steadily rose to 240 to 250 million tons in recent years. This would mean that during the last ten years, i.e., between 1963 and 1973, the average annual rate of growth in grain production was 3.1 percent. This would represent an acceleration in the rates of growth as compared to the First Five-Year Plan figures.

Before my visit to China, I tended to be rather skeptical of these figures and tended to discount somewhat the claims of recent years. I was more inclined to accept the estimates published by various United States Government agencies, placing grain production in the neighborhood of 220 million tons. However, based on what we saw, I am now more inclined than I was before to credit the Chinese figures.

Those parts of China we had access to, i.e., the whole eastern portion of the country running from north to south, seem to be fully electrified. Rural electrification has really taken hold. This then has far-reaching implications for water resource management. Rural electrification has permitted the spread of a network of small pumping stations. This then in turn makes possible the improved distribution of water for irrigation and drainage, thus significantly contributing to flood control.

With better control of water, it was possible to introduce double cropping in areas which used to be single cropped and triple cropping in many areas that used to produce two crops a year. A major role in the expansion of double cropped and triple cropped areas is also played by the increasing application of chemical fertilizer. Therefore, the combination of better water management and increasing chemical fertilizer application has almost certainly contributed to the rise in yields per acre and the total growth in farm production.

Some Aspects of Commune Organization

It always seemed to me that I had a fairly good understanding and a reasonably clear picture of commune structure and organization. However, following actual visits to communes, I was struck by how abstract and skeletal my vision of rural organization was. In effect, the obvious became clear, and what was already clear became clearer. In a certain sense, my view and understanding of communes was not altered, but was sharpened and came into better focus. In many ways, the commune as an institution and as a mode of rural organization combines elements of continuity and change in the Chinese countryside.

The basic pattern of rural life has remained in many respects unchanged. On the whole, the rhythm of life in the Chinese countryside still revolves around natural villages that have existed for a long time. These natural villages seem to maintain close relationships with market towns which serve as marketing centers for a group of villages. Frequently or perhaps typically, the market town also serves as the political and administrative center for the commune. On the basis of our extremely limited observation, it would seem that the framework developed by Skinner in his seminal work on the marketing system of traditional and contemporary China may indeed capture many elements of Chinese reality today.[6] Depending on topography, geographic configuration and density of settlement, a natural village may coincide with a production team; or two small villages may comprise a team; and in the case of a quite large village, it may be equivalent to a production brigade.

As noted above, the commune center performs a number of administrative, political and economic functions. It is the marketing center; it is also where the credit cooperative is located and therefore where the banking functions are performed. This is where the peasant households place their deposits and where the commune engages in its financial transactions. It also serves as the party center for the population of the whole commune. Very importantly, the commune serves as a communication center; it has a telephone which links the area to the outside world, to the party and government hierarchy. It is a most essential ingredient for transmitting directives, messages and for an exchange of views between cadres at varying levels. Next to the telephone is the broadcasting center of the commune, which in many areas is linked to loudspeakers found in every peasant home. This communications network provides an effective means for education, indoctrination and introduction of new techniques. It is one of the instruments through which social control is extended in the countryside and through which political and innovative influences can permeate even relatively remote rural settlements.

In conversations and briefings with commune cadres, I was struck by their innovative spirit. For instance they described for us how they tried to introduce one technique which did not work; they gave it up and tried something else, and when that did not turn out well, yet experimented with other approaches until they hit on one which suited local conditions. In general, one was left with the strong impression that a key task of the commune is to serve as a source for innovation and experimentation. It is probably the avenue through which new techniques of production are introduced into the countryside. This innovative function is reinforced by the fact that the commune center may usually be also the seat of rural industry.

The administrative functions of the commune center also fall into place if one explores the relationship between the commune, the *ch'ü*, the *hsiang* and the large *hsiang*. There seems to be some variation in this respect between different areas, but at least in the places we visited, the Advanced Agricultural Producers Cooperative corresponded to the *hsiang* prior to commune organization. When the commune was established, this became the production brigade. The commune in turn encompassed the *ch'ü* or the large *hsiang*. In all of the commune briefings, we were left with the impression that the functions and responsibilities of the production brigade are quite unclear and shadowy. Perhaps with the exception of those brigades which coincide with natural villages, the brigade may be a somewhat artificial administrative creation, with possibly less historical continuity than the team and the commune.

Agricultural Planning

There is no detailed central planning of production in Chinese agriculture. In this respect communes have significantly greater autonomy than industrial enterprises. Some information on the agricultural planning process was obtained by us on a visit to a commune in the distant suburbs of Shanghai. Farm production targets are passed down to the commune by the *hsien*. The target figures for grain and cotton are stated in different terms. For grain, the target is specified in terms of total output and the quantity to be sold to the state. The state pays a procurement price of 11.4 fen per catty for paddy and 13.4 fen for wheat. It pays a premium price of 30 percent more for grain sold to the state that is over and above the compulsory procurement quota. The cotton target is specified in acreage terms, since virtually all of the cotton is sold to the state. There is also a national cotton yield target for each area, including the one into which this commune falls.

We were told that generally the commune tends to exceed this yield target and also that there has been no change in cotton acreage since 1960. The procurement quota for grain is set once every five years, based on the grain output level for each area, after allowances are made for the food requirements of team households and for fodder and seed. As a way of stimulating food production, the purchase price of grain was increased in recent years. It went up by 10 percent since 1969. On the other hand, the cotton price was not increased. With the present price relationships between cotton and grain and given the fact that in this commune three crops of grain are produced per year, the gross output value per mou for grain and cotton is about the same, although cotton output value still tends to be somewhat higher.

Once the commune obtains the target from the *hsien*, these are distributed to the brigades and by the brigades to the teams. All production teams allocate roughly the same acreage ratios to cotton and grain. Usually, the *hsien* quotas and targets are a little lower than the commune can fulfill.

The state supplies chemical fertilizer to the commune based on the acreage sown. The cadres in this particular commune considered the chemical fertilizer supplied sufficient, given the availability of organic fertilizer. The state attaches no condition to the use of chemical fertilizer, and the production teams are free to allocate it as they wish, but they are encouraged to apply it to cotton. The allocation of chemical fertilizer is 60 catties per mou, which represents a 20 to 30 percent increase since 1965.

Rural Industries in the Commune

To me, one of the most illuminating features of rural development in China was to see the burgeoning of small and medium scale industries in the countryside, mostly located in the market towns. On the basis of our very limited sample of observations, it was hard to draw any generalizations, but one certainly was reminded of the development of small scale industry in Japan. Whether consciously or not, one was left with the impression that after a process of trial and error beginning with the Great Leap and stretching through the 1960s, the Chinese may have gradually evolved a pattern of rural industrial development, which is closely integrated with the agricultural sector. At the same time, some portions of rural industry are related to the national economy as a whole in two ways. Some of the output enters export channels and thus becomes a provider of foreign exchange, while certain other products are manufactured for large scale industry on a sub-contracting basis. During our visit, we did not come across any commune factories which operated on a sub-contracting basis, but we did find plants producing for export and for local needs. Combining what we saw with documentary evidence available concerning the development of small scale industry in China, it would seem that this type of industry may be making a similar contribution to China's industrial and economic development as occurred at an earlier stage in Japan. There is no question that these industries play some role in employment absorption and in meeting the rural demands for many types of producers goods and consumer goods as well.

In the communes we visited, we came across plants that manufactured farm tools, engaged in farm machinery repair, manufacture of farm machinery parts and even some production of complete farm machinery such as threshers. Quite clearly, rural industries play a crucial role in providing for the still relatively simple farm equipment needs of Chinese agriculture at its present stage of development. One also runs across other kinds of machine repair shops which manufacture parts for many different kinds of machinery used in the countryside. Some of these manufacture small generators which are installed in the pumping stations referred to above. There are also some quite primitive foundries using very backward and unsafe methods of producing pig iron to meet local needs. It was unclear as to whether the quality of the pig iron and steel thus produced could meet minimum standards. One of the most frequently found rural industries is basket weaving, leading to the manufacture of a wide variety of products, such as large basket containers for the storage of grain, smaller baskets for carrying materials from and to the fields and last but not least, the manufacture of a wide variety of straw products with lovely designs for export. Interestingly enough, in some places, basket weaving is based on the putting-out system. The plant located at the commune center provides the design, the model and the materials, but the product is actually woven in the household as a spare time activity, usually by the peasant women. The plant also exercises quality control and stores the finished product until it is shipped to the import-export corporation.

In conclusion, a trip of this kind opens up new horizons and raises many questions. It adds a new dimension of reality and depth of understanding that cannot be obtained in any other way. At the same time, it is doubtful that this depth of understanding can be acquired unless it is preceded by considerable background and foreknowledge of China.

Notes

Chapter 1

1. Data for Japan estimated by Irene Taeuber in *The Population of Japan,* Princeton, N.J., 1958, p. 41; for China, see Roland Pressat, "La population de la Chine et son economie," *Population,* Vol. 13, No. 4, October-December 1958, p. 570. However, this figure officially released by the statistical authorities to Pressat may represent something of an underestimate. This presupposition seems to be borne out by the fact that for most of the nine cities for which vital statistics were given to Pressat the rates were higher for most years between 1952 and 1956.
2. According to S. B. Simon's *Studies in the History of Education, 1780-1870,* A British Select Committee found that as late as 1837 in the major industrial towns, only one child in four or five was ever getting to school. (Quoted by R. P. Dore, *Education in Tokugawa Japan,* University of California Press, Berkeley and Los Angeles, 1965, p. 291.)
3. The British figure is based on the 1801 estimate made by Phyllis Deane and W. A. Cole in *British Economic Growth, 1688-1959, Trends and Structure,* Cambridge University Press, 1964, Table 72, p. 282. Their original estimate was converted into 1959 British prices (from the 1865–85 prices in which they were stated) on the basis of implicit deflators given by Deane and Cole in Table 90. These were then converted into United States dollars at the exchange rate prevailing in 1959 and to this an inflation factor was added for 1959–69.
4. The figure would vary somewhat from country to country, particularly in the light of the fact that some regions of Western Europe were more advanced than others at particular points in time during this period. Relevant data, establishing ranges of plausibility, are provided by Simon Kuznets in his book on *Modern Economic Growth: Rate, Structure and Spread,* New Haven, 1966, pp. 63–72 and 390–99 and most particularly Tables 2.5, 7.1 and 7.5.

5. This is based on T. C. Liu and K. C. Yeh's GDP estimate for 1933, *The Economy of the Chinese Mainland: National Income and Economic Development, 1933–1959*, Princeton, N.J., 1965. The range of indeterminacy in these per capita estimates may in part be ascribed to the difficulty of estimating the appropriate exchange rates for converting yuan product figures into dollars. This problem is greatly aggravated by the uncertainties surrounding estimates of population size for 1933.
6. Kuznets, *op. cit.*, Tables 2.3 (p. 43) and 2.5 (p. 65).
7. *Ibid.*, p. 384, fn. 6.
8. Derived from an estimated per capita product of $700 for 1958 and per capita product rates of growth for 1860 to 1813 and 1913 to 1958 as given in Kuznets, *op. cit.*, Table 7.1 and Table 2.5 and then converted into current dollars.
9. This and closely related aspects of the problem received a great deal of attention in the symposium volume edited by E. A. G. Robinson, *Economic Consequences of the Size of Nations*, New York, 1960.
10. See Kuznets, *op. cit.*, pp. 300–304, and K. W. Deutsch and A. Eckstein, "Industrialization and the Declining Share of the International Economic Sector, 1890–1957," *World Politics*, January 1961.
11. For an excellent analysis of the industrialization debates in the Soviet Union, see Alexander Erlich, *The Soviet Industrialization Debate, 1924–1928*, Cambridge, Mass., 1960.
12. For instance, Chou En-lai in his report to the Fifth Session of the First National People's Congress stated that "The Soviet Union has decided with full confidence to catch up with and surpass the United States in the output of the most important industrial products in fifteen years. *The Chinese people is striving to catch up with and surpass Britain in the output of steel, iron and other major industrial products in a period of fifteen years or slightly more*." (Report delivered on February 10, 1958 under the title "The Present International Situation and China's Foreign Policy," NCNA, February 11, 1958.)
13. See Ma Yin-ch'u, *My Economic Theory, Philosophical Thought and Political Position*, Peking, Finance Publishing House, 1958.
14. *Ibid.* and his article "A New Theory of Population," *Hsin-hua pan-yüeh k'an* (New China Semimonthly), No. 15, 1957, pp. 34–41.
15. A great deal of light was thrown on these economic policy disputes by Red Guard newspapers and other documents which have become available to students of Chinese mainland developments since 1966.
16. See Mao Tse-tung, *The Question of Agricultural Cooperation*, a report delivered at a meeting of Party secretaries on July 31, 1955, published in English by Foreign Languages Press, Peking, 1956.
17. "Communique of the Sixth Plenary Session of the Eighth Central Committee" and "Resolution on Some Questions Concerning the

People's Communes" in *Sixth Plenary Session of the Eighth Central Committee of the Communist Party of China*, Foreign Languages Press, Peking, 1958, pp. 1–49.

18. For detailed discussions of statistical problems and reliability in China see C. M. Li, *The Statistical System of Communist China*, Berkeley, 1962; Alexander Eckstein, *The National Income of Communist China*, New York, 1961 and *Communist China's Economic Growth and Foreign Trade*, New York, 1966, Appendix A; T. C. Liu and K. C. Yeh, *The Economy of the Chinese Mainland*, Princeton, N.J., 1965.

19. For an excellent discussion of the issues involved see the comments by Robert Dernberger, Dwight Perkins and Anthony Tang with T. C. Liu's reply in P. T. Ho and Tang Tsou, eds., *China in Crisis*, Vol. 1, Bk. Two, Chicago, 1968, pp. 650–90.

20. According to my national income study cited above, grains comprised 52 percent of China's gross farm production value in 1952. The Liu-Yeh calculations suggest a higher ratio—about 60 percent both in 1952 and 1957. It should be noted that the Chinese use the term grains and food crops interchangeably. These include rice, wheat, millet, kaoliang, coarse grains and sweet potatoes converted to a grain equivalent on the basis of a 4:1 ratio.

21. The uncertainty arises from the fact that total livestock value product estimates based on official Chinese data show no rise between 1952 and 1956 and then jump sharply between 1956 and 1957. While these official figures are somewhat implausible, the Liu-Yeh adjustment is purely arbitrary and devoid of any economic rationale. (See T. C. Liu and K. C. Yeh, *op. cit.*, Appendix Table E–2.) For the 1960's there are virtually no data, except that it is clear from qualitative statements that livestock numbers were decimated during the 1959–62 food crisis. One would expect that their recovery, particularly for cattle, horses, mules and donkeys, would necessarily be slow.

22. The population estimates are based on official data for 1949, 1952 and 1957 as given in Chen Nai-ruenn, *Chinese Economic Statistics: A Handbook for Mainland China*, Chicago, 1967, Table 1.3, p. 124. The 1957 to 1968 population data are taken from Department of State, Bureau of Public Affairs, Issue No. 4, *Communist China*, Washington, D.C., 1969, p. 13 and from John S. Aird: "Population Policy and Demographic Prospects" in *People's Republic of China: An Economic Assessment*, Washington, D.C., U.S.G.P.O., May 18, 1972, p. 328. In citing the latter population figures, one must bear in mind that the Chinese Communist authorities did not publish any population data for the 1960's, so that these estimates are subject to large margins of error just as all other statistical series for the past decade.

23. Estimates for 1914–18 to 1931–37 are based on Dwight H. Perkins, *Agricultural Development in China, 1368–1968*, Chicago, 1969, Table D.32, p. 289.

24. Data concerning output in Japanese agriculture were taken from Yujiro Hayami and Saburo Yamada, "Technological Progress in Agriculture" in L. R. Klein and Kazushi Ohkawa, eds., *Economic Growth, The Japanese Experience Since the Meiji Era*, Homewood, 1968, Table 5A–1 and 5A–2, pp. 156–57 and Kazushi Ohkawa, "Phases of Agricultural Development and Economic Growth" in K. Ohkawa, B. F. Johnston and H. Kaneda, eds., *Agriculture and Economic Growth, Japan's Experience*, Princeton, N.J., 1969, Table 1, p. 6.

25. Phyllis Deane and W. A. Cole, *British Economic Growth, 1688–1959*, Cambridge, 1964, Table 38, p. 170.

26. Based on data in the *United Nations Statistical Yearbook* for 1967, New York, 1968, Table 183, pp. 572–74.

27. The data for India are based on foodgrain production stated in physical terms. These in turn represent official Indian government statistics as cited in The Ford Foundation, *Data on the Indian Economy*, New Delhi, January 1970, p. 3.16.

28. See R. M. Field, "Chinese Communist Industrial Production," in *An Economic Profile of Mainland China*, Washington, D.C., 1967, pp. 293–94 and Chen and Galenson, *op. cit.*, Table III–7, p. 66.

29. For a discussion of Field's methodology see R. M. Field, *op. cit.*, and his paper on "Labor Productivity in Industry," in A. Eckstein, W. Galenson and T. C. Liu, eds., *Economic Trends in Communist China*, Chicago, 1968.

30. Chao Kang, *The Rate and Pattern of Industrial Growth in Communist China*, Ann Arbor, 1965, Chap. III.

31. Chao, *ibid.*, Tables 26 and 27, p. 101.

32. The Indian rates are based on the officially published index of industrial production cited from The Ford Foundation, *Data on the Indian Economy*, New Delhi, January 1970, p. 4.01.

33. R. M. Field, "Chinese Communist Industrial Production," *op. cit.*, Table 3, p. 274.

34. R. M. Field, "Chinese Industrial Development," in *People's Republic of China, An Economic Assessment, op. cit.*, Table B–1, p. 83.

35. *Ibid.* For chemical fertilizer the lower figure is from Field and the higher from Premier Chou En-lai's interview with Edgar Snow, *New Republic*, March 27, 1971, p. 20.

36. For a detailed analysis of foreign trade statistics and their complexities see Alexander Eckstein, *Communist China's Economic Growth and Foreign Trade*, New York, 1966, Chap. 4–6 and Appendix B and C.

37. The series in Table 5 differs for most years to a small extent from those compiled by Dernberger and Eckstein: see Robert F. Dernberger, "Prospects for Trade between China and the United States," in A. Eckstein, ed., *China Trade Prospects and U.S. Policy*, New York,

1971, Table A–1, pp. 276–77 and Alexander Eckstein, *Communist China's Economic Growth and Foreign Trade,* New York, 1966, Table 4–1, pp. 94–95. These differences can be traced to differences in the methods or derivations of the F.O.B. and C.I.F. adjustments for China's different trading partners and/or to differences in the estimates of China's trade with North Korea, North Vietnam, Outer Mongolia and Albania. Since the series presented in Table 5 is more up to date than the others referred to, it is used.

38. United Nations, *Statistical Yearbook, 1962,* New York, 1963, Table 152, pp. 428–31.

39. A. Eckstein, *op. cit.,* pp. 93–94.

40. United Nations, *Statistical Yearbook, 1967,* New York, 1968, Table 13, pp. 67–68.

41. Data for world and Indian trade are drawn from the United Nations, *Statistical Yearbook, 1967,* New York, 1968, Table 148, pp. 384 and pp. 390–91 and from Ford Foundation report cited earlier, p. 7.01.

42. For a careful critique of Liu and Yeh's estimate see Robert Dernberger's review of their book in the *Journal of Political Economy,* Volume 78, No. 4, August 1966, pp. 419–21.

43. See T. C. Liu, "Quantitative Trends in the Economy," in Eckstein, Galenson and Liu, eds., *op. cit.,* Table 21, p. 164.

44. See John S. Aird, "Population Policy and Demographic Prospects in the People's Republic of China," in *People's Republic of China: An Economic Assessment,* pp. 220–331 and Leo Orleans, *Every Fifth Child,* London, 1972, p. 56.

45. For a more detailed discussion of this foreign exchange problem and the sources of these data see Appendix in A. Eckstein, *op. cit.,* New York, 1966.

46. All of the figures for India are based on the aforecited Ford Foundation report, p. 2.01 and 2.02. It must however be noted that all national product estimates for India must be used with great deal of caution and may be subject to considerable margins of error. Therefore, these national product comparisons for China and India must necessarily be considered as quite tentative.

47. For average long-term growth rates of these countries see Kuznets, *op. cit.,* Table 2.5, pp. 64–65.

48. See S. Kuznets, "Quantitative Aspects of the Economic Growth of Nations, II, Industrial Distribution of National Product and Labor Force," in *Economic Development and Cultural Change,* Supplement to Vol. V, No. 4, July 1957, Tables 3 and 10.

49. T. C. Liu, "Quantitative Trends in the Economy," in A. Eckstein, W. Galenson and T. C. Liu, eds., *Economic Trends in Communist China,* Chicago, 1968, pp. 123–28.

Chapter 2

1. This scale effect is, of course, both crucial and indeterminate, in the sense that what will be the operationally significant range will inevitably vary from country to country, depending upon size, institutional framework, etc.

Chapter 3

1. Economic backwardness can of course be described or defined in terms of a number of mutually interrelated criteria such as GNP per head, share of labor force in agriculture, average product per worker, etc. For internationally comparable measures of structural change associated with economic growth see Simon Kuznets, *Modern Economic Growth: Rate, Structure and Spread,* New Haven and London, 1966; particularly Chap. 3.
2. There are various ways in which the scope and extent of internal trade could be measured. In this context I am thinking of the share of output entering marketing channels, and within this share the proportion sold in local as compared to regional or national markets.
3. Thus a premodern polity such as that of Imperial China, embedded in a premodern economy based on traditional techniques of production, could exert far-reaching control over a vast area but with minimal penetration at the sub-*hsien* level.
4. In this context the *ceteris paribus* assumption must be strongly underlined. Therefore it would be erroneous to jump to the conclusion that economic and political mobilization would be impossible. In fact, as both Soviet and Chinese examples illustrate, ideology and organization can compensate for technical backwardness at least up to a point.
5. In thinking through these definitions of needs and demands I have been greatly influenced by, and have profited from, studying the burgeoning literature in the field of political development. I am referring to the first five symposia sponsored by the Committee on Comparative Politics and published by Princeton's University Press, to David Apter's *The Politics of Modernization* (Chicago, 1965), and to *Comparative Politics, A Developmental Approach* by Gabriel Almond and G. Bingham Powell, Jr. In working on this paper I have particularly benefited from reading Lucian Pye's most stimulating essay on *Aspects of Political Development,* Boston, 1966.
6. Mobilization is of course very closely associated with industrialization. I am treating it here as a separate concept since mobilization may be directed not only towards economic growth but political development as well. Moreover, it may go beyond that and serve as a means of sustaining a permanent revolution.

7. Alexander Gerschenkron, *Economic Backwardness in Historical Perspective, A Book of Essays,* Cambridge, Mass., 1962, Chap. 1, p. 24.

8. For instance, this was most apparent in Communist China during the Great Leap Forward (1958–59) when the whole state and economic management apparatus became highly politicized with numerous tasks and responsibilities transferred to direct Party control. At the same time ideological exhortation and indoctrination was greatly stepped up and the Party with its cadres was mobilized to a fever pitch. In turn, it was the task of the cadres thus imbued to mobilize the masses. (See Franz Schurmann, *Ideology and Organization in Communist China,* University of California Press, Berkeley and Los Angeles, 1966, Prologue pp. xlii and xlv, and Introduction, pp. 1–9.)

9. Sigmund Freud, *Group Psychology and the Analysis of the Ego,* Liveright Publishing Corporation, New York, 1967, p. 61.

10. I am indebted to Professor Gregory Grossman for calling this to my attention. In considering this problem it may be important to bear in mind that the leaders ideal is a communist man who is both *red* and *expert.* However, particularly in underdeveloped communist countries such as China, where technical and skilled manpower is very scarce and where technical backwardness itself severely limits the technical learning opportunities, such an ideal may be unattainable.

11. In introducing this notion of degree of "potency," I of course recognize the obstacles to translating it into measurable magnitudes. Theoretically, i.e., provided that the data are available, rising input applications and input productivities can be measured. If more intensive ideological indoctrination were the only instrument to be used in inducing input changes, the measurement problem would be relatively simple. However if, as is more probable, ideology is used in combination with other instruments, it may be extremely difficult—if not impossible—to separate out the effects of the former from the latter. This difficulty arises both from the fact that ideological and other inputs may be inter-correlated and that applications of ideology can hardly be quantified. One can of course quantify the number of workers engaged in indoctrination (i.e., party cadres engaged in ideological work), but this can hardly serve as an adequate measure of the factor mobilization or factor productivity effects of ideology. It would be even more difficult to measure the degree to which input mobilization and productivity effects are traceable to spontaneous rather than coercive adherence.

12. Karl Marx, *Contribution to the Critique of Political Economy,* Charles H. Kerr and Co., Chicago, 1911, p. 11.

13. For instance in discussing the role of primitive accumulation in the development or rise of early capitalism Marx states that "*Force is the midwife of every old society pregnant with a new one. It is itself an*

economic power" (italics supplied). *Capital,* Vol. 1, Chicago, Charles H. Kerr and Co., Chicago, 1921, p. 824.

14. This ambiguity was clearly recognized by Engels in the much referred-to four letters written by him after Marx's death in response to the critics of Marxist theory. In these letters he again reiterates the role that ideology, religion and philosophy may play in a society's economic development. At the same time he re-emphasizes that the interaction between cultural elements and production forces is "on the basis of economic necessity, which *ultimately* always asserts itself." (See Karl Marx and Friedrich Engels, *Selected Correspondence, 1846–1895,* translated by Dona Torr, New York, 1942, pp. 475–518.)

15. "Of all things in the world, *people are the most precious,"* in Mao Tse-tung, *Selected Works,* Vol. 4, Peking, Foreign Languages Press, 1961, p. 454; emphasis added.

16. In Lifton's words there are certain psychological assumptions long prominent in Mao's thought but never so overtly insisted upon as during the Cultural Revolution. One of these assumptions is an image of the human mind as infinitely malleable, capable of being reformed, transformed and rectified without limit. Another is a related vision of the will as all-powerful, even to the extent that in Mao's own words, *"the subjective creates the objective."* That is man's capacity for both undergoing change and changing his environment is unlimited; once he makes the decision for change, the entire universe can be bent to his will. (Robert J. Lifton, *Revolutionary Immortality, Mao Tse-tung and the Chinese Cultural Revolution,* New York, 1968, pp. 70–71.)

17. This point was most dramatically driven home during the Great Leap of 1958–59.

18. See Amitai Etzioni, *A Comparative Analysis of Complex Organizations,* 1961, p. 66.

19. I am indebted to Professor Richard Lowenthal for this particular way of formulating the problem.

20. Professor Skinner goes well beyond this in his most suggestive policy cycle theory based on shift patterns of this appeals mix in different phases of the cycle. See G. W. Skinner and E. A. Winckler, "Compliance Succession in Rural Communist China, A Cyclical Theory," in Amitai Etzioni, ed., *Complex Organizations,* Second Edition, New York, 1969, pp. 410–38.

21. See Egon Neuberger, "Libermanism, Computopia and Visible Hand," *American Economic Review, Papers and Proceedings,* May 1966, pp. 131–44.

22. See Philip Selznick, *TVA and the Grass Roots,* Berkeley, 1949.

23. Something like this seems to have taken place in Czechoslovakia between January and August 1968.

24. In no sense does this, however, imply a unilinear pattern of development or an inevitable line of progression. Clearly at any one point the

process is reversible provided the communist leadership is prepared to pay the price for such reversals.

Chapter 4

1. *Economic Journal,* LXVI, 261, 1956, pp. 25–48.
2. Cambridge, Harvard University Press, 1959.

Chapter 5

1. This point was first developed by Professor W. W. Lockwood in his article on "Japan's Response to the West, The Contrast with China," *World Politics,* Vol. IX, No. 1 (October, 1956).
2. *Ibid.* For a good study of social mobility in China see P. T. Ho, *The Ladder of Success in Imperial China,* New York, 1964.
3. For a discussion of the significance of growing points or modes in economic development see Albert Hirschman, *The Strategy of Economic Development,* New Haven, 1958.
4. For a definition of "modern economic growth" see Simon Kuznets, *Six Lectures on Economic Growth,* Glencoe, Ill., 1959.
5. See Henry Rosovsky, "Japan's Transition to Modern Economic Growth, 1868–1885," in *Industrialization in Two Systems, Essays in Honor of Alexander Gerschenkron,* New York, 1966.
6. Rosovsky, *op. cit.,* p. 64; *The Chinese Year Book,* Premier Issue, Shanghai, 1935, pp. 1423–27; Frank Tamagna, *Banking and Finance in China,* New York, 1942.
7. G. C. Allen and A. G. Donnithorne, *Western Enterprise in Far Eastern Economic Development,* New York, 1954, Chap. VI.
8. C. C. Chang, *An Estimate of China's Farms and Crops,* Nanking, 1932.
9. J. L. Buck, *Chinese Farm Economy,* Chicago, 1930; and *Land Utilization in China,* Nanking, 1937.
10. See also T. H. Shen, *The Agricultural Resources of China,* Ithaca, 1951.
11. For an analysis of these economic changes approached within a somewhat different framework see the preceding chapter.
12. See P. T. Ho, *Studies on the Population of China, 1368–1953,* Cambridge, Mass., 1959.
13. *Ibid.,* p. 13.
14. E. O. Reischauer and J. K. Fairbank, *East Asia, The Great Tradition,* Vol. I, Boston, 1960, p. 212.
15. *Ibid.,* pp. 214–15.
16. L. S. Yang, *Money and Credit in China,* Cambridge, Mass., 1952.
17. Benjamin I. Schwartz, *In Search of Wealth and Power, Yen Fu and the West,* Cambridge, Mass., 1964, pp. 10–11.
18. R. H. Tawney, *Land and Labor in China,* London, 1932, p. 48.
19. G. W. Skinner, "Marketing and Social Structure in Rural China," Parts

I and II, *Journal of Asian Studies,* Vol. XXIV, No. 1 (November 1964), and No. 2 (February 1965).

20. P. T. Ho, "The Salt Merchants of Yang-chou: A Study of Commercial Capitalism in Eighteenth Century China," *Harvard Journal of Asiatic Studies,* XVII, No. 1–2 (June 1954).

21. G. W. Skinner, *op. cit.*

22. P. T. Ho, *The Ladder of Success, op. cit.,* pp. 41–52.

23. G. W. Skinner, *op. cit.,* and J. L. Buck, *Land Utilization in China, op. cit.,* p. 357.

24. K. Ohkawa and H. Rosovsky, "The Role of Agriculture in Modern Japanese Economic Development," *Economic Development and Cultural Change,* Vol. IX, No. 1, Pt. II (October, 1960).

25. J. K. Fairbank, *Trade and Diplomacy on the China Coast, The Opening of the Treaty Ports, 1842–1854,* Cambridge, Mass., 1953; and Michael Greenberg, *British Trade and the Opening of China, 1800–42,* Cambridge, Eng., 1951.

26. C. F. Remer, *The Foreign Trade of China,* Shanghai, 1926, p. 27.

27. C. M. Hou, *Foreign Investment and Economic Development in China, 1840–1937,* Cambridge, Mass., Chap. 7.

28. C. M. Li, "International Trade," in H. F. McNair, ed., *China,* Berkeley, 1946, p. 501. According to Li, citing Sargent, merchandise imports amounted to 25 million Chinese dollars in 1841 and exports to 13.3 million Chinese dollars, with the difference covered by silver exports.

29. Mary C. Wright, *The Last Stand of Chinese Conservatism,* Stanford, Calif., 1957.

30. E. G. Beal, *The Origin of Likin,* Cambridge, Mass., 1958.

31. Cited by P. T. Ho in *Studies on the Population of China, op. cit.,* p. 154.

32. Wright, *op. cit.,* p. 158.

33. The term *tsu-ch'iang* was first used by Feng Kuei-fen in 1860; see S. Y. Teng and J. K. Fairbank, *China's Response to the West,* Cambridge, Mass., 1954, pp. 50–53.

34. Teng and Fairbank, *op. cit.,* p. 28.

35. *Ibid.,* p. 62.

36. Albert Feuerwerker, *China's Early Industrialization,* Cambridge, Mass., 1958, p. 16.

37. *Ibid.,* p. 174.

38. See A. Feuerwerker, *op. cit.,* Chaps. 4 and 5, and K. C. Liu, *Anglo-American Steamship Rivalry in China, 1862–1874,* Cambridge, Mass., 1962.

39. C. F. Remer, *The Foreign Trade of China,* pp. 38–45.

40. Y. K. Cheng, *Foreign Trade and Industrial Development of China,* Washington, D. C., 1956, Appendix I, p. 258.

41. Remer, *op. cit.,* Tables 2, 3, and 6.

42. Computed by the author on the basis of trade figures given by Y. K. Cheng, *op. cit.*, p. 258.

43. Remer, *op. cit.*, pp. 48 and 89–90.

44. Cheng, *op. cit.*, p. 17.

45. Allen and Donnithorne, *op. cit.*, p. 107.

46. Actual number computed by author on the basis of the number of American residents and their share in the foreign population as given by Remer, *op. cit.*, Table 25, p. 338. Treaty ports were not only open to foreign trade but were subject to extraterritoriality, under which foreigners and their activities in China were subject to foreign and not to Chinese law.

47. Allen and Donnnithorne, *op. cit.*, pp. 145–47.

48. D. K. Lieu, *The Growth and Industrialization of Shanghai*, Shanghai, 1936, pp. 421–22.

49. Remer, *op. cit.*, p. 93.

50. C. F. Remer, *Foreign Investment in China*, New York, 1933, p. 54.

51. Kia-ngau Chang, *China's Struggle for Railroad Development*, New York, 1943, pp. 23 and 24; and H. B. Morse, *The Chronicles of the East India Company, Trading to China, 1635–1834*, Vols. III and IV, Oxford, 1926–29.

52. Feuerwerker, *op. cit.*, Table 17 and p. 290, and United Kingdom, Naval Intelligence Division: *China Proper*, Vol. III, July 1945.

53. The foreign share in total modern shipping was 77 percent in 1897 on the basis of tonnage of steamers entered and cleared through maritime customs. See C. M. Hou, *op. cit.*, Table 28.

54. Rhoads Murphey, *Shanghai, Key to Modern China*, Cambridge, Mass., 1953, pp. 47–49.

55. F. C. Jones, *Manchuria Since 1931*, London, 1949, p. 101 and Allen and Donnithorne, *op. cit.*, p. 267.

56. Based on data in the South Manchurian Railroad *Report on Progress*, p. 48 and Y. K. Cheng, *op. cit.*, pp. 258–59.

57. The selection of commodities for inclusion was governed by the availability of data. The following are included in the index: coal, iron ore, pig iron, steel, antimony, copper, gold, mercury, tin, tungsten, cotton or cotton cloth, flour, cement, crude petroleum, and electric power.

58. Yen Chung-p'ing, *Chung-kuo chin-tai ching-chi shih t'ung-chi tzu-liao hsuan-chi* (Selected statistics in China's modern economic history), Peking, 1955, pp. 134–36 and Tables 21 and 30.

59. T. C. Liu and K. C. Yeh, *The Economy of the Chinese Mainland, National Income and Economic Development, 1933–1959*, Princeton, 1965.

60. Yen Chung-p'ing, *op. cit.*, pp. 124 and 130–31.

61. Liu and Yeh, *op. cit.*, Tables 8, 11, and 21.

62. This conclusion emerges from Ou Pao-san's and Liu-Yeh's national

income studies for 1933; it is confirmed by the author's own national income study for 1952 and by some other more specialized monographic studies as well.

63. P'eng Tse-i, ed., *Chung-kuo chin-tai shou-kung-yeh shih tzu-liao, 1840–1949* (Some materials on the modern history of Chinese handicrafts), Vol. 3, Peking, 1957, Appendix 3.

64. Yen Chung-P'ing, *op. cit.*, and Hou, *op. cit.*, Chap. 7.

65. Y. K. Cheng, *op. cit.*, pp. 258–59.

66. To avoid misunderstanding, my argument is not intended to imply a zero elasticity of supply, but merely that it may be assumed to be well below unity. Thus I am not saying that the traditional peasantry does not respond, or is not capable of responding to price changes and changing market conditions; the point is merely that such responses tend to be delayed and slow.

67. All the quantitative data, unless otherwise indicated, cited in this section dealing with agriculture are drawn from Buck's study on *Land Utilization in China*.

68. Liu and Yeh, *op. cit.*, Table 21.

69. J. L. Buck, *Land Utilization in China, op. cit.*, p. 354.

70. The errors and estimated biases incurred by converting China's per capita product into dollars are shared by similar conversions for other low income countries. Therefore, while the particular GNP figure thus obtained is undoubtedly subject to a large margin of error, this need not affect the relative standing of a country on a comparative per capita scale. Conversion of early national income estimates for currently developed countries is subject to similar kinds of biases. Of course, conversion of late seventeenth-century product estimates into current prices is fraught with a host of additional hazards. Nevertheless, given a 100 to 200 per cent differential, it is improbable that the margins of error would be so large as to nullify the point made; namely that in 1949 China's GNP per capita was lower than that of pre-industrial England. These early British figures are from Phyllis Deane and W. A. Cole, 1962, p. 3; they represent a revised and adjusted version of Gregory King's original estimates.

71. For comparative data on interindustry composition of GNP and labor force, see Simon Kuznets, "Quantitative Aspects of the Economic Growth of Nations, Industrial Distribution of National Product and Labor Force," *Economic Development and Cultural Change*, Supplement to Volume V, July, 1957.

72. Phyllis Deane and W. A. Coale, *British Economic Growth, 1668–1959*, Cambridge Eng., 1962, p. 41.

73. J. L. Buck, *Land Utilization in China, op. cit.*, pp. 383–87.

Chapter 6

1. Alexander Gerschenkron, "Economic Backwardness in Historical Per-

spective," in *The Progress of Underdeveloped Areas,* ed. by Bert F. Hoselitz, Chicago, 1952, p. 5.

2. These figures, as well as all national income estimates throughout this article, are based on preliminary findings emerging from a detailed study of Communist China's gross national product which the author is in the process of preparing.

3. D. H. Perkins, *Agricultural Development in China, 1368–1968,* Chicago, 1969, p. 16.

4. A. K. Chiu, "Agriculture," in *China,* ed. by H. F. MacNair, Berkeley, Calif., 1946, p. 469.

5. This seems to have been the practice at least as far back as the Han dynasty.

6. J. L. Buck, *Land Utilization in China,* Shanghai, 1937, pp. 181–85 and 267–73; C. C. Chang, *An Estimate of China's Farms and Crops,* Nanking, 1932.

7. H. D. Fong, "Rural Industries in China," *Problems of the Pacific,* 5th Conference of the IPR, Banff, Alberta, 1933.

8. Li Choh-ming, "International Trade," in *China, op. cit.,* p. 498.

9. G. B. Cressey, *China's Geographic Foundations,* New York, 1934, p. 26.

10. Julean Arnold, in *Chinese Economic Journal* (October 1930), p. 1069.

11. Buck, *op. cit.,* p. 349.

12. U.S. Department of Commerce, *Foreign Commerce Yearbook,* 1937, Washington, 1938. Subsequent findings incorporated in preceding chapter.

13. F. C. Remer, *The Foreign Trade of China,* Shanghai, 1926, pp. 222–23.

14. A. K. Chiu, "Agriculture," in *China, op. cit.,* p. 474.

15. *China Handbook, 1950,* New York, 1950, pp. 581–83.

16. Buck, *op. cit.,* Table 18, p. 462.

17. Report delivered at the session of the National Committee of the Chinese People's Political Consultative Conference of June 6, 1950, in *New China's Economic Achievements,* 1949–1952, Peking, 1952, p. 6.

18. Edwin W. Pauley, *Report on Japanese Assets in Manchuria to the President of the United States,* July 1946, p. 37.

19. This is based on the official index compiled by the Central Committee on Financial and Economic Affairs. See "Economic Development in Mainland China, 1949–1953," in *Economic Bulletin for Asia and the Far East,* published by the United Nations Economic Commission for Asia and the Far East, November 1953.

20. See Li Shu-cheng, "New China's Achievements in Agricultural Production During the Past Three Years," in *New China's Economic Achievements, op. cit.,* p. 188.

21. Ch'en Yun, "The Financial and Food Situation," in *ibid.,* pp. 53–54.

22. For coal, official statements admit a shortfall.
23. Power for household use is strictly rationed, particularly in Manchuria.
24. The arithmetic behind this estimate is as follows:

Peak Manchurian finished steel capacity	910,000 MT
Finished steel capacity after dismantling	325,000 MT
Capacity which must be reinstalled to produce 1952 output	475,000 MT
Capital requirement per ton of finished steel	$US 400
Total capital requirement for reinstallation of capacity	$US 190,000,000

However, about half of this capital investment is for structures, which have been left more or less intact, so that one should only count equipment costs, which may be estimated as:

$US 95,000,000

Add to this a replacement allowance of 10 per cent per year on old capital which was not removed. For two years:

$US 65,000,000

Total cost of replacement and reinstallation:

$US 160,000,000

25. Shen, *op. cit.*, p. 308.
26. Po I-po, "Three Years of Achievement of the People's Republic of China," in *New China's Economic Achievements, op. cit.*, p. 158.
27. Hsüeh Mu-ch'iao, "China's Great Victories on the Economic Front During the Past Three Years," in *ibid.*, p. 281.
28. The "cash and currency control plan" placed the People's Bank in the position of a central clearinghouse for all transactions and a repository of all capital, including current working capital, for the state enterprise system.
29. The victory bond units, known as fen, are composed of 6 catties of rice (millet in Tientsin), 1.5 catties of flour, 4 feet of white shirting, and 16 catties of coal. The fen is quoted nationally every ten days, with the value based on the wholesale prices of these items in Shanghai, Tientsin, Hankow, Sian, Canton, and Chungking; in computing the fen, the commodity basket values in these cities are given the following weight: Shanghai—45; Tientsin—20; Hankow, Canton, and Chungking—10 each; Sian—5.
  Unlike the fen, parity deposit and wage units are separately quoted for all large cities. The exact composition of these varies from

city to city, but they all include some grain, staple, cloth, vegetable oil, and coal.

30. Chung Kan-en, "The Success of the State Bank's Policy on Interest Rate," *Economic Weekly,* Shanghai, July 3, 1952, as summarized in Chao, ed., *Source Materials from Communist China,* III, October 1952, p. 62.

31. *Ta Kung Pao,* Shanghai, June 10, 1949.

32. For an analysis of the Soviet case, see F. D. Holzman, "The Burden of Soviet Taxation," *American Economic Review,* XLIII (September 1953), pp. 548–71.

33. It must also be borne in mind that part of this increase is due to price rises. The rise in the wholesale price level may be crudely estimated at about 20 per cent between 1950 and 1951, and 30 per cent between 1950 and 1952.

34. Following Western fiscal practice, we treated all expenditures not covered by regular revenues as deficits which had to be covered by extra-budgetary levies, bond issues, or bank overdrafts.

35. I am indebted to Dr. Joseph Froomkin for calling this to my attention.

36. This was not true prior to 1953, when the Manchurian transport system was under joint Sino-Soviet management.

37. Based on an article in *People's China* of September 1, 1953, by Hsu Hsueh-han. This figure may include, however, substantial military equipment paid for by Peking.

38. This observation applies, of course, only to small net imports or exports.

39. For an excellent analysis of the Soviet Industrialization debate, see Alexander Erlich, "Preobrazhenski and the Economics of Soviet Industrialization," *Quarterly Journal of Economics,* LXIV (February 1950), pp. 57–88.

40. Bruce F. Johnston, "Agricultural Productivity and Economic Development in Japan," *Journal of Political Economy,* LIX (1951), pp. 498–513.

41. Shigeto Tsuru and Kazushi Ohkawa, "Long-term Changes in the National Product of Japan since 1878," *Income and Wealth,* Series III, Cambridge, Eng., 1953, pp. 19–44; Yuzo Yamada and Associates, *Notes on the Income Growth and the Rate of Saving in Japan,* Mimeo. 19, Tokyo, 1953, p. 1.

42. *China Yearbook, 1948,* Nanking, 1948; United Nations, *World Iron Ore Resources and Their Utilization,* New York, 1950; W. S. and E. S. Woytinsky, *World Population and Production,* New York, 1953.

43. Edwin W. Pauley, *Report on Japanese Assets in Manchuria to the President of the United States,* July 1946, p. 98.

44. The first portion of this railroad, running from Chungking to Chengtu,

is an exception inasmuch as it links the Szechuan rice basin to the rest of the country. Generally, the reasons for concentrating on this western line are probably primarily strategic and political, designed to bring these remote areas under closer control by the center.

45. United Nations, *Demographic Yearbook, 1952,* pp. 224–31 and 264–69; Woytinsky and Woytinsky, *op. cit.,* Tables 63, 82, and 86.

46. United Nations, *Demographic Yearbook;* Kingsley Davis, *The Population of India and Pakistan,* 1951, pp. 36–37.

47. There were recurrent reports in the Chinese Communist press, in the spring and summer of 1954, that a sharp fall in the death rate has occurred. See, for example, *New China News Agency,* Peking, March 10, 1954, for a report on partial census results.

48. See *Estimates of the Capital Structure of American Industries,* 1947, prepared by James M. Henderson and others, Harvard Economic Research Project, June 1953 (hectograph).

49. See the section on the Five-Year Plan below.

50. The agricultural and all other value products in this article were estimated in terms of Chinese Communist currency (JMP) and then converted into dollars at the official rate of exchange. Therefore, they reflect the 1952 price relationships in mainland China, with their peculiar institutional distortions. For this reason alone, if for no other, these value products are not internationally comparable.

51. T. H. Shen, *Agricultural Resources of China,* Ithaca, N. Y., 1951.

52. Pierre Gourou, "The Development of Upland Areas in China," in *The Development of Upland Areas in the Far East,* IPR International Secretariat, New York, 1949, p. 10.

53. As a matter of fact, the first collective farm in China—"The Spark"—was established in this region.

54. Shen, *op. cit.,* p. 363.

55. See the statement by Teng Tzu-hui, head of the Chinese Communist Party's Rural Work Department, noted in *New York Times,* November 2, 1954, p. 9.

56. Johnston, *op. cit.*

57. E. B. Schumpeter et al., *The Industrialization of Japan and Manchukuo, 1930–1940,* New York, 1940, p. 251; Shen, *op. cit.,* p. 38.

58. "Economic Developments in Mainland China, 1949–1953," in United Nations, *Economic Bulletin for Asia and the Far East,* IV, No. 3 (November 1953), pp. 17–31.

59. For a fuller discussion of these cooperatives, see A. Doak Barnett, "China's Road to Collectivization," *Journal of Farm Economics,* XXXV (May 1953), pp. 188–202.

60. "Decision on the Development of Agrarian Production Cooperatives," December 16, 1953, reported in *China News Analysis,* Hong Kong, February 12, 1954.

61. "Order of Government Administrative Council for Enforcement of

Planned Purchase and Planned Supply of Grain," issued November 23, 1953, published by *New China Agency,* Peking, February 28, 1954.

62. United Nations, Economic Commission for Europe, *Economic Survey of Europe Since the War,* Geneva, 1953, p. 166, and Chart 13, p. 177.

63. As of November 1954.

64. Po I-po, "The 1953 State Budget of the People's Republic of China," *Supplement to People's China,* March 26, 1953; Chou En-lai, "Report at the Fourth Session of the National Committee of Chinese People's Consultative Council," in *Ta Kung Pao,* Hong Kong, February 5, 1953.

65. Speech at the Fifteenth Congress of the All-Union Communist Party (Bolshevik), Moscow, 1927; verbatim report, p. 67.

66. Compare Po I-po, *op. cit.;* Chia To-fu, "Report to the 7th Session of All-China Trade Union Congress," in *New China News Agency,* September 25, 1953; Wu Lun-hsi, "New China on the Road to Industrialization," in *Ta Kung Pao,* Hong Kong, October, 1953.

67. This "general line" was first announced in an editorial of the *People's Daily,* on October 1, 1953, under the title "Struggle for the Distant and Great Goal of Socialistic Industrialization." Incidentally, all of our references to collectivization include producers' cooperatives, on the assumption that the de facto distinction between the two is slight.

68. The new bond issue valued at six trillion JMP (about U.S. $240,000,000) was launched in December 1953. See *New York Times,* December 10, 1953, January 23, and February 9, 1954.

69. *New China News Agency,* Peking, September 15, 1953.

70. Harry Schwartz, "Soviet Aid to China," *New York Times,* October 5, 1953.

71. Text of the Soviet-Chinese Communist Communique on 7 Accords, *New York Times,* October 12, 1954.

72. See Table 7 and Woytinski and Woytinski, *op. cit.,* pp. 118–21.

73. United Nations, Economic Commission for Latin America, *Study on Iron and Steel Industry,* II, E/N, 12/293, Santiago, 1952, Add. 2 and 3. This study gives the investment cost per ton of finished steel in a plant with a 250,000 ton capacity at U.S. $400. The investment cost per ton of crude steel is estimated at U.S. $170, all in terms of 1948 prices. In the 1,000,000 ton plant at Sparrows Point, Maryland, unit investment cost is estimated at U.S. $283 per ton of finished and U.S. $126 per ton of crude steel.

74. United States Federal Power Commission, *Steam-electric Plant Construction Cost and Annual Production Expenses,* Washington, D.C., 1950

75. Input-output studies for the United States economy, conducted by the Harvard Economics Research Project, would tend to indicate that about one-third of the new investment required per unit of increased output in steel and power production would consist of complex types

of equipment. It was assumed that this equipment could not be manufactured in China and would, therefore, have to be imported from the Soviet Union.

76. This relates the share of gross investment to gross national product. Derived from M. Mukharjee and A. U. Ghosh, "The Pattern of Income and Expenditure in the Indian Union," *Bulletin of the International Institute of Statistics,* XXXIII, No. 3 (December 1951), pp. 49–68.

77. Soviet investment figures cited here refer to the period of the first two Five-Year Plans and are based on Norman Kaplan's study, *Capital Investments in the Soviet Union, 1924–1951,* Rand Research Memorandum 735, Santa Monica, Calif., November 1951.

78. Capital-output ratios used here specifically refer to incremental ratios designed to measure the increment in product associated with a given amount of additional (new) net investment.

79. See Alexander Eckstein and Peter Gutman, "Note on the Soviet Incremental and Average Capital-Output Ratios," CENIS Econ. Devt., A.I.6, Cambridge, Mass., March 18, 1954 (mimeograph).

80. Shigeto Tsuru and Kazushi Ohkawa, "Long-term Changes in the National Product of Japan Since 1878," *Income and Wealth,* Series III, Cambridge, Eng., 1953; Yuzo Yamada and Associates, *Notes on the Income Growth and the Rate of Saving in Japan,* Mimeo. 19, Tokyo, 1953; Colin Clark, *The Conditions of Economic Progress,* 2nd ed., London, 1951, pp. 136–38.

81. See W. W. Lockwood, *The Economic Development of Japan,* Princeton, N.J., 1954, pp. 25–34.

82. Koh Tso-fan, "Capital Stock in China," *Problems of Economic Reconstruction in China,* China Council Paper No. 2, IPR, Eighth Conference at Mont Tremblant, December 1942; Edwin W. Pauley, *Report on Japanese Assets in Manchuria to the President of the United States,* July 1946.

83. This applies to Japan approximately between 1890 and 1915 and to the Soviet Union between 1928 and 1938.

84. See Teng Hsiao-p'ing, "Report on the 1954 State Budget," in *NCNA Daily Bulletin,* Supplement No. 204, London, June 29, 1954.

85. Abram Bergson, ed., *Soviet Economic Growth: Conditions and Perspectives,* Evanston, Ill., 1953, p. 9.

86. The term "resource base" is used here in its broadest sense. Thus, China is comparatively better endowed with mineral resources, while Japan faced an expanding world market and a different international climate. For further details, see Table 7 and Section IIIA.

Chapter 7

1. Ishikawa Shigeru, "A. Ekusutain: Chugoku Keizai no Seicho Moderu" in Koshinkoku Kaihatsu no Riron, ed. by Ajia Kyokai (Nikkan Kogyo

Shinbusha, 1956). Ishikawa Shigeru, "The Prospects for Communist China" in *Asian Affairs*, Vol. I, No. 3, September 1956, pp. 308–14.

2. For an interesting attempt to investigate this problem see an article by Ishikawa Shigeru in the January 1957 issue of this journal.

3. Frank Lorimer, *The Population of the Soviet Union, History and Prospects*, League of Nations, Geneva, 1946, pp. 133–37.

4. Naum Jasny, *The Socialized Agriculture of the U.S.S.R., Plans and Performance*, Stanford, 1949, Chart Tables 4, 5, 6, and 37 in the Appendix.

5. "Doklad o Natural'nom Naloge 15 Marta" (Report on the Tax in Kind, March 15, 1921), *Sochineniya*, XXVI, 246.

6. Gregory Grossman, "Soviet Agriculture Since Stalin," *The Annals of the American Academy of Political and Social Science*, January 1956, pp. 62–74.

7. For an interesting discussion of the national income implications of these rural-urban shifts see Simon Kuznets, *Economic Change,* Chap. 6, New York, 1953.

Chapter 8

1. For an analysis of some of the reasons that produced the divergent patterns of collectivization in China and Russia, see the author's "Manpower and Industrialisation in Communist China, 1952–1957," in *Population Trends in Eastern Europe, the USSR and Mainland China*, Milbank Mem. Fund, 1960, pp. 158–60.

2. For a detailed analysis of Chinese Communist population policy, see Irene Taeuber, "Population Policies in Communist China," *Population Index*, October, 1956, and W. Parker Mauldin, "Fertility Control in Communist Countries," in *Population Trends in Eastern Europe, the USSR, and Mainland China*, Milbank Mem. Fund, 1960, pp. 197–208.

3. R. R. Nelson, "A Theory of the Low-Level Equilibrium Trap," *A.E.R.*, December, 1956.

4. R. S. Eckaus, "Factor Proportions in Underdeveloped Areas," *A.E.R.*, September, 1955, pp. 559–60.

5. For an official statement of policy, spelling out the new strategy, see Liu Shao-ch'i's *Report on the Work of the Central Committee*, delivered at the Second Session of the Eighth Congress of the Chinese Communist Party on May 5, 1958.

6. See for instance, Ma Yin-ch'u's "A New Principle of Population," *Jen-min jih-pao*, Peking, July 5, 1957.

7. *Ibid.*

8. This aspect of the new strategy was officially enunciated in the Communique of the Sixth Plenary Session of the Eighth Central Committee of the Chinese Communist Party issued on December 17, 1958.

Chapter 10

1. *Report on Food Situation,* Tokyo, Japanese Ministry of Agriculture and Forestry, November 14, 1945.
2. I am indebted to Mr. David Bau for calling these facts to my attention, documentary support for which can be found in *Food Position of Japan for the Rice Year 1946,* Tokyo, SCAP, 1946, p. 6.

Chapter 11

1. I wish to express my thanks to Doak Barnett, Abram Bergson, Morris Bornstein, Walter Galenson, Gregory Grossman, Saul Hymans, Edwin Jones, Simon Kuznets, T. C. Liu, B. M. Oza, Dwight Perkins, Peter Schran, Warren Smith, and Ezra Vogel for their most helpful comments on an earlier draft.
2. Alexander Eckstein, "Comment on Professor Reinhart Bendix's Paper Entitled 'The Cultural and Political Setting of Economic Rationality in Western and Eastern Europe'," *Value and Plan,* ed. Gregory Grossman, Berkeley, University of California Press, 1960, pp. 262–66.
3. Josef Goldmann, "Fluctuations and Trends in the Rate of Economic Growth in Some Socialist Countries," *Economics of Planning,* 4, No. 2 (1964), pp. 88–89. Goldmann, who is a Czechoslovak economist, has written several other articles in Czechoslovak economic journals. For different approaches to economic fluctuations in socialist economies see: Julio H. G. Olivera, "Cyclical Economic Growth under Collectivism," *Kyklos,* 13, fasc. 2 (1960), pp. 229–55; L. M. Fallenbuchl, "Investment Policy for Economic Development: Some Lessons of the Communist Experience," *Canadian Journal of Economics and Political Science,* 29, No. 1 (February, 1953), pp. 26–39; Alfred E. Oxenfeldt and Ernest van den Haag, "Unemployment in Planned and Capitalist Economies," *Quarterly Journal of Economics,* 68, No. 1 (February, 1954).
4. Fluctuations in rates of change in economic activity are often referred to in the business-cycle literature as *Kuznets cycles* because of the latter's pioneering work in this field. See W. A. Lewis and J. O'Leary, "Secular Swings in Production and Trade, 1870–1913," *The Manchester School,* 23 (May, 1955), pp. 113–52; and Simon Kuznets, *Capital in the American Economy, Its Formation and Financing,* Princeton N.J., Princeton University Press, 1961; also Simon Kuznets, *Secular Movements in Production and Prices,* Boston and New York, Houghton Mifflin Co., 1930. *Kuznets cycles,* however, usually refer to long swings for periods up to 20 years, while our references to economic fluctuations in rates of growth refer to much shorter periods.
5. Therefore, whenever the term *cycle* or *cyclical fluctuations* appears in

this paper it is intended to refer to economic fluctuation as defined in this and the preceding section.

6. These definitions of cyclical concepts are largely based on R. A. Gordon, *Business Fluctuations*, 2nd ed., New York, Harper, 1961, Chaps. 8, 9, and 10, with some slight modifications.

7. Mao Tse-tung, *Selected Works*, Vol. 4, Peking, Foreign Languages Press, 1961, p. 454; this is an extract from an editorial dated September 16, 1949; emphasis added. For more detailed references, see Stuart R. Schram, ed., *The Political Thought of Mao Tse-tung*, New York, Praeger, 1963, p. 251.

8. See Benjamin Schwartz, "Modernization and the Maoist Vision—Some Reflections on Chinese Communist Goals," *China Quarterly*, No. 21 (January-March, 1965), pp. 3–19.

9. Wu Chiang, "Pu-tuan ko-ming lun-che pi-hsu shih ch'e-ti pien-cheng wei-wu lun-che," (Theorists of Uninterrupted Revolution Must be Thorough Theorists of Dialectical Materialism) *Che-hsueh yen-chiu*, No. 8, 1958, p. 25, as quoted by Schram, in *The Political Thought of Mao Tse-tung*, p. 54. It is very interesting to note that this transformist view of man, society, and nature assumed growing importance in Stalin's mind after World War II. This was evidenced in the so-called "Stalin Plan for the Transformation of Nature" formulated in 1949, and in Stalin's approach to biology, linguistics, and psychology. As Robert Tucker puts it in his most thoughtful essay on "Stalin and the Uses of Psychology," in *The Soviet Political Mind*, New York, Praeger, 1963, "People were not responding in the expected way to the technique of political education and indoctrination. This led the Stalinist mind to seek a formula for making people respond properly. If Russians were failing to respond to the goals set before them, then something was the matter with the Russians and with the means employed to elicit their response. *Their minds had to be remolded to the point where inner acceptance of the Soviet ideology and all the behavior patterns it imposed would come as a matter of course* [emphasis added]."

10. "Preface by Mao Tse-tung to the book *Socialist Upsurge in China's Countryside*, December 27, 1955." The English text is reprinted as Document No. 4, pp. 117–19 in Robert R. Bowie and John K. Fairbank, *Communist China 1955–1959: Policy Documents with Analysis*, Cambridge, Mass., Harvard University Press, 1962.

11. A. S. Chen, "The Ideal Local Party Secretary and the 'Model' Man," *China Quarterly*, No. 17 (January-March, 1964), 229–40.

12. For the quote from Liu, see Conrad Brandt, Benjamin Schwartz, and John K. Fairbank, *A Documentary History of Chinese Communism*, Cambridge, Mass., Harvard University Press, 1952, p. 336. For the quote from Ch'en Yun, see the same source, pp. 330–31; emphasis added.

13. For a more detailed analysis of China's economic backwardness see Alexander Eckstein, *Communist China's Economic Growth and Foreign Trade,* New York, McGraw-Hill, 1966; and *Economic Trends in Communist China,* ed. Alexander Eckstein, Walter Galenson, and Ta-Chung Liu, Chicago, Aldine Publishing Co., 1968.
14. The terminology and use of these concepts (i.e., *remunerative* and *normative* appeals) were derived from an unpublished paper by G. William Skinner, "Leadership and Compliance in Communist China." In this paper, Skinner develops a cycle theory of policy behavior in sociological and organizational terms rather different from ours. Yet Skinner's and my analysis mutually complement rather than contradict each other.
15. See Kenneth R. Walker, *Planning in Chinese Agriculture, Socialisation and the Private Sector, 1956–1962,* London, Cass, 1965.
16. This point is well developed by Benjamin Schwartz in "Modernization and the Maoist Vision."
17. For instance Liu Shao-Ch'i states in his "Report on the Work of the Central Committee of the Communist Party of China to the Second Session of the Eighth National Congress," that "The development is U-shaped, i.e., high at the beginning and the end, but low in the middle. Didn't we see very clearly how things developed on the production front in 1956–1958 in the form of an upsurge, then an ebb, and then an even bigger upsurge or, in other words, a leap forward, then a conservative phase and then another big leap forward," in *Second Session of the Eighth National Congress of the Chinese Communist Party,* Peking, Foreign Languages Press, 1958.
18. See, for instance, Walker, *Planning in Chinese Agriculture, Socialisation and the Private Sector, 1956–1962,* Chap. 1.
19. For detailed discussions of China's statistical system, its strengths and weaknesses, see Choh-ming Li, *The Statistical System of Communist China,* Berkeley, University of California Press, 1963; T. C. Liu and K. C. Yeh, *The Economy of the Chinese Mainland,* Princeton, N. J., Princeton University Press, 1965, and Alexander Eckstein, *Communist China's Economic Growth and Foreign Trade,* Appendix A.
20. Walker, *Planning in Chinese Agriculture,* p. 62.
21. See, for instance, the directive of September 12, 1956, "On Strengthening the Building of Organization and Control over Production in the Cooperatives," *Hsin-hua pan-yueh-k'an* (hereafter cited as *HHPYK*) 93, No. 19 (1956), pp. 53–59.
22. See Chou En-lai's "Report on the Second Five Year Plan for the Development of the National Economy," *HHPYK,* 94, No. 20 (1956), pp. 35–49.
23. Teng Tzu-hui, "On Internal Contradictions of Cooperatives and Democratic Management," *HHPYK,* 109, No. 11(1957), pp. 94–100, and Standing Committee of the NPC, "Decision on Increasing Members'

Plot in Cooperatives," June 25, 1957, *HHPYK*, 112, No. 14 (1957), pp. 153.

24. State Council Decision "On Not Allowing Commodities Subject to State Planned Purchase and Planned Supply and Unified Purchase Alone with Other Commodities to Enter the Free Market" issued August 9, 1957, *HHPYK*, 116, No. 18 (1957), pp. 207–8.

25. See Alexander Eckstein, *Communist China's Economic Growth and Foreign Trade,* Chaps. 2 and 3. See also P. P. Jones and T. T. Poleman, "Communes and the Agricultural Crises in China," *Stanford Research Institute Studies,* 3, No. 1 (February, 1962), p. 4.

26. See *Jen-min jih-pao* editorial, "The Three Level Ownership System with the Production Brigade as the Basic Level Is the Basic System for People's Communes at the Present Stage," *Jen-min jih-pao,* December 21, 1960, and *Jen-min jih-pao,* editorial, "Conscientiously Implement Policies of Rural People's Communes," *Jen-min jih-pao,* April 2, 1961, and the New Year's editorial in *Jen-min jih-pao,* January 1, 1962.

27. This is brought out in an as yet unpublished paper by Peter Chen based on an analysis of documents captured during a Nationalist raid on Lien Chiang *hsien* in Fukien Province.

Chapter 12

1. Elliot J. Berg, "Wage Structures in Less Developed Countries," in A. D. Smith, ed., *Wage Policy Issues in Economic Development,* London, 1969, p. 303.

2. United States Department of Labor, Bureau of Labor Statistics, *Handbook of Labor Statistics, 1973,* Washington, D.C., 1973, Table 45, p. 108.

3. Berg, *op. cit.,* p. 320.

4. These prices were collected by Bruce Reynolds, who, at the time of his visit to China was a graduate student in economics at Michigan, and is now Assistant Professor of Economics, at Union College.

5. Barry M. Richman, *Industrial Society in Communist China,"* New York, 1969.

6. G. William Skinner, "Marketing and Social Structure in Rural China," *Journal of Asian Studies,* XXIV, Part I, November 1964, pp. 3–43; Part II, February 1965, pp. 195–228; Part III, May 1965, pp. 363–99.

Index